Ted Barris divides his time between teaching at Toronto's Centennial College in the journalism department and writing/broadcasting professionally. His work on CBC and TVO is well known (he has earned a Billboard Radio Documentary Award and numerous ACTRA Award nominations) and his bylines appear in such publications as the *National Post* and *Globe and Mail*, and the *Legion*, *Beaver*, and *Air Force* magazines. He has published 16 non-fiction books. In 1993, he received the Canada 125 Medal "for service to Canada and community." In 2004, the Remembrance Service Association of Halifax recognized Ted Barris and his military history writing with its annual Patriot Award. In 2006, the 78th Fraser Highlander regiment awarded Barris its annual excellence award, the Bear Hackle Award, to recognize his "contribution to the awareness and preservation of Canadian military history and traditions."

DUNDURN
TORONTO

ALSO BY TED BARRIS

MILITARY HISTORY

Days of Victory: Canadians Remember, 1939–1945
(with Alex Barris, 1st edition, 1995)

Deadlock in Korea: Canadians at War, 1950–1953

Canada and Korea: Perspectives 2000 (contributor)

Juno: Canadians at D-Day, June 6, 1944

Days of Victory: Canadians Remember, 1939–1945
(Sixtieth Anniversary edition, 2005)

Victory at Vimy: Canada Comes of Age, April 9–12, 1917

Breaking the Silence: Veterans' Untold Stories from the Great War to Afghanistan

OTHER NON-FICTION

Fire Canoe: Prairie Steamboat Days Revisited

Rodeo Cowboys: The Last Heroes

Positive Power: The Story of the Edmonton Oilers Hockey Club

Spirit of the West: The Beginnings, the Land, the Life

Playing Overtime: A Celebration of Oldtimers' Hockey

Carved in Granite: 125 Years of Granite Club History

Making Music: Profiles from a Century of Canadian Music
(with Alex Barris)

101 Things Canadians Should Know About Canada (contributor)

Behind the GLORY

CANADA'S ROLE IN THE ALLIED AIR WAR

Ted Barris

DUNDURN
TORONTO

Library and Archives Canada Cataloguing in Publication

Barris, Ted

Behind the glory : Canada's role in the Allied air war / Ted Barris. — 1st pbk. ed.

Includes bibliographical references and index.
ISBN 978-0-88762-723-1

1. British Commonwealth Air Training Plan — History. 2. World War, 1939–1945 — Aerial operations, Canadian. 3. World War, 1939-1945 — Aerial operations. 4. Aeronautics, Military—Study and teaching — Canada — History.
I. Title.

UG639.C3B37 2010 940.54'4971 C2010-905882-8

Maps showing the location of BCATP stations are reprinted from *The Creation of a National Air Force: The Official History of the Royal Canadian Air Force*, by W.A. B. Douglas, vol. 2 (Toronto: University of Toronto Press, 1986). Used with the permission of The Department of National Defence.

We acknowledge the support of the Canada Council for the Arts and the Ontario Arts Council for our publishing program. We also acknowledge the financial support of the Government of Ontario, through the Ontario Book Publishing Tax Credit and Ontario Creates, and the Government of Canada.

Printed and bound in Canada.

Dundurn
3 Church Street, Suite 500
Toronto, Ontario, Canada
M5E 1M2

To Kay and Alex, whose generation served so that their son's and granddaughters' wouldn't have to

CONTENTS

Preface

From its first appearance in 1992, this book created a stir.

Originally considered a niche subject, *Behind the Glory*'s story of wartime aviation instructors immediately struck a chord with reviewers and readers. While on a coast-to-coast tour of Canada that fall, I gave 150 interviews in just over two weeks. Reporters seemed drawn to the unsung heroism of the story. Reviewers loved the Hollywood angle. And broadcasters scoured the book's pages for former instructors willing to go on-air. Even as much of that media went to air or press, copies of the book seemed in short supply. By mid-autumn I was besieged with calls from people desperate to find the book, including from a commercial pilot who flew from Sarnia, Ontario, to Montreal to pick up a reserved copy. *Behind the Glory* had captured people's imagination.

Just as important, however, the book kindled long overdue recognition for the nearly forgotten instructors from their air force community. In 1993, for example, many of the 12,000 members of the Allied Air Forces gathered at the Royal York Hotel in Toronto. At its 23rd annual reunion, the association dedicated much of the honours program to those who served in Training Command, in particular, instructors in the British Commonwealth Air Training Plan (BCATP). In a keynote address to AAF members, I highlighted the contribution of Canada's "unknown soldiers" and reminded the air force veterans present how much they owed their original instructors for their survival. As part of my tribute to the role of instructors, I echoed words of support offered by a former navigational instructor to a graduating class of airmen bound for service in the BCATP in 1942:

> "The difference between an operational flyer and an instructor, can be the equivalent to that between a single rifleman and a Bren gunner," he said. "The operational flyer can fight with only his own brain, his own hands. The instructor can fight with the brains and hands of all the hundreds he influences and teaches."

That air forces reunion speech proved a watershed. Since its publication, *Glory*'s research has been the source of many presentations about the BCATP and its neglected instructors. The book became an entrée to similarly address such organizations as the Canadian Aviation Historical Society, the Canadian Warplane Heritage Museum, the Aircrew Association of Canada, the Air Force Association, the Billy Bishop Museum, the Canadian Harvard Aircraft Association, the Royal Canadian Legion, the Canadian Club, the Empire Club, as well as BCATP commemorative societies in Nanton, Alberta, and Yorkton, Saskatchewan. On occasion, the book's content was presented in support of instructors seeking veterans' status and pension benefits. During 2005—Canada's designated Year of the Veteran—History Television aired the documentary "Bomber Boys: A Commonwealth of Heroes" based in part on *Behind the Glory* content.

Among the hundreds of responses that have inspired the reprinting and publication of this book, was a letter from the son of a former BCATP flying instructor. His correspondence recounted the story of his father's instant connection to the book. When *Glory* came his way, the son said, the father apparently immersed himself in its stories cover to cover. He read it again and again, feeling it spoke to him more than other wartime chronicles. Then, when his father's health faltered, the son said the BCATP veteran eventually became bedridden in hospital. All he requested from home in his last days was his copy of *Behind the Glory*. It was there in his room when he died.

In the years leading up to its publication and since, the book has yielded hundreds of acquaintances among veterans of the air training plan. At first their stories attracted me. Sometimes their flight logs, diaries, and photo collections did too. But it was their personalities and their passion to keep the BCATP story alive that had me coming back. Several close friendships resulted with, among others, former instructors Charley Fox, Charlie Konvalinka, John Campsie, Joel Aldred, Ted Arnold, Russ Bannock, Henry Gordon, Jack Harris, Norm Harrison, Bob Hesketh, Eric Johnston, Margaret Littlewood, Fred Lundell, John Neal, Don Rogers, Dick Ross, Al Stirton, Ross Truemner, John Trull, and Babe Woollett. Some of these friends are gone now. Gone . . . but still giving my work impetus.

I'm sure that reader response to two other Second World War volumes—*Juno: Canadians at D-Day, June 6, 1944* and *Days of Victory: Canadians Remember, 1939-1945*—released by Thomas Allen Publishers in 2004 and 2005 respectively has helped us reach a decision to reprint *Behind the Glory*. For that momentum I sincerely thank the editorial, production, marketing and sales teams at Thomas Allen. Nevertheless, I believe it's the clarity of those original instructors' recollections and the honesty of their reflections on the unique plan they built that have convinced us a new edition was viable.

Though the British Commonwealth Air Training Plan officially came to an end sixty years ago, its legacy served Canadian aviation long after. Similarly, as the inscription on the BCATP memorial gates at Trenton, Ontario, suggests—"Their shoulders held the sky suspended/They stood, and earth's foundations stay"—the legacy of the plan's instructors gives this book renewed life.

Ted Barris
Uxbridge, 2005

Acknowledgements

As Harvard 3222 took off and gained altitude, I watched the concrete runway slowly fall away. For miles around the Tillsonburg airstrip, a sea of corn was ripening in the sunshine. The aircraft, which had rolled off the North American Aviation assembly line in California in June 1941, roared into the sky to lead four Harvard trainers in a formation exercise.

It was November 4, 1990.

As a non-pilot, I was in the second cockpit. At the controls was Norm Beckham, a pilot who taught himself to fly Harvards after the Second World War. Harvard 3222 had seen more instructors and student pilots and flown more training sorties than either Norm or I would ever know. But this was my very first flight in a Harvard, the workhorse aircraft of RCAF Training Command during the war. It was also an introduction to the British Commonwealth Air Training Plan and to the instructors who helped implement the plan and win back air supremacy for the Allies. *Behind the Glory* is the result of that trip back into the wartime memories of those who taught and learned in the BCATP.

First of all, my thanks to the Ontario Arts Council's Writers' Reserve Grant program for providing funds towards the research of this book.

As I began the search for original sources, several military aviation associations helped me. The executives and membership of the

Canadian Harvard Aircraft Association, the Aircrew Association, and the Canadian Aviation Historical Society offered encouragement and lists of contacts to get me started. Along the way, numerous other organizations provided advice, leads, archival material, and support. Groups such as the Canadian Warplane Heritage Museum, Canada's Aviation Hall of Fame, the Norwegian Consulate, the Italian Cultural Institute, the Toronto Harbour Commission, the Niagara Falls Bridge Commission, the Canadian Jewish Congress, the National Film Board of Canada, the North Bay *Nugget*, the Uxbridge-Scott Historical Society, Western Canada Aviation Museum, Aviation World bookstore, and the Royal Canadian Military Institute gave me data on international and national aviation as well as life inside and around BCATP stations.

Several individuals at the Directorate of History, Department of National Defence, provided valuable advice and assistance. My initial contact, Norman Hillmer, provided direction as well as some of his own research, and at the DND itself, Carl Christie and W.A.B. Douglas helped me verify details of the plan.

Early on, as I attempted to tap the memories of a group of veterans—BCATP instructors, who have rarely, if ever, come forward to talk about their wartime experiences—I was allowed to broadcast my appeal for first-hand information on CBC Radio; in particular, I wish to thank Bill McNeil and Bob Burt for providing support and air time.

A number of individuals provided me access to their private files, diaries, log books, letters, films, photographs, and book collections and gave me introductions to instructors not previously quoted in published material on the BCATP. Among them were D'Alt Swift, Gerry Anglin, Bill Coffman, Frank Turner, Jean Bruce, Jeanne Muldoon, Eddy Souris, Don Cooper, and especially Dave MacDonald. My correspondence with Brian Howard, Rob Schweyer, Ken West, John Neal, Shirley Mills, and Iris Barr yielded valuable background stories and yet more contacts. Jack Meadows, John Evans, and Ken Smith allowed me to quote their personal memoirs freely. Babe Woollett travelled halfway around the world to tell me the story of the Air Observer Schools. Joe Clark helped me reconstruct the tale of *Captains of the Clouds*. Stevie Cameron offered unique material on her father Whitey Dahl. Bert Adkins provided information and leads on Buff Estes. Byron Christopher helped me reach the plan's only woman instructor. Mary Jane Varo dug up material on eastern Canadian training stations. In particular, because of their long experience with the publication of aviation history, I am grateful to Larry Milberry and Hugh Halliday for their pathfinding work in this field.

Before I could write a single word of the manuscript, I was entirely dependent on a group of eager and dedicated transcribers—Margaret Gammon, Catherine Cripps, Kristine Morris, Jenny Kanis, Marlene Lumley, and Donna Morgan. In an extraordinarily short time, they waded through 150 audio cassettes and provided me with transcripts of more than 200 hours of interviews with former participants in the BCATP.

I was fortunate to meet three knowledgeable BCATP instructors: Charlie Konvalinka, Charley Fox, and John Campsie. Each knew the subject from a different perspective. Each understood the story I wished to tell. And each provided direction, comment, analysis, criticism, and advice on how to tell it best. I owe each of them a debt of gratitude for the hours they spent on the project. As BCATP instructors they helped scores of airmen win their wings, as unofficial editors of my work, they have given this book its wings.

The people at Macmillan Canada involved in this publication gave more than their job descriptions set out. Cover artist Garfield Ingram, designer David Montle, and editorial assistant Nancy Ceneviva all threw themselves whole-heartedly into this book. Above all, my greatest praise goes to editor-in-chief Philippa Campsie. Her initial discovery of the project, her ceaseless encouragement for its author, her critical eye for its detail, and her genuine love of its subject-matter helped advance this work from a six-page outline to a bound and printed book.

Through two and a half years of digging, chasing, organizing, and writing, I relied heavily on the encouragement of many people. Most of the instructors I interviewed or corresponded with endorsed the work right away. Others, who had little working knowledge of the BCATP itself, confirmed my belief that it could be done and befriended the venture from beginning to end. Among the most loyal friends of *Behind the Glory* are David Ross, Peter Jennings, Bill Edgar, Tom Best, Terry Clifton, Barb Pratt, Rob Mowat, Aaron Milrad, and, right from the beginning, Barry Broadfoot. I include my family—Jayne, Quenby, Whitney, and Kate—among the book's and my best friends. But I give greatest thanks to my mother, Kay, for her steadfast confidence in me, and to my father, Alex, for the countless hours he spent checking library sources, transcribing interviews, proofreading copy, and believing in this work and its author.

Ted Barris
Uxbridge, 1992

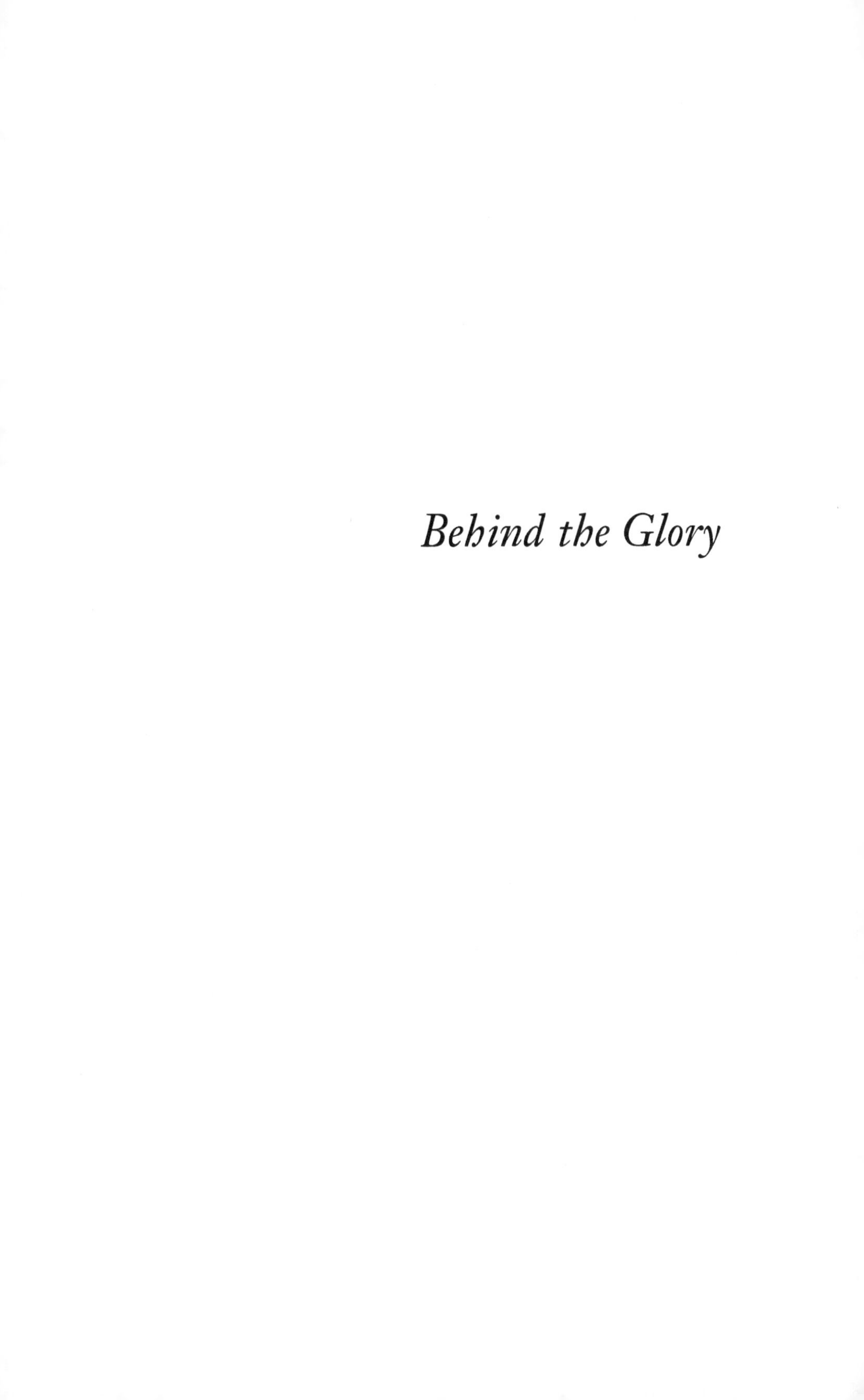

Behind the Glory

1

CALLING CARDS FOR HITLER

IN THE SUMMER OF 1944, the troopship *Aquitania* completed a transatlantic crossing from Halifax to Scotland. Up the Firth of Clyde at the wartime docks of Gourock, she discharged a precious human cargo—thousands of freshly trained Allied air crew now ready for operational training and ultimately for active combat in the air war against Germany.

Among the thousands of disembarking servicemen was a young RCAF officer named Charlie Konvalinka. Three generations before, his ancestors had left Europe for a new life in America. Until now, he had never paid a return visit. Konvalinka's first experience of Britain was a train ride in the middle of the night through blacked-out cities and villages. In the morning, he and his fellow air crew members arrived at the seaside resort town of Bournemouth, on the south coast of England.

Bournemouth was full of Canadians. For nearly four years, RCAF airmen like Konvalinka had arrived by the thousands to be billeted at city hotels. Wartime had transformed Bournemouth into No. 3 Personnel Reception Centre, and as such became the temporary quarters for air crewmen from Russia, Australia, New Zealand, France, Poland, South Africa, and the United States, but mostly from Canada.

With each new group of airmen that arrived in Bournemouth, there was processing to be done. Within the first few days of Konvalinka's arrival, he and several hundred other former flying instructors were assembled for a briefing in one of Bournemouth's old motion-picture theatres. The newly posted operational pilots were informed it would be a kind of orientation session, at which they would be told what life was like overseas. When all the pilots had taken their seats, out came an RCAF officer—a flight lieutenant, like Konvalinka—to begin the session.

"Well, you instructors are finally out here now," he began. "Bloody bunch of cowards!"

This wasn't at all what Konvalinka and his colleagues had expected.

"You guys probably don't have the guts to do what we do," the officer went on. "To fly a bomber on a straight and level when everybody's shooting at you, or take on the enemy in a fighter one-on-one."

The theatre remained silent. Konvalinka felt his blood boiling.

"If you had any guts at all you'd have been over here fighting. We're the brave ones. You're not!"

Konvalinka couldn't restrain himself for another second. Before he realized what he was doing, he had called out, "And who, for Christ's sake, taught you to fly? God?"

The presiding officer peered out into the theatre in search of the speaker. "Who said that?" he stormed.

Konvalinka stood up immediately and said to the sea of astonished faces around him, "I did. I said it!"

Charlie Konvalinka had never flown a combat mission in his life. Yet he had accumulated more than 1,850 hours of flying time; he was expert at the controls of every aircraft used for training service pilots in the Allied arsenal—aircraft such as two-seater Harvards, twin-engine Ansons, Lockheeds, Cessna Cranes, Airspeed Oxfords, and even biplane trainers such as Tiger Moths and Fleet Finches. At the age of twenty-six, Konvalinka was considered old by a fighting air force whose combat pilots were mostly nineteen, twenty, or twenty-one.

Before he received his overseas posting, Konvalinka had been an RCAF flying instructor. In four years of service in the British Commonwealth Air Training Plan, he had taught perhaps a hundred other young men to fly. He'd shown some of them how to dodge and weave and throw a fighter aircraft around the sky to elude an enemy closing in for the kill. He'd instructed others how to bring a multi-engine aircraft home on just one engine. In short, he'd taught them how to survive.

Some of his students, now on operations, had flown fighter cover in the campaign to retake North Africa. Others in Bomber Command had completed full tours—thirty missions or more—over Brest, Hamburg, and Berlin. Still others of his students—Australians and New Zealanders—had gone home to squadrons in the South Pacific and were flying operations into Burma, over Singapore and even hit-and-run bombing raids on the Imperial Japanese Navy. And yet here it was, the beginning of 1944, and RCAF Flight Lieutenant Charlie Konvalinka had never fired a shot in anger, had experienced no combat duty.

From the beginning Konvalinka had had his heart set on becoming a fighter pilot. He had the physique of a fighter pilot—a short, compact build—a legacy of his days as a sprinter competing for Canada on the international track and field circuit. He had the right attitude too. Anything his taller friends could do, he could do better. And it was only half in jest that he claimed: "I'm the best pilot I ever saw." But all he really wanted to do was get his hands on the control column of a Spitfire and put it through its paces.

He had joined the Royal Canadian Air Force early enough, a few months after Canada declared war on Germany in September 1939. When he'd taken his school documentation and a couple of letters of recommendation to the RCAF recruiting centre on York Street in Toronto, it was the time of the "Phony War." The Germans had invaded Poland and Czechoslovakia (including Bohemia, the birthplace of his great grandfather). The Low Countries had fallen before the Blitzkrieg, and most people thought France would need lots of pilots to fend off the Germans. So there would still be plenty of time for Konvalinka to get into the thick of it. Still lots of Spitfire time to log.

Charlie Konvalinka had not joined the air force because he wanted to kill Nazis. At a pivotal moment in his training, late in 1940, while the Battle of Britain escalated between Churchill's "few" and Göring's mighty Luftwaffe, Konvalinka had been interviewed about his wartime aspirations. He could have given the patriotic answer ("To go fight for the King and to shoot down Nazis"), but he didn't. He was honest enough to say he'd joined because his passion was to fly. And he was marked high for his honesty. However, the one thing Konvalinka had learned even in the first months of his training: the air force sent you where *it* wanted, not where *you* wanted.

And so, in late 1940, when Charlie Konvalinka graduated with a "distinguished pass" at No. 2 Service Flying Training School at Uplands, near Ottawa, and received his wings, he wasn't posted to an operational training unit and sent overseas to shoot down Messerschmitts. The RCAF sent him to Central Flying School (CFS) in Trenton, Ontario, to become a military flying instructor.

As an instructor he had worked at CFS, then in Moncton, New Brunswick, Stanley, Nova Scotia, and Souris and Gimli in Manitoba, from the middle of 1941 until July 1944. Perhaps to alleviate the initial disappointment of not being sent overseas himself, he referred to the scores of pilots he'd trained as his "calling cards for Hitler."

Charlie Konvalinka had never expected any reward for being an RCAF instructor. The DFC (Distinguished Flying Cross) and the DSO (Distinguished Service Order) were the recognition reserved for successful combat pilots and crew. And only a few instructors were ever decorated with the AFC (the Air Force Cross) for outstanding service in Training Command at home. Nor was there ever in Konvalinka's mind a sense that teaching young men to fly military aircraft was as heroic as getting shot at on a fighter sortie or bombing mission over Europe. He did, however, believe himself to be a professional. And he had proved it the very first time he got into trouble in a Harvard trainer during the summer of 1941.

"I had just begun instructing at Trenton [RCAF Central Flying School]. A sergeant pilot named Charlton was my very first student. I was training him to be an instructor," Konvalinka said.

"We'd gone up this one day to do the sequence on spins. The little red patter book says that you're supposed to climb to around 6,000 or 7,000 feet. And you go through the patter—the instructional jargon that we used. And right from the book Charlton recites: 'I will now do a spin to the right and the recovery.' So he throttles back, pulls the nose up until just above stalling speed, then applies full rudder to the right, and the Harvard falls into a spin.

"Now, a Harvard spin is a bone-shattering experience under normal conditions. It bounces and jumbles its way around when it spins. But this one didn't. It was like a knife cutting through butter. And it was new to me. I'd never experienced anything like it.

"I guess we were down around 4,000 feet and I got on the intercom tube and said 'That's good. Take her out now.' And I hear this shaky voice from the rear cockpit say, 'I'm trying . . .'

"I said, 'I have control' [and took control via the dual controls in the front cockpit].

"The standard recovery for a spin to the right is to kick on full opposite rudder—in this case the left rudder—push it down all the way, and centre the control column laterally. The Harvard will then kick out to the left. And as soon as it does, you centralize the rudder pedals, stand on them, hold them straight, and let the airplane find its way out of the spin . . .

"Well, I did all this. Nothing happened. It just didn't work. But I knew there were secondary things you could do. Use the engine. When it's spinning you've got the power off. So I put the power on. No good. I tried everything: put the flaps down, then up. Nothing. Then finally a combination of flaps and using the engine, and it started to come out, awfully damn low. There was no way we could have bailed out and made it. We were below a thousand feet and coming down fast."

When Konvalinka returned to the station and reported the Harvard's extraordinary spin conditions to the Trenton aircraft riggers, they concluded that the wing had been "out of rig" (that is, improperly aligned). This resulted in an aerodynamic instability, which produced the nearly uncorrectable spin. In other words, the wing could easily have torn itself right off and the Harvard would certainly have crashed, taking both Konvalinka and his student to their deaths.

So although Konvalinka couldn't yet claim to have faced the cannon and guns of a Messerschmitt 109 in a dogfight, nor to have steered an eighteen-ton Lancaster bomber through a sea of exploding flak, he'd faced death in the cockpit of a Harvard trainer.

"In that emergency," Konvalinka said, "I had gone cold. The emotions were entirely deadened. The brain took over."

On the day his son was born in a mission hospital in Gimli, Manitoba, in July 1944, Flight Lieutenant Charlie Konvalinka got the news he'd been waiting for. At long last the air force had posted him overseas to operational duty (or "ops" as it was familiarly called). He would see England and prepare himself for what he called "the most dramatic and traumatic event of a lifetime." (Other combat pilots described ops as "long periods of boredom interspersed with a few seconds of sheer terror.")

All his experiences seemed to flash before him, however, when he was called a coward in a Bournemouth movie theatre.

Konvalinka and the orientation officer were hustled from the theatre and into the office of the station commander for an explanation. His years as a flight instructor and a flight commander told Konvalinka how to deal with this kind of confrontation. He described the theatre incident as "a difference of opinion between two officers of equal rank." Apparently, the station commander didn't see the need to discipline either man for his outburst. The issue was dropped. Charlie Konvalinka advanced to operational training and eventually realized his dream to fly Spitfires.

But the question remained: who had taught this pilot and nearly 50,000 other Allied military pilots to fly? Who had trained the nearly 150,000 qualified navigators, wireless operators, bomb-aimers, air-gunners, and ground crew who were poised for the invasion of France, Italy, and Japanese-occupied Asia? Who had turned the tide of the air war after the retreat from Dunkirk, near-defeat in the Battle of Britain, the devastation of the Blitz, and the air routs at Pearl Harbor and Hong Kong? In short, who had transformed the Allied air forces into the most powerful weapon in the world? The answer: Konvalinka and hundreds of instructors like him in the British Commonwealth Air Training Plan.

Rooted in the First World War, when thousands of airmen were recruited and trained for the Royal Flying Corps (later the Royal Air Force) in Canada and the United States, and then formally planted in Canada with much greater Canadian control at the outbreak of war in 1939, the BCATP (or JATP for Joint Air Training Plan, or EATS for Empire Air Training Scheme) was a program to standardize the training of air crew for military service.

In its five-and-a-half-year lifespan—from December 1939 to September 1945—the BCATP would expend about $2 billion in the training of air crew from nearly every nation of the free world. It would ultimately deliver air superiority to the Allied war effort. The product of its training—nearly a quarter of a million air and ground crew—would spearhead the major land and sea operations to take back Europe, North Africa, and much of the Pacific. It would supply RAF Bomber Command with the trained airmen for a third of a million sorties. It would produce some of Canada's 160 fighter aces who accounted for more than a thousand victories in the Second World War. It would help sustain the flow of bomber and fighter aircraft to the European theatre of war by supplying trained pilots and navigators to Ferry Command. And it would ensure the success of military operations on all fronts with the qualified airmen of Transport Command and Coastal Command. It would, in Winston Churchill's words, be "one of the major factors, and possibly the decisive factor of the war." And it happened almost entirely in Canada.

Nobody could have foreseen the plan's success in 1939.

Even though a confederation of four Canadian provinces had negotiated national independence from its colonial parent in 1867, and had grown politically to nine provinces and geographically from the Atlantic to the Pacific by the twentieth century, Great Britain maintained a strong military presence in Canadian air space.

Even though the first controlled flight in the British Empire had been recorded by a Canadian in Canada in 1909, it went down in history as the achievement of a British subject, John McCurdy.

Even though Canada had trained and sent 2,500 pilots overseas to serve the Allies in the First World War, Canadian airmen never flew in combat in a Canadian flying service. Ten of the twenty-seven leading Allied air aces were Canadian, but even W.A. "Billy" Bishop, the most decorated Canadian airman in the First World War, flew missions against the Germans as a member of the Royal Flying Corps.

Even though by 1915 pilot training was being carried out at two flying schools in Canada—at Curtiss Aviation in Toronto and the Aero Club of British Columbia—the instruction and graduation of military pilots and air observers remained under British authority. Instructors and students were duty-bound solely to the War Office in London, England. The entry qualifications, the training syllabus, and the graduation standard (or awarding of "wings") were all set by the Royal Naval Air Service or the Royal Flying Corps (amalgamated in April 1918 as the Royal Air Force).

At the Armistice, Canada's air strength consisted of 110 airplanes, twelve airships, six kite balloons, some camera equipment donated by the British government, and about 1,700 air crew returning from the European war. That number declined in the peacetime years that followed. In 1920, under the jurisdiction of a Canadian government air board, Camp Borden opened an air training facility, offering a combination of ground school and flying instruction aboard either SE5a fighters or de Havilland 9a bombers. Service in Canada's non-permanent air force consisted of no more than four weeks' training every two years. Moreover, its objectives were largely non-military—to license pilots for civil aviation, to conduct government air operations (forestry and fish patrols and photographic surveys), and finally, should the need arise, to defend Canada.

Encouraging recruits to enlist was not a priority, so young men did not flock to join Canada's ad hoc air force. Even though the Canadian

Air Force gained permanent status from the government in 1923 and, in 1924, permission from the King to be called the Royal Canadian Air Force, in 1931 the RCAF graduated only twenty-five pilots—and because of restricted budgets granted only one of them an active appointment. Canadians were still given an option to join the RAF; each year, Britain reserved permanent commissions for two Canadian university graduates. However, during the general prosperity and relative peace of the 1920s and then the depression of the 1930s, Canadians did not rush to train and serve in the RAF.

An emphasis on air training re-emerged in the late 1930s. The British government, aware of the renaissance of the German air force, planned the construction of seven air training schools. One would be located in Canada. It also launched an RAF recruiting program in the Dominions; under its Trained in Canada Scheme, fifteen candidates for the RAF would be selected by the RCAF, sent to the facilities being built at Trenton, Ontario, and trained according to the RAF regimen.

Group Captain Robert Leckie, a Canadian member of the RAF, was among the first to promote the advantages of permanently establishing military flight training in Canada. His service as a distinguished flying-boat pilot in the Royal Naval Air Service during the First World War and his postwar appointment as Superintendent of RAF Reserves gave him plenty of credibility. His "Proposal to Establish a Flying Training School in Canada" had three selling points: first, Canada was fairly close to the United Kingdom; second, it was close to a highly industrialized United States; and third, revitalized training in Canada would increase the flow of air crew into the RAF.

The proposal was shot down by Prime Minister Mackenzie King, who disapproved of the use of Canadian territory to train British airmen. Throughout 1938, despite repeated pitches by British industrialist J.G. Weir and the British high commissioner in Ottawa, Sir Francis Floud, King maintained that Canadians were "prepared to have our own establishments here and to give in those establishments facilities to British pilots to come and train here. But they must come and train in establishments which are under the control of the government of Canada." King also refused to make any decision that committed Canada to enter any future European war on the British side. He felt that by siding with Britain, he ran the risk of angering the French-speaking Quebec electorate.

The prime minister's outwardly staunch Canadian nationalism signalled his commitment to keep any training scheme in Canada Canadian-controlled and his determination to be personally involved in its orchestration. Thus began the political give and take. In July 1938, Mackenzie King invited another British delegation to negotiate an acceptable air training program. The British secretary of state for air responded by sending Group Captain J.M. Robb, commandant of the Central Flying School of the RAF, to discuss training facilities in Canada.

This move did not bring the two sides any closer together. Britain still wanted Britons and Canadians trained in Canada for the RAF; King still would not commit Canada to training pilots for Britain. The prime minister also felt that the proposed scheme undermined Canada's own defence requirements and—if the RCAF were required to recruit for the RAF—the autonomy of the RCAF. (Even though the RCAF came into being on April 1, 1924, as a successor to the Canadian Air Force, it remained under the control of the Canadian Army until December 13, 1938.)

By January 1939, the two sides were back where they had started. All they had to show for many months of negotiation was a lot more misunderstanding and thirteen new military pilots (graduates of the Trained in Canada Scheme) trained by the RCAF under the RAF syllabus for RAF service. Two months of renewed negotiation followed, resulting in an agreement to jointly train fifty British pilots for the RAF and seventy-five Canadians for the RCAF.

These negotiations resulted in alterations to the RCAF training organization. Instead of the existing RCAF ten-month pilot training course, pilots would now be trained in three stages of sixteen weeks each, according to a revised RAF syllabus. The most innovative feature of the joint training plan was that the elementary training would be contracted out to eight civilian flying clubs across Canada. This was the idea of another Royal Flying Corps veteran of the First World

War, Major Murton Seymour. A Canadian, Seymour had trained in Vancouver at one of Canada's first two civilian schools; that connection would help establish civilian leadership in what became the Elementary Flying Training Schools of the British Commonwealth Air Training Plan.

This first attempt at joint air training never really came to fruition. Of thirty-three Canadian student flyers who entered elementary flying at the civilian aero clubs, twenty-seven were due to receive their RCAF pilot's flying badges when war broke out in September 1939. Meanwhile, the fifty British pilot trainees who were destined for service training in Canada never left England. In late 1939, they finished their training at home and were immediately posted to RAF operations against Germany.

However, the 1939 bilateral pilot training proposal capitalized on the strengths of both the RAF and the RCAF training traditions to develop a common training approach. Both sides had discussed requirements and the availability of training aircraft. Civilian flying schools had proved their worth in sharing the training load with both air forces. Canada had come to understand Britain's anxiety over the growing air power of Germany. And the RAF had come to understand the RCAF's aspirations for autonomy in air crew training in Canada.

Partly as a statement of national autonomy, the Canadian Parliament made its own declaration of war on Germany a week after Britain. On that day, September 10, 1939, discussions between the British Air Ministry and Canadian air force officials began in London to build upon the RAF-RCAF joint training experiment of the previous twelve months. British Air Ministry officials calculated the number of pilots each Commonwealth dominion might contribute to the war effort. All agreed that three or four times the number now being produced in the dominions would be required to counteract the German threat.

The discussion turned to Canada's role in training air crew, including the effect of Canadian winter conditions on flying training, where instructors and trainer aircraft would come from, how American flyers might be recruited, and what airfields would be available. The influence of Mackenzie King prevailed; it was agreed that any air training in Canada would be under the control of the RCAF.

The notion of a "commonwealth" air training plan arose three days later. Vincent Massey, the Canadian high commissioner to the United Kingdom, spoke with his Australian counterpart, Stanley Bruce, about Britain's weakness in the air. They then talked to RCAF Group Captain A.E. Godfrey and to two Australian officers, and finally to the Dominion Secretary, Anthony Eden, and other members of the British cabinet.

Massey claimed to have been the first to propose "that Canada might be able to make a decisive contribution to the common war effort by training Commonwealth airmen." At a high commissioners' meeting on September 16, 1939, the Canadian and Australian representatives together suggested that Eden consider "a scheme whereby Canadian, Australian and New Zealand air forces should be training in Canada on planes to be specially built in Canada."

When British prime minister Neville Chamberlain sent a telegram containing the Massey-Bruce air training plan to Mackenzie King, he concluded his request for Canadian approval by saying, "We trust therefore, that this co-operative method of approach to the problem will appeal to your Government. The knowledge that a vast air potential was being built up in the Dominions where no German air activity could interfere with expansion might well have a psychological effect on the Germans, equal to that produced by the intervention of the United States in the last war."

The proposal appealed not only to King's sense of history, but also to his sense of political survival. As Canada's major contribution to the Allied war effort, the mounting of a commonwealth air training scheme would not result in long casualty lists, nor would there be the political risk of conscription for a large army, because the Canadians in the RCAF would be volunteers. On September 28, King presented the proposal to his cabinet and wired Chamberlain Canada's acceptance of the plan in principle, with a proposal for further discussions.

The horse trading began when the British negotiating team, led by industrialist Lord Riverdale, arrived in Ottawa in October 1939.

Riverdale began by laying out the round numbers; the British proposal called for the training of 29,000 air crew (pilots, air observers, and wireless operator/air-gunners) each year. Elementary flying training would be conducted in Canada, Australia, and New Zealand, with all service flying training to be done in Canada. In Canada, there would be twelve Elementary Flying Training Schools (EFTS), twenty-five Service Flying Training Schools (SFTS), fifteen Air Observer Schools (AOS), fifteen Bombing and Gunnery Schools (B&GS), three Air Navigation Schools (ANS), and a large Wireless School. Five thousand training aircraft would be required and 54,000 air force personnel. The total estimated capital and maintenance cost for three years (the length of time the war was expected to last) would be almost $1 billion, with three-quarters of that paid by Canada, Australia, and New Zealand. While most felt the components of the scheme were appropriate, it was the bottom line that caught the Canadians off guard.

Mackenzie King and his finance minister, J.L. Ralston, proposed scaling down the costs and getting Britain to shoulder more of the financial burden, since this "was not Canada's war in the same sense that it was Great Britain's." At the same time, the Canadian government expected Britain to buy more Canadian wheat, and it demanded that a ceiling be put on the amount of Canadian credit extended to the United Kingdom for war purchases. Riverdale had to weigh the value of this vital air support scheme against the loss of some credit purchasing power and increased spending on weapons and wheat. The plan won out. In return for this commitment, however, Britain asked that the air training scheme be given the highest priority in Canada.

The second phase of negotiations began when the Australian and New Zealand delegations arrived in Ottawa with their counterproposals. The plan's price tag was on their minds too. Not only was it too high but so was the ratio of trainees they were expected to contribute. These figures were recalculated to reflect actual population ratios—57 percent of the trainees would come from Canada, 35 percent from Australia and 8 percent from New Zealand. Consequently, the size of the scheme was adjusted. Generally, the number of schools was reduced: the number of SFTSs was cut from twenty-five to sixteen, the AOSs and B&GSs from fifteen to ten, and the ANSs from three to two. There would be twenty-six smaller EFTSs instead of thirteen large ones, and four Wireless Schools instead of one large one. As well, the aircraft requirement was scaled down. The overall projected cost was pared back to just over $607 million—of which Britain would pay $185 million, Canada $287 million (excluding EFTS costs), Australia $40 million, and New Zealand $28 million—from the inception of the plan to its agreed termination on March 31, 1943.

Because of Mackenzie King's earlier demands, there was no question about the control of the training plan. It would be administered by the Canadian government and commanded by the RCAF. With that battle apparently settled, the British wanted the agreement initialled as an "essential step forward in our joint war effort." However, the Canadian prime minister was not yet ready to give his blessing. Mackenzie King wanted to protect his political interests at home (particularly among those Anglo-Canadians who might question the emphasis on an air training plan over and above the traditional mustering of a large land force). Just as the British had demanded that the plan be given top priority by Canada, King expected the British government to reciprocate by stating "that the air training plan should take priority over all other Canadian commitments not already entered into." Believing this to be the last hurdle, Prime Minister Chamberlain agreed.

But King wasn't finished. Even as the British Commonwealth Air Training Plan document was being put into its final form, he had second thoughts about the status of Dominion squadrons in the field. The agreement suggested that the United Kingdom would "initiate discussion" on the matter later. That wasn't good enough for King. He was afraid that Canadian graduates of the BCATP would lose their RCAF identity completely and, after overseas posting, be swallowed up by RAF operational squadrons. The British Air Ministry dug in its heels. Even if an operational squadron were manned largely by RCAF air crew, its ground personnel would be largely RAF and would consequently outnumber the RCAF air crew; thus, the ministry would refuse RCAF designation of such a squadron. By December 15, 1939, the two sides had come to a stalemate.

Riverdale was at his wits' end. King was adamant, but he wanted the agreement signed. He telegraphed Anthony Eden, the Dominion Secretary, to say that the entire BCATP was "imperilled." The telegraph and telephone lines between London and Ottawa buzzed with new urgency. British Air Ministry officials huddled. King entreated the Governor General, Lord Tweedsmuir, who was ailing and bedridden at Government House, to support the Canadian position.

In spite of his political and nationalistic posturing, King was determined to finalize the BCATP agreement by mid-December. His resolve had little to do with the priorities of the Canadian government or the growing air war. December 17, 1939, would be his sixty-fifth birthday, and he wanted the agreement completed in honour of that occasion. He succeeded. By midnight on December 16, Lord Riverdale presented a formula to the effect that "Canadian pupils when passing out from the training scheme will be incorporated in or organized as units of the Royal Canadian Air Force in the field." For the time being, though not forever, Mackenzie King had preserved the Canadian factor in the creation of the BCATP.

On Sunday evening, December 17, 1939, the prime minister addressed the Canadian people, stressing the important role the BCATP was about to play in the war. "In making provision for this vast undertaking," he said, "the government has done so knowing that nothing can be left to haste or to chance. The intricate machine must be perfect. In every phase of their work, the men must be trained by the highest skill, and under the best conditions it is possible for the country to provide.

"Let there be no mistake about the significance of the present war. It is a desperate struggle for existence itself. On its outcome will depend the fate not of Canada alone, nor even the British Empire . . .

but of humanity itself. To save mankind from such a catastrophe, the airmen of the British Commonwealth, whether setting their course by the North Star or the Southern Cross, are dedicating their lives."

Just before the prime minister retired for the night, he recorded in his diary that "it was certainly a memorable birthday. I suppose no more significant Agreement has ever been signed by the Government of Canada, or signature placed in the name of Canada to [such a] definitely defined obligation."

2

COUNTDOWN TO ZERO DAY

IT WAS A CRISP WINTER'S MORNING when the power-brokers who had negotiated and signed the British Commonwealth Air Training Plan agreement assembled for a photograph on the steps of the Parliament Buildings in Ottawa. Lord Riverdale, chief negotiator for the United Kingdom, stood with J.V. Fairbairn, Australian minister for air, Prime Minister Mackenzie King and his key cabinet ministers—including J.L. Ralston, Norman Rogers, and C.D. Howe—and representatives from the Royal Australian, Royal New Zealand, Royal Canadian, and Royal Air Forces. Bundled up in heavy winter coats, gloves, and fedoras, this assembly of politicians, bureaucrats, and military brass turned to smile at the camera.

Even though Prime Minister King basked in the limelight as the individual most responsible for launching the plan, the BCATP did not owe its success to the negotiating sessions in London and Ottawa in 1938 and 1939, nor to the politicians and military strategists who signed it. The credit for the success of this massive scheme belonged to thousands of anonymous men and women who, like Charlie Konvalinka, shared the love of flying.

In that sense, the plan originated in 1927, when a lanky, soft-spoken aviator landed his Ryan NYP monoplane, the "Spirit of St. Louis," at Le Bourget Airport in Paris, after a 3,600-mile non-stop flight from New York. Inspired by Charles Lindbergh's achievement, a young architecture student from Auburn, New York, abandoned his education to pursue a flying career. Maury Dillingham was one of many Americans who joined the RCAF before Pearl Harbor and who served as a flying instructor in the BCATP.

An innovator of another sort captured the imagination of Argentine-born Ted Arnold. The summer of the Lindbergh flight, when he was on vacation from his British public school, Ted got an invitation to visit an airfield just outside Southampton on the south coast of England. He'll never forget seeing "this aeroplane with a great revolving wing on top.

"The pilot was an amiable Spaniard. The aircraft had a regular motor and propeller on the front. But just before he began to move forward along the ground, they pulled a rope to get this big wing on top revolving. And it helped lift the plane into the air. I had the feeling I had just seen the future."

Young Ted Arnold was right. The aviator was Spanish aeronautical engineer Juan de la Cierva. The crash of his trimotor plane in 1919 had led Cierva to develop the autogiro, a more stable form of aircraft. The prototype that Ted had seen in 1927 gained wide use in France, Germany, Japan, and the United States before the Second World War and was the forerunner of the helicopter. Although Cierva was killed in an airliner crash at Croydon aerodrome near London in 1936, Ted was not dissuaded from flying; he went back to Argentina, later joined the RCAF, and instructed scores of pilots in the BCATP.

The passion for flying affected youngsters even in remote regions. Ren Henderson spent his childhood on the island of Samarai, at the eastern end of Papua New Guinea, where his father was the magistrate, dispensing Australian justice. In the 1920s there were few roads and no cars, so there were really only two ways to get around—on foot and by air. The first aircraft Ren ever saw was "a weird-looking contraption that belonged to the Australian Air Force, with the engine and propeller pointing backwards. It had two wings and all these damn wires. You could have let a cockatoo go in there, and it would never have found its way out through all those wires.

"I remember a native standing there watching this thing land on the water and taxi up to the beach," Henderson said. "He turned to someone beside him and said, 'It's the motor car that belongs to Jesus Christ.'"

Ren Henderson was among about 10,000 Royal Australian Air Force air crew shipped to Canada for BCATP training. Like nearly all of his mates from home, Henderson was itching for an overseas combat posting. Instead, he was one of the first three RAAF pilots to become a BCATP instructor. Ren finally got a crack at flying fighter sorties in mid-1944, and there, in the skies over Dieppe, "it was what I learned as an instructor that saved my life."

For Jack Meadows, flying was like "a germ spreading" through his life. As a boy in England his favourite books included a 1910 history of the *Daily Mail* London-to-Manchester air race, stories about the aircraft in the Great War, and biographies of such flyers as McCudden, Mannock, Ball, Bishop, Boelcke, Immelmann, and Richthofen. When he was about ten he attended Alan Cobham's Flying Circus and invested his month's allowance—five shillings—for a "joy ride" in the rear cockpit of an Avro 504K. He studied aviation periodicals, and one—*The Aeroplane*—published his account of an air display at Ipswich Airport.

The "germ" grew at prep school when he was riveted by the sight of a close formation of Bristol Bulldog fighters flying overhead, and at college when he participated in anti-aircraft drills, firing blanks from a .303 Enfield rifle at an attacking Hawker Audax. Flying became "a full-blown fever" in 1937, when he invested his life's savings—£35—in flying lessons at the Ipswich Aero Club. Meadows had set his sights on an RAF career, carrying on the military aviation traditions of his bookshelf heroes. Instead, he would log 1,600 hours instructing Allied pilots on thirty aircraft types across England and Canada before he eventually went day-fighting in Spitfires in 1943 and later night-fighting in Beaufighters and Mosquitoes.

For Gene Vollick, who lived in Hamilton, Ontario, a summer morning when he was nine years old changed his whole life. Somewhere between six and eight o'clock on the morning of August 11,

1930, the British dirigible R100 motored overhead en route from Toronto to Niagara Falls as part of its North American publicity tour to promote commercial airship flights. Gene was thunderstruck. From that moment on, he abandoned his old hobby of collecting baseball cards and began to collect aviation cards. When the war began, he enrolled in an aero-engineering course at the Galt Aircraft School, but later remustered into air crew and trained RCAF pilots at the Service Flying level until the war ended.

The R100's trip over southern Ontario affected many others who saw it. The night before, August 10, the dirigible passed over Ottawa, and as she reached the Peace Tower on Parliament Hill six powerful searchlights illuminated her silver shape, creating an unforgettable sight. American millionaire Howard Hughes was rumoured to have offered $100,000 to have the R100 do a fly-past over New York. Toronto motorists got a free look as they stopped their cars in the streets to watch her circle the city.

One of the best spots for dirigible viewing was a house in the Cabbagetown section of Toronto. As the R100 circled the city, thirteen-year-old Allister Rutherford scrambled to the rooftop of his Winchester Street house and gazed at it until it was a speck in the distance. Rutherford lived with his bicycle at the ready; whenever there was the slightest indication of air traffic at the Leaside Aerodrome, he and his friends were off like a shot, pedalling uptown to watch what they called "the flying circus." His fascination for flying as well as mathematics led him into navigation instruction for the wartime RCAF; he served the Air Training Plan from coast to coast, from Chatham, New Brunswick, to Comox, British Columbia.

The Roaring Twenties and the Dirty Thirties—the best and worst of times—provided youngsters with plenty of opportunity to fall in love with flying. Wing-walkers, barnstormers, transoceanic daredevils, former First World War aces, aerobatic teams, and flying circuses of every shape and size gave demonstrations and shows all across Canada. On June 5, 1928, Amelia Earhart stopped in Halifax en route from Boston to Wales; on June 17, she became the first woman to cross the Atlantic by air. Ford Trimotor airplanes conducted

National Air Tours that stopped at centres all across North America in the 1920s. In April 1930, the RCAF inaugurated a demonstration flight of Siskin fighters; they were Canada's first touring aerobatic team. In July 1933, Charles Lindbergh made short stopovers in Halifax and St. John's on his way to Greenland, and Edmonton's Blatchford Field welcomed Wiley Post and his Lockheed Vega "Winnie May" in the midst of a solo round-the-world flight.

Owen Sound, where teenager Charlie Krause attended high school in the 1930s, was the birthplace of Canada's most celebrated fighter pilot, Billy Bishop. Krause remembers one of Bishop's homecomings, when he landed in a farmer's field on the outskirts of town. But the event that left a greater impression on him was a fly-past that didn't land in Owen Sound.

In July 1933, pioneering Italian aviator General Italo Balbo launched his historic Second Atlantic Aeronautica—a six-week mass transatlantic flight of seaplanes from Orbetello, Italy, to Chicago and back. Balbo wanted to commemorate the first decade of fascism in Italy and to impress his superior, Benito Mussolini. About noon on Saturday, July 15, Balbo's aerial armada of twenty-four Savoia Marchetti seaplanes (en route from Montreal to Chicago, where a huge reception awaited them) passed the southern edge of Georgian Bay, right over Charlie Krause's home town. "I always wanted to fly," Krause recalled, "I guess because for a country kid growing up on the farm, airplanes were fascinating. But the day that Italian outfit flew over town, that sort of sealed it." Eight years later Krause would join the RCAF, serve several years as a pilot instructor in the BCATP, and still make it overseas in time to fly night operations in Mosquitoes and survive the war.

Young Charley Fox of Guelph, Ontario, used to listen to his father's war stories. Thomas "Will" Fox had fought in the Boer War, serving with the British cavalry in the 10th Hussars, the same regiment as Lord Baden-Powell. As a result, Will Fox raised his sons, Ted and Charley, in a pretty strict fashion. But Charley's decision to join the war effort had much more to do with a summer day in 1934 when the RAF paid an unexpected visit.

"I never was one to make airplane models, or even think of getting up in the air," Fox said. "In fact, one time when they offered me a flight over the fair in Hamilton, I said, 'No. I'm afraid I'll be sick.' But that year there was a flight of Hawker Furys visiting from No. 1 Squadron of the Royal Air Force. I had read about them. They were silver-coloured fighter biplanes. They were doing demonstrations over Ontario and Quebec. And all of a sudden one day I hear this roar. Five silver airplanes came zooming from over the top of College Hill, glinting in the sunlight. Then swoosh . . . they were gone. But I never forgot it." By the time No. 1 RAF Squadron was in full combat back in Britain in 1940, Fox had enlisted in the RCAF. Before he went overseas in 1943 to fly Spitfires, he taught scores of BCATP trainees how to prepare themselves for the toughest flying assignments of their lives.

Others caught the aviation bug in more casual ways. Alan Stirton, the third son of six children in a Saskatchewan farm family, was smitten by flying entirely by accident. Each weekday he would hitch up the family pony, Fanny, to a buggy and head out for the Petrolia schoolhouse near Moose Jaw.

"One day in the fall of 1930, luck was with me. I was driving home from school, and a small airplane landed in our neighbour's stubble field. We hustled old Fanny into the barn and ran across the fields to admire this wonderful machine. Lo and behold, if the pilot didn't offer me a ride. What a thrill. I was only twelve at the time. But from then on I dreamed of becoming a pilot." Stirton did learn to fly, but getting his pilot's licence was a painful experience.

In spite of British prime minister Neville Chamberlain's assurance from Hitler in September 1938 that there would be "peace in our time," the Canadian government prepared for war by offering private flying clubs a $100 grant for every student pilot who received a licence. Dick Ryan, a First World War fighter pilot who managed the Moose Jaw Flying Club, placed ads in local newspapers offering to split the grant with any aspiring pilots.

"One free ride to assess your ability to become a pilot," Ryan promised, and offered a private pilot's licence if the trainee passed the tests after twenty hours of flying time. Total cost to the student: $150. The ad attracted a local RCMP constable, a couple of auto-mechanics, and a few others, including Al Stirton, who admitted, "I didn't know a rudder from an aileron." But it didn't take him long to scrape the cash together, and by October 1 he was airborne in a ten-year-old Gipsy Moth with Ryan himself. After seven and a half hours of dual instruction, Stirton did his first solo flight. And on November 14, 1938, he took his private pilot's test from an examiner visiting Moose Jaw from Edmonton.

"In those days," Stirton remembered, "no examiner dared risk his life by riding in the airplane with a student, but stayed on the ground and 'observed' the flight from the seat of his car. I was instructed to climb above the aerodrome, do a medium turn to the left, then one to the right, followed by a steep turn each way; then put the aircraft into a spin and recover; then fly to Ross Collegiate about one and a half miles distant and back; then circle the water tower in figure-eight turns; then do a spot landing back at the aerodrome.

"The examiner had positioned a square canvas sheet with a red X on the field. When I was downwind, he would wave a white flag and I was to close the throttle, glide down, land, and stop within fifty feet of the spot. All went well. And I stopped with the spot under the right wing."

At that point, Stirton noticed the instructor, Bob Eddie, speeding towards the Gipsy Moth in his car. Eddie leapt out of the driver's seat and proceeded to tear a strip off the pilot trainee.

"What did you do that for?"

"Do what for?" Stirton asked.

"I'll give you credit for getting down to the spot," Eddie fumed, "but you were turning at too low a height. You know you can't turn below 400 feet. Go up again, and if you're too high, side-slip off some height. But for God's sake don't turn so close to the ground!"

"A side-slip," Stirton repeated. "Okay." And off he went.

Unfortunately, Stirton had never been taught how to side-slip. On the second approach to the field, he throttled back, turned the Gipsy Moth to line up with the examiner's canvas sheet, noticed he had a bit too much height and lowered his left wing to slip sideways down closer to the ground.

"Suddenly, the aircraft stalled and sank like a brick," Stirton recalled. "I had forgotten to lower the nose to maintain flying speed as I came out of the side-slip, and the poor Gipsy Moth hit the ground so hard that the undercarriage was punched up into the fuselage. The wings drooped down onto the grass. And I cracked three ribs."

The crash of Gipsy Moth CF-ADI nearly put an end to Stirton's flying ambitions. But by January 18, 1939, the aircraft had been repaired and was flying again, and Bob Eddie's blood pressure was back to normal. Al Stirton passed and received his pilot's licence. In May, he had accumulated seventy hours on airplanes at the Moose Jaw Flying Club, and earned his commercial licence. But flying jobs were few and far between that summer, so he just took friends for rides to build up his hours.

If he had stopped flying after that crash landing, Stirton might never have been invited to join the British Commonwealth Air Training Plan. He wouldn't have taught the basic principles of flying to hundreds of young military pilot trainees at St. Catharines Elementary Flying Training School or flown any anti-submarine patrols in Sunderland flying boats with No. 423 RCAF Squadron over the North Atlantic.

In fall 1939 the Blitzkrieg against Poland began in Europe. Britain declared war on Germany on September 3. A week later Canada did the same. And that's when the war came looking for Al Stirton. The day after Canada declared war—September 11—Stirton received a telegram from the minister of national defence inviting him to serve in the Royal Canadian Air Force. Naturally, he answered yes, "thinking that I'd become a hero as a fighter pilot."

Similar missives arrived on the desks of flying clubs and private aviation companies from Halifax to Vancouver to Yellowknife. Just about everyone who was anyone in the commercial flying business in Canada received a telegram.

Wilfrid "Wop" May received one in Edmonton. A former Royal Flying Corps pilot, May had returned from the First World War a hero with a DFC and twelve enemy aircraft to his credit. The following year he had launched the first air service at Edmonton's Blatchford Field. May is credited with the first commercial flight from Edmonton, the first freighting flight for Imperial Oil into the Northwest Territories, and the first commercial passenger flights into the Peace River district of Alberta. May's mercy mission of flying diphtheria vaccine in an open cockpit Avro Avian from Edmonton 500 miles to Fort Vermilion on January 3, 1929, captured world attention; as did his participation in the pursuit and apprehension of Albert Johnson (dubbed the Mad Trapper) in 1931. Wop May, like Al Stirton, answered the telegram (and for his role in the BCATP was eventually awarded the American Medal of Freedom).

Ottawa also sent for Clennell Haggerston Dickins in Winnipeg. At the time "Punch" Dickins was in his thirties and working as the general superintendent of Canadian Airways. He was in charge of all air mail service from the Great Lakes to the Pacific and the Arctic. Dickins, like May, was a First World War veteran in the Royal Flying Corps with a DFC to his credit and had pursued his aviation career in the bush, flying in and supplying prospectors in the North. His flight for Dominion Explorers in 1928 was the first ever to survey the barren lands of the Arctic. In 1929 Dickins had been the first pilot to fly over the Arctic Circle in Canada. The call from Canadian Pacific president Sir Edward Beatty about "a wartime job" for Dickins turned out to be crucial to the launching of the Atlantic Ferry Organization.

Calls also went out to a couple of commercial pilots flying in Quebec—Charles Roy Troup and Walter Woollett. "Peter" Troup had served in the RAF's peacetime No. 39 Bomber Squadron but had resigned his commission, emigrated to Canada, and pursued a career in Quebec's bush country with Fairchild Aviation. Not long thereafter,

"Babe" Woollett did the same, leaving No. 29 RAF Fighter Squadron to seek his fortune at Fairchild in Canada.

Between them, Troup and Woollett did every conceivable kind of flying in the 1920s and 1930s. Troup raced seaplanes at the Canadian National Exhibition and led the Trans Canada Air Tour of eight Bellanca aircraft as part of a sales promotion. Woollett flew some of the first survey crews into northern Quebec and Labrador, flew an international mail route, and led countless rescue missions, including one to locate and retrieve his friend Peter Troup. But the greatest of their collaborations cast Troup and Woollett as co-designers of the BCATP Air Observer Schools, right after war was declared.

The skill of the air observer was viewed by the RAF military establishment with awe that bordered on reverence. In its air crew training manuals the British Air Ministry went so far as to say that "in many respects the air observer has the most responsible and exacting task in a bomber aircraft. . . . Mentally he must always be on the alert. . . . He must estimate and plot the course, be able to take snap readings, judge weather conditions, look out for ice and keep alternative objectives and landing grounds in the back of his mind . . . He must show a marked ability to handle figures, and be sufficiently skilled in signals to take a portion of work off the wireless operator. Above all he must never make mistakes . . . He is a wise and considerate pilot who appreciates the difficulties of his air observer." Few flyers had greater respect for the air observer than did Babe Woollett.

Woollett's high regard for the skills of air observation came from one of his earliest flying experiences. As an RAF elementary flying student training at Duxford EFTS in 1924, Woollett quickly adapted to doing "circuits and bumps" with the instructor in the second cockpit of his trainer aircraft, an Avro 504K biplane. On the day he soloed, leaving his instructor, Flight Lieutenant Sutherland, on the ground, Woollett became so enraptured by the sights of nearby Cambridge that he headed for home in the wrong direction. After buzzing the horseracing crowd in the grandstand at Newmarket on Classic Race Day, "my main concern became finding my way home. Fortunately, I happened to know that the main road from Newmarket to London ran right through the middle of Duxford Air Force Station." When he finally landed back at Duxford he was nearly court-martialled for flying so low over the standing-room-only Newmarket grandstand; but he gained a life-long respect for those who navigate aircraft to and from given points on the map.

Probationary Pilot Officer Woollett advanced from his Avro trainer to the presentation of his RAF wings and confirmation as a pilot officer. After five years of peacetime service in No. 29 RAF Fighter Squadron, he emigrated to Canada in 1929 and spent ten years "flying in the backwoods of [northern Quebec and Labrador with its] uncharted lakes. . . . We'd go through the ice, hit rocks and driftwood . . . through a lot of very dangerous and dashing flying." In addition to navigating his way around the bush, Woollett had worked his way up to operations manager of Dominion Skyways, based in Rouyn/Noranda. But in 1939 he was prepared to leave all that behind to fly once again with the RAF.

Two things prevented his repatriation to England: at thirty-three he was too old by air force standards for Fighter Command, and secondly he was encouraged by an old RAF friend to stay in Canada to play a much larger role in the war. "Air Chief Marshal Sholto Douglas wrote back to me," Woollett said, after appealing directly to Douglas to pull a few strings and get him back into the RAF. "Douglas explained that . . . the same way they were going to call on the private aero clubs [in Canada] to operate the elementary flying training schools in the BCATP . . . they were going to call on civil air operators to help set up another dimension of the BCATP. . . . They felt that from this colossal group of experienced and resourceful people—the mechanics [or air engineers] and bush pilots—they could develop schools [in Canada] operated without drawing on the people with potential fighting or military value." That's how "Dougie," as Woollett knew him, wanted him to fight the war.

Thus, as Lord Riverdale and the British delegation grappled with Prime Minister Mackenzie King over quotas, national identity, and the budget of the air training plan, the civilian operators were invited to study the requirements for running Air Observer Schools (AOSs), to draft construction and operating plans, and to submit tenders to the government.

The original BCATP document, signed December 17, 1939, called for ten AOSs, capable of graduating 340 observers a month, or about 4,000 a year. Most AOSs would be at municipal airfields, sometimes sharing facilities with EFTSs. The RCAF would supply the basic facilities and equipment, while the former bush flying companies would organize and carry out all operating services—from catering to classroom maintenance. In addition, the civilian companies had to hire civilian pilots to chauffeur the air observers on training flights.

"We gathered in Ottawa," Woollett remembered. "All the major bush contractors throughout Canada were requested to submit estimates to the Department of Defence: Dominion Skyways, Yukon Southern, Canadian Airways, Wings, Prairie Airways, Mackenzie Air Service, Starratt Airways, Leavens Brothers, Ginger Coote Airways, Quebec Airways, and others. . . . While a lot of us were under the umbrella of Canadian Pacific, the companies retained their individual identities . . . ensuring the government a real competition, plus a variety of approaches and totals from which to choose."

Peter Troup and Babe Woollett virtually lived at the Château Laurier hotel in Ottawa as they dug up every shred of information they could to win for their company, Dominion Skyways, the business and the honour of organizing the Air Observer Schools. Among the big questions facing the "Château Rats," as they were called, was the cost of heating. None of the bush operators had heated more than sheds and hangars to that point, and the BCATP required the heating of administrative buildings, mess halls, barracks, classrooms, and other structures at each of the planned ten schools. Feeding the AOS recruits posed another problem. How could the schools guarantee the highest quality of food—such as meat—for air observer students, while such food was rationed in the civilian communities where the schools were to be located? Then there was the janitorial problem. What would it cost to hire staff to clean everything from sheets and kitchens to washrooms? On the flight line they had to estimate the costs of aircraft maintenance, fuel and oil consumption, and maintenance crew salaries, all "pretty monumental considerations for a bunch of half-assed bush pilots.

"Eventually, our group had to wind up our effort to make the presentation deadline for the Department of Defence," Woollett said. "We bundled the necessary sets of papers into their separate envelopes, and I stood waiting to take over the baton, like a chap in a relay race. With only about thirty minutes to get over to Defence Headquarters, some meticulous member of our team suddenly gasped: 'My God! We haven't any sealing wax, and they have to be sealed!'

"Finally, I had to run over to this office and hand in our submission without sealing wax, but with the prescribed number of copies all sealed in separate envelopes with tape . . . I was out of breath as I handed the bids over to some rather stuffy old general, who refused to accept them because they were not all sealed with red sealing wax . . . I rushed to the outer office where they helped me get the damn things sealed . . . and got it signed in. There was only five minutes left before they lowered the boom."

The proposals varied widely from company to company. Some of the highest bids were ten times that of the lowest. Other submissions were presented on a single sheet with only the bottom-line figure attached. The Department of Defence tossed them all out, but recognized the sensible cost breakdown in the Dominion Skyways bid.

"He called us back in and explained they were not satisfied, but would we sit down with Leonard Apedaile, who was financial adviser to the minister, and thrash this thing out . . . [so] the operators could handle the scheme without making a colossal profit . . . [nor] go belly up." Woollett and Troup were asked to form a subsidiary company, Dominion Skyways Training Ltd., to operate the first Air Observer School on a non-profit basis.

They opened No. 1 AOS at Malton, Ontario, on May 27, 1940. It became the template for the nine AOSs that followed, and in Woollett's view "one of the most important factors in the success of the whole cooperative effort between the RCAF and the civilian operators." By New Year's Day 1941, the Troup/Woollett-managed Dominion Skyways Training school (and three others up and running in

Edmonton, Regina, and London) had graduated 115 air observers, who, unlike Woollett on his first solo, could guide an aircraft home.

Scores of other civilian flyers were contacted by the minister of national defence. Johnny Fauquier left a charter operation on the lower St. Lawrence to teach instructors at Trenton and then became one of the RCAF's leading bomber pilots. Matt Berry left bush flying to run the No. 7 Air Observer School at Portage La Prairie. Moss Burbidge was called out of retirement after 15,000 flying hours to become chief flying instructor at No. 16 EFTS in Edmonton. Stu Graham went from pilot testing to designing BCATP aerodromes. Don Watson left Canadian Airways to assist technical training. Dennis Yorath, a pilot with the Calgary Flying Club, took up duties as manager of No. 5 EFTS Lethbridge. Fred McCall helped organize Canadian flying clubs to support the EFTS system. Harry Kennedy left Trans-Canada Airlines to teach instrument and night flying. Arthur Wilson brought his skills as a flying club instructor to several Service Flying Training Schools. R.S. Grandy left commercial flying in Newfoundland to instruct pilots at Camp Borden. Jock Palmer stopped flying explosives into the north to instruct pilots in the BCATP. Romeo Vachon, who had pioneered air services along the north shore of the St. Lawrence, organized aircraft overhauls. And Grant McConachie, who had pioneered air mail and passenger service from Edmonton to Whitehorse, later became responsible for managing Canadian Pacific Airlines' western operations, including four Air Observer Schools.

That summer, one of Grant McConachie's part-time pilots at Yukon Southern Air Transport was nineteen-year-old Russ Bannock from Edmonton. He'd grown up within cycling distance of Edmonton's Blatchford Field, where he'd witnessed the early comings and goings of the best bush pilots in the North—Punch Dickins flying his Fokker Super Universal, Leigh Brintnell aboard his tri-motored Fokker, and Wop May and his Junkers W34. And he'd been dazzled by the aviation celebrities who had passed through Blatchford, men such as movie actor Wallace Beery flying his Bellanca Skyrocket, Wiley Post on his around-the-world solo flight, or American speed pilot Frank Hawks arriving at the 1930 Air Show with his Travel Air Mystery Ship, the Texaco 13. He'd seen the fleet of ten Martin B-10 bombers en route to Alaska, the Ford Reliability Tour, and the Pitcairn Autogiro.

Although he loved flying, Bannock had his sights set on a job in mining, and he settled down to a routine of school in the winter months and summer jobs to earn the money for tuition. In 1937 he landed a summer job as a bar steward aboard a Hudson's Bay Company steamer heading north down the Mackenzie River. The *Distributor* made two trips each summer, pushing a cluster of barges loaded with supplies for the communities along the river. On the second trip, he heard that a company in Yellowknife, Consolidated Mining & Smelting, was recruiting workers for mineral exploration work. So he jumped ship in Fort Smith and looked for a way to Yellowknife.

The only quick route north across Great Slave Lake to Yellowknife was by air. Bannock bought a ticket and went to the seaplane dock on the Slave River, where he found Stan McMillan loading his Fairchild 71 for the next leg of his freighting trip to Yellowknife. McMillan was another of the flying legends of the North. Although he began flying in the officers training corps and earned his military wings with the fledgling RCAF in the mid-1920s, Stan really cut his teeth in aviation by flying mail, men, and supplies to Hudson Bay and the Arctic. In late 1929 he had flown one of two aircraft for Colonel C. MacAlpine of the Dominion Explorer Company. The north-bound expedition planned to survey 12,500 square miles of uncharted territory from Churchill on Hudson Bay to Aklavik at the mouth of the Mackenzie River. Along the way, weather forced the eight-man expedition down, and it took them fifty-four days to trek out of the frigid Arctic wilderness to Cambridge Bay on Victoria Island. (McMillan would later join the BCATP to manage several Air Observer Schools.)

Bannock watched McMillan packing the Fairchild and wondered whether there'd be room enough for a passenger.

"I thought I was supposed to go on this flight," he said to the pilot.

"You are," McMillan said.

"Where am I going to sit, then?"

McMillan pointed at the freight compartment, where there was just enough space for a man to lie flat between the pile of freight and the roof of the airplane. "Just climb on top of the load," he said.

All Bannock can remember of his first plane ride was the cramped space and the rough ninety-minute ride to Yellowknife. "The weather was bad, so we flew across Great Slave Lake and never got above a hundred feet. I'll never forget it."

Bannock made it to Yellowknife and joined Consolidated for the summer. That fall, back in Edmonton, he told his father he was going to become a flying geologist, and he took lessons at the Northern Alberta Aero Club for his pilot's licence. By the summer of 1939 he had earned his commercial pilot's licence. Then Grant McConachie asked him to join Yukon Southern Air Transport. Bannock accepted and that summer he flew as co-pilot and mechanic for McConachie between Edmonton and Whitehorse. He earned little but learned a lot. When he heard that the Calgary Auxiliary Squadron was flying Westland Wapiti bombers, he applied there. But before he could be accepted, his telegram arrived from the minister of national defence.

Even though the full extent of his flying experience was two summers in the bush—one in mineral exploration, the other as a co-pilot flying mail for Grant McConachie—Bannock was prime material for the Royal Canadian Air Force, a force desperate for trained pilots. At the outbreak of war, the RCAF total strength was 298 officers and 2,750 airmen, with an auxiliary force of 1,013. Its flying arsenal consisted of 270 aircraft.

As well as an obvious shortfall in aircraft and trained airmen, when the war began the RCAF had only five operating aerodromes and half a dozen under construction, and there were only two construction engineers in its employ. With a scheme of such mammoth proportions before them, the air force called on the experience of private industry for help.* The RCAF formed the Directorate of Works and

---

* Because much of the BCATP training would be done in winter, there was also a sudden demand for aircraft skis on elementary training aircraft. Coincidentally, in Sioux Lookout, Ontario, boat builders Warner and Carmen Elliott had perfected a

Buildings and appointed R.R. Collard (the vice-president and general manager of a Winnipeg construction firm) as its first commander.

Despite the impossible deadlines, congested working conditions, and a shortage of staff, Collard's group produced more than three-quarters of a million blueprints and 33,000 drawings, which were used to build 8,300 hangars, drill halls, and barracks blocks. From fall 1939 through to spring 1940, an army of engineers, teamsters, carpenters, plumbers, and thousands of other tradespeople excavated and graded sites, dug wells for water, erected and framed buildings, and poured enough cement to have made a twenty-foot wide highway from Ottawa to Vancouver. So rapid and massive was the BCATP site construction that communities such as Rivers, Manitoba (where a navigation school was built) compared the arrival of the BCATP to the arrival of the railway at the turn of the century.

However, at the end of 1939, the master scheme—the British Commonwealth Air Training Plan—that would deliver a force of professional military air crew to the war effort was still just a piece of paper.

It would be another six months before the organization could start processing BCATP trainees at its seventeen recruiting centres. It would be just as long before raw recruits arrived by the thousands at three Manning Depots across the country to be introduced to air force discipline and guard duty. The seven Initial Training Schools were not yet ready to stream men into the three basic air crew functions: pilot, observer, and air gunner. The elaborate and expensive scheme to have civilian aviation organize twenty-six Elementary Flying Training Schools and ten Air Observer Schools was still being thrashed out at the Château Laurier in Ottawa. And the first of more

---

wood lamination process in the manufacture of aircraft skis for legendary bush pilot Harold "Doc" Oaks and for Admiral Richard Byrd's three Antarctic expeditions in the 1930s. When BCATP authorities found out about their work, the Elliott brothers were astonished to receive orders from de Havilland for 400 sets of skis; local service station operator, Bill Fuller, converted his service bays into an assembly line and the ski orders were met.

than forty Service Flying Training Schools wouldn't put their first trainees into Harvards until mid-1940.

The British Commonwealth Air Training Plan, what one journalist of the time later called "the greatest single achievement of the Canadian people since our provinces came together in the Confederation that is Canada," was a long way from delivering on its promise of 19,500 trained air crew a year, let alone delivering a death blow to the Luftwaffe.

In December 1939, the British Commonwealth Air Training Plan consisted of committee minutes, accounting ledgers, designer blueprints, munition requisitions, manpower quotas, and a legislative document with a deadline. What it needed was a core flying force whose experience wouldn't be used in fighter sorties over the English Channel nor in bombing runs over Germany, but in training the air crew that would. Consequently, although it was never really announced as such, building a nucleus of military flying instructors became one of the early objectives of the wartime RCAF. There was no time to lose.

Zero Day, the day on which training under the plan was to begin, was April 29, 1940. The first fully trained graduates were scheduled to receive their wings that autumn at the earliest. In the meantime, civilian flyers from the bush, from commercial aviation, from the barnstorming circuit, and from the string of small flying clubs across the country were lining up to become military pilots and get into the fighting. They would have to fill the gap until the plan began to produce new pilots.

"Civilian pilots were the initial backbone of the training plan," Russ Bannock said. "Most of them, like myself, had never been in the air force. The regimentation was quite strange at first. I was sent to a coastal squadron equipped with Avro Avians. But when they realized I had only forty or fifty hours of flying experience, I was seconded to the flying club in Vancouver.

"There [at the British Columbia Aviation School] I was taught basic aerobatics and instrument flying, the equivalent to the Elementary Flying Training School in the plan. We were the first wartime course; it was called the provisional pilot officer course. None of us had any uniforms. We were all in civilian clothing, but we were still called pilot officers."

The RCAF had traditionally enrolled pilot recruits as provisional pilot officers, or PPOs, perhaps to make up for the air force's shortage of official uniforms. But a month after Russ Bannock arrived at Trenton for officers' school, he was in uniform. At the beginning of 1940, he was on his way to Camp Borden, near Barrie, Ontario, the only service (or advanced) flying level school in Canada at the time.

"My first instructor at Camp Borden was a sergeant pilot. He wasn't a very good instructor. In fact, he scared himself whenever he put a Harvard into a spin. It was the same with aerobatics. One time he was trying to teach me a loop, and it must have been a bad one, because we fell into a spin. So he never attempted to teach me loops again. I had to teach myself once I went solo."

Another PPO who came to Borden from civilian flying was a twenty-one-year-old Nova Scotian, Fred Macdonell. Both of his parents had served in the medical corps during the First World War—his father as a doctor, his mother as a nurse—and Fred was born in London, England, in May 1918. On the night of the armistice, November 11, 1918, Macdonell's parents went to the theatre to see *Peter Pan*, and his father fell sick with influenza. He died four days later. Fred had intended to follow in his father's footsteps, to become a doctor. But the declaration of war in September 1939 changed his plans too. Once they signed him up, the air force sent him for basic flying instruction to the Halifax Flying Club and then on to Camp Borden early in 1940.

"I trained on Anson Is," Macdonell explained. "They were pretty primitive. The brakes worked on air pressure, so they had to fill up tanks [with compressed air] so you had brakes when you landed. And each time you used the brakes, the pressure would go down.

"I remember I had my first solo at the island airport in Toronto. It was a really tiny runway for an airplane like an Anson. And with those funny air brakes in the Anson, I had visions of going off the end of the runway. I thought I wasn't going to land without going into the water.

It wasn't really frightening. You were young and you sort of took it in stride. You were more on an edge then."

Frank Montgomery was quite used to "primitive" aircraft. His family had farmed near Vanda, Saskatchewan, where he was born in 1916, but a series of crop failures forced them to move to Saskatoon. There he discovered the Saskatoon Aero Club and started flying, financing his lessons by doing odd jobs—painting houses and picking rocks from farmers' fields. He flew a Gipsy Moth and a Waco 10. He took his flight test for his private pilot's licence in an old Avian, while the district inspector, who'd travelled up from Winnipeg, watched from a deck chair on the Saskatoon airfield.

Montgomery was working on his commercial licence when he received his telegram from National Defence on November 3, 1939. He got on the train in Saskatoon and arrived at Camp Borden three days later.

"They put me right into a Harvard," Montgomery said. "Now, I'd flown nothing but Gipsy Moths and that old Waco. Well, it didn't make any difference [to them]. You were supposed to be able to fly. If I'd had more experience, I might have said, 'Hey, what about a check flight?' But in those days, if you could hack it, you were in. If you couldn't, you were gone."

Experience in the air was a rare commodity in Canada. Even a few extra hours and a slightly higher designation made all the difference to an individual's prospects. For example, twenty-three-year-old Don Rogers had his civilian instructor's licence from the Hamilton Aero Club, so when the RCAF contacted him in August 1939, he was offered a special course at Camp Borden. Rogers was checked out and quickly reassigned back to the Hamilton Aero Club, where "in mid-September we received the first four of a year-long series of PPOs to train to the equivalent of private pilot's qualifications."

Another seasoned flyer pressed into early military service was Len Trippe. Like Peter Troup and Babe Woollett (who had left the RAF in England to fly bush runs along the lower St. Lawrence and north into Quebec), Trippe left the Air Force Reserve in England, arrived in Canada, and joined the Ontario Provincial Air Service based in

Sudbury. He did his first bush piloting in flying boats in 1924. In the late 1920s he began instructing at various southern Ontario flying schools. When times got tougher and flying students fewer in the 1930s he barnstormed to boost business. Trippe and his colleagues dreamed up "death-defying" acts, including parachute jumps and wing-walking, and improvised stunts such as the one they used to entertain a crowd at a Victoria Day celebration at Port Dalhousie on Lake Ontario. "We tied an inner tube to the undercarriage of the Moth," Trippe recalled. "Then once we were in the air over the water [parachutist George Bennett] crawled out of the cockpit, hooked his legs through the inner tube and hung head down, no parachute or anything. George couldn't even swim a stroke."

By the late 1930s Trippe found himself at one of the busiest private airfields in southern Ontario—Barker Field, in what was then northwest Toronto. Three aviation firms ran businesses there: Patterson and Hill, Fred Gillies Flying Service, and Leavens Brothers, where Trippe found work instructing. President Clare Leavens toured the countryside with a sound truck selling flying lessons and passenger flights at a cent a pound. On any given Sunday there'd be twenty-four or more aircraft taxiing around Barker Field, taking off and landing without the aid of air traffic control. There was never an accident.

"In 1939, the government came to Leavens Brothers," Trippe said, "and asked if Leavens could gather up all the private pilots they could possibly find that were interested in becoming instructors for the RCAF. These pilots [the provisional pilot officers] were given a living-out allowance, AC2 [Aircraftman 2nd Class] pay, and their flying free—a hundred hours with us—still in civilian clothes.

"So we gathered up a bunch of pilots, including private pilots from the States. We bought six Tiger Moths and the RCAF gave us six Fleet Finches. All we had to do was supply the gas and oil and service our own aircraft. We had about fifteen students there at a time. And we rushed them through."

"For us as instructors," Don Rogers added, "there were the few minutes of nervous tension, watching your student's first solo, and the extended period of tension, waiting for him to return safely from his first solo cross-country flight. Yet we knew we were performing an essential task for the war effort. It seemed like a relatively lowly first step to operational flying."

Operational flying, or combat flying, was the objective for nearly all young pilots joining the RCAF in fall 1939. They didn't have to read the editorial columns in the *Globe and Mail* or listen to Lorne Greene's "Voice of Doom" on CBC Radio news broadcasts to realize that RCAF-trained fighter and bomber pilots would soon be on their way to Britain in support of the Royal Air Force and the British Expeditionary Force in Europe.

Bush pilot Russ Bannock wanted to be a fighter pilot. Medical student Fred Macdonell wanted to be posted overseas as his father had been in the Great War. Saskatoon Aero Club pilot Frank Montgomery had grown up listening to stories of First World War combat from his neighbour, former RFC/RAF fighter pilot Vic Graham, and he longed for the same kind of adventure. And Don Rogers figured a short stint teaching PPOs elementary flying was a sure stepping stone to an operational posting.

It wasn't to be. The irony was that their experience and eagerness to enter the RCAF worked against these ambitions. Because they were so quick to enter the air force, which was now committed to producing nearly 20,000 qualified air crew a year, their dream of flying combat missions at the controls of Hurricanes or Spitfires could not be realized. For many of the qualified pilots who joined the RCAF in 1939 as provisional pilot officers or civilian instructors, there was a much less heroic and yet more crucial role to play.

The RCAF dragnet for pilots qualified to teach caught a former Winnipeg barnstormer named Wess McIntosh just as he'd made up his mind to fly in the air force. Six years before, his grandmother had died and left him $500, and he'd convinced his father to let him invest the money in flying lessons at the Northwest Aeromarine flying school in Winnipeg. Within a year he had earned his certificate of competency. His first flying job was with the flying club in Winnipeg, doing test flights of various aircraft. By 1935 he was barnstorming, taking up thirty to forty customers on a good day at $1.50 per ride.

"Sometimes, I would go into factories and sell tickets for 25 cents each," McIntosh recalled. "Then as soon as I sold a dollar-and-a-half's worth, I'd put the names in a hat and draw out the name of the guy who'd won the airplane ride. He'd come out to Stevenson field and he'd get a flight over Winnipeg and back. We didn't play around at all. No aerobatics . . . I didn't know how to, anyway."

By 1939 McIntosh had 407 hours' flying time. But try as he might to get more substantial work with Connie Johansen's air chartering company or Punch Dickins's Western Canada Airways at Stevenson Airport in Winnipeg, it never worked out. McIntosh joined the Canadian Naval Reserves, who were looking for volunteers to ship out overseas to take delivery of a destroyer that the Canadian government had purchased. If all else failed, McIntosh figured he might get an interview in Britain with Imperial Airways, who were hiring Canadians.

"Just as I got to Halifax, war was declared," McIntosh continued. "So they shut the gates on us. We sat there for the seven days it took Canada to declare war on Germany." McIntosh believed that the Canadian government deliberately declared war on Germany a week later to allow its two destroyers—the *St. Laurent* and the *Fraser*—to steam from the Pacific through the American-controlled Panama Canal to the Atlantic without jeopardizing American neutrality. While in Halifax, McIntosh got permission to transfer to the air force.

"The air force said they'd take me on as a sergeant pilot, if I got released. (I didn't know it at the time, but they'd already sent a pilot's commission to my home.) So, I got paraded before my Navy CO, who said, 'We need you here. Why do you want to leave for the air force?' I showed him my logbooks and explained that I'd get an air force commission if I joined, and he said, 'Permission granted.'

"I was discharged from the navy on the twenty-ninth of September, 1939. And it's a good thing, because if I had shipped out on the destroyer *Fraser*, I wouldn't be here." (On that trip, the *Fraser* was rammed and sunk.)

Within two weeks, instead of being at the bottom of the Atlantic, Wess McIntosh was 5,000 feet in the air—a student again—flying as many training aircraft as the air force could scrape together—Fleet Finches, Harvards, and Airspeed Oxfords.

In the instructors' cockpits, at the second set of controls, were the best civilian and military flying instructors the RCAF could find. During those first weeks at the Borden and Trenton air force stations, McIntosh took instruction from Canadian bush pilot Johnny Fauquier (later decorated for his "pathfinder" operational flights over targets in Europe) and then from a Royal Air Force flight lieutenant named Dick Waterhouse.

"Dick was an Englishman," McIntosh said. "He'd been in the RAF quite a while and he was just good, that's all. In theory, we were flying with an officer. But after the first salute in the morning, that was it. He was the instructor, I was the student. But we didn't have to salute and stand at attention all the time. He treated me well. Dick had a dog called Pluto, a beautiful black lab. This dog could come into the mess and pick up a glass of beer in its mouth and take it to Waterhouse."

For McIntosh's course of civilian students, unnecessary saluting was a waste of effort, and time for beer in the mess was limited. Zero Day was fast approaching, and the quota of fully trained flying instructors seemed unattainable. When McIntosh completed the elementary program at Borden there was no ceremony to mark the beginning of his advanced flying at Trenton. The RCAF wartime agenda overlooked the graduation of his class and McIntosh's Category C instructor's designation.

"They realized we hadn't had our wings [graduation]," McIntosh said. "I think they had actually forgotten. So they had a quick wings parade. There weren't many of us. They just lined us up in a hurry in a hangar and sort of said, 'Here, you're a military pilot now.'"

On March 18, 1940, McIntosh conducted a familiarization, or introductory, flight with his first student, a pilot officer named Rhodes. Rhodes was the first of more than 500 students McIntosh would teach in the British Commonwealth Air Training Plan. His official blue RCAF Pilot's Flying Log Book eventually recorded more than 3,000 hours of instruction flying.

"The strange part," McIntosh remembered, "was that I was still a sergeant pilot. Here I'm an instructor. Here's my first student—a pilot officer. We had been in the air force before them, but we were junior to them. They were all provisional pilot officers. But there wasn't time to worry about it.

"I had six students at a time. I used to fly six times a day, day in and day out [because] the big push was on. It looked like they would need every pilot they could get their hands on in England."

It would be another eight months before the first BCATP graduates arrived in Liverpool, England, for posting to operational units. A great deal more planning needed to be done. There were aerodrome sites to be selected, as the RCAF had only five of its own at the beginning of the war. Barracks, hangars, and other station buildings had to be designed and built. Supply systems to support the operation of more than a hundred planned air training stations—everything from hot and cold running water to parachute packing to mail delivery and laundry facilities—had to be organized.

Because the air force owned only a few dozen of the projected 3,500 training aircraft it would need, Tiger Moths, Fleet Finches, North American Harvards, Avro Ansons, and Fairey Battles had to be procured for the millions of instructional hours that lay ahead. The recruiting system itself had to be streamlined; indeed, in November 1939, recruiting had to be suspended to allow overworked officers at the recruiting centres to take stock. And more qualified instructors were always needed. Fortunately, though, for Wess McIntosh, his fellow instructors, and the RCAF, an accident of history gave the BCATP—newborn in December 1939—time to mature and deliver its first offspring to the war effort before it was too late.

3

ABANDON HOPE ALL YE WHO ENTER HERE

SIXTY-THREE MINUTES after the expiry of Britain's ultimatum to Germany on September 3, 1939, a British Blenheim reconnaissance bomber flew from Wyton airfield to photograph German shipping north of Wilhelmshaven. It was the Allied Bomber Command's first sortie of the Second World War.

The same day eighteen Hampden and nine Wellington aircraft searched for but found no German warships in the North Sea. That night Whitley bombers dropped 5.4 million propaganda leaflets over Hamburg, Bremen, and nine cities in the Ruhr valley. The next day, twenty-nine Blenheim and Wellington bombers returned to Wilhelmshaven to attack the battleship *Admiral Von Scheer* and the cruiser *Emden*. A quarter of the aircraft were lost, and Bomber Command recorded its first casualties of the war. It was nearly six weeks before German bombers made their first attack on British territory, damaging two cruisers in Scotland's Firth of Forth.

The opening months of the war in western Europe were in stark contrast to the violent clashes of arms that had taken place twenty-five years before. In 1914 Anglo-French forces had faced an immediate German invasion, so they struck eastward with great force; they were repulsed with heavy casualties. In fall 1939 and early 1940 the French and English Allies moved cautiously up to the Westwall (the German border fortifications) and then retreated to the dubious safety of the Maginot Line. What followed were months of relative inactivity—a period dubbed by the Germans "*Sitzkrieg*" and by American journalists the "Phony War."

On the ground, operational activity consisted of building defences from scratch between the end of the existing Maginot Line on the Belgian border, northwest towards the North Sea. This kept the Allied defenders busy, but out of combat, in the autumn and winter. However, there was one weapon with which the Allies could strike directly at Germany—the bomber.

During the Phony War between September 3, 1939, and April 8, 1940, RAF Bomber Command continued to conduct reconnaissance, dropped more leaflets and seventy-one tons of bombs, and attacked Germany's North Sea shipping and a number of its seaplane bases. The pilots made 996 daylight sorties and 531 night sorties. Sixty-two aircraft were lost, which represented 4 percent of RAF Bomber Command's engaging aircraft. However, that figure does not reflect the air crew casualties—pilots, navigators, wireless operators, and gunners. They numbered in the hundreds, in just seven months of hit-and-run air warfare.

One survivor of those first thousand Bomber Command sorties was a young Canadian RAF pilot officer. During the late 1930s, when the RCAF offered very few opportunities for aspiring military pilots, W.J. "Mike" Lewis, from Welcome, Ontario, managed to get to Britain via a program that offered short-service commissions for Canadians in the RAF. Just as the war broke out, Lewis completed his training as a bomber pilot and was immediately posted to No. 44 RAF Squadron at Waddington in Lincolnshire.

"I flew one of the first Hampden missions against German shipping," Lewis recalled. "But it was extremely frustrating. The British government wouldn't let us drop bombs on Germany, only targets at sea."

Pilot Officer Lewis's impatience to "get on with it" was shared by most RAF air crew. Along with the general excitement, Lewis recalled the tireless efforts of his commander early in the war. Newly appointed RAF Air Vice-Marshal Arthur Harris was a constant presence at No. 5 Group Bomber Command stations involved in the early action. The two met, and Mike Lewis, far from family and home in Canada, was invited to the Harrises' home for Christmas dinner in 1939.

"It was a social occasion," Lewis said. "Very little talk of the war. But the frustration was obvious to all of us."

The orders not to bomb German land targets seemed all the more unreasonable when British Air Ministry officials assembled all the air crew at Lewis's station for an announcement about the potential severity of the war. Lewis remembered the ministry representative saying that "if Britain went beyond the Phony War to a full war, [the ministry] expected that Bomber Command in strength would be wiped out twelve times during the first year of hostilities." In other words, Lewis was told, "You've got a month to live."

The escalation in the number of sorties, the rising fatality statistics, and the harsh realities recognized by the Air Ministry were further proof that as the air war intensified, qualified air crew would be desperately needed. And if seven months of bomber and air crew losses and a plea from British officials were not enough to strengthen the resolve of the BCATP organizers, then an incident in the skies over England certainly was.

At the time, Jack Meadows, an RAF flying instructor, was teaching prospective fighter pilots on North American-built Harvards. "At No. 15 Service Flying Training School at Kidlington, just outside Oxford," Meadows said, "[we were] insulated from the battle and [knew] little more than we read in the papers. We had our own job to do, teaching the pilots to replace the casualties. We got on with it, vaguely aware that if an invasion ever happened we would be trying to strafe the beaches in our 150-mph Harvard advanced trainers, with one fixed forward .303 Browning gun and eight small bombs hung on external racks.

"A pupil in an Anson, on his first night solo from our satellite airfield, [was] shot at by an intruding Junkers 88 and, almost certainly accidentally, collided with it. The episode became worked up into a case of a gallant deliberate ramming by the unarmed RAF pilot.... Enemy activity often stopped night flying."

It was tough enough for young trainees to keep their attention focused on cockpit instruments without having to scan the night sky for intruders looking for quarry. It was tougher still for an instructor to build student confidence in the air when his classes were constantly grounded by the threat of Luftwaffe attack. The death of the Anson pilot trainee and others like him underscored the need to get Canada's fledgling air training plan and its nucleus of experienced instructors off the ground.

Canada was 3,000 miles from the front; instructors there could coax their novice students into the air without fear of enemy intrusion. Flying conditions were ideal. Canada was situated centrally in the Commonwealth and strategically close to the largest industrial power outside Europe—the United States. All the plan needed were updated facilities and aircraft and enough instructors qualified to operate them.

The first military experience of many Canadians who went on to become those much-needed instructors was Manning Depot (or Manning Pool). One of the recruits was Livingston Foster, who turned twenty a couple of weeks after Canada declared war on Germany. His first experience of flying had occurred on the Niagara escarpment west of his family's farm near Grimsby, Ontario, in 1934. On a lazy afternoon late that spring, he and a bunch of his school chums saw an odd-looking contraption come down and land in a field. The pilot of this Pitcairn Autogiro—a forerunner of the helicopter—was barnstormer Walt Leavens, of the Leavens Brothers outfit at Barker Field in Toronto. Leavens was willing to offer rides. Foster and his chums were game, until the moment they entered the machine.

"Cap" Foster, as he was known (named after his godfather, Captain Livingston, a veteran of the First World War), didn't want to appear frightened. "The apprehension inside me bordered on sheer terror," Foster later wrote. "Even though I was shaking in my boots, I wasn't going to let my friends see it. I was going up, come hell or high water. The strange part of it, though, was that once we got airborne, the most wonderful feeling came over me—sublime enjoyment—and it lingered long after my flight was over." (Leavens later recorded in his makeshift log—a spiral notebook—that on "6 June 1934 . . . one little chap went up in the Giro. He had been weeding onions to pay for his ride—ten cents a long row. I gave him as long a ride as possible.")

The other discovery Foster made that day was that "I would never back down or show my fear. I had managed to put on a credible display of casual but false bravado. And later I would use that same casual bravado for the benefit of student pilots assigned to me for instruction."

When rumours of another war in Europe began buzzing around his community in 1939, Foster decided it was time to rekindle that feeling he'd had aboard the barnstormer's autogiro. He and two close friends—Dave Heathcote and Bob Aldrick—had seen some Royal Air Force recruiting folders and had fallen in love with the look of a Supermarine Spitfire depicted on the cover. They immediately wrote away for RAF brochures and application forms.

Neither of Foster's friends would ever fly a Spitfire. Dave Heathcote was killed in a Harvard crash during pilot training and Bob Aldrick became an air gunner, was shot down overseas, and became a prisoner of war. When Cap Foster finally slipped into the confined cockpit of his beloved Spitfire in early 1943, the fighter aircraft nearly killed him. What ultimately saved him was the experience of thousands of hours of instructional flying and the instincts and reflexes that instructing had developed. It all began when the RAF refused him, but recommended that he join the RCAF.

"I had two very strong and long-standing reasons for joining the air force," Foster said. "First, I wanted to fulfil that dream I'd had ever since my ride in the autogiro. And second, I had a score to settle with the Germans. In the First World War, my father was gassed and taken prisoner at the Second Battle of Ypres. He spent thirty-eight months working eighteen hours a day in German salt mines at Bienrode, and during that time he was beaten and tortured by German prison guards." Foster's father was Mohawk, a full-blooded descendant of

Chief Joseph Brant, and Foster maintained that the colour of his father's skin had provoked the abuse he'd received as a POW at Bienrode. His introduction to air force life might well have suggested he was up against a similar prejudice.

"I reported to No. 1 RCAF Manning Pool, located on the Canadian National Exhibition grounds in Toronto," Foster wrote. "My first few days there were spent shovelling out sheep pens and then sleeping beside the piles of manure."

The 352 acres of the Canadian National Exhibition grounds had been the site of a yearly exhibition and fair. The Ex had always boasted one of the finest amusement parks in North America, one of the most popular grandstand shows on the entertainment circuit, and one of the biggest livestock competitions in the world. When war was declared, a week after the 1939 CNE closed, the grounds took on a brand new identity—No. 1 RCAF Manning Depot—and the space used for housing thousands of prized cattle, pigs, horses, and sheep became the new barracks for a mustering air force.

While Cap Foster cleaned sheep stalls, a young photographer from east-end Toronto managed to escape the clean-up because his medical revealed varicose veins. Ken Smith, who later instructed pilots in aerial photo reconnaissance, remembers the extraordinary renovations going on at the Coliseum, the main livestock quarters of the CNE.

"For several weeks," Smith wrote in September 1939, "each morning [they were] hosing down the bullpen, where the cattle had been and where the [military] drilling would be, and scrubbing up the General Exhibits area, which was to be the bunkrooms. The upstairs had been the poultry show, and it meant pushing along the cracks in the wooden floor with a long stick with a nail on the end to push out the chicken lice, vacuuming the floor, and then washing it down. This took a number of mornings.

"Double bunks were eventually installed . . . 1,000 bunks upstairs and 1,000 down. Soon, although my home was in Toronto, we all had to live in. The bunkrooms were not always quiet late at night. Along the end of each bunkroom was a row of washbasins and taps for morning ablutions, etc. I was in the lower bunkroom. And every once in a while one of the tin washbasins would come sailing over the railing to land with a satisfying (for those upstairs) crash on the cement floor, fairly close to our bunks. They put up chicken wire to forestall this habit."

"I was in where they used to put feed for the pigs," Harvey Timberlake said. At the outbreak of war, he had taken his six-foot-two, 110-pound frame to the recruiting office. They took one look at him and told him to "go home, drink beer and milk, and put some weight on." When he was at last accepted, he was marched down Bay Street, straight to the CNE and "Manning Depot, where they put us into the pigpen. They had long troughs in the pens and that's where you all stood up and urinated.

"As soon as we got there, it was, 'Shirts up, pants down, peckers out.' Imagine a couple of hundred men standing in the horse ring with their pants down, waiting to receive short arm inspection. I didn't care; I'd been delivering groceries to prostitutes when I was ten. But most of the boys cried."

Medical officers were anxious to prevent any outbreaks of disease. The air force doctors often assembled recruits in the drill hall and conducted elementary sex education (what an Edmonton recruit called "cock and ball lectures"), during which the medical officer would lecture on the consequences of failing to use condoms and show graphic pictures of genitalia covered with VD sores.

There were 1,400 RCAF Aircraftmen 2nd Class (AC2s or "Acey Deuceys") in the converted pigpen barracks with Timberlake. Plenty of them joined up initially because of patriotism; there was still enough anti-German sentiment left over from the 1914–18 war to fuel a young man's emotions and patriotic fervour. Many came from parts of Canada that had limped through ten years of depression; the air force offered the first potential paying job and regular meals in a decade. Some who enlisted were in search of adventure as far from Canada as they could get. Others responded to peer pressure to sign up, or joined to get away from girl troubles or tensions at home. But the new world they entered was daunting at first.

"All the stabbing of my arms, the endless series of vaccinations": that's Chuck McCausland's memory of his first days at Manning Depot. Unable to enlist right away, because he worked with Ontario Hydro (considered an essential service), McCausland had finally been called up to Toronto; he remembers that "you went in one day and it would be a smallpox shot in the left arm, the next day German measles in the right arm. I don't think there was anything they didn't inoculate you for."

Harold Lancaster, a farm boy from Elgin County, in southwestern Ontario, had had scarlet fever shots at school, but "when they checked me in the air force, I tested positive. A bunch of us tested positive, so they moved us to the Automotive Building and quarantined us there for three weeks. I'll always remember one of those first mornings, when that old bugle went, I thought, 'What in hell have you got yourself into, Lancaster?'"

The routine that Lancaster and thousands of his fellow recruits soon got used to was an indoctrination to air force life—a sort of boot camp—where you marched and cleaned animal pens, paraded and washed latrines, got vaccinations and learned to salute with your left arm while the right arm was sore from the vaccine, drilled in the horse arenas, and got your head shaved. The object was to reduce every volunteer to the lowest common denominator so that the air force could rebuild you in its own image. In most cases, the architect of that rebuilding was a foul-mouthed, raspy-voiced, unsympathetic senior drill sergeant. After a while the endless vaccinations and embarrassing crotch examinations seemed a picnic by comparison to a day "down on the parade square with the sergeant-major, who really thought he was J.C.," as AC2 Timberlake remembered.

"From the first day, this was the guy who was going to make men out of us. He was out to break our spirit. He'd march us around for hours on end, put us all in a row, slap us between the shoulder blades, and yell 'Stand up' till some of the boys started to cry."

"Our sergeant-major stood up on the mezzanine [of the cow palace]," Harold Lancaster said, "watching and pacing and shouting out commands. And he always said, 'How in hell do you guys ever expect to fly aircraft in formation when you can't even walk in a parade?'"

"Most of us hated his guts," Timberlake agreed; but they soldiered on despite the insults, the blistered feet, and the exhaustion, because the reward for enduring the drill sergeant's abuse was that first set of regulation boots and air force blues. That uniform, no matter how ill fitting, no matter how scratchy around the neck and down the legs, seemed to compensate for the weary muscles and bruised egos.

"When you were issued your uniform," Chuck McCausland explained, "you immediately headed downtown to Adelaide Street, just east of Victoria. There was a little tailor shop there. With the big woollen socks that you were issued, when you pulled the pant leg down, it pushed the sock down. So, the tailor would put a gusset in there for $1.50 so your socks would fit under the pantleg of your uniform." That modified uniform saw Chuck McCausland through training, overseas onto Spitfires, and back to Canada as a flying instructor until the end of the war.

With or without a gusset, ill fitting or not, the RCAF uniform could barely contain the pride of the Aircraftman 2nd Class inside. That too was something the air force (knowingly or unknowingly) counted on, because built into the blues that the recruits wore was a new-found sense of esprit de corps and responsibility.

Yet, as rigidly as air force regulations governed things and as busy as the blow-hard drill sergeant kept his recruits, there was bound to be trouble; as former lacrosse and football player Jeff Mellon painted it, "that's where a kind of mob rule took over. People would steal wallets. And snipping wrist-watches was pretty common. But if a guy was ever caught stealing, he'd be taken into the shower and roughed up pretty good, with eight guys standing guard at the door."

"I remember one night we found a guy lifting stuff out of a bunk," Bob Hesketh recalled; he had joined the air force because it seemed the most glamorous of the services, but an introduction to barracks justice quickly changed his view. "Six or seven of us chased this guy all over the barracks. We finally caught him and kicked the shit out of him. It was never reported."

"Everybody knew if you got caught, that's what happened to you," Bill Lennox confirmed. Employed before the war in the pulpwood camps outside Port Arthur, Ontario, Lennox was familiar with the severity of life and justice in a work camp. Manning Depot justice was the same, because "there were thousands of guys down there. If a guy got started stealing, well then, you couldn't leave anything any place. The rule was, if you caught anybody stealing, just make sure he's got one breath of life left in him when the medical officer got there.

"I saw one guy drummed out of the service at Manning Depot. Holy Jeez, it was impressive. He was paraded with the slow roll of the drums into the Coliseum. It was packed with airmen. And they led this fellow in and just stripped him of everything that was air force. They stripped his brass off. Stripped off everything he had. His buttons came off and everything else."

Each day's procedure and activity was carefully laid out for air force volunteers. When a recruit was officially inducted at Manning Depot, he was handed a sheet of paper that itemized seventy procedures, from procuring socks and shirts to getting X-rays and inoculations. Each procedure had to be completed, each item on the list initialled. (Somebody calculated that if each procedure were actually followed to the letter, it would have taken Manning Depot two years to process recruits.)

New acronyms entered the air recruits' vocabulary. They learned KRs and ACIs—the King's Regulations and Air Council Instructions. They had to pay close attention to DROs—the Daily Routine Orders—and specifically to the back pages of those orders, to discover which recruits would staff the kitchen, when they'd clean latrines, or where they'd conduct ground policing. There was an expression that very much summed up life in the air force in those early weeks at Manning Depot: "If it was on the ground, you picked it up. If you couldn't pick it up, you painted it. If you couldn't paint it, you saluted it."

"I learned a valuable air force lesson one day," Jack Harris recalled. He'd grown up in the west end of Toronto, not far from the CNE grounds. (In fact most of his air force career would be served within a hundred miles of his Humber Bay home as a service flying instructor.) "They had this French-Canadian corporal who had us all lined up. And he says, 'How many of you fellas can drive trucks?' Well, three of us put our hands up, because we figured we were going to get an interesting assignment. And he says, 'There's a pile of asphalt that's got to be removed, so here's the wheelbarrow and the picks. Get at it, guys!' So I learned early in the game: *Never volunteer.*"

Of course, air force days weren't all KP, PT, and BS. Within weeks of its opening, No. 1 RCAF Manning Depot had an auditorium with a stage run by Oscar Pearson of the Central Toronto YMCA, who supplied various types of entertainment. Soon a library was assembled, lounges arranged, and soccer teams organized for games in the CNE parking lots. From among those recruits who excelled at the rhythm and discipline of parade drill, the air force assembled precision drill teams to perform at the CNE grandstand and the annual Grey Cup football game at Varsity Stadium.

The moment that New Brunswick recruit Dick Ross remembered best was his introduction to a "wet canteen."

"'What the hell's that?' I asked.

"'We can go there and get a drink,' they said.

"'You mean liquor?'

"'Well, beer,' they said.

"So we go in. You could cut the smoke, it's so thick. And the rattle and smell of things, it's incredible. Anyway, I got a bottle of beer and sat there and drank it. And the waiter came around and said, 'Have another?'

"'I don't think so,' I said. 'I'm already feeling this.'

"'How many have you had?' the waiter asked. I held up one finger and he said, 'How can just one bother you?'

"I said, 'When I look up at the lights, they're flickering.'

"And he asked, 'Where you from?'

"'Moncton.'

"And he laughed as he said, 'That's it. You're used to sixty-cycle electric power. We've got twenty-five up here, twenty-five times a second. Your eyes aren't accustomed to it. But they will. So you can have another beer all right.'"

There were many such discoveries at Manning Depot. Jim Coyne had experienced a lot in his nineteen years before joining up and coming to the CNE barracks. He had hunted and fished and thrived on backwoods cooking at his home at The Pas, Manitoba. Air force food, he discovered, would never be as good. John Clinton had been in the Royal Hamilton Light Infantry Reserve before he enlisted in the RCAF and came to Toronto, but he still couldn't believe the sheer numbers of men, the confusion, or the twenty-four-hour-a-day poker games at the Coliseum barracks. And in the quiet of one evening at the Horse Palace at No. 1 Manning Depot, Herb Liebman was sitting on his bunk, when "a blond fellow from up North came up and sat down beside me.

"'Are you Jewish?' he asked.

"I said, 'Yes, I am.'

"And he said, 'I've never seen a Jew before. My father warned me before I left home. He told me to be careful of the Jews.'

"I talked with him a long while. It was a totally innocent question. There was nothing malicious about it. He was a nice fellow, and we were quite friendly after that. Things like that happened in those days."

Tolerance had its limits, however. George Bain had already begun his career in journalism as a stringer for the Toronto *Telegram*. He remembered Manning Depot in the dying moments of one of those first event-filled days, when, as thousands of physically drained recruits were near sleep, someone would yell into the silence: "Anybody here from the West?"

"Yes, sir," would come back some lone, naive voice.

And everyone in the place would yell back, "Fuck the West!"

Wherever he was from, the day a civilian arrived at Manning Depot, his life changed permanently. However, for Cap Foster, the self-proclaimed master of "casual bravado," things didn't change completely until the day *after* he arrived at the CNE.

"I had been a boxer all the way through high school," Foster recalled, "and I used to spar with Harry McLean, the welterweight champion at Queen's University. The day I joined the air force, I was on the card at Maple Leaf Gardens. So I went to ask permission to fight that night. They didn't give it to me. But I snuck out anyway and won my fight by a first-round knock-out.

"Next morning, I was called in and asked about it. Fortunately, the newspaper had misprinted the name of the winner of the fight the night before. They wrote that 'Jack' Foster had won the bout. But the officer told me straight, then, 'Son, from now on, all your fighting is going to be done in the air force.'"

During those first weeks in the air force, nearly everybody was assigned to guard duty at some point. RCAF aircraftmen were dispatched from Manning Depot to act as sentries at air force installations across Canada. Whether or not those installations were actually at risk, guarding an aircraft, a hangar, or a runway (four hours on, four hours off) was itself an extension of air force discipline. At the very least, these temporary postings gave a military organization that was swamped with bodies and a backlog of paper time to clear the pipeline.

For Willy Clymer, who had just quit a job at Canada Wire in Toronto to answer his call-up, guard duty was actually a substitute for the livestock stables at the CNE Coliseum, because "they had a diphtheria epidemic down there at Manning Depot, so they couldn't take us.

"We went straight on to Dartmouth, Nova Scotia, for guard duty. God, it was awful. Two and a half months standing out at the end of Runway No. 2, out in the boonies at night, all night. From two till six in the morning. You'd almost think the Germans were going to come over the end of the runway."

At the other end of Nova Scotia, the air force stored its fleet of coastal patrol aircraft—Northrop Deltas, Westland Lysanders, and Lockheed Hudsons. An RCAF recruit posted to guard duty at Sydney admitted: "We never knew what we were doing. Nobody ever told us what we were supposed to be guarding. We marched around the airport carrying old [Enfield] rifles that nobody had showed us how to fire." Yet the thrill of seeing these bush planes, sub-chasers, and bombers up close for the first time in his life made up for the boredom of sentry work.

Aircraftman Harold Lancaster got more than a look. After surviving both scarlet fever and the quarantine quarters at the CNE Manning Depot, he was posted to guard duty at Fingal, Ontario, "where an aerodrome was going up. They didn't have the personnel for security police, so we just walked around at night with a gun in our hands. But that's where I had my first flight in the air force. A fellow was testing [a Fairey Battle] after an engine overhaul. He offered me a flight around the countryside while he tested everything, so I just rode along in the back gun turret."

Jeff Mellon got his first flight while on guard duty too, but he had to earn it. When he was a kid, growing up in east-end Hamilton, he had won the right to hang around the air club's Gipsy Moth by running errands. Tarmac duty at No. 5 Service Flying Training School in Brantford worked pretty much the same way. "They were flying Anson [Is] there. We had to [supply the aircraft with] high-pressure air, which was the power for operating the flaps and brakes. Our job was to run in between the propellers, keeping your head down, jam in this tube from a dolly where the pressure was generated, and fill the Anson's tanks with the air. Then you'd back out and hope you weren't close to the props. We did this day and night, but it was especially fun on ice. We used to get a lot of flights that way. You could fit one or two extra bodies in the back of an Anson and the instructors were good about giving us a free flight."

As dangerous as dodging props might seem, at least Mellon and his AC2 buddies had some of the comforts of home at the Brantford station. When a former employee of the Coca-Cola Company named Pat McLean arrived for guard duty at Portage la Prairie, at what was to be No. 14 Elementary Flying Training School, "the station was still under construction. There was a barracks block being built, but beds weren't up. We had to scramble around and unpack the bunkbeds and put them together. No electricity in the building. No running water. We ate our meals with the construction crew. The black, black soil there was either blowing dust or mucky gumbo. We had rifles. They weren't loaded. And we walked around on 3-hour shifts all night.

"We got to the point where we thought we saw things too. This was near a German settlement. One night we saw a light flashing across the airport. We thought, 'Uh-oh, could be sabotage here.' So we called out the Mounted Police. They came out and investigated. They found a man walking to his barn with a lantern, and the light was flashing between his legs."

While the German threat to airman Pat McLean and the muddy airstrip at Portage la Prairie was imagined, the one in Europe was real. On January 10, 1940, Adolf Hitler informed his commanders that his plan to attack the Allies would begin within the week. The same day, a German light aircraft made a forced landing at Malines in Belgium; the plane's occupants carried details of the proposed attack. The danger to Holland and Belgium was real. On January 27, Hitler tabled Operation *Weser*, the plan to invade Norway. The Phony War was becoming less so.

In the early months of 1940, the RCAF raced to keep pace. By then its strength had doubled from 4,000 officers and airmen to 8,000. The first RCAF Overseas Headquarters were established in London, England, in January. In February, No. 110 Army Co-operation "City of Toronto" Squadron sailed from Halifax, the first of forty-eight RCAF squadrons to serve overseas during the war.

To implement the BCATP, the air force organized four Training Command regions: No. 1 TC headquarters was in Toronto, No. 2 TC headquarters in Winnipeg, No. 3 TC headquarters in Montreal, and No. 4 TC headquarters in Regina. And in mid-April, two weeks before Zero Day, when the BCATP was to be officially christened, the RCAF opened its first Initial Training School (ITS) in Toronto and soon after that, its second in Regina. Each one used borrowed premises for accommodation—an equestrian facility (the Eglinton Hunt Club) in Toronto and a teachers' college in Regina. Later on, a Catholic convent in Victoriaville, Quebec, and a school for the deaf in Belleville, Ontario, became ITS facilities.

After a month in the mud of southwestern Manitoba, Pat McLean and the rest of his course arrived at No. 2 ITS Regina to begin preflight training. This was a critical time and place for the RCAF volunteer. It was here that AC2s were promoted to LACs (Leading Aircraftmen) with a pay increase from $1.70 a day to $2.00 a day (plus 75 cents a day flying pay). Here, the ranks were culled and the best recruits streamed into one of three air crew careers: pilots, observers (navigators), or wireless operator/air gunners. For most, no other designation but "pilot" mattered. Four weeks at ITS would determine which it would be.

When the BCATP began, only applicants with junior matriculation—those who had completed high school—were considered. ITS specialty training took on the atmosphere of a postsecondary or university education. Aircraftmen left the business of cleaning livestock pens behind them and attended their first lectures. The content and tone of these sessions immediately reflected the serious nature of the commitment they'd made at the recruiting centre.

With lectures and textbooks, instructors introduced them to the science of aerial navigation and the business of determining "reliable fix"—the location of an aircraft at any moment. Given a compass, a divider, and a Dalton computer (a manual calculator that a pilot strapped to his leg), they dealt with longitude, latitude, and vectors, and their instructors gave them rhymes to help convert magnetic compass bearings to true compass bearings: "Variation east, magnetic least. Variation west, magnetic best. Deviation west, compass best. Deviation east, compass least."

Any Morse code they may have learned as boy scouts was dredged up from their memories, as ground instructors had them practise on table buzzers and Aldis lamps to a rate of at least eight words per minute. The manual *Meteorology for Pilots and Navigators* put out by the Department of Transport gave them a basic knowledge of meteorology, from cloud formation and ice accretion to wind variation, line squalls, and vertical currents. There were official presentations on LDAO (Law, Discipline, Administration, and Organization in the RCAF). Leading Aircraftmen also took classes in armament, aircraft recognition, aerodynamics, and airmanship. Between classes, the school disciplinary officer led them through daily physical training (PT) and, of course, parade drill.

All this training was designed to determine if the recruit was "air crew material." In fact, the opening line of Pitman's *Flying Simply Explained* read: "Will I make a pilot?" The syllabus was demanding, but the new official Leading Aircraftman status did wonders for the confidence and the ego.

"At ITS we received the coveted 'flash' to wear in the front of our field service cap," Don Suthers wrote. He had graduated from McMaster in Hamilton and had worked as a clerk with Westinghouse for four years, but, up to that point in his life, nothing equalled the prestige of that simple little triangle of white cloth, which was inserted into the front of the cap to signify air crew in training. "Some of the more jealous non-air crew types bruited it about that the white flash indicated that the man was under treatment for syphilis."

The white flash meant a lot to ex-infantryman John Clinton. "It indicated you were air crew. That was important. You were on your way. . . . We took advantage of it with the ladies."

It was also the first time LAC Clinton felt completely inspired by what he was doing. He came from a family of United Empire Loyalists and had just scraped through high school with a "50.1 percent average. I had no motivation at all. But suddenly at ITS, this was sort of it," Clinton said. "I enjoyed everything about ground school. We learned meteorology, math, principles of flight. I'm not sure what my marks were, but somewhere in the high 70s or low 80s."

High marks strengthened a Leading Aircraftman's hand for the coming selection process, yet there was still one other stiff challenge to meet at ITS—the Link trainer. "It was just like an airplane," Clinton remembered. "The Link trainer had a fuselage, wings, and an open cockpit with all the normal controls," but it was a simulator that never left the ground.

The Link trainer and its inventor, Edwin Albert Link, might never have enjoyed the prominence they did had it not been for the near desperate need of the BCATP in late 1939. Edwin Link had grown up during the 1920s in Binghamton, New York. Half the time he worked in his father's organ and piano factory, the other half he learned how to fly. But flying lessons were very expensive at the time—$25 an hour. So, in 1929, Link patented a cockpit-like contraption with a simulated instrument panel and control stick, all of which floated on a set of organ bellows he had borrowed from his father's factory. The result simulated the movement of an aircraft in flight.

In the 1930s Edwin sold six simulators to Casey Jones at the Curtiss-Wright aircraft company. Then he took a prototype to Washington with an idea that the United States Army Air Corps might be interested. When that venture fell through, he decided to raise the Link's profile by installing one in the Long Island town of Rye, as an amusement ride for a quarter a flight.

One of Link's contemporaries, New York test pilot and instructor Jack Charleson, contended that "if you could fly this unstable little monster, you could fly a stable airplane in straight and level flight." In January 1940, that notion captured the imagination of Air Vice-Marshal Robert Leckie, on loan from the RAF as the director of training for the BCATP. Leckie decided to buy 200 Link trainers, "an unheard-of order at the time." The first fifty were made in the United States and subsequent ones in Ontario at a factory near Gananoque.

Leckie's order proved to be a turning point for the Link trainer, which is credited with training more than two million military and commercial pilots. And for the infant BCATP, without a large supply of training aircraft at its disposal, the Link trainer became an essential training tool for determining potential pilots and for honing basic instrument skills—that is, flying with only a turn-and-bank indicator, a magnetic compass, and an air speed indicator.

"They had a cyclorama—a circle of boards about ten feet high and about forty feet in diameter," John Clinton said, remembering the Link trainer room. "It had painted scenery and a horizon on it, as if you were looking out over the landscape. They would start up the motor. If you pressed the rudder control it would turn in that direction. [When you manipulated the control column] it would bank, and the nose would come up or go down, just like an airplane. It was amazing.

"The instructor would sit over to one side with a recording device hooked up. One session took about twenty or thirty minutes. It really could give you the idea of coordinating the controls of an airplane. The first time [though], I was just all over the place. I couldn't coordinate the turning and the nose. I came out soaking wet, I had been trying so hard. I remember telling myself I had blown it, that I would probably be washed out [of the course]."*

Clinton eventually mastered the Link as well as a score of other training and operational aircraft. He served three years as a flying instructor in Training Command and then flew missions for the South Atlantic Ferry Command and Transport Command.

"The Link was extremely sensitive, as sensitive as any aircraft," said Link instructor Dick Tarshis. "It did everything that the aircraft would do. If you made a mistake in the air, it was serious; if you made a mistake and crashed the Link, it was only on paper."

Tarshis's job as Link instructor kept him close to the airplanes he loved but could not fly. As a boy he had spent his summers at a cottage on Hanlan's Point on the Toronto Islands, where he watched aircraft of all shapes and sizes taking off and landing at the Island Airport. After high school he worked with Regal Films, the Canadian outlet for Metro-Goldwyn-Mayer, booking Hollywood movies into Toronto theatres. This job helped pay for flying lessons, and by 1938 Tarshis had his private pilot's licence. When he enlisted, the RCAF put him on a train to Brandon, Manitoba, for Manning Depot, to Carberry, Manitoba, for guard duty, and on to ITS at Regina. The Link was never a problem. It was Tarshis's incurable air sickness at Elementary Flying Training School that did him in.

"I tried everything, triple bromides, everything," Tarshis said. "But the medical officer at EFTS said that my system just couldn't stand it. And eventually, I was washed out. I felt very badly when I realized I wasn't going to be a military pilot. So I took my discharge out of the air force, but I came back a year later as a Link trainer instructor." By the war's end he had instructed for about 2,700 hours

* Washing out was officially known as CT or "ceased training."

and worked with nearly 2,000 RCAF students on the Link.

"There were probably twelve Link trainers in a room," Tarshis explained. "The student would report to me, then walk up the steps into the Link. I'd start up the motor for the bellows, go back to my desk, communicate with the student by headphones, tell him to demonstrate level flight, climbing, gliding, and basic turn and banking moves. Then I would record his manoeuvres at my desk.

"Inside the Link was an exact replica of an aircraft [cockpit], with an instrument panel that lit up, a regular stick, and rudder pedals. If the student moved the stick, it would let out air on one side and so it would bank. The student also knew that if he made a turn, the outer wing would go faster than the inner wing, and he could stall and spin to the ground. The Link would actually rotate and spin, so the student had to get control, do the right things and bring it out of the spin. It was just like really stalling an aircraft. It really created all the hazards of flying, without leaving the ground."

Flying capability, as the instructor viewed it, was partly a product of instinct and partly a matter of hand-eye-foot coordination. For LACs such as Chuck McCausland, who had played half-back for the Queen's University Golden Gaels in the 1930s, or Jeff Mellon, who had played semi-professional lacrosse with the Hamilton Tigers, the Link trainer was "a piece of cake." Nor was the manipulation of the control column and rudders a problem for young airmen such as Harvey Timberlake, who had driven a car from the age of twelve.

Later on in the life of the BCATP, Link training took on a new dimension when instructors installed a hood over the cockpit so that the pilot had to fly by instruments only, as he would in bad weather or at night. Decorated fighter pilot Jackie Rae recalled a day of training in the Link, when "I was doing my exercises with the coupe-top closed, so that I was flying absolutely blind. I was doing everything well, I thought, until [in my headphones] I heard this horrible crash. My instructor had taken a strawberry box, held it up to his microphone, and squashed it. It made the most terrible noise. I jumped a foot inside the Link. Then he said, 'You have just landed 300 feet under the ground.' I guess I had taken my eyes off the altimeter . . ."

The struggles of airmen coping with this peculiar craft moved one Link student to record his observations in poetic form in spring 1940. Having been a newspaper editor in Val d'Or in northern Quebec, airman Carrol McLeod described the antics of the Link and its students in an exaggerated Habitant accent. The result was a poem entitled "Dat Goddam Bird de Link," and included the lines:

For two t'ree mont' my brudder Pierre,
Take course on "Link" to fly de h'air
Dat "Link" she's plane of speciale make,
On first solo your nerves he's shake,
You take him off wit' nose to sky—
But dat goddam t'ing to floor she's tie.

McLeod mastered the Link, but never gave up the pen; his cockeyed poetry continued to appear in the RCAF *Wings* magazine. Later, when he became a flying instructor himself, his observations of the air force and its massive training scheme became the subject of a book called *Dat H'ampire H'air Train Plan*.

"At the end of the flight," Dick Tarshis summed up, "I would go over what [the student] did right and wrong. You had a chart that had recorded all his moves. We tried to impress upon them that this was going to help them greatly in their flying, that they'd be a hell of a lot better flyer. But students were not that excited about flying the Link trainer. What they wanted was to really fly."

After four weeks of facts and figures, lectures and Link flights, meteorology and Morse code, fitness and hygiene, studying and saluting, or, as Fred Lundell put it, "learning your A-B-C's and minding your P's and Q's," an airman's future in the RCAF depended on an interview on his last day at ITS. LAC Fred Lundell, from Revelstoke, British Columbia, figured he was ready. His father had flown in the Royal Flying Corps during the First World War, and Lundell had devoured his stories as well as books about air aces Billy Bishop, Ray Collishaw, and Don MacLaren. When war came again in 1939, most of Lundell's graduating class at Revelstoke High School joined the services; he enlisted in the RCAF. Manning Depot set him back with scarlet fever and the measles. Finally, he seemed to be getting airborne at ITS. But all his ambitions to be a military pilot like his father and his storybook heroes depended on how he fared at his "Selection Day" interview. There, in a few short minutes before a panel of instructors, officers, and the CO, his fate would be decided. Would he go on to become an observer? A gunner? Or, best of all, a pilot?

"Hours were spent polishing shoes, adjusting ties, and achieving an appropriate cap angle," Lundell remembered. "Then the solid oak doors opened. There sat the panel—grey-haired, bald-headed, more ribbons and wings than one could imagine—and somewhere a voice announced: 'LAC Lundell, Frederick W.'

"Good God, I thought. If I were able, I should cross myself. It's like Brandon's funeral parlour, on which we painted 'Abandon Hope All Ye Who Enter Here.' I smiled and stopped shaking.

"There were stern faces. Searching questions. 'Did quite well in your courses, Lundell.'

"'I think I was second or third in the course.'

"'Want to be a pilot?'

"'Everyone wants to be a pilot.'

"'What special abilities do you have for a pilot, Lundell? Can you drive a car?'

"'No, sir.'

"'Why not?'

"'We didn't have a car, sir.'

"'Hmmm. No proven abilities.'

"'Oh, but sir, I can hit the front door of a house with the Vancouver *Province* from fifty feet, riding my bicycle, no hands.'

"A couple of suppressed grins . . . I saluted smartly and was dismissed . . . [I stood] outside those massive doors for what seemed the proverbial eternity, trying to kick myself—'riding a bicycle, no hands' . . . you made a real ass of yourself.

"Suddenly the doors opened.

"'LAC Lundell. . . . We don't think you will make pilot, or navigator, but perhaps bomb-aimer . . .'

"I knew I shouldn't have mentioned hitting a door at fifty feet . . .

"'. . . but we have decided to give you a go at pilot training anyway.'"

LAC Fred Lundell, like the thousands before and after him, collected his ITS rewards—his navigation, mathematics, and aerodynamics marks, as well as his RCAF-issue two-piece fire-resistant flying suit, flying gloves, fleece-lined flying boots, goggles, and helmet—and then "began the repetitive ritual of completing another giant step towards gaining my wings and an eventual ops posting, and of saying goodbye to friends acquired during this phase of training."

4

A GREAT TIDE OF AIRMEN

On June 5, 1940, the Canadian aviation fraternity—flyers and administrators from the air force, commercial aviation, and private flying clubs—gathered in Ottawa for a special meeting. The highlight of the Wednesday luncheon was the annual presentation of the McKee (or Trans-Canada) Trophy. The three-foot-high trophy in the form of a winged figure flying over the globe had been created to honour Captain James Dalzell McKee, who had completed the first seaplane flight across Canada in 1926. Each year following that flight, the trophy was awarded to the person "rendering the most meritorious service in the advancement of aviation in Canada." At the 1940 luncheon, the minister of national defence, Charles Gavan "Chubby" Power, rose to address the gathering and to announce the winner—Murton A. Seymour, the president of the Canadian Flying Clubs Association.

Murton Seymour's lifelong association with Canadian aviation began in 1915, when he helped organize Canada's first flying club, the Aero Club of British Columbia, near his home in Vancouver. That summer he took flying lessons by sitting on the wing of an OX-powered Curtiss pusher airplane while his instructor, William Stark, conducted ground demonstration runs. Seymour then practised by taxiing along the ground and making short hops of three or four feet off the ground. In September he successfully soloed in the Curtiss, and in November he graduated.

By this time the First World War was a year old, and the Royal Flying Corps came to Canada to set up a training program. The Aero Club of British Columbia became a training school, and Seymour was recommended for a commission in the Special Reserve of the Royal Flying Corps. He proceeded to Central Flying School at Upavon, England, in 1916, flew single-seater fighters for No. 41 Royal Flying Corps Squadron, stationed at Abeele, Belgium, until early 1917, then returned to Canada and became major in charge of all flying and technical training for the RAF in Canada.

After the war he completed his studies in law and was admitted to the bar in both British Columbia and Ontario in 1919. He established his law practice in St. Catharines, Ontario, and helped the local flying enthusiasts set up the St. Catharines Flying Club in 1928. He was its first president.

This was a critical time for civilian flying in Canada. It was clear that air transport—private, commercial, and military—would be of increasing economic importance, and that trained pilots would be needed for peacetime aviation as well as a vital resource should any military need arise. To begin filling the need for trained pilots at the end of the 1920s, the Canadian government, following the British example, launched the Light Aeroplane Club Scheme. This scheme had three goals: to establish aerodromes across Canada, to create an awareness of air transport among Canadians, and to create a reserve of partially trained pilots for defence in the event of war.

Each aero club had to provide a flying field, hire an instructor, have ten qualified pilots in its membership, and find thirty members prepared to qualify as pilots. In return, the government would provide two airplanes and a $100 grant to each club for each member who qualified as an ab initio pilot. (It was this arrangement that had enticed Al Stirton to sign up at the Moose Jaw Flying Club in 1938.)

The combination of his wartime posting with the Royal Flying Corps, his postwar direction of flight training, and his experience in organizing civilian aero clubs put Murton Seymour at the centre of the scheme. By fall 1929, Seymour had helped to organize sixteen aero clubs across the country into the Canadian Flying Clubs Association. The association advertised for potential pilots and organized the Trans-Canada Air Pageant, involving twenty aircraft and a picked air crew from the RCAF, which staged twenty-six aviation performances from the Maritimes to Vancouver.

In the late 1930s, when hostilities were looming in Europe, Seymour, as the CFCA president, lobbied the government to expand the flying club activities in elementary flying training for defence purposes. In June 1939, Seymour and the Department of National Defence arranged for eight of the association's twenty-two clubs to undertake the elementary flying training instruction of a number of provisional pilot officers (PPOs). Eight club instructors were put to work in dual cockpits to train the first thirty-two PPOs for the RCAF. Seymour didn't stop there; he toured the country inspiring the rest of the member clubs to help carry out this training in the national interest.

At eight o'clock on Sunday morning, September 3, 1939, the telephone rang at Murton Seymour's home in St. Catharines. Wing Commander George Howsam of the RCAF in Ottawa was on the line. "The balloon's up," he said. "Come to Ottawa immediately." Seymour spent the next twenty-four hours sending and receiving telegrams. By Monday morning, the remaining fourteen CFCA members were ready to assume responsibility for the elementary stage of flying training of pilots for the RCAF.

The training given by the clubs formed the basis of the Elementary Flying Training Schools of the British Commonwealth Air Training Plan. Before the official inauguration of the BCATP, civilian-run EFTSs had trained more than 500 provisional pilot officers and leading aircraftmen; by the end of the war the number totalled 41,000. That spring afternoon in Ottawa, when Chubby Power presented the McKee Trophy to Murton Seymour, Seymour's brainchild—a nationwide system of elementary flying training schools—was already giving shape to the RCAF's amorphous air training plan.

In the muddy fields on the outskirts of St. Catharines, Seymour's own aero club hired its first manager and chief flying instructor. Until that spring, Fred Pattison had been working for $18 a week as a mechanic at Frank Murphy's garage in downtown St. Catharines; when he took the manager's job his salary jumped to $40 a week. Meanwhile, the club put the call out across southwestern Ontario for flying instructors to teach the first batch of RCAF provisional pilot officers. A twenty-seven-year-old commercial pilot named George Dunbar drove down from London and applied.

"Hell, I didn't think I had enough experience," Dunbar admitted, "I didn't even know where St. Catharines was, and had a devil of a time finding it. But they hired me on the spot—$50 a week and $2 an hour for every hour I flew."

Dunbar had logged many flying hours by spring 1940. As a kid growing up near London, he had wheedled his way into becoming a sort of roustabout at Lambeth airfield. He served an apprenticeship as an aircraft engineer and in the mid-1930s had learned to fly, earning his commercial pilot's licence in less than two years. George's mentor was the London Flying Club's chief flying instructor, Captain Tom Williams, who, although he had started his career in the cavalry, claimed to have flown in 500 dogfights as a Royal Flying Corps fighter pilot during the First World War. As a bush pilot he took only the toughest contracts; he hauled nitroglycerin into northern mining camps (where even the ground crews would vacate the airstrip until Williams had safely landed and shut down his Waco freighter).

"Tommy had the same sort of cavalier approach to teaching," Dunbar remembered. "I know I soloed before I ever did a spin in an airplane. People were talking about spinning, and I didn't know what the hell they were talking about. So he says 'Okay, get your helmet and let's go.' And away we'd go. He'd spin to the left and spin to the right. And he'd say, 'Now you do them.' And I did them. And that was that. I guess that's what I learned from him. It didn't take me long to know exactly when [a student] was ready to do something in the air."

As ready as George Dunbar was to instruct, as eager as Defence Minister Chubby Power was for success, as desperate as RCAF Wing

Commander George Howsam was for pilots, and as confident as Murton Seymour was in the entire aero club plan, the scheme experienced early growing pains. The day before St. Catharines EFTS got its first manager, a windstorm blew in from the northwest and flipped two of the club's aircraft on their backs, damaged the club hangars, and brought down another of the club's aircraft in downtown St. Catharines, killing both the pilot and his passenger.

"The school just wasn't ready," George Dunbar said. "Where the airport was situated was quite low—it's only a foot or two above the waterline of the lake so it was very difficult to fly. You'd smash airplanes up quite easily, because they'd get stuck in the mud and go over on their backs." Even after the staff sent photographs of the muddy field to Ottawa, asking the government to macadamize the runways, there were problems. "Overnight the construction crews would dig a hole for a sewer and leave it unmarked. And next morning we'd be watching an aircraft coming in after a flight and all of a sudden it would fall into one of these holes, break a prop or a wingtip, and there'd be another airplane out of commission."

Nevertheless, flyers from all parts of Canada, eager to fly in the RCAF, responded to the military emergency. Some accepted their provisional pilot officer status and went back to flying school. Flyers such as Frank Montgomery, who had hopped the train in Saskatoon when National Defence telegraphed him, and Wess McIntosh, whom fate had snatched from the RCN destroyer *Fraser* before she sank, got their PPO commissions and took preliminary training at Camp Borden and the main RCAF station at Trenton. PPO Russ Bannock from Edmonton went to the Aero Club of British Columbia, and PPO Fred Macdonell took elementary flying at the Halifax Flying Club. By the middle of 1940, all four of them were informed that they would not be sent to operational training units overseas; the system was so desperately short of flying instructors that they would be ploughed back into the program as the first crop of BCATP flying instructors.

Shortly after it began accepting its first trainees, St. Catharines welcomed ten former RCAF ground crewmen to their club hangar. At their home station, Trenton, the ten recruits had been standard tradesmen assigned to general duties, but when they heard about the flying club schools, they had requested permission to remuster as air crew and qualify as pilots. J.A. Sully, their commanding officer at Trenton, granted them ten days' leave. They pooled what money they had; one of them contributed the money he'd made by auctioning off a car he'd won in a raffle. Dunbar remembered them "trickling in one Sunday afternoon after hitchhiking to St. Catharines. They didn't have enough money for lodging . . . and the first night made arrangements to sleep in the hangar. Next day, Fred Pattison and some of the boys scrounged some tents and helped rig them up at a tourist camp a couple of miles from the field. We thought everything was okay, but a couple of days later, another instructor overheard that they were not all getting three squares a day because of insufficient funds. [Pattison] took the problem to local clubs, whose members immediately agreed to provide dinner for the group every day.

"They were an enthusiastic gang; they had to get through the course in so short a time. They were so enthusiastic that when they didn't have any studying to do at night, they would come back and help the ground crew service the aircraft they were flying." By the end of the course, seven of the ten had qualified for pilot licences.

Nearly all of those who graduated from the aero clubs' elementary flying training advanced to become RCAF pilots or air crew and served under the RAF in the early days of the war, some in Operation Dynamo (the evacuation of the British Expeditionary Force from Dunkirk) or the Battle of Britain in the summer and fall of 1940. Of the seven Trenton tradesmen who qualified at St. Catharines, three were reported missing-in-action, one became a prisoner of war, and one won the Distinguished Flying Cross.

Meanwhile, events in Hitler's *Weser* plan were accelerating. In February 1940, General von Falkenhorst had assumed command of the German expedition to invade Norway. In March, the French and British planned the mining of Norwegian waters. And on April 7, the RAF spotted German ships steaming north towards Narvik and Trondheim.

Thirty-seven-year-old Fridtjov Loberg was stationed at Trondheim air base with the Royal Norwegian Air Force. Loberg had joined the air force when he was twenty and had learned to fly in a Farman aircraft, which he remembered looking like "a scaffold with an engine sitting in the middle of it"; he and his fellow cadets were not issued parachutes because "the air force was afraid we might run out of them." When the Germans invaded six of Norway's seaports on April 9, 1940, Loberg and his colleagues at Trondheim were still ill equipped.

"We got a phone call at the airfield," Loberg remembered, "that there was a four-engine plane coming in our direction. We had two eighteen-year-old Fokker aircraft and quickly sent them up. But when the German aircraft came over at about 6,000 metres altitude, our planes had only managed to reach 3,000 metres in all that time. I guess the Germans were laughing their heads off. They knew we didn't have anything to fight back with."

The Norwegians recognized that counterattack was futile. So Loberg and thirty-four other pilots of the RNAF were instructed to evacuate. They took to the sea and spent the next four weeks making their way to Britain by freighter and fishing boat, and were eventually escorted by a British coastal vessel to Lerwick in the Shetland Islands.

Norwegian land forces had had better luck on the first day of the invasion—a coastal battery sank the German heavy cruiser *Blücher* in the Oslo Fiord. On that day, April 9, twenty-two-year-old Harald Jensen was about to write his sergeant's exam at the Oslo military school. He witnessed the thwarting of the first German assault.

"Next morning, we got out on the parade ground and planes were circling overhead. One came down quite low—it looked like a Heinkel. I was on my way to a machinegun post. I had been ordered out to a railway station. I commandeered a car to get to the station, and when we arrived at the machinegun post, it was already manned and there were three German planes coming down in perfect formation. But the whole thing was completely silly. They landed at Fornebu airport and captured Oslo within a few hours."

Jensen was allowed to go home to Larvik, but he decided to search out resistance forces. With the equivalent of about five dollars in his pocket he trekked through Sweden trying to get into the fighting. He made his way to Stockholm, where he remained for eight months before he managed to get hired on board the *Taurus*, one of five ships planning to run the gauntlet from Sweden, past Denmark, and up the Skagerrak to the North Sea and England.

The morning the ships weighed anchor, "it was supposed to be snowing. . . . We were steaming along the Norwegian coast past Sola, the biggest air base the Germans had in northern Europe at that time, and the weather started to clear. Next thing we know there's a warship bearing down on us. We all ran up on deck. We could see the ship's bow drawing closer and closer. The captain was going to [open] the sea-cocks and sink our ship, when the warship swung broadside, and we saw she was flying the British navy flag. She was a light cruiser."

Jensen and all the crewmen of the *Taurus* became instant celebrities in the British press. They received the Norwegian War Medal for bravery. Five modern freighters had broken the German blockade of Norway and Denmark at a time when Britain had a dwindling number of ships in its merchant marine and even fewer successes against the German invasion of Europe.

It took the Germans sixty-two days to complete the seizure of Norway. In the course of those two months there were 2,600 German and 7,000 Allied casualties. However, the government of Norway survived. Almost the last to leave the country was King Haakon, who immediately formed a government-in-exile in London, England.

Fridtjov Loberg and Harald Jensen had become expatriates too. Yet they and thousands of their countrymen would return to emancipate their homeland five years later. Their route to victory would begin 3,000 miles away, at a military flying training station in Canada as part of the British Commonwealth Air Training Plan.

From April through June 1940, the flow of Norwegian military personnel aboard planes, pleasure boats, fishing vessels, and merchant marine ships to Britain was constant. They were a people without a home and a military force without a place to regroup. In Britain, the RAF had its hands full. Europe was falling and British authorities could offer no surplus planes, equipment, instructors, or training fields to help rebuild a Norwegian air force.

The commanding officer of the Norwegian army air arm, Captain Bjarne Oen, had fled to England aboard the same Norwegian fishing vessel as airman Loberg. From the moment he arrived on May 12 he began a campaign to reorganize Norwegian flyers. At first he negotiated them into the RAF Volunteer Reserve. But when Norway capitulated on June 7, Britain cancelled all plans to train Norwegians, since the RAF needed all its pilots, aircraft, and aerodromes for combat flying, not training. Oen approached the French for training facilities, but they were in disarray. However, diplomatic contacts in Washington and Montreal were already working to solve the problem of the homeless Royal Norwegian Air Force.

Canada and the RCAF had just launched the BCATP. The Canadian government agreed to provide the airfield on the Toronto Islands as a potential training facility for the RNAF. The Toronto Harbour Commission offered land adjacent to the airport rent-free for any required buildings to house the Norwegians. Aircraft, purchased by Norway before the outbreak of war and on order from American factories, would be sent to Toronto. In Britain, the Norwegian government-in-exile made plans to train both naval and army flyers at the Toronto Island Airport. The British government agreed to accept graduates as reserve flyers in the RAF.

The first 120 naval and army flyers of the RNAF-in-exile crossed the Atlantic aboard two former Norwegian coastal steamships—the 800-ton *Iris* and the 1,200-ton *Lyra*—in August 1940. Fridtjov, or, as he became known in Canada, Fred Loberg, was with the first contingent sent to establish a pilot training station for the RNAF in Toronto. Organizers of the Norwegian training camp were first headquartered at the Royal York Hotel, while the Norwegian army and naval servicemen were temporarily barracked at Lakeside Home, a Toronto Island summer home for the patients of the Sick Children's Hospital, and aboard the *Iris*, which had managed to navigate the St. Lawrence Seaway up to Toronto harbour.

Beside the airport "was mostly vacant land," Loberg remembered, "so we immediately started building the camp there. We had to build a barracks, mess hall, and equipment depot" before the pilot training could begin. There was training of another sort going on in the vicinity—no sooner was Loberg's office up "next to the Maple Leaf Baseball Stadium, than I found baseballs breaking through the windows of my office." The baseball players had the jump on the airmen in another respect too. They had uniforms. Procuring RNAF uniforms was Loberg's next assignment.

"How many men can I count on?" Loberg asked the chief officer.

"You can guess just as well as I can," was the reply.

So Loberg threw what little commercial experience he had at the problem. The Norwegian air force colour was green; their uniforms were also tailored much like German military uniforms, and that would never do. So, first Loberg sought permission from the RAF to use their air force blue for RNAF officers' uniforms.* Then he assembled a uniform that would fit a man of his stature; it was a battle-dress uniform with a bloused top that was buttoned to the pants.

By fall 1940, the Loberg-styled uniforms had been manufactured and distributed, and elementary flying training had begun at Camp "Little Norway." Trainees studied at the ground school and later in the wireless school (known popularly as "Radio City"), while they upgraded their physical training in the station's new gymnasium-sauna facility (later named Haraldshallen because it was christened by Prince Harald). The first pilot trainees took one of the world's shortest ferry rides, across the narrow channel to the island airport, for their elementary flying sessions in Moth and Fleet biplanes borrowed from the Toronto Flying Club.

---

* Air force legend attributes the adoption of blue uniforms to Russia. In 1917, at the time of the Revolution, the Russian cavalry had ordered a million yards of blue cloth from Britain for their officers. Because of the upheaval in Russia, the cloth was never delivered and sat in British warehouses until the British air force appropriated it. Royal Air Force blue uniforms made their first appearance in October 1919; later Commonwealth, European, and American air forces adopted it.

The Battle of Britain was in its sixth week when Little Norway took delivery of its first American-built Fairchild PT-19 Cornells. Soon after, the first three Douglas light bombers arrived, and then a freighter full of Curtiss Hawk fighters. Still later, patrol bombers on pontoons arrived for the naval branch. In all, about $20 million worth of aircraft (financed by gold spirited out of Norway when the Germans invaded) got RNAF instructors and students off the ground. Training was well under way by November 10, 1940, when the Norwegian and RAF flags were raised at the official opening of the Royal Norwegian Air Force Training Centre.

During the months that followed, a steady parade of new aircraft and Norwegian royalty made their way to the island airport to bolster the training fleet and the morale. Whenever royalty showed up, so did the bevy of newsreel cinematographers, ready to document the unveiling of each new blue-and-yellow Fairchild Cornell. For propaganda purposes the RNAF hired a film crew and renowned American journalist Lowell Thomas to narrate how "Crown Princess Martha opens the christening ceremony for a number of gift airplanes," while pointing to the fuselage inscriptions that read "Fra Nordmenn—Argentina" and "Fra Nordes Venner—Minnesota." As the paper was ripped away to reveal more inscriptions on Cornells, Thomas said, "And five-year-old Prince Harald performs his first official act . . . unveiling more planes bought with funds contributed by Norwegians or friends of Norway in South America and the United States."

High on the list of the friends of Norway was the citizenry of Toronto. By the time the camp was fully operational, around Christmas 1940, training flights of blue-and-yellow Cornells and all-green Hawks were a common sight across the Toronto skyline. Although some officials in the city warned of "the risks of aviation over the bay," on most pleasant, sunny days Torontonians congregated along the waterfront to watch the bombing and strafing manoeuvres. So did many RCAF recruits, newly inducted at the main Toronto Manning Depot nearby. Navigation recruit Al Rutherford remembered several drill parades disintegrating into total chaos as recruits craned their necks to see the Norwegian flyers instead of paying attention to their marching steps. In fact, around Toronto, some air force recruiting posters that read "Join the Royal Canadian Air Force" had been chalked with the addition "and watch the Norwegians fly."

Despite the language barrier, Toronto families often invited airmen of the RNAF over for home-cooked meals. People were so hospitable that "we didn't have enough boys to send to all the dinner invitations," Fred Loberg explained. "I remember being to five different events in one day, starting at noon. I kept saying that I had to get back to camp; then I'd go on to the next address just to make an appearance."

Not far from the barracks on King Street, some of the Norwegians discovered European cooking and a warm welcome at Oscar's restaurant (later Winston's Theatre Grill). The restaurant's co-owner, Cornelia Berceller, recalled singing to the pilots and said that they used to order extra bread and ketchup to help extend their meals. Many Toronto organizations staged teas and dances for these first foreign servicemen in their city. Groups such as the Canadian Jewish Congress offered non-alcoholic beverages to all servicemen at the George Street canteen. They considered it a public service and contribution to the war effort. However, for teenager Sonia Ramstein, who persuaded her parents to let her serve the airmen iced water at the canteen, it afforded a golden opportunity "to see all those tall, handsome, blond-haired airmen" close up.

When training started, there were about 300 Norwegians in the camp. Almost immediately Little Norway began to receive telegrams and letters of inquiry from expatriate Norwegians around the world; all were invited to enlist. In 1941 the Norwegian government-in-exile ordered the general conscription of Norwegian citizens, and soon they began arriving from Norway by way of Brazil, Argentina, Mexico, Australia, South Africa, India, China, Egypt, Portugal, Iceland, and the Faeroe Islands. The experience of a young Norwegian aircraft engineer named Viggo Ullmann was typical; when Norway fell, he was in Tokyo, but he soon took his family (including his daughter Liv, who would later become famous as an actress) to Toronto to serve at

Little Norway.* The camp's population soared to capacity at 700 men in 1941 as more aircraft arrived—more Cornells, Hawks, and Douglases, and six Northrop patrol bombers on twin pontoons.

"Taking off from the water was always tricky," Loberg explained. He had left his quartermastering duties behind and was instructing in everything from Link simulators to aircraft recognition. "It was quite strange taking off in the direction of Tip Top Tailors," at the west end of Toronto harbour.

Gary Bekkevold remembered that seaplane training with the Northrop bombers was made all the more difficult by the boat traffic in the harbour. Bekkevold, like so many of his Norwegian army countrymen, had been taken prisoner in spring 1940; but he had escaped from the Gestapo, fled through Sweden, across Russia and Siberia, then through China and Japan to North America. At Little Norway he was an instructor at the recruit school, where he led physical training and weapons training.

One sunny spring day he looked out at the harbour just as an instructor, Flight Lieutenant Finn Strand Kjos, did his pre-flight check with student pilot Tron Harsvik in the dual cockpits of a Northrop float plane. Kjos had more than a thousand hours' flying experience, and his student had flown sixty solo hours to date. The two pilots turned the Northrop into the southwesterly wind and began to throttle up. About a half-mile away, the Toronto harbour ferry *Sam McBride* was plying between Wards Island and the mainland. Capacity on the ferry was 1,000 passengers, but on this trip there were barely thirty-five aboard.

Fred Dickie happened to be watching the take-off from atop the Bank of Hamilton building on Yonge Street near the waterfront; he felt uneasy that the seaplane was taking a long time to lift off the water. The same was clear to the skipper of the *Sam McBride*, now

---

* Ullmann stayed with the Little Norway training centre until 1943 when he accidentally walked into a moving airplane propeller and suffered injuries that were eventually fatal.

about a third of the way across the harbour. Captain Ernest Straker spotted the Northrop "heading straight for our bow. When I saw it was going to hit us, I put my helm hard to starboard. . . . It was really a sympathetic gesture. There was no hope that they would not hit us.

"The plane first struck a lifeboat davit," Captain Straker said. "Then it lost its wings, one against the funnel and one against a mast," as it continued its upward course. The ferry was hit above the waterline and stayed upright and afloat, but what was left of the Northrop hit the water about 300 feet beyond the ferry and "disappeared in ten or fifteen seconds at the most," drowning the two Norwegian pilots.

At the coroner's inquest that followed, Captain Straker and a lifeguard witness testified that the sun was directly behind the ferry and that the glare off the harbour may have blinded the pilots and hidden the ferry's approach. Yet the greater issue debated at the inquiry was the very existence of Little Norway. Chief Coroner Dr. Smirle Lawson criticized the placement of an air training facility so close to downtown Toronto. Lieutenant-Commander Haahon Joergensen, the officer in charge of the Little Norway seaplane base, defended his pilots, claiming that "this accident was one of those rare things which would probably not happen again in 100 years." However, the jury, while commending "the part the Norwegian flyers are playing in this war," concluded by warning of the continued "hazards involved when inexperienced flyers are manoeuvring in and around Toronto bay and its environs."

The inquiry noted two other recent RNAF training crashes near Toronto, one the previous week at Clarkson, and another beside the Queen Elizabeth Highway, but the ferry crash seemed to end the happy honeymoon between Toronto civic officials and the RNAF. As well, given the heavy social schedule many of the Little Norway recruits were experiencing, it was apparent to men such as RNAF wireless operator Kal Pedersen that "the great metropolis proved too much of a temptation for activities unrelated to serious training of air force personnel."

By spring 1941, a 430-acre recruit training and recreation camp for the RNAF was carved out of the forest sixteen miles from Huntsville in the Muskoka district north of Toronto. In January 1942, the elementary flying training of Norwegian recruits was transferred from Toronto Island Airport to the Muskoka airport outside Gravenhurst.

The war in Europe escalated quickly. On May 10, 1940, seven Panzer, three motorized, and thirty-four infantry divisions, as well as 2,700 combat aircraft from Germany's *Luftflotten* (air fleets), began the invasion of Belgium and Holland. That evening Neville Chamberlain resigned. The new British prime minister, Winston Churchill, formed a national coalition government. Churchill ordered the RAF to attack targets west of the Rhine to hamper the German advance. Two days later the leading Panzers crossed into France. On May 14, the Luftwaffe bombed Rotterdam; on May 15, the Netherlands surrendered; on May 17, the Germans entered Brussels; and by May 20, German armoured divisions had split the defending British and French armies in two and were preparing to invade France. On May 20, an advance party of No. 112 "City of Winnipeg" Army Co-operation Squadron sailed from Montreal on its way to Liverpool. In early June, as Hermann Göring's Luftwaffe concentrated its attacks on the retreating British Expeditionary Force at Dunkirk, No. 1 Fighter Squadron, augmented by personnel from No. 115 "City of Montreal" Squadron, and a rear party of No. 112 (AC) Squadron prepared to sail for Europe.

Russ Bannock and a number of his PPO colleagues were packing at Rockcliffe to join No. 112 Squadron embarking in Halifax. According to Bannock, their Lysander aircraft were "supposed to go over to France and land with the first Canadian Division to do reconnaissance work and to focus artillery from the air." Attached to No. 1 Fighter Squadron was reconnaissance photographer Ken Smith, who remembered being secretly ferried across Halifax harbour in a freighter before boarding the *Duchess of Athol*. But just before the convoy was due to leave, it was delayed by two events.

"One morning," Smith wrote, "we saw a tremendously high bow of another ship next to us. This ship was the *Empress of Britain*, and on it, coming out from England for her first wartime tour of Canada, was

Gracie Fields. When she found out there were Canadians going overseas on the ship below, she came to the front of the bow above us and sang several songs for us; we were the first to hear her in Canada."

Then, just before the convoy of ships (including the *Duchess of Bedford*, the *Samaria*, and three French ships—the aircraft carrier *Baern*, carrying 120 American warplanes for France, and the cruisers *Emile Bertin* and *Jeanne d'Arc*) weighed anchor, grim news arrived from France. The Royal Navy, the RAF, and thousands of British ferries and pleasure craft had evacuated nearly 340,000 British, French, and Belgian troops from the shores of France, but 200 ships and 177 aircraft had been lost. The fall of France was imminent. Bannock's mission was scrubbed, he never got to Halifax, and "most of us pilots, who had been added to the squadron, were sent off to become flying instructors. At that point the Air Training Plan was just getting off the ground."

As Ken Smith and the rest of No. 1 RCAF Fighter Squadron and No. 112 Army Co-operation Squadron steamed out of Halifax for Liverpool, Britons and North Americans read or heard the June 4 broadcast of Churchill's defiant speech: "We shall fight on the beaches . . . we shall fight in the fields and in the streets, we shall fight in the hills; we shall never surrender." For Russ Bannock and those assigned to the ranks of the BCATP, the fight would be against time over the airfields of Canada.

It was now June 1940. Zero Day, the day the BCATP officially began, had passed at the end of April. A second Manning Depot had opened its doors in Brandon, Manitoba. (Later there would be others at Edmonton, Lachine, and Quebec City.) There were still just two Initial Training Schools, in Toronto and Regina. Several of the flying clubs officially became BCATP Elementary Flying Training Schools that month (No. 1 at Malton, No. 2 at Fort William, No. 3 at London, and No. 4 at Windsor Mills, Quebec). Camp Borden was still the only Service Flying Training School in the system. Peter Troup and Babe Woollett of Dominion Skyways had opened No. 1 Air Observer School at Malton in May. There was one Wireless School, in Montreal, which had been open since February. And the system's only Air

Navigation School and its only Central Flying School (CFS) were up and running in Trenton.

"I was disappointed that I wasn't going overseas," said Russ Bannock, who was immediately posted from Halifax to CFS Trenton in June to instruct instructors. It seemed to him a waste of time showing other pilots—pleasure flyers, commercial flyers, bush pilots, one-time barnstormers, PPOs, and the first BCATP service-level pilots—how to be teachers, when the greatest need was in the skies over Britain. What good was Prime Minister Mackenzie King's promise that the BCATP would be working at full capacity—churning out 19,500 pilots, air observers, and wireless operators a year—by April 1942 if there was no Britain to send the airmen to? Canadian government officials and the RCAF responded to the crisis at Dunkirk and the possible invasion of Britain by offering to send BCATP instructors and administrators into the RAF immediately.

Churchill responded with characteristic calm resolve. "We can defend ourselves for some time to come, but we count on the training plan to supply a great tide of airmen when our strength, and that of our enemy, begins to wear and tear. We would prefer a thousand pilots from you later, than ten today."

Consequently, instructors like Russ Bannock and his student instructors at Trenton Central Flying School could not take part in the titanic struggle between RAF Fighter Command and the German Luftwaffe. In the summer and fall of 1940, they had to concentrate on the promise "to supply a great tide of airmen."

Despite his initial disappointment at being pulled off the Britain-bound convoy, Bannock was proud to have been selected as an instructor. "I realized you had to be a better pilot than the others, and it appealed to me, teaching other pilots to be flying instructors. We flew a variety of aircraft, too—EFTS trainers like Tiger Moths or Fleets, and SFTS Harvards, Ansons, and Oxfords. We had a bit of everything.

"The work was like being in a factory. We started at eight a.m. and finished at five. You'd take a student up for an hour, debrief him, and then you were up with another—probably six different flights a day. We operated about 150 aircraft on the aerodrome, which had no runways, just a big grass field, which wasn't difficult in the summertime, but in the winter became a skating rink. There were no radios or control towers. We had control officers in little huts on a van at the end of the runway flashing green, red, or yellow lights. It wouldn't be uncommon for a hundred aircraft to land on that aerodrome between 11:45 and 12:00 noon [at lunch time] and not have a single mishap."

No mishaps, perhaps, but some near misses. Among those early pilots training to become an instructor at Trenton was Al Stirton, who had pranged the Gipsy Moth on the airfield at Moose Jaw. Two years later, flying his Fleet Finch trainer, he was still feeling apprehensive about final approaches. The flying circuit—or "circuits and bumps" as it was affectionately known—was common to all levels of instruction. The flight pattern was simple enough: take off into the wind, climb to 500 feet, turn left, climb to 1,000 feet cross-wind, fly downwind parallel to the airstrip, descend to 500 feet on the base leg, turn into the wind at 500 feet, throttle back to glide on the approach, and land well into the field. Unfortunately, Stirton had a bad habit of undershooting the landing area, coming in too low on the approach, and having to add power to clear the last row of fenceposts before reaching the end of the runway. After one of these near tangles with the airfield perimeter fence, his instructor lost his temper.

"Stirton," fumed Flying Officer Jack Wickett from the instructor seat of the Fleet, "you will *never* undershoot this airfield again!" He taxied the Fleet to the flight line back in front of the hangar, climbed out of the cockpit, and said to Stirton, "Keep your parachute on, and walk around this whole airfield. Slap every fencepost as you pass it. No short cuts. I'll be watching you."

It was a hot summer day, but off Stirton went on his four-mile trek along the fence line. He was faithful to his instructor's orders for the first while, but about halfway around the airfield, he ducked in behind some trees and took a short cut back. He sat in the hangar for another thirty minutes, stowed his parachute away, and then made his way to the barracks. But he had learned his lesson. He never undershot the airfield again.

The Category Test was the instructor trainee's next hurdle. It was as much a test of a man's verbal ability as of his flying skill. Stirton and all student instructors had to master the "rote method," which meant memorizing each exercise with a set "patter" word-for-word from the official *Principles of Instruction* or CAP (Canadian Air Publication) No. 1 book. All instructors had to use exactly the same patter for each exercise, talking and demonstrating at the same time.

Stirton took the test on his twenty-fourth birthday. He arrived at the hangar punctually at 8:30 in the morning, picked up his parachute, and waited for the senior officer. He spent a nerve-racking hour and fifteen minutes before the arrival of Squadron Leader Bradshaw, who took one look at Stirton in his standard civilian clothing and shook his head. "You civilians have no respect for a parachute. And yours is a disgrace. How long have you been waiting?"

"An hour, sir," Stirton replied.

"An hour? And you couldn't find time to get the parachute stick and tuck in those corners to save the silk that's sticking out? I hope you don't have to jump with it." Whereupon Bradshaw grabbed the parachute, tucked in the corners, and packed it into the proper RCAF condition.

Bradshaw watched Stirton do his pre-flight walk-around check, then climb aboard and start the engine.

"You are now the instructor," Bradshaw explained, "and I am your student . . . so demonstrate each exercise with the appropriate patter."

The taxiing demonstration went fine. Take-off was okay. Stirton then took the Fleet trainer out of the circuit, climbed to 4,000 feet, and demonstrated a stall, a spin, steep turns, and the basic flying manoeuvres. He was just beginning to feel at ease when he noticed a problem with the Fleet's engine.

"Our oil pressure's dropping, sir," he pointed out.

"Damn," complained Bradshaw, "Back to the airport. We'll have to change aircraft."

Back at the Trenton airfield there were only a couple of Fleets left on the flight line, all ten-hundred series Fleets. Stirton made the mistake of suggesting they were underpowered for aerobatics.

"If you can't do a roll in a ten-hundred, you can't do a roll!" Bradshaw snapped. "You'll get lots of these when you're teaching at Elementary [Flying Training] School. Let's go."

Another pre-flight check, taxi, take-off, and climb for aerobatics demonstration. So far so good. Stirton demonstrated a forced landing (which is a simulated emergency landing, in which the pilot brings the aircraft down to about a hundred feet before turning the power back on and pulling up), but Bradshaw shook his head and then demonstrated one himself. Bradshaw's forced landing demo reminded Stirton of his own undershooting days. As Bradshaw glided powerless to the forced landing target, he didn't even make the field before he had to power back up and pull away. It was all Stirton could do to keep his smirk from turning into a laugh. Instructors were human too.

"A very good test," Bradshaw wrote on Stirton's graduating Instructor's Certificate. "After some experience with pupils, plus continued effort . . . he should become a very capable instructor." Five days later, Al Stirton, with only 146 military flying hours under his belt, was a sergeant pilot and full-fledged instructor on the staff at the EFTS operated by the St. Catharines Flying Club, with students of his own.

The RCAF had officially opened No. 9 Elementary Flying Training School at St. Catharines the week Stirton arrived. He and two other novice instructors from Moose Jaw reported to Chief Flying Instructor George Dunbar and joined fellow Trenton CFS graduates Bill Zaleschook and Bruce Pallett as RCAF sergeant pilots "on indefinite leave without pay." (Although they were officially RCAF-trained and ranked, most EFTS instructors remained civilians, operating in civilian clothing, in the civilian employ of the EFTS at a civilian wage of about $200 a month.)

Bruce Pallett was a farm boy from Dixie, Ontario, whose family was of United Empire Loyalist stock. As a teenager in the 1930s, he had fallen in love with flying. Every day after his farm chores, he collected garbage at fifty cents a load to pay for his flying lessons at Barker Field in Toronto. He took lessons from former Ontario Provincial Air Service pilot and barnstormer Len Trippe; once around the field for 65 cents.

At the height of the market season, young Pallett would get up at two in the morning, load the truck with produce, drive to the market in Toronto, sleep in the truck until the market opened at six o'clock, sell the produce, fill the truck with gas, and present his father with the day's take of $15 or $20. His father would always give him a dollar or two back to finance his flying lessons. By that time he'd earned the nickname "Banty" because, just like a bantam, he never stood still. In the dead of winter, Pallett would arrive in his rubber boots for a lesson at Barker Field, and Trippe would kid him by asking, "Banty, how you gonna keep your feet warm?"

"I've got a forkful of horseshit in each boot," Pallett would say.

By 1937, Banty Pallett had his private pilot's licence and 135 hours' flying time, just fifteen short of the requirement for his commercial licence. That's when he heard about the government-funded program that helped private pilots reach that magic 150-hour target and a commercial licence. Pallett was also just short of the required junior matriculation, but he cajoled his principal at Etobicoke High School into writing a letter claiming he had the equivalent of junior matriculation. It worked. He got his commercial licence and soon after the war broke out was shipped off to Trenton CFS to become an instructor.

Banty Pallett moved into locker No. 1 when No. 9 EFTS officially opened at St. Catharines. Bill Zaleschook was the second staff instructor. On the second day of EFTS operations, the Fleet Aircraft company (based in Fort Erie, Ontario) delivered thirty-two Fleet Finch trainer aircraft. That meant that Pallett and Zaleschook had to test-fly sixteen Fleets each in twenty-four hours, because on day three, No. 9 EFTS would receive its first official BCATP students—a score of ab initio students from England. The pace accelerated, and in the first three days of instruction "Banty and Bill were in the air twenty-one hours," explained Pallett's wife, Joyce. "Banty had lost his voice, because he'd been hollering down the gosport [rubber intercom] tube for twenty-one hours, instructing those greenhorn British students. On the morning of the fourth day, it was raining. They couldn't believe their luck. Flying was washed out that day."

The morning that Al Stirton, Dwight Buckmaster, and Allan Miller arrived from Trenton to augment the staff to five, No. 9 EFTS was in an uproar. The whole station seemed to be under construction and swamped in mud. There was no running water in the students' barracks. The heaters weren't working. The mess hall had a chef but very little kitchen equipment. The flight room in the hangar wasn't even close to operational. A handful of Canadian LACs wandered about trying to orient themselves, while a dozen British trainees gorged themselves on Orange Crush and McIntosh's toffee, which they'd just discovered in the station canteen. Chief Flying Instructor George Dunbar was delighted when the three new instructors arrived and presented their credentials.

"Good," said Dunbar briskly. "Now grab a parachute while I assign you some students and you can go right to work."

"Hold it," Stirton said. "Can't we have a couple of days to settle in? We have to find living accommodation, learn our way around, and get oriented."

"Okay," said Dunbar, relenting. "Take the rest of the morning off, but be back here at one o'clock ready to fly!"

After lunch Al Stirton got the first students of his instructor's career, a young Haligonian named Purves, an Ottawa recruit named Corcoran (who was later shot down twice while flying bombers), another Ottawa recruit named O'Connell (who won the DFC in 1942), and a fourth student named Goodwin.

To the four neophytes Stirton was god. He could do no wrong. They depended on him to help them survive and to coax them, in a matter of eight or ten hours in the air, to fly the Fleet solo. At the same time, the four helped break Stirton into his first instructor's job. As they learned the basics of elementary flying, he experimented with his patter and teaching techniques. The relationship between instructor and pupil, like so many in the early months of the BCATP, was symbiotic.

Nevertheless, bad weather and the condition of the airfield continued to play havoc with the momentum of instructors' teaching and trainees' learning at St. Catharines. The flying club had originally procured its site because it was too swampy for either city development or farming. Since most of the grass had been scraped away to level the earth for the airfield, whenever it rained No. 9 EFTS turned into a quagmire. Inevitably, that cancelled training flights. And it extended the time required to get trainees up solo and on their way to the next training level.

To complicate matters, halfway through the first course of students, a second course arrived. With the addition of only two instructors—Sergeant Pilots Fred Wellington and Donald Whitaker—Stirton and his fellow instructors worked the first month without a single day off. When that well-deserved break arrived, Stirton bought a used car and headed for Niagara Falls.

He remembered that as he drove past the station "I was thankful that my students wouldn't lose any time on my account because it was a dull day with low cloud. So probably no flying."

Station procedure required a weather test flight at the beginning of each training day. Because there were low cloud conditions this particular day, Banty Pallett took a Fleet up to investigate. The ceiling was less than a thousand feet, not enough room for elementary flying, and there was no sign the weather would move out. So the day was rescheduled for ground instruction.

"About noon," CFI Dunbar recalled, "I had to go to town. I left [Wellington] in charge [of further weather testing]. Around 1:45, he took another instructor [Whitaker] and the two of them went up to do the weather test."

"Wellington and Whitaker went up together," Al Stirton continued, "and the ceiling was still low; so they made a quick circuit and landed. They turned to taxi in, just as Art Vincent [assistant to the RCAF CO] took off to fly to Hamilton. As Vincent got airborne, he made a low pass over the other Fleet. This was an invitation to a dogfight. So Wellington and Whitaker turned around, took off, got on Vincent's tail, and the dogfight was on. In trying to shake them off his tail, Vincent did a series of loops, but at low altitude because of the low cloud. The boys followed him."

Aerobatics were strictly forbidden over an airfield, and to engage in dogfighting at such a low altitude was particularly foolhardy.

Nonetheless, with the station's staff and students grounded because of the weather, it wasn't long before the two Fleets, chasing each other over the field, drew a crowd of spectators. For the officers and ground crew, high jinks like this were not unusual, but the EFTS trainees were witnessing an exhibition of aerobatics by their instructors for the first time.

Among the spectators were instructors Banty Pallett and Bill Zaleschook. Pallett had offered to go up for the midday weather test, but because he had done the morning check, Wellington and Whitaker had insisted it was their turn. As they watched, Zaleschook was the first to express concern. He told Pallett that with the extra weight in their Fleet, Wellington and Whitaker were getting closer to the ground with each pass. "One more loop," Zaleschook said, "and they've had it."

Vincent's Fleet led the chase through one more loop and "pulled out just above the ground," recalls Stirton, "but the boys went straight in."

The Fleet exploded and burned on impact. A fire crew with extinguishers was there in a matter of seconds, but the heat was so intense that no one could get to Whitaker and Wellington, even if they had survived the crash. Their bodies were burned so badly that the crash investigation couldn't determine which pilot was in which cockpit, nor who had had control of the Fleet during the dogfight. No blame was assigned, but Art Vincent soon left St. Catharines for good.

5

COCKPIT CLASSROOM

DONALD WHITAKER AND FRED WELLINGTON were among the first of many that the BCATP would kill along the way. Regulations prohibited tail chasing, yet instructors and students did it anyway. One foggy day George Dunbar had taken a student in a Fleet well above the smog and cloud for instruction, when suddenly a Fairey Battle trainer screamed across in front of them; it was none other than Dunbar's old London Flying Club instructor, Tom Williams. Dunbar told his student to hang on, and a dogfight ensued.

Low flying was restricted to designated areas, but instructors still introduced their students to the sensation of being "right down on the deck" whenever the opportunity or the challenge presented itself. Al Stirton and fellow-instructor Keith Patman once got together under a 500-foot ceiling of cloud en route from St. Catharines to London. The two instructors hedge-hopped over country roads, chased cows and horses through farmers' fields, scattered chickens and ducks, leap-frogged over motorists along the highway, and dropped low enough alongside a locomotive to wave to the engineer.

"Another time, Bruce Woods and I were up together on a mutual instrument practice," Al Stirton remembered. For at least thirty minutes a month, instructors were required to fly exclusively by instruments—that is, two instructors would go up, one in the rear seat flying on instruments "under the hood" (or covered by a cloth canopy so that no visual reference could be made with the ground or the horizon), and the other in the front seat as instructor and look-out. Normally "at half time, we would return to the airport, change seats, and take off for the second half-hour.

"This day, it was getting close to noon, and as we were some distance from the airport, we decided to change seats in the air to save time. We left the power on and I got out on the right wing [while Woods got on the left. We] changed seats and finished our flight. When we landed, the ground crew couldn't figure out how we came back in different seats, as it was very muddy from rains so they knew we hadn't landed anywhere. We never explained."

There was always an element of risk in these exploits. But it was encouraged in certain trainees. The fact is, if some of these new young pilots hadn't learned to handle the risks, there would have been no Spitfire, Hurricane, or Mosquito ace pilots. Certain pilots calculated the risk, dealt with it, and defied it better than others. This made the difference between learning and mastery, and sometimes between life and death.

Although the crash that killed Whitaker and Wellington wasted two valuable pilots, their deaths jolted the naive young trainees who had not yet faced the realities of their eventual role in the war. If they hadn't realized it before then, they discovered that day that taking the controls of an aircraft, learning to survive in the air with a piece of military machinery, and training for victory was dangerous work.

That's why the staff at St. Catharines had every trainee flying again as soon as possible after the crash. It not only made up lost time in the training schedule, but it distracted the young trainees and prevented them from grieving too long, refocused their attention on the job at hand, and prepared them for dealing with death in their midst. Trainees had to recognize danger without buckling in the face of it. Only expert instructors and an aircraft like the Fleet Finch could achieve this.

During the early days of the Elementary Flying Training Schools, the Fleet Finch did yeoman service getting BCATP trainees from the Link trainer to their first solo flight. Were it not for the forgiving nature of this biplane workhorse, which some called "the backbone of the training plan," many of the BCATP's earliest trainees might not have made the grade, or worse, might have been injured or killed by pilot error.

In the first year of the war, Fleet Aircraft of Canada Ltd. delivered 335 Finch IIs to the RCAF. Each one was built for maximum stability and recoverability under training conditions. There were, however, certain flaws in its character, as the instructors at No. 7 EFTS Windsor discovered.

Cyril Cooper, the civilian manager of the Windsor Flying Club, and RCAF Commanding Officer Abner Hiltz had received their quota of Trenton CFS graduates and begun training operations. Among the first Windsor instructors were Brick Bradford, Frank Vines, Gus Bennett, and Bob Eaton. In August 1940, instructor Eaton took a student from the second course up for a sequence of basic aerial manoeuvres, including spins. The object was to stall the Fleet in mid-air, have it fall into a spin, and demonstrate the standard recovery technique. This day, as the Fleet fell into its spin, it also flipped on its back. Bob knew how to bring the Fleet out of an inverted spin, but no matter how hard he worked, the Fleet did not respond. He told his student to bail out; then he did the same. Not a moment too soon. Bob's chute popped about fifty feet from the ground; in fact, he and the Fleet hit the ground simultaneously. Bob Eaton's student landed safely, Bob fractured his ankle, and the Finch was a write-off.

A few days later, Windsor's chief flying instructor, Al Lewis, and the assistant CFI, Paul Hovey, put another Fleet Finch into an inverted spin. The same thing happened, except that when they popped off the perspex coupe top over the cockpits, it rolled across the wing, putting just enough weight on that wing so that the Fleet righted itself and they landed safely. But an unexpected flaw had been revealed in the RCAF's principal elementary training aircraft.

Instructor Gus Bennett recalled that soon after, a group of air force experts known as a Visiting Flight arrived from Trenton. "They conducted experiments, pasting threads all the way along the surfaces of the wings so that they could see the airflow in a stall condition. They also got into an inverted spin and managed to get out all right; but they weren't very happy. They immediately said not to teach any more inverted spins."

What Bennett and the rest of Training Command soon learned was that although the Fleet Finch had been designed for a heavy 160-horsepower motor, a lighter 130-horsepower motor had been installed. As a result, under certain conditions of weight distribution (such as a heavier-than-normal pilot in the rear cockpit), the Fleet would stabilize in an inverted spin and never recover. Eventually the Fleet Finch's tail section was modified to compensate for this defect, but not soon enough for two of Windsor's pilots.

"Stormy Fairweather was giving a test to a young student from Brantford, an LAC named Axler," Bennett recalled. "It involved some aerobatics. They were doing a roll-off-the-top, where you do a loop and then at the last second, at the top of the loop, you roll out right side up and level. We figured because of his weight, the Fleet just flipped into an inverted spin instead of rolling out. And once they got into it, with his heavy weight in the back and the light student in front, they couldn't get out of it. He didn't have enough altitude, less than a thousand feet. They crashed and both were killed."

Once again, an entire station mourned. Students had lost a barracks-mate. The young instructing staff had lost a colleague. The air force had to notify relatives and return a husband and a son home in coffins. Training Command had lost more time, another valuable teacher, and a potential pilot for operational duty in Fighter or Bomber Command overseas.

A.H. Fairweather and D.R. Axler were two of several thousand fatalities* recorded during the existence of the BCATP, compared to overall Canadian air crew losses during the war of about 10,000.

---

* During the Second World War in the United Kingdom, more than 25,000 air crewmen were lost in non-operational flying accidents. Throughout their entire involvement in the war, the American Air forces lost more aircraft in training and routine flights than they did in combat. And in the last twelve months of the war, the Germans lost 25 percent of their total aircraft production in ferrying accidents.

However, at this early stage of the war, there were as many pilots dying in training as in combat. About the same time that Fairweather and Axler were killed in Windsor, and Whitaker and Wellington in St. Catharines, the RCAF recorded its first battle casualty in Britain.* Both kinds of losses were troubling. Both underlined the need for qualified pilots for the war effort. Both increased the pressure on the plan and its instructors to produce more pilots.

At No. 7 EFTS Windsor the pressure was evident right from the beginning. As with other early stations, the barracks blocks for trainees were incomplete, aircraft were in short supply, and the student-to-instructor ratio, as in St. Catharines, was unmanageably high. Nevertheless, the civilian manager expected his instructors to deliver trained pilots like bus drivers delivering passengers. (Cyril Cooper was also the owner of a bus line between Windsor and Toronto.) The flying instructors felt slighted because their civilian employer "considered us the same as bus drivers," Gus Bennett explained. "Cooper didn't realize that we were 'exalted' professional pilots.

"There were a lot of start-up problems. One was, there were only hard benches in the instructors' flight room. We felt we should have proper chairs. We were a little brassed off over things like that. We had a meeting one day and decided this wasn't very good. So I was delegated to write a note to management and present it. Well, Cooper didn't take too kindly to that. He just considered us his bus drivers.

"The other thing was that after six months we were supposed to get a raise in pay. Well, at the end of six months we didn't get our raise, nor after seven months, nor after eight. So all the instructors went on strike."

Gus Bennett wanted to be treated like the experienced professional he felt himself to be. He had taken his first flying lesson in the

---

* On August 26, 1940, the first RCAF squadron went into action: No. 1 Fighter Squadron engaged Luftwaffe fighter aircraft in the Battle of Britain that day, destroyed three and damaged four German aircraft. The pilot lost was F/O R.L. Edwards, the RCAF's first battle casualty.

mid-1930s when he "liberated" two dollars of his mother's money for a lesson in a Cirrus Moth at the Brantford Flying Club. Flying quickly became his passion, in spite of his father's insistence that he stay in school to improve his chances of employment during the depression. Father and son struck a deal: he would study commerce at Queen's University for a year. After a year, when he discovered that he wasn't "built for the halls of higher learning," Bennett borrowed enough money from his father to get his commercial pilot's licence.

When war was declared, Bennett answered the call for instructors and got into Trenton Central Flying School. A month later he was on the flight line at Windsor instructing his first three trainees at No. 7 EFTS. However, although Bennett's determination, individuality, and sense of humour commanded great respect from students, the same was not true from management.

"Because it was a civilian-run school, we didn't wear uniforms," Bennett said. "Our uniform consisted of our civilian clothes plus air force-issue flying coveralls, helmet, and boots. But we wanted a uniform. We felt that we should have a uniform to walk about the streets, because after all, we were in the military service. But there was no uniform provided.

"So we designed our own uniforms. We got air force officers' material and had our EFTS wings and crest sewn on, which all looked strangely like RCAF officers' uniforms. We'd put on our 'uniforms' and the air force blue trench coat, and we'd wear them over in Detroit. Customs just waved us right through. We shouldn't have been there looking like that, but we were heroes over there. We'd walk into a bar and everybody'd buy us a drink.

"It was great, until a Visiting Flight came down one day from Trenton. We thought we'd impress these people, so we all wore our 'uniforms.' Well, the stuff really hit the fan. There was a picture in the Windsor *Star*. The chap who saw it at Training Command Headquarters was not the least bit impressed at our trying to impersonate an officer of the RCAF." That was the end of the public use of the EFTS air force uniform. Still, Bennett and the Windsor staff had made their point. Headquarters sent officers to investigate problems at the Windsor station. They removed Cyril Cooper. And conditions improved, even if the pace didn't slacken.

When the British Commonwealth Air Training Plan officially opened stations such as St. Catharines and Windsor, school capacity was set at forty-eight students. However, the needs of the air war and the growing efficiency of the system later pushed the average to ninety trainees. The EFTS staff at each school handled two classes at all times, graduating one class and accepting another every four weeks. The original eight-week syllabus included about 180 hours of ground instruction and fifty hours of air training, half of it dual (with the instructor accompanying the student) and half solo.

A BCATP trainee was expected to solo after about eight hours of dual instruction. This phase of instruction was among the most stressful times in the entire training regimen. It was as much a test of a new instructor's effectiveness as of a trainee's potential flying ability. Yet instructors agreed that "God watches over first solos."

If the Deity factored into a successful first solo, it was only after an instructor felt his student answered all other criteria. Was he familiar with the instruments? Was he light-handed on the control column? Did he have natural hand-foot coordination for the stick and rudder pedals? Could he apply the throttle evenly? Could he taxi smoothly? Did he know always to take off into the wind? Was his straight and level flight effortless? Did he demonstrate ease through climbing, gliding, and stalling manoeuvres, side-slipping, medium turns, steep turns, and climbing turns? Was his precautionary landing ability effective? Could he handle both powered approach and gliding approach to landing smoothly? Did he exhibit a combination of healthy self-confidence and a sense of caution? When an instructor felt that his student met these criteria after their first eight hours in the air together, he let him go solo.

The way his heart pounded, his stomach flipped, and his mind raced during that first EFTS solo experience stayed with a trainee pilot for a lifetime. Instructor Bob Hesketh described his own solo experience as a combination of fear and exhilaration. Decorated

RCAF pilot Hugh Godefroy remembered, "When [my instructor] stepped out of the back seat that fateful day and secured the empty safety belts in the back, my heart came up in my mouth. Slowly he turned to me and looked me squarely in the eye. For a second his eyes softened and his leathery face broke into a smile. 'Now, see if you can get it down so that you can walk away from it, will ya!'"

Fighter pilot Bill Olmstead recalled that "my first solo lasted only ten minutes, but in that short space of time, I saw the light, as head, hands, and feet performed perfectly, never to bother me again." An American, Len Morgan, who joined the RCAF and soloed at EFTS St. Catharines, remembered the exhilaration. "I twisted twice to look into the empty back seat and laughed loud enough to hear myself above the engine's roar."

Instructor John Clinton recalled his first solo ruefully because "as we came in to land, I brought the aircraft down and I held it there, and held it there, until it stalled and landed. The only problem was, I was about ten feet above the ground."

Coastal Command Sunderland pilot Jack Bowers remembered his instructor watching his approach at the edge of the field. "I started to come in for a landing, and said to myself, 'I'm too high.' I flew over the field, looked at my instructor, wondering if he'd wave his arms as if to say, 'Go around and try again,' but he just stood there with his arms folded, as if to say, 'You make the decision.' He had decided to cut the cord."

"I was up solo," airman Harold Lancaster said, "and got down fine. Taxied up to the line. Came in a little too quickly. Hit the brakes too hard. And the aircraft tail went up. I shut off the motor. Did everything according to Hoyle. The thing teetered for a moment on the end of the propeller and then gently went down. No damage. My instructor took a picture and on the back he wrote 'Ace Lancaster.'"

At the end of his first test as a pilot, RCAF instructor Ken Summerville remembered writing to his mother. He began the letter in blue ink, but when he wrote down, "This is my red letter day," he rewrote it in red ink.

Euphoria was another apt description reflected in letters home. Trainees who successfully soloed after eight hours often claimed that their "feet didn't hit the ground for hours and days after." Ahead there were many great hurdles yet to clear: the twenty-hour test, the fifty-hour test, graduation from elementary flying to service flying, and ultimately—the Holy Grail of military flying—the wings test. Still, a first solo was a moment to savour, provided the exhilaration didn't swell the trainee's head. Instructors agreed there were numerous danger points in a pilot's career, plateaus where he felt he had mastered the machine, times when he sensed he could do almost anything up there with an airplane. At this stage, confidence was a healthy acquisition; cockiness was not.

Robert Letson soloed at No. 7 EFTS Windsor in 1940. He relishes it as "a never-to-be-forgotten moment," but his confidence was shaken one day soon after when "aloft solo and revelling in the experience, I became aware of something above me. Glancing up I could see nothing except two wheels within ten feet of me! I have often wondered if the other Fleet Finch pilot knew how close we came to selling the farm that day." (Letson went on to instruct in both RCAF and RAF Training Command.)

Letson didn't bother to tell his instructor, Frank Vines, about his near miss. Even if he had, it probably wouldn't have surprised the seasoned instructor. Vines had grown up in Goderich, near Sky Harbour airstrip (later the site of No. 12 EFTS). When he was fourteen, his father paid London Flying School instructor Tom Williams six dollars to take Frank up for a spin. Williams told Frank and his father that Frank had "talent as a pilot." By 1938, after numerous twelve-dollar flying lessons in Williams's Gipsy Moth, Vines had his private licence, and by 1939 he nearly had his commercial ticket. When he discovered that the air force wanted him as an instructor, he thought, "Great. I'll instruct for six months, get a few more hundred hours, and then whoopie, I'm off and running overseas." Two years and nearly 2,000 hours of instructing later, Vines was posted overseas to No. 233 RAF Squadron on Coastal Command. In the course of those 2,000 hours, he trained a young student named Croll Taylor.

According to Vines, LAC Taylor demonstrated early on that he was "a hell of a good pilot." He took to the controls naturally and soloed early. Then, one day that first summer at No. 7, Vines sent Taylor off on some solo aerobatics practice. A few minutes after the Fleet left the airstrip, a farmer southeast of the station called; a trainer aircraft had crashed. Abner Hiltz, the commanding officer, his assistant, and the station's medical officer immediately raced away in search of the farm, the plane, and its pilot.

"When they got there," Vines said, "they found the airplane. It had crashed straight in, but it hadn't burned. Hiltz turned white as they tried to decide which one of them would look into the cockpit, when all of a sudden across the field comes this guy in white pants and white shirt, lugging a parachute. He approached Hiltz, saluted him, and said, 'Sir, I'm sorry about the airplane.' Everybody brightened up as Hiltz said, 'Don't worry about it, son.'

"Of course there was a court of inquiry. But they never called me, and I was his instructor. They just took a statement from him. Croll said, 'I don't know what happened, but at the top of a loop, I must have stalled and gone into a spin and wasn't able to get out, so I bailed out.' I thought this was strange; he was one of my better students. And I got disciplined by the air force for not teaching him how to come out of a spin.

"Meanwhile, Croll left within a week and I never flew with him again. I didn't see him again until I was in Ferry Command in 1945. I was in Prestwick, and lo and behold, there is Croll Taylor. So I bought him several Scotches and he bought me several Scotches. I finally said, 'Croll, tell me the truth. What really happened that day you supposedly got into a spin? Your mother even wrote me a letter calling me a murderer for not teaching her son properly.'

"'Well,' said Taylor, 'it was a hot day. And those safety straps were digging into me. So I took the harness off. Then it got even hotter, so I put the coupe top back—'

"'Then,' I said, 'you started doing loops and all of a sudden you parted company with the airplane. Is that what happened?'

"'That's exactly what happened,' Taylor said." Croll's confident attitude had put him near the head of his class. It had pushed him through his solo easily. Yet when it turned to cockiness while looping his Fleet that summer day in 1940, it nearly buried him and the career of his instructor, Frank Vines. However, they both survived, partly because, as Vines commented, "We thought we would live forever. I never thought I'd get killed in an airplane. By an irate husband, perhaps, but never by an airplane."

A bit of that same bravado soon after paid off for Vines. He and another student had just completed their pre-flight check. They taxied into position, throttled up, and headed down the runway. Just as their Fleet left the ground, one of its two wheels fell off. If it had happened a second earlier, the aircraft might have ground-looped (spun around on its wingtip) or cartwheeled and crashed. Initially Vines had no idea there was anything wrong until "all of a sudden, I see a Fleet flying formation with me. It was Al Lewis, the CFI, and Syd Hutnick, our chief engineer, who, of course, is responsible for the Fleet's airworthiness. Hutnick is alongside holding a wheel in his hands and pointing down. At first, I wondered what the hell he was doing with the wheel. Then I looked down and saw they had meat wagons and fire trucks coming from all directions, and I realized.

"I wasn't thinking about dying. I thought what a wonderful opportunity to test my skills—how to land on one wheel. I had seen it done in a movie serial once, so I figured I could do it too."

"Frank came down knowing the condition of his aircraft," remembered friend and fellow instructor Gus Bennett. The entire school was watching as "he made a beautiful cross-wind landing on one wheel. He kept the plane on that one wheel, just to the very last second. Then it settled down and he did a slow ground loop. Beautiful job of flying!"

The citation from station management congratulated Vines for "the masterful manner in which you averted what might have been a very serious accident. . . . The coolness and skill which you exhibited in handling your machine, certainly calls for our loud praise." Unfortunately, loud praise did not translate into recognition from the air force, nor an opportunity to be promoted away from his instructor duties, nor a crack at RCAF service flying and a pair of RCAF wings, nor ultimately a posting overseas. It didn't even help him earn his overdue raise. Still, his presence of mind had saved his life and his student's.

Demonstrations like Vines's one-wheel landing taught a student pilot a great deal. Any emergency flying—a forced landing because of engine failure, restarting an engine in flight, recovery from stalls and spins, or abandoning an aircraft—was instructive. With the exception of bailing out, all these procedures were part of the training syllabus. Then there were the intangibles—the flying tips that no aviation textbook ever contains.

Some of the earliest instructors at Wop May's Edmonton and Northern Alberta Flying Club had been bush pilots who had helped Wop launch flying in the north. Flyers such as Maurice "Moss" Burbidge were aviation pioneers, living legends, and by the first crop of students at the newly christened No. 16 EFTS Edmonton, they were treated with reverence. Moss Burbidge had flown both bombing and fighter aircraft in the First World War. As a result, the RAF had made him an instructor at No. 1 Flying Training School in England. In 1928 he had accepted the CFI position at the Edmonton and Northern Alberta Flying Club but continued flying commercially, inaugurating air mail service to Fort McMurray, Fort Chipewyan, Fort Smith, Fort Resolution, and Aklavik down the Mackenzie River. Burbidge retired in 1939 with more than 15,000 hours of flying in his log. But with the war that year, he was called back into service at No. 16 EFTS in Edmonton.

That's where PPO Hadley Armstrong took instruction from him. Armstrong was ready for the RCAF; he was strong physically and emotionally. His father had died in an auto garage explosion and Hadley had learned to be the family breadwinner at a young age. He had excelled in gymnastics at home in Gananoque, Ontario, and had become both a competitor and a coach. But neither his experience nor his agility could equal his first experience with Moss Burbidge.

"I was in the back seat of a Tiger Moth as his student, when the engine started coughing," Armstrong remembered. "Right away, Moss says, 'Excuse me. I'll be back in a minute.' And out he came with a bale of wire in hand and climbed out on the wing. Suddenly, I'm the only guy flying the plane, when I didn't know the first things about flying. Moss fixed whatever it was, climbed back into the cockpit, and off we went. He was a character."

If nothing else, the experience gave Armstrong the confidence to fly no matter what was going on around him. Moss Burbidge's tips and stunts made enough of an impression on young Armstrong that he completed his training in record time, earned his wings that September, and went on to become both an elementary and advanced flying instructor, training scores of RCAF combat pilots until early 1944.

Notwithstanding the impressive style of instructors like Burbidge, the aircraft cockpit was a terrible classroom. The racket and vibration from even the smallest of the Fleet Finch's 130-horsepower Kinner 5-cylinder radial engines drowned out instructions spoken through the gosport tubes.* More often than not, the instructor had to yell his directions to be heard. Any abnormal weather conditions—strong winds, intense summer sun, or bitter winter cold—also created problems. EFTS instructor Stan Castle found he couldn't operate in winter in the unheated cockpit without "a pair of socks, fur slippers (my girlfriend gave me), flying boots, service-issue winter underwear, pajamas, battle dress, two flying suits, and silk gloves under mitts and goggles. Of course, you could hardly move. And with all this, you're supposed to feel the light touch on the controls."

A twenty-year-old bank teller and part-time saxophone player who enlisted in 1940 and devoted the rest of his working life to wartime and peacetime training in the RCAF (eventually reaching the rank of brigadier general in the Unified Services, the equivalent of air commodore) was nearly washed out of pilot training because

---

* The Gosport Communications System originated in the pre-First World War training aircraft of the Royal Naval Air Service station located at Gosport on the south coast of England.

the instructions he received in the cockpit didn't get through to him. A perceptive elementary instructor at No. 19 EFTS in Virden, Manitoba, recognized Ross Truemner's problem, sat him down in the flight room, and soon realized that Truemner had no idea how to land an airplane.

"Tomorrow morning," he explained, "you and I are not going to fly. Instead, we are going on a little trip. Meet me at the flight line at daybreak."

Truemner was punctual. The instructor was too. Together they left the hangars and walked across the airfield into the tall grass of the open Manitoba prairie. The instructor sat Truemner down and asked him to pretend they were in an airplane.

"What way are you going to point the plane when you take off?" he asked.

"Into the wind," Truemner said.

"What's your take-off procedure?"

"First, the cockpit check . . ." And so it went. From take-off to climbing to turning to descending to landing, the instructor talked him through. That morning, before the planes were lined up outside the hangar for the day's flying, Truemner had gone through three complete circuits while sitting in the grass; he had imprinted the procedure step-by-step from start to finish in his memory. Now all he had to do was carry out the procedure in a real flight.

"He had me talking like an instructor," Truemner marvelled. "It registered on me. I didn't realize until years later, but what he was doing, and eventually what became a regular part of pilot training, was called 'ground briefing.' This man knew the secret."

After eleven hours of patient ground and airborne briefing with his instructor (well beyond the prescribed eight-hour limit), Truemner flew his first solo without a hitch, "and from then on, I talked to myself in the airplane." He never stopped talking. He talked to himself throughout the rest of his EFTS training at Virden and later at No. 10 SFTS Dauphin, through his wings test, during his instructor's course at Trenton, and throughout his three years as an instructor at

No. 16 SFTS Hagersville. He was ploughed back into the BCATP as a ground instructor, an examining officer, an instrument instructor, and a Standard Beam Approach instructor. Ross Truemner became so proficient at flying and teaching flying that he earned the sobriquet "Mr. Instrument Flyer." Although he never flew a single overseas mission, he earned the Air Force Cross in part because he helped hundreds of trainees break through that first psychological barrier to understanding flight, by talking them through it.

While the Moss Burbidge school of instructing left an indelible impression, it wasn't necessarily the best way to teach pilots. As trainee Ross Truemner found, the best elementary instructor was patient, methodical, and innovative. Even when he was furious with a student's carelessness or miscalculation, a capable instructor rarely exploded with anger.

Banty Pallett was well known for his tolerance. He realized that there was little point adding to the pressure on a student by ranting and raving through the gosport or at a ground briefing. Particularly with his first crop of English students, who were often emotionally distracted by events at home, Pallett took great pains to offer constructive criticism and encouragement. He never yelled at them. On days when weather washed out flying, Pallett sat with students in the hangar and dealt with their problems. This "hangar flying" technique built their confidence. He also let them make minor mistakes in the air, so they could learn from experience; in fact, he would not let a student go solo until he had made at least one bad landing; a student's ability to get himself out of trouble was more important than making consistently perfect landings.

As hectic as the days became, an instructor couldn't allow the daily routine to siphon away his energy. The long hours, the repetition, the constant shouting into the gosport tubes over the roar of the aircraft engine, and the need to stay alert, watching for other aircraft in the skies around a training station as well as being on constant guard for a student's unexpected errors—all took their toll. Civilian EFTS instructors lived away from the station, some sharing rooms with colleagues in a hotel, some renting modest flats or digs in rooming houses. They needed those few hours of rest away from the station.

Pallett paid for his long days in a Fleet cockpit, as his wife, Joyce, attested. "I used to rub his feet at night. His feet were on the rudder pedals all day. The vibration would just drive him crazy. So when he got in, I'd just massage his feet to relax him. He never complained about the pain. But often it kept him from going to sleep." Nonetheless, in fifty-two months of training scores of EFTS pilots, Pallett didn't wash out a single one.

Banty Pallett was never completely successful in separating one aspect of his life from the other and often brought his work home with him. He corresponded with scores of young EFTS graduates after they left St. Catharines and made their way up the training ladder and beyond. Pallett's students went on to service flying stations around the continent—at Yorkton, Moncton, and Dunnville and at schools in the United States. Others went on to distinguished flying in Fighter, Bomber, Transport, and Coastal Command from Scotland to Khartoum. But they never forgot "the Skipper."

Letters from his old pupils to their "favourite instructor" gave Banty a running commentary about their graduation to heavier, faster, more powerful planes. Some reminisced about the simpler Fleet flying and less-disciplined life they had enjoyed at St. Catharines. One of his former students followed in his footsteps to become a pilot at No. 7 Bombing and Gunnery School in Paulson, Manitoba; Art Browne finished a letter by commenting that "I learned more from you than I've learned since." And just before he received his wings at Dunnville, another Pallett protégé, Dave Duffy, wrote to say, "I owe you plenty, Mr. Pallett."

Al Stirton's philosophy in the instructor's cockpit was as positive as Banty's; he attempted "to lead rather than drive my students, something I learned from my favourite schoolteacher at our prairie school. I tried to be patient and not too critical . . . I tried to be friendly with my students . . . but avoided becoming pals." Perhaps most important of all, "I learned how far I could let an error go before taking over the controls."

Landings were particularly tricky, because "if [students] levelled out too high, the aircraft would drop in heavily and one had to be quick to add power to cushion the landing. If they failed to level out or 'flare' in time, the aircraft would fly into the ground, bounce badly, and then stall in heavily. Again, quick use of the throttle was the remedy. The Fleet was a sturdy trainer and could take the abuse, so I let them bounce all over the field. Then I'd ask, 'What did you do wrong this time?' If they realized the mistake, they soon learned."

One of Stirton's students was a very quick learner. He stood out in the crowd of trainees partly because he was tall and slim, but also because of his good manners, his popularity with his classmates, and his natural ability as a pilot. When Stirton took him up, he remembers the young man's gentle, smooth control of the Fleet. He scored well on instrument flying, and his cross-country from St. Catharines to Mount Hope (near Hamilton) and back was "a piece of cake.... He flew it as though he'd done it many times."

However, Stirton remembered that there was an unpredictable side to LAC John Gillespie Magee. Born in Shanghai in 1922 and educated at St. Clare boarding school and Rugby Public School in England, Magee was above average scholastically and so well read he could quote Plato and Aristotle. The war began while he was in America preparing for a career at Yale, and he grew restless and homesick for England. He decided to join the RAF early in 1940. The American State Department refused him a visa, so he tried the RCAF. After first being refused for being underweight, he was accepted as Aircraftman 2nd Class late in 1940. Under Stirton and the rest of the St. Catharines instructor crew, Magee proved himself, soloing after only six and a half hours; the minimum time for most students was eight hours.

"At this time, Magee was in the junior course," Stirton said, "and had listened to the senior course discussing their aerobatics—loops, rolls, spins—and comparing notes on how to do them. So Mr. Magee, on his second or third solo, decided to do a roll. He knew the rules did not allow aerobatics below 3,000 feet, so he climbed to 5,000, looked over the side, and decided 6,000 would be better, looked again, and went on up to 8,000 to attempt his roll . . .

"He got into an inverted spin, where the blood rushes to the head and the pilot can 'red out'—the opposite of a 'black out,' when the blood is drawn away from the head and brain. He struggled with the controls and finally recovered at about 600 feet above the ground.

"Meanwhile he had been sent up for thirty minutes and an hour had gone by. His instructor, A.K. Patterson, became anxious and watched for his return. On landing, Magee bounced badly and taxied in. His instructor went out to him and demanded, 'Why the ropey landing?' The lad was as white as a sheet and shaking badly. He told A.K. what he had done and was taken to the medical officer, who said, 'Take him right back up.' He shook for two days, then recovered, and after a reprimand resumed flying."

Despite his temperamental nature and overzealousness, Magee graduated from No. 9 EFTS at the top of his class in both flying and ground school. He did his service flying and received his wings at No. 2 SFTS Uplands. When he got his commission, he was posted overseas in mid-1941, did his advanced training on Miles Masters in preparation for operational service with No. 412 RCAF Squadron.

"Then on December 11, 1941," as Al Stirton learned from dispatch sheets received from overseas, Magee "was in a flight of seven Spits on a formation flight practice routine above the clouds. Their leader found a hole in the cloud base and led them down through it. Magee was number three in the formation and as he cleared the clouds, he collided with an Oxford training aircraft flown by a student and both were killed."

It was only after Magee's death that Al Stirton and most of the rest of the aviation fraternity learned how the young pilot had channelled his impulsive energy. As a schoolboy he had written a ten-page diatribe against society in blank verse—called "Brave New World"—that had won a poetry prize. "Maggie was a smart cookie," said Jim Coyne, one of Magee's guard duty mates at Trenton. "He always had a way with words." George Dunbar, the CFI at St. Catharines, recalled Magee as "the poet." So it did not surprise them to learn that when Magee was overseas he used the long waits between sorties to make model airplanes and used his poetry prize money to buy books. His poetry recorded air combat experiences, which he called "high blue battle." Three months before he died, John Gillespie Magee wrote the lines that are now recited by flyers around the world.

> Oh! I have slipped the surly bonds of earth,
> And danced the skies on laughter-silvered wings.
> Sunward I've climbed and joined the tumbling mirth
> Of sun-split clouds—and done a hundred things
> You have not dreamed of—wheeled and soared and swung
> High in the sunlit silence. Hov'ring there,
> I've chased the shouting winds along and flung
> My eager craft through footless halls of air.
> Up, up the long delirious, burning blue
> I've topped the wind-swept heights with easy grace
> Where never lark, nor even eagle flew;
> And, while with silent, lifting mind I've trod
> The high untrespassed sanctity of space,
> Put out my hand, and touched the face of God.

It's debatable whether any more or different instruction in the British Commonwealth Air Training Plan could have helped John Magee survive the war. It's arguable that his eagerness to fly beyond his ability contributed to his death. And yet, Al Stirton, one of his earliest and most observant instructors, worried about his temperamental nature, while admiring his intelligence and his gift as a natural pilot.

Just as an AC2 recruit at Manning Depot learned that you never volunteered in the air force, the BCATP's instructors learned that you never, or rarely, got to go where you wanted, when you wanted. For flyers such as Ross Truemner and Banty Pallett (who also received an Air Force Cross for service as an instructor), there would be no shooting war. For scores of others, such as Russ Bannock, Cap Foster, Gus Bennett, Frank Vines, and Al Stirton, overseas postings had to wait until the air force decided to let them go. For now, as BCATP instructors, their wartime role was to "shoot" patter, fill a student's mind with enough knowledge to advance in his training, fly hypothetical missions over the Channel and Europe, battle the limited time available to build up a pupil's flying hours, survive a student's mistakes in the air, and win the war of numbers by replenishing the Allied side with more ready pilots than the Germans could. As Ross Truemner commented, "I fought the war by teaching kids to go fight the war for me."

If he felt hard done by, Truemner wasn't alone. At the end of September 1940, when the air force awarded wings to the first BCATP-trained graduating class at No. 1 SFTS Camp Borden, most pilots were posted throughout the BCATP network as SFTS instructors. Out of a total of 203 Canadians who graduated during 1940, only twenty were posted to operations in Britain. A small number went to home defence squadrons. But 165 either went off to Central Flying School in Trenton to become BCATP instructors or became staff pilots at Bombing and Gunnery Schools or Air Observer Schools in the BCATP. It was clear, with trained military pilots and instructors in such high demand and in such short supply, that recruiting outside Canada would be necessary.

6

RECRUITING AT THE WALDORF

JOHN COOPER joined the air force on impulse, hoping to work in an RCAF air crew. (In time he became a BCATP instructor and later a heavy-bomber pilot. In 1944 he was shot down and became a prisoner of war at Stalag Luft 3, in Sagan, Germany.) What sparked his impulse was witnessing a clandestine operation.

Before the outbreak of war in September 1939, the RCAF had purchased thirty Harvard trainers from the North American Aviation factory in California. Factory pilots had flown the first fifteen up the Pacific coast to Vancouver, where RCAF pilots took over for the trans-Canada flight to the two main RCAF training stations in Ontario. But the second batch of Harvards (and any purchased subsequently by the BCATP) left sitting in California after September 10, 1939, posed a real problem. Canada was at war. The United States was not, and its Neutrality Act prohibited aerial delivery. How could a belligerent nation take receipt of its purchased airplanes from a non-combatant nation?

Not long after he finished high school in the small Saskatchewan town of Qu'Appelle, John Cooper filled out a questionnaire asking for his career preferences. One of the three preferences he indicated was "pilot." Flying appealed to him at the time because a family acquaintance, John Berven, was already in the RCAF. Berven returned home to Qu'Appelle in spring 1940, and his Norwegian parents had told everyone in town that he would be flying over on a certain day at a certain time.

"At that early stage of the war," Cooper explained, "the U.S. was not directly involved. However, Canada was buying aircraft from the States. In order to maintain a sort of neutrality, the aircraft being purchased were not allowed to fly over the border into Canada. Instead, they were flown to northern North Dakota and Montana, right up to but not over the border. Then a team of horses on the Canadian side were hitched to the aircraft on the American side and [the airplanes were] pulled over to Canada. From there, they were flown to RCAF [stations] at [Camp] Borden and Trenton, Ontario."

The practice violated the United States Neutrality Act. However, at that time in America, there was law and there was business. And if there was a loophole to be found, business would find it.

That's why Flying Officer Berven had come back to Qu'Appelle. Along with other RCAF pilots and BCATP instructors, he went to the prairies to rendezvous with American factory pilots. The Americans had flown the Harvards up from the North American Aviation plant at Inglewood, California. Some of the aircraft already had RCAF markings on them; others were covered with waterpaint that was later washed off to reveal RCAF insignia.

Out there on the prairies, where the only border between the two countries was an imaginary line, the Harvards were hauled across the international boundary and flown by Canadians to their eastern destinations.

"We picked up three Harvards that came across the border at Sweetgrass," John Berven remembered. "We had no radios. But we flew in loose formation over Qu'Appelle and then we just followed 'the iron compass' (the railway) across northern Ontario back to our home base at Camp Borden. It took three days." Berven had been party to a circumvention of the United States Neutrality Act. And John Cooper had witnessed it. "As the formation flew over, it sealed my desire," Cooper said. He went to Regina and applied to join the air force that same spring. John Berven went on to log 2,000 hours as a flying instructor for the rest of the war and earned an Air Force Cross for his service. Meantime, North American Aviation continued to do business with the RCAF this way, narrowly avoiding an international incident every week, from the day Canada declared war on Germany until the day after the Japanese attacked Pearl Harbor.

Running the risk of an international incident on the 49th parallel was the least of the RCAF's problems at that point. As the Battle of Britain gave way to the Blitz in fall 1940, the pressure mounted on the Mackenzie King government and the BCATP to come through with its promise of pilots. Yet the problems that had plagued the plan at its inception remained. There were plenty of raw recruits, but too few training aircraft and even fewer qualified instructors to train the massive air armada that Churchill had dreamed of. Nevertheless, the neighbour who had posed legal problems to the delivery of trainer aircraft proved to be the BCATP's greatest ally in terms of manpower in its first eighteen months of operation.

Although President Franklin Delano Roosevelt had officially declared his nation neutral on September 3, 1939, he was unofficially anti-fascist and pro-British. So were many of his countrymen. The very next day—September 4—Billy Bishop, who had been made an honorary air vice-marshal in the RCAF in 1936 (he later became an honorary air marshal), contacted a former American comrade-in-arms, Clayton Knight. Knight had flown in Britain's Royal Flying Corps during the First World War, was a renowned aviation artist, and was well connected with the pilot fraternity in the United States. Bishop also reached another acquaintance, Canadian First World War flyer Homer Smith, who was then living in the United States. Within a week, the threesome had booked a room at New York's Waldorf Astoria Hotel to act as recruiting headquarters. Knight and Smith also embarked on a nationwide tour of flying schools to survey American pilots' opinions of RCAF recruitment in the United States. Eight months later, when the Phony War ended with the fall of France, and when the demand for qualified instructors and staff pilots in the BCATP was urgent, Knight and Smith had compiled a list of 300 experienced American pilots eager to come to Canada. The Clayton Knight Committee to recruit Americans for the BCATP got down to business.

Thus during the same period that the RCAF was "importing" Harvards across the international border from such places as Sweetgrass, Montana, to Coutts, Alberta, it also began "importing" the products of Clayton Knight's recruiting drive—American airmen. Their numbers and contribution were substantial. On December 8, 1941—the day after the attack on Pearl Harbor—there were 6,129 Americans serving in the RCAF (more than 6 percent of its strength), nearly 900 Americans had graduated from the BCATP, another 650 were working as staff pilots and EFTS instructors, and 668 were RCAF ground personnel. Of course, because of United States neutrality, these were not highly publicized statistics.

Beginning in late 1940, without fanfare or ceremony, airmen from all the forty-eight states and with every conceivable flying background—private aviators from small clubs, commercial air mail and airline pilots, and stunters from the heyday of barnstorming—began to make their way to RCAF recruiting stations.

Among the thousands who came to Canada to swell the ranks of BCATP instructors was Charles Purcell. Though Charlie was born in the farming country of Parker, South Dakota, his ancestors (on both sides of his family) had made the "run for homesteads" in Oklahoma Territory in 1893. In 1930, sixteen-year-old Charlie Purcell had spotted a First World War Curtiss Jenny circling near Parker. When the aircraft landed, Purcell gave the pilot directions to the airfield at Sioux City, Iowa. In return, Charlie offered his last five dollars from summer camp allowance and asked the barnstormer for a joy ride. That flight, complete with rolls, loops, and spins, convinced Purcell he was going to be a pilot.

"When World War II broke out," Purcell recounted, "I immediately wrote to Ottawa, telling them what a hot pilot I was. (I didn't bother telling them I only had about forty hours' flying.) They wrote back saying they couldn't recruit outside the Empire, but if I just happened to be in Canada, to drop in and talk."

The Clayton Knight Committee was created to help people such as Charlie Purcell. From the original hotel room in New York City, the committee had expanded to branch offices at hotels in Spokane, San Francisco, Los Angeles, Dallas, San Antonio, Kansas City, Cleveland, Atlanta, and Memphis. In time, the CKC hired secretaries and recruiter-interviewers. However, Charlie Purcell's first request for assistance to get to Canada was turned down because the committee required a minimum of 200 hours' flying experience.

"I had about given up," Purcell said, "when one evening at a local dance hall where I was tending bar, a young fellow walked up, introduced himself, and told me he was ferrying Cessna Cranes to Winnipeg. He advised me there were thousands of Americans in Canada now, and that you didn't lose your American citizenship [by joining the RCAF]. He said if I was interested, he'd stop overnight on his next trip and fly me up to Winnipeg with him.

"So, next trip the pilot, Prentice Cleaves, called saying he was in town and would leave about ten o'clock the next morning. I met him at the airport and we flew into Winnipeg. Got a hotel room where he had a few RCAF pilots over for a drink of bourbon. I sat with my mouth agape, listening to the stories and names I'd read about. Here were guys who had flown with them and knew them personally.

"One officer told me he knew the recruiting officer, a Group Captain Baskerville, and would call him to set up an appointment for me the next morning. He told me how to get to the office, told me not to get in line but rather to walk right up to the front and tell them I had an appointment. . . . As I approached the desk, a sergeant came over and rather haughtily asked my business. His manner changed when I told him I had the appointment. He alerted G/C Baskerville and showed me into his office. He was a small RAF type with a handlebar moustache. . . . He told me he could give me a sergeant rating and start me out, after the Instructors' Course at Trenton, as an elementary instructor." Purcell refused the offer saying, "I want to fly the big stuff."

Charles Purcell was shipped to Manning Depot in Toronto, where his flying career was briefly sidetracked while he performed as a member of a precision drill team that put on a nightly show in the fall at the Canadian National Exhibition grandstand. Purcell enjoyed an advantage over other LACs, since the team was excused from reveille and KP. Next, he weathered ITS in Toronto and even the Selection Day tribunal, which recommended that, if he didn't make the grade at EFTS, he be washed out and sent to Air Observer School. When he reached No. 20 EFTS Oshawa, "it was December 7, 1941, Pearl Harbor day. The non-Americans at the station kidded us, saying, 'Well, now you Yanks will get into the war, too.' I had no idea where Pearl Harbor was." Unlike the 1,500 Americans who immediately repatriated, Charlie Purcell remained in Canada with the BCATP as an SFTS instructor, stayed with the RCAF when he went overseas in 1943, and eventually flew "the big stuff."

The Clayton Knight Committee did not advertise. Americans discovered its aims through word of mouth and in pamphlets that were distributed to flying schools around the country. The committee was careful to be seen recruiting civilians to fill positions in Canadian aviation as instructors and staff pilots. To be seen as a pipeline for recruiting potential RAF fighter pilots would have upset isolationist sentiment in the United States and undermined the work of the committee altogether.

The American re-election of Roosevelt in November 1940 helped the committee's cause, for even though the United States remained neutral, President Roosevelt, in a December 1940 "Fireside Chat" broadcast, described the American role in the war as the "arsenal of democracy." By the end of the year, the RCAF had accepted 321 American recruits.

Not far from the British embassy in Washington lived another American whose interests lay north of the border. Jim Buchanan had studied aeronautical engineering during the depression years. With the outbreak of war in September 1939, he had applied to join the United States Corps of Army Engineers in Guam. The Corps never responded. He tried the United States Naval Reserve, but an old motorcycle injury to his ankle made him unfit for service at sea. That's when he tried his neighbours at the British embassy.

"Where can I enlist?" Buchanan asked an embassy official.

"We're not a recruiting station," the official said. "It's illegal to recruit in a non-combatant country." However, he invited Buchanan to leave his name and phone number.

Four days later, an embassy official called back and said, "We want to talk to you about your paper." An aviation magazine in the United States had just published a report on de-icing aircraft surfaces written by Jim Buchanan. Someone at the embassy had read it and since the RAF wanted to ferry aircraft across the Atlantic without losing any to wing icing, the official gave the young American specific instructions about how to enlist.

"I was told to go to a specific store, buy a uniform, and report to Ottawa, where they gave me two Hudsons [light bombers] and a big hangar and I was assigned this task—to develop my de-icing theories, to use the exhaust from the aircraft engines and pipe it through the wings to keep them warm enough that ice wouldn't form on them."

Whether his experiments yielded the results the British hoped for, Buchanan can't say. But before long he escaped the routine of de-icing tests for the routine of flying instruction at No. 6 SFTS Dunnville, in southwestern Ontario.

Others of his countrymen came to the BCATP from American naval flying schools. In his travels Clayton Knight discovered that the United States Navy set standards so high at its schools that many recruits washed out of the program early; he believed that some might still make the grade if they were given a second chance.

The BCATP desperately needed staff pilots at bombing and gunnery schools (B&GS) in Canada to fly wireless operator/air-gunner and air observer trainees on practice missions. The BCATP also needed "air chauffeurs" to fly Westland Lysanders for target towing, Bristol Bolingbrokes and Fairey Battles for gunnery practice, and Avro Ansons for simulated bombing runs. In particularly short supply were pilots qualified to fly twin-engine aircraft, such as the Bolingbrokes and Ansons. The United States Navy had more than enough twin-engine candidates, so the Clayton Knight Committee was able to stream some into the BCATP. By the end of 1940, 242

Americans were serving in the RCAF as "air chauffeurs;" in January 1941, after six months in operation, No. 1 B&GS at Jarvis, Ontario, reported that it had fifty-five Americans on its pilot staff of seventy.

No doubt one of those seventy B&GS staff pilots will remember a unique Christmas gift he received in December 1942, from RCAF trainee student George Penfold. After scoring poorly on his Link trainer tests at ITS, Penfold was shipped off to Jarvis to try his hand as an observer. He wasn't much good at that either. The cramped Frazer-Nash turret in the Bolingbroke aircraft, he found, was no place for a 210-pound Canadian in a bulky flying suit and his gunnery scores reflected this fact. On his first training mission over Lake Erie, he was unable to hit the moving target and scored a perfect zero.

"I discovered that we must achieve one score of 4 percent hits to graduate," Penfold explained. "However, I could visualize spending the rest of the war in the student section of No. 1 B&G School.

"Fortunately, due to a series of near-miraculous passes in the barracks ablutions crap game, I was able to purchase a forty-ounce bottle of rye, and repaired to the drogue pilots' section suitably armed. I explained my predicament to an understanding chap who, after my presentation of the votive offering, agreed to speak to his colleagues to see what might be done to help. I told him the time of my next ordeal.

"Lo and behold, the Lysander pilot waved a friendly acknowledgement as we lined up for the firing run. The next manoeuvre caused the drogue to move from its regular distance so that the cable from the Lysander came exceedingly close to the Boley's starboard wing tip. I merrily emptied the required belt of M.G. ball directly at the stationary target, no lead necessary, as the drogue was about twenty feet from my guns.

"To say that I was delighted to find that my accuracy had immeasurably improved that day is a considerable understatement. LAC Penfold had achieved 9 percent hits and could go on with winning the war." Meanwhile, at least one staff pilot at Jarvis enjoyed an unexpected bottle of Christmas cheer.

Among the Americans at Jarvis was a Californian named Hennessey, who had come to Canada in the summer of 1940. Because he was already a licensed pilot, Hennessey got preferential treatment when he arrived at Manning Depot in Toronto. The RCAF decided he was officer material, so he wasn't sent to the barracks along with the thousands of AC2s but was lodged in a double room with Canadian recruit Allister Rutherford.

The red-haired Rutherford (or Rusty as he was automatically nicknamed), arrived at the CNE barracks with a University of Toronto degree and a teaching certificate from the Ontario College of Education. He was going to help fill the BCATP's shortage of navigation instructors. As Rutherford recalls, Hennessey's story was typical of Canada-bound flyers.

"Hennessey, who was known everywhere as Three Star Hennessey, of course, had been scooped up by the Clayton Knight Committee. Three Star had been at the University of California, paying twenty dollars an hour to fly what he called a 'pipsqueak' airplane. 'And now here I am, in Canada,' he said. 'They'll be paying me all kinds of money to fly a really decent airplane.'

"The air force decided that one of the things they should do was teach us how to be gentlemen. So they assigned a fellow to teach you how to carry your hat, wear your uniform, et cetera. After all, we're officers.

"We ate in the officers' mess. Linen and candelabra on the table and waiters. In fact, each morning, a balding man knocked on your door and gave you a cup of tea. What a life!"

After learning officers' etiquette at Manning Depot, Three Star Hennessey went on to B&GS to become a staff pilot, and Al Rutherford was put on an officers' sleeper hooked to the transcontinental passenger train and sent West to join one of the first courses in Central Navigation School at "a goddam boondock" near Rivers, Manitoba.

Recruits from the United States also began filling the trainee ranks, sometimes dominating the numbers there too. Len Morgan, a BCATP recruit from Terre Haute, Indiana, arrived at St. Catharines EFTS in the summer of 1941. Of the forty-one LACs in his course, a dozen were American; however, "we were never asked to swear allegiance to the King . . . [just to sign] agreements to serve for the duration and a period of demobilization of up to one year," Morgan said. Because they numbered nearly a third of the course, "the sign over the main gate was altered one night to read: 'Royal California Air Force,'" which made the point, but cost Morgan and his buddies a few extra hours of parade drill.

American pilots, too, soon assumed instructor positions in the BCATP. Eric Johnston, who was posted to teach elementary pilots at No. 9 EFTS St. Catharines in 1941, has memories of American instructor Bart Reynaud, "a pilot who had been flying fish from northern Maine to Boston. He was able to spit tobacco through the eye of a needle."

At No. 7 EFTS in Windsor, instructor Brick Bradford remembered flying with several American imports, including Golden Gloves boxing champion Milt Levitch and two former United States Navy flyers, Ken Jarvis and Walt Pague. Pague "took his training with the Navy at Pensacola, Florida. He secretly got married while he was at the base. Because you couldn't be married as a trainee, he was kicked out of the Navy," but he resurfaced in the RCAF.

The Americans sometimes brought a little extra colour and excitement to a BCATP station. Bradford remembers "a big American student who chased me around the hangar with a fire axe for washing him out." A couple of recruits, Rodion Rathbone (son of movie star Basil Rathbone) and a friend named Bradley, who arrived from Hollywood to get their elementary training at Windsor, "used to entertain the troops by having fencing duels in the barracks. They'd grab their foils and do the old movie scene trick, jumping up on tables and beds and fencing like mad men."

Other RCAF trainees remember American flyers in the BCATP for their humourless, hard-bitten approach to life. George Bain, a respected newspaperman before and after the war, was not at all mechanically inclined as an elementary student at No. 13 EFTS St. Eugene, Ontario. In 1941 he ground-looped a Fleet Finch. His American instructor, Welchel, "a failed pilot trainee of the United States Navy course at Pensacola, was very tough and bawled the hell out of me. I thought I was going to be washed out, but I wasn't.

"I think it had a good effect on me. I remember when he was lecturing me about this grave offence, having ground-looped the aircraft, he said: 'Don't look at me like a scared rabbit.' He had intimidated me. He was aggressive. But he pounded a lot of essentials into my head and made me rather a careful pilot. That may have been good too. I'm still alive, in any event."

Chuck McCausland's instructor at No. 10 EFTS Mount Hope, Ontario, had worked as a bush pilot in the United States. He had a sharp tongue that was constantly lubricated by stick after stick of Wrigley's Spearmint gum. His name was Howard Hughes (no relation to the eccentric aircraft manufacturer and movie producer).

"We've got to get you flying solo," Hughes said to McCausland, while the two were up in a Fleet. "What a dunce you are!"

McCausland was fed up. Seated in the front cockpit and in full view of Hughes behind, he took his hands off the stick and said, "You can take the damn thing. I'm finished." McCausland just sat there as the Fleet went up and up.

"Aren't you going to turn it?" asked Hughes.

"Nope," said McCausland sulkily.

"Turn around."

The student turned to see his instructor chewing gum, sitting with his arms crossed. Nobody was flying the plane.

"I wondered if you had any spunk. Good! Now come on, take me back," said Hughes, smiling.

McCausland took the control column of the Fleet, turned, and landed, and Hughes told him to go up alone. "I wasn't five feet in the air," McCausland said, "when I let out a great war whoop." Neither the instructor nor the student had lost in the stand-off. But McCausland had gained a little confidence and won grudging respect from his gum-chewing American instructor.

New York City hoteliers did well by the RCAF in the first year of the war. The Clayton Knight Committee (renamed the Canadian Aviation Bureau in 1941) remained tenants at the Waldorf Astoria at the expense of the RCAF through a bank account in Homer Smith's name. The nearby Gotham Hotel also welcomed a couple of Canadian civilians, who booked into a large suite for about a week late in 1940. The register indicated only two signatures, a couple of businessmen from Canadian Pacific Airlines. However, in the days that followed, the suite was visited by about a hundred pilots.

Babe Woollett and Peter Troup had come to New York to recruit staff pilots for the Air Observer School at Malton, Ontario. Although the agreement struck between the minister of defence and the AOS operators guaranteed that the RCAF would supply equipment, the civilian companies had to find pilots—sometimes referred to as taxi pilots—to fly air observer students on training missions.

"It was done as quietly as possible," Woollett recalled. "We were looking for people with twin-engine experience, night flying, and instrument flying, which we didn't have in Canada. We interviewed them in the suite. They came in by appointment, one at a time, and each for about a half-hour. We had an advance sheet with the number of hours they'd flown, the type of aircraft, even the number of accidents.

"I remember a very smart bloke, neat-looking. Leroy came in with tunic shirt, pressed pants. He was very well turned out and articulate. He had a lot of experience with good commercial airlines, passenger and mail. We made him chief pilot right away because he was the type of fellow that could take charge of things."

Not all of the pilots arriving for interviews at the Gotham Hotel were as spick-and-span as Leroy. In fact, many of the American flyers applying for AOS jobs had been dismissed by their airline employers for any number of offences, most commonly drinking. At one point during their week-long stay in New York, Woollett interviewed an Irish fellow named Danny Duggan, who looked scruffy and unkempt—"a sloppy joe type." Still, there was something endearing about him, something Woollett knew would make him a favourite among air observer students. And when Duggan's affinity for alcohol later became a problem, Woollett knew exactly how to deal with it.

"Please give me another chance," Duggan pleaded.

"You've had a couple of chances," Woollett said.

"I'll behave."

"Okay," Woollett relented, "but I catch you drinking at all anywhere, anytime, on duty or off, and you're out. You'll fire yourself."

"God bless you," Duggan said, as he nearly hugged Woollett for the one last chance. And he was as good as his word. Woollett was right. The students loved Duggan and he never "fired" himself; although later he transferred away from No. 1 AOS Malton and was killed while flying with Ferry Command.

Of the hundred American pilots Woollett and Troup interviewed in New York, twenty returned to Toronto ready to join the staff of No. 1 AOS Malton. Even though one of the American pilots fell out a window at the Park Plaza Hotel and broke his neck on his first weekend in Toronto, Woollett still called the Americans "a God-send to the Plan."

Among them was United States presidential hopeful Wendell Wilkie's nephew, Jim Hamilton; a flyer named Harlon Buettner, who later went to Pan Am; Oscar Zegetie, who signed after the war with United Airlines; Ray Cleveland, later a pilot for Eastern Airways; and Bill Odom and Chuck Banfe, later famous for their round-the-world flights.

Meanwhile, another Canadian military pilot, hired as a civilian manager with Canadian Pacific Airlines soon after September 3, 1939, arrived at a Park Avenue apartment in New York on a similar mission. While Woollett and Troup needed taxi pilots for air observer instruction, C.H. "Punch" Dickins was sent to the United States to hire "aerial truck drivers" to fly Lockheed Hudson bombers across the Atlantic for the aircraft-starved RAF.

Dickins had been in touch with American flyer Jacqueline Cochran,* whose husband offered him the New York apartment, while she volunteered to fly him around New England in her Beechcraft to meet prospective pilots for the Atlantic Ferry Organization (Atfero).

---

* In September 1942, Cochran was appointed director of Women's Flying Training in the USAAF.

In the course of his recruiting mission, Dickins met senior executives of United, Pacific Western, Continental, and American Airlines who "let it be known that if any of their captains wanted to go and volunteer to join Atfero as ferry pilots, they were quite at liberty; and they guaranteed them their jobs would be there when they got back."

By fall 1940, Dickins had assembled his first Atfero pilots and established a training centre at St.-Hubert airfield near Montreal. There he and his crew checked out American pilots and mechanics on multi-engine aircraft in preparation for the transatlantic Hudson flights. All that was needed were the bombers themselves.

On November 10, 1940, at a makeshift airfield known as Hattie's Camp (later Gander aerodrome) in Newfoundland, Air Vice-Marshal D.C.T. Bennett stepped into the cockpit of a brand-new Lockheed Hudson bomber. He taxied away from five old railway cars that were functioning as an operations room, radio quarters, weather bureau, offices, and barracks, and led six other Hudsons into the night-time sky over Newfoundland. A little more than ten hours later, Bennett and his group of Atfero ferry pilots landed all seven Hudsons at Aldergrove, Northern Ireland. The delivery of the Hudsons—from American factory to British warfront—had taken several days, not the usual four to five months.

It was Armistice Day, 1940.

Three nights later—on November 14—Coventry was bombed. About 450 German bombers flew over the heart of the city in a raid that killed or wounded 1,100 civilians, destroyed twenty-one factories, and rendered a third of the houses of Coventry uninhabitable. The relatively small size of the city compared to the scale of the attack shocked Britons and marked a turning-point in the war, not in the tide of winning or losing but in the tactics of both sides. Coventry was the latest victim of the war's escalation.

Halfway through the Battle of Britain—during which Göring intended to eliminate RAF fighter resistance—German bombers had dropped bombs (apparently by mistake) on central London. The next night—August 25-26, 1940—about fifty RAF bombers raided Berlin. Until then, both sides had concentrated their attacks on factories, harbours, and military installations. That early form of strategic strike ended then and there and the Blitz began. For fifty-seven consecutive nights—from September 7 to November 3, 1940—an average of 200 German bombers a night pounded London. More than 15,000 Londoners were killed and more than 250,000 people became homeless.

By November 15, it was clear that civilian centres were targets and the air raids had produced an addition to the wartime lexicon of Britain and Germany: the verb "Coventrate" (*Coventrieren* in German)—to physically and psychologically destroy a city.

As desperate as things became in Britain in 1940 with the retreat of the British Expeditionary Force at Dunkirk, the heavy losses sustained during the Battle of Britain, and the destruction caused by the Blitz, not all RAF personnel were thrown into the fray at home. The RAF sent some of its best to help accelerate air crew training in the BCATP. Not all of them were flying instructors, however.

Jack Hunt was an expert in aircraft engines and air frames. A native of Birmingham, he had enlisted in the permanent force during the Depression, gone through basic and technical training, and been posted to several operational squadrons. In 1939 he was a ground crew instructor. In 1940, Hunt was one of a draft of about 250 officers and NCOs bound for Canada to inaugurate ground crew training at the BCATP's new Technical Training School in the recently completed $7 million mental hospital south of St. Thomas, Ontario.

"Chaos reigned," Hunt said. "There were thousands of volunteer Canadian troops and very little equipment to teach them with. It was necessary to run two shifts of instruction, one from 8 a.m. to 4 p.m., and another from 4 p.m.to midnight, which led to some interesting episodes when the 'wet canteen' opened during the supper break about eight o'clock."

Hunt and his colleagues trained aircraft engine mechanics (engine fitters), air frame mechanics (riggers), aircraft instrument repairmen, and welders, among others. In all, the school would process and graduate between 40,000 and 45,000 ground crewmen for BCATP stations and overseas duty at the front. However, the greatest problem that instructors at St. Thomas faced, like everyone else in the Allied war effort, was the shortage of aircraft parts.

George Barrett discovered this problem the day he began the course at St. Thomas. The twenty-year-old Barrett had always enjoyed tinkering with engines, and the moment he had enlisted he was whisked away to the RCAF station at Trenton to work as an engine fitter. When the school at St. Thomas opened, he was transferred there to upgrade his training. He remembered that the hospital facilities had been converted to engine rooms, machine shops, and woodworking areas, "full of wrecks, or aircraft that wouldn't fly."

The makeshift classrooms and broken pieces of aircraft were less of a challenge to Barrett than "the communication gap" between the British instructors and the Canadian recruits. As he put it, when the RAF instructors at St. Thomas "used technical language, it wasn't technical language that anybody could understand. You couple that with a really broad Lancashire accent, and words came out of the classrooms that were never in any dictionary—words like 'chunnick,' meaning a lump of steel. But it was really entertaining. I ate the whole thing up and I discovered that I could pick these people's brains and find out what they really were talking about. And that's how I learned."

The one thing St. Thomas had plenty of was space. Rigger Roy Legassicke, who was among the first recruits at St. Thomas, remembered that in addition to the buildings on the grounds, "the place was all connected with underground tunnels. The network was so long and spread out you could get lost down there."

At Christmas 1940, when authorities at the school cancelled all forty-eight-hour leave, more than a thousand AC2s went absent without leave. Military Police were called in from other RCAF stations to round them up, and the entire third floor of a training building was converted into a guard house for the recruits who had gone AWL.*

Later on, when the St. Thomas Technical Training School was hit with a diphtheria epidemic, an entire barracks block (conveniently

---

* Absent without leave is "AWL" in the RCAF; Americans call it "AWOL."

outfitted with bars in the windows) was transformed into a huge quarantine ward for several hundred recruits.

In spring 1940, when Honorary Air Marshal Billy Bishop arrived for an official inspection, 5,000 airmen were summoned from the school barracks to assemble in the quadrangle of buildings at the centre of the station. An RCAF band arrived for the ceremony. Barrett recalls the occasion vividly, because that day the air force finally delivered on a long-standing promise. Like all RCAF recruits, Barrett had dreamed about getting his first air force uniform. He was at first issued with an armband to signify that he was an airman. Six months before his posting to St. Thomas, air force stores issued him a pair of Oxfords and a twenty-five-year-old Royal Flying Corps uniform; it was a faded bluish-grey, and one shoulder was an inch and a half higher than the other.

Air Marshal Bishop spotted Barrett as he inspected the ranks and asked, "Son, how long have you been in the service?"

"I enlisted October 14, 1939," Barrett piped up.

"Don't you think it's about time they gave you a uniform?" Bishop asked, making sure that St. Thomas authorities could hear.

Within half an hour, George Barrett was issued his official RCAF parade blues—"and my feet didn't touch the ground."

Like engine fitter Barrett, Henry Gordon was mechanically inclined. Growing up on St. Urbain Street in Montreal, Gordon had discovered radio and become fascinated by its technical capabilities. He worked in a knitting mill and a lamp manufacturing plant, but he always kept his radio theory book in a desk drawer nearby, just out of the boss's sight. Eventually, he had enough savings to take a commercial radio operator's course, and by the time he graduated in 1939, he could send and receive Morse code at twenty-five words a minute. He considered a radio operator's job in commercial shipping, but U-boat attacks on shipping in the Atlantic changed his mind.

It seemed that all his studies in radio would be wasted, until a day in September 1940 when Gordon and his girlfriend passed the RCAF recruiting centre on St. Catherine Street in Montreal. Inside, a bored-looking NCO sat at a desk. Gordon asked for enlistment information, and the NCO casually asked him, "Do you have any trade?"

Without thinking, Gordon said, "I'm a radio operator."

"You are!" said the recruiter, perking up. And when Gordon told him his Morse code speed, he was quickly escorted into another office to meet another recruiter, this time an officer.

"We are badly in need of wireless operators," the officer pointed out. "Would you like to join the RCAF? We would be glad to have you."

"Sounds interesting," Gordon answered.

The officer grabbed a Bible, put Gordon's hand on it, swore him in, shook his hand, and announced, "You are now a member of the RCAF."

As soon as the new airman had signed the recruitment papers, the NCO handed him an envelope and said, "Here's your railway ticket to Brandon for Manning Depot. Your train leaves tomorrow."

"Congratulate me, Zita," he announced to his girlfriend when he got outside. "I'm a member of the RCAF. I'm leaving tomorrow." She burst into tears. His mother cried when he told her the news. He told his father and he cried. The next day, at Windsor Station, they all cried again as Gordon's family saw him off on the train for Brandon.

After three weeks at Manning Depot, Gordon was shipped to No. 2 Wireless School at Calgary with 200 other recruits. By November he had his RCAF Wireless Electrical Mechanic's sparks badge and had his duffel bag packed (he thought) for overseas service. However, he and five other wireless grads—the top-scoring students in the WEM course—were summoned to the CO's office. There, they were each handed two stripes (as corporals) and a tome entitled *King's Regulations* and told to get ready to teach classes. Gordon recalls that the KR book was about 700 pages long. "I was up all night trying to study it. The first few weeks, I was learning the night before what I was going to teach the next day."

Just as he was becoming familiar with the syllabus, not to mention his new surroundings in Calgary, Training Command shipped him out to Winnipeg in February 1941, to open up No. 3 Wireless School.

"We arrived late one night at the Main Street Station. It was thirty degrees below zero. We travelled on what seemed like a country road and arrived at one of these big old buildings that had been an institute for the blind. We slept on the floor that night."

If it was tough for a Quebecker to survive Winnipeg's February weather, Gordon had it easy compared to his students—a group of newly arrived Australian and New Zealand recruits, who had left their countries in summer to come to wintry Canada. During those first days at Winnipeg, they got not only their first radio theory but also scarves and boots.

The weather was no better that winter in Montreal, where recruit John Bigham had just arrived at No. 1 Wireless School, a converted school for the deaf. "The snow was literally up to our armpits. . . . During that winter, someone left a window open in one of the laboratories where a tap had been left dripping. Combine that with twenty-below weather and voilà—broken pipes and a flood. Water covered the floors, the halls and cascaded down the steps. We had to bail out four inches of water before it froze. We were successful, but then along came the measles and chickenpox."

Bigham was familiar with both cold and disease. He had been born in the Canadian prairie town of Weyburn, Saskatchewan, where his father was a doctor (among the babies he delivered was author W.O. Mitchell in 1914). Bigham survived the barracks flood at No. 1 Wireless School in Montreal, but "the school was still quarantined and some of us ended up in hospital at Ste-Anne-de-Bellevue in the chickenpox ward." When training resumed some weeks later, "we quickly settled in to the routine of reveille, breakfast, morning parade, classes, lunch, classes, dinner, possibly additional classes for those who needed extra help, and finally freedom until the pattern was repeated the following day."

With the high demand for instructors, John Bigham (like Henry Gordon) was quickly scooped up by Training Command, even before he got his Wireless School graduation sparks, and was shipped off to another school as a rookie instructor. In a matter of hours he went from being a student training in a former school for the deaf in Montreal to being an instructor teaching in a former convent in Victoriaville, Quebec.

"We took over the Collège de Sacré-Coeur. It became an Initial Training School for wireless operators. My job was to teach Morse code to a gang, literally, of unwilling students. They were unwilling simply because the class sizes were horrendous. Can you imagine a chapel full of teenagers? The chapel was my classroom and I would have as many as 150 men in the chapel at times. Someone went snooping one day and discovered the sacramental wine cache. It was a wingding of a celebration."

Parties were regular events for Henry Gordon's wireless/air-gunner students (WAGs) from the South Pacific. At No. 3 Wireless School in Winnipeg, Gordon roomed with his Australian and New Zealand students (including a few members of the famous All-Blacks rugby team). The only privilege he enjoyed was a partitioned area at one end of the barracks block. But he had no privacy, especially when his students found out that he'd proposed to his girlfriend, Zita, and had made plans to travel back East to marry her.

"It was the night before I was to leave for Montreal. It was lights-out at ten o'clock," Gordon recalled. "I went to my little room that night, and as I was reading I heard some strange noises. It went on for a little while, then there was a knock on my door. I came out and found that they had gone to the mess hall and stolen two big coffee urns. Somewhere they had got some liquor and poured it into the urns. They had found something to eat. And so they put on a surprise party for me in the dark."

The Wireless School at Winnipeg was not unlike the Technical School at St. Thomas. Plenty of eager students. Lots of space. But never enough equipment. Acting Sergeant Henry Gordon taught his Aussies and New Zealanders radio theory "in a school-like classroom with about twenty-five students. To show them the different instruments that we didn't have, I had to draw much of the material on chalkboards. When you taught in the lab, where we had some transmitters and receivers, you worked on Morse code. But because we were short of equipment, it was slow work."

Newfoundland wireless instructor Walter "Paddy" Sellars worried about sending his students off to combat duty. He served at three of the four Wireless Schools in the BCATP and remembered "seeing every prospective graduate face-to-face for his final exam, and often feeling guilty at graduating young men to face dangers I was not allowed to face." Sellars recalled a photograph published in a 1940 edition of a Montreal newspaper "of the first WAG class at Montreal [Wireless School]. . . . All but eight of the 120 [graduates] were casualties within twelve months—either KIA [killed in action], MIA [missing in action], or wounded."

Guilt was a common feeling among BCATP instructors. Although they knew they were equipping young men with the mental tools of war, pilot instructors, air observer instructors, wireless/air-gunner instructors, and ground instructors experienced strong misgivings about their roles. Particularly in the early days of the plan, most instructors worked in relative isolation, grinding out class after class, course after course, month after month, seldom recognizing the importance of the long hours they put in. The value of their efforts seemed to be belied by the long lists of casualties coming back from Fighter Command and Bomber Command overseas. Only rarely did their work seem to have a direct use.

Twenty-nine-year-old Welshman Bill Dunphy had honed his trade in the backwoods of northern Ontario. The young engine fitter had left Britain a year before war broke out and between November 1938 and fall 1939 he had been employed by Starratt Airways, maintaining all ten of the bush company's aircraft at their base in Hudson. In September 1939 he went to Ottawa, joined the RCAF, and was commissioned as an engineer flying officer. Three months later he was posted to Vancouver, "the wrong way from where I wanted to go," to set up the repair depot at No. 6 Torpedo Bomber and No. 4 Ground Reconnaissance Squadron.

Although he was not officially assigned as an air engine instructor, Dunphy found himself the head of a repair crew that had little or no experience in maintaining combat aircraft. Shortly after he arrived, he noticed "a number of Hawker Hurricanes that were in storage there for Vancouver's No. 1 RCAF Fighter Squadron. The aircraft had not been serviced in a long time. The engines in particular looked to be in bad shape. I looked up the exhaust manifold of one, saw the exhaust valves were all rusty. I had a lot of men who'd never had any air engine experience. So I thought it would be a good idea to teach them, as well as to fix up the engines. I had no authority, but I thought, 'We'll give the Hurricanes a top overhaul.'

"When we took the tops of the engines off, we could see evidence that the engines had been overstrained. The damage was pretty obvious. The valves were not only rusted, but they were bent as well. So we took them all apart and fixed them all. The very day after we finished the job, I got orders to crate the Hurricanes right away, because they were needed by the RAF in the Battle of Britain."

Bill Dunphy's timing had been perfect. As an impromptu instructor, he had whipped his repair depot crew into shape; he had upgraded a squadron of air-weary Hurricane fighter aircraft to battle readiness; and in the process he had enhanced RAF air strength when it was desperately needed. However, Dunphy said, "If those orders for the Hurricanes had come a few days earlier, when all those engines were being stripped on the hangar floor, I think I'd have been out of the air force right then." Instead, the fighter aircraft "reached Britain safely and performed extremely well."

The Commonwealth decision to entrust Canada, the RCAF, and its instructors (official and otherwise) with the responsibility of training Allied air crew had delivered one of its first dividends. There would be many more and much greater to come. All the BCATP needed was a little more time to produce and a few more believers.

7

HOLLYWOOD HEROES

IT'S A BLUSTERY MORNING early in 1941 at an RCAF training station in eastern Ontario. Two air force officers are taking stock of the Harvard training fleet lined up on the airfield in front of them. Despite the United States Neutrality Act, North American Aviation factory pilots have flown most of these Harvards to just south of the United States–Canada border, where "democracy and a stout rope did the rest."

Overhead the unmistakable roar of another Harvard trainer is heard. One of the officers on the airfield notices this unexpected arrival just as the Harvard makes its final approach, lands, and taxies to the flight line in front of the station hangars.

A sprightly, clean-cut pilot, dressed in waist-length leather jacket and stylish sunglasses, emerges from the cockpit to greet the RCAF officers.

"Hi," says the dashing young pilot. "I was told to deliver this ship here. So here she is."

"Here?" one officer asks.

"Yes. This is Trenton, isn't it?" says the civilian pilot.

"Yes. Trenton, Canada."

"Canada?" repeats the startled pilot. "Well, now, what d'you know about that? I was looking for Trenton, New Jersey. My compass must have gone haywire."

How this flyer came by the Harvard and why he happens to be flying over eastern Ontario are never clear. As it turns out, it doesn't really matter.

The pilot, or at least the man mimicking a pilot, is none other than swashbuckling movie hero Tyrone Power. No, the Hollywood matinee idol is not fleeing across the border to seek asylum in Canada, nor running away to join the RCAF and win the war. Power is doing the next best thing. He and his long-time Hollywood employer-producer, Darryl F. Zanuck at 20th Century Fox, are putting the war in Europe on the silver screen, in the hope that a still complacent and generally isolationist American public might buy into the war, at least at the box office.

The movie plot line, written by Zanuck under the pseudonym Melville Crossman, tells the story of a brash young American test pilot who enlists in the Royal Air Force and is killed in the early days of the Battle of Britain. Zanuck wrote the screenplay under the title "The Eagle Squadron," but British government officials, who were cooperating in the production, persuaded him that the pilot should not die in the story and that *A Yank in the R.A.F.* was a better title. What made the film historic was not its artistic merit, nor its box office receipts.* It was the first time that the Allied nations at war—Britain and Canada—participated (however minimally) in a Hollywood movie production about the war. It also marked the screen debut, if only in a ludicrous plot angle, of the British Commonwealth Air Training Plan.

Late in 1940, the plan's profile among flyers—military and otherwise—couldn't have been raised much higher. For private, commercial, and bush pilots who considered enlisting, the path was clear:

---

* When 20th Century Fox released *A Yank in the R.A.F.* in September 1941, New York *Herald-Tribune* critic Howard Barnes wrote: "It is neither imaginative nor conventionally captivating. . . . What makes *A Yank in the R.A.F.* a rather stunning entertainment is the fact that it keys right in to the memorable events which constitute the present chapter in history. . . . [It] may be warmongering. That's what makes it worthwhile screen entertainment."

train in the BCATP en route to a pair of RCAF wings and an overseas posting. However, the growth and modest success of the plan were not winning favour with the general public in Canada. Shipload after trainload of Canadian infantrymen departing for Europe—by the end of 1940, a full division in total—drew far more press and flag-waving well-wishers than the fledgling air training plan. Of 203 Canadian pilots who received their wings in 1940, a total of twenty were posted overseas.

As admirable as the plan's achievement was after just eight months of official operation, twenty trained pilots, compared with the fall of France, the Battle of Britain, and the thousands of Canadian soldiers who were already overseas, seemed insignificant. What Canadian taxpayers did notice was the fact that they were paying three-quarters of the estimated $33,000 required to turn one recruit into a fully trained pilot. The plan also continued to fly through unfriendly political skies by hiring American pilots in contravention of United States neutrality laws. As a result, the press and opposition politicians in Ottawa began to criticize the BCATP; Hansard from late 1940 shows that the BCATP occupied Parliament more than any other aspect of Canadian military policy.

The effect of these negative perceptions convinced Minister of National Defence Chubby Power and the Deputy Minister for Air James S. Duncan "that the whole plan . . . with its schedules and . . . somewhat incomprehensible delays . . . had to be sold to the public through well-planned . . . publicity." They hurriedly created the RCAF Directorate of Public Relations.

Put at the helm of the face-lifting team were veteran newspaperman Norman Smith of the Ottawa *Evening Journal* and the director of sales from the advertising firm Cockfield, Brown and Co., Joseph W.G. Clark.

Power and Duncan couldn't have made a better choice than Joe Clark. He had military credentials; during the First World War he had gone overseas as a bombing officer with the 75th Battalion at Vimy Ridge; he had transferred to the Royal Flying Corps, had been shot down three times, and had finished the war as a flight commander with the Distinguished Flying Cross. He had communication skills as a former newspaperman with the Toronto *Star* and as an advertising executive. Joe Clark also had a knack for making things happen.

Within weeks of his arrival in his new PR position, Clark managed to convince *The Saturday Evening Post* magazine to assemble a splashy feature on the British Commonwealth Air Training Plan. The *Post* assigned associate editor Richard Thruelsen and celebrated colour photographer Ivan Dimitri to the job. Clark arranged for the RCAF to fly them across the country for the best shots. The resulting article, entitled "Canada's Open Secret," was a dazzling spread drawn from hundreds of Kodachrome transparencies.* While perusing this collection of still photographs, Joe Clark had another idea, which turned into the RCAF's biggest promotional scheme of the war.

Opportunity knocked in December 1940, when Clark found Hal Wallis, the executive producer of Warner Brothers pictures, sick in bed in a New York hotel. Clark dropped in to see him, opened his briefcase, and showed Wallis the Dimitri transparencies, recently published in the *Post*. "The effect on the sick man," reported the Montreal *Standard*'s A.W. O'Brien, "was magical—he fairly raved over them and proposed a technicoloured short on the subject. But Clark kept on talking and Wallis finally agreed that a short wouldn't do the subject justice. A full-length, technicolour feature would be the thing."

Hollywood had never been reluctant to exploit current events for promotional and financial gain. However, before Pearl Harbor, the big moviemakers approached the Second World War rather gingerly. Anti-Nazi movies such as Warner Brothers' *Confessions of a Nazi Spy* and MGM's *The Mortal Storm* and *Three Comrades* acknowledged the

---

* Clark's PR Directorate later approached *Maclean's* magazine with the same idea. Assistant editor Gerry Anglin helped assemble the September 15, 1941, rotogravure insert entitled "Men Take Wing," which depicted the story of the BCATP in twelve pages of pictures and captions. The air force had the printers run 100,000 copies of the special section, so that the extra copies could be used as recruiting pamphlets. Not long after, Anglin was snapped up by the air force and became the first editor of the RCAF *Wings* magazine.

realities of war while paying lip-service to American neutrality. When the RAF began to engage the Luftwaffe over British soil in the summer of 1940, the American public was suddenly captivated and so, consequently, were American moviemakers.

By early 1941, Hollywood had gone beyond stories about training American servicemen in such films as Paramount's *I Wanted Wings* and rushed to film stories of Americans joining up to fly alongside the British. That year, Warner Brothers released *International Squadron*, in which Ronald Reagan played a ne'er-do-well American flyer who joins the RAF and becomes an air ace. Universal kept pace with *Eagle Squadron*, featuring Robert Stack as a member of the unit of American flyers who formed their own fighting unit within the RAF. Meanwhile, 20th Century Fox starred Tyrone Power as the wrong-way-Corrigan who follows the war and co-star Betty Grable to Britain in *A Yank in the R.A.F.*

As interested as 20th Century Fox, Universal, MGM, and Paramount appeared to be in the war, it was Harry, Jack, and Abe Warner who actually committed film and resources to the Allied cause. Early in the war, Warner Brothers had sent money to Britain to purchase two Spitfires for the RAF* and produced a fund-raising documentary called *London Can Take It* at their Teddington studios. The Warners had also demonstrated their sympathies by producing several films with anti-Nazi and patriotic themes.

On January 28, 1941, Joe Clark (on behalf of the RCAF) and Hal Wallis (representing Warner Brothers) met in New York to sign the contracts for a feature-length film "to illustrate the gallant work of the Canadian air force in the war against Germany." Fully aware of the cooperation symbolized by this move, Clark and Wallis met and signed the deal at the Waldorf Astoria Hotel, the American headquarters for the Clayton Knight Committee.

The general thrust of the feature, as Wallis later described it, was to show Canadian "bush pilots at work, turning their skills to military

---

* Of all the major studios, Warner Brothers were most friendly to the Roosevelt administration and hence most interested in aiding Britain.

uses in wartime." Canadian actor Raymond Massey had already drawn Wallis's attention to that theme; he'd spotted it in a magazine article on bush pilots by Arthur Horman. Wallis purchased the rights to the piece and hired Canadian-born novelist Norman Reilly Raine to write a screenplay with the working title "Bush Pilots." Because Massey was under contract to Warners, he seemed the ideal candidate to star in the picture.

In February, Raine began work on the script. A veteran of the First World War himself, Raine had a number of hits to his credit, including *Dawn Patrol*, *The Adventures of Robin Hood*, and *The Fighting 69th*, which had starred James Cagney. Perhaps with Cagney in mind, Raine fashioned a script that told the story of a fast-talking bush flyer named Brian MacLean who moves in on a competitor's business and his girlfriend; then, caught up in the fervour to defend his country, MacLean dashes off to join the RCAF, only to find he is too old for combat duty. He is relegated to becoming an instructor, bucks the rules and protocol of Training Command and is court-martialled, but eventually dies a hero's death while ferrying a Hudson across the Atlantic.

While his Hollywood instincts carried Raine through the rather predictable first half of the movie script, he needed to do research for the sequences involving life in the BCATP, which would dominate the second half of the screenplay. Joe Clark eagerly obliged; almost immediately his press office in Ottawa began assembling and forwarding to Hollywood an exhaustive history of the RCAF. Clark sent along descriptions of Wings Parades and training sequences; details of air force procedure and language from syllabus to slang; stills of the exteriors and interiors of buildings, training aircraft, crash trucks, and ambulances; data on the drill squad and the band; aerial photographs of locations; and samples of uniforms, badges, and buttons. In the midst of his scavenging expedition, Clark asked Chief of Air Staff Lloyd Breadner to collect pictures of control towers, instructors' quarters, an airmen's Christmas dinner, and recruiting posters for use in the film. Finally he asked Breadner to borrow portraits of Canadian war aces Barker, Collishaw, and McLeod, adding, "Rob them from Billy Bishop's office if necessary."

By this time Honorary Air Marshal Billy Bishop was deeply involved in promoting RCAF endeavours. As a non-serving officer he was not restricted by military dictates, but the prestige of his high rank and his own fame gave him the authority to pursue whatever propaganda activities he wished. For five years he had argued frequently and passionately that Canada's "most valuable contribution [in wartime] would be a trained air force." Bishop had been instrumental in soliciting American pilots to the BCATP via the Clayton Knight Committee as early as 1939. Then in 1940, just a week before the RCAF–Warners movie deal was signed in New York, Bishop's mission to make Canada "a nursery of air crews" was given a real boost; he became the RCAF's director of recruiting and indirectly contributed to the brand-new Warner Brothers feature about the BCATP.

As a blizzard of paper flew back and forth between Los Angeles and Ottawa in early 1941, Hal Wallis and Joe Clark grappled with the fine print of the movie contract. Clark insisted that the feature not tarnish the image of either the RCAF or the RAF and that there be no interference with BCATP training schedules. Accordingly, the final lines of Raine's first script summary explained that "the girl goes out of the picture before the RCAF sequences commence." Air Vice-Marshal Robert Leckie read the script and passed judgement on Hollywood's version of the BCATP, commenting, "I suppose a picture can be made from tripe like this, but God only knows how."

Unlike *A Yank in the R.A.F.*, a great effort was made to be authentic. The Directorate of Public Relations hired Flight Lieutenant Owen Cathcart-Jones (a renowned long-distance flyer who had served the British Navy in its Fleet Air Arm) as technical adviser and script consultant; Cathcart-Jones became responsible for the accurate depiction of every aspect of the RCAF in the film—including which BCATP stations and which RCAF aircraft were to be filmed. Among other things, he ensured that all locations representing Canada were real, not Hollywood backlot mock-ups.

As smoothly as the pre-production phase seemed to be going, several issues remained unresolved. Who would be cast in this movie? And what would it be called? In May 1941, Joe Clark received Hal

Wallis's first batch of suggested titles, ranging from "Shadow of Their Wings" to "The Fighting RCAF." The RCAF responded with all the imagination that a bureaucracy preoccupied with wartime statistics could muster; Chubby Power offered "Winged Bridge" and "Wings of Canada," while Lloyd Breadner came up with such gems as "Bush Pilots Over the Sea," "Tails Up," and "Atlantic Ferry." However, the search ended unexpectedly when Hal Wallis happened to pick up a copy of the Canadian motion picture periodical *Motion Picture Digest*; its editors had reprinted portions of a Victory Loan campaign speech, which appealed to "every man and woman to do their duty by supporting the loan . . . [and] those glorious captains of the clouds, the youngsters of our Empire, who, against vastly superior numbers, saved . . . not only . . . Britain, but civilization for the whole world." The author was none other than Billy Bishop.

Cameras were due to roll on the first scenes of *Captains of the Clouds* at No. 2 SFTS Uplands in July 1941. Throughout the early summer, producer Hal Wallis worked to assemble a production team for what he described as "by far the most extensive and difficult venture in location work undertaken by Warners since the silent period." Hungarian-American Michael Curtiz (who later won an Oscar for *Casablanca*) would direct. Italian cameraman Sol Polito would shoot the film (although there was some difficulty admitting him to Canada because Italy was an Axis power). The team of cinematographer Elmer Dyer and stunt pilot Frank Clarke would supervise aerial filming; the two were renowned for the greatest dogfighting sequences ever filmed in Howard Hughes's First World War epic *Hell's Angels*. Aerobatic sequences would be supervised and in some cases performed by stunt pilot Paul Mantz; Mantz's credits during his ten years in Hollywood included flying a Stearman through a hangar in the movie *Air Mail* as well as crash-landing another Stearman between two trees for *When Willie Comes Marching Home*. The supporting cast included Warners' stock actors Dennis Morgan, Alan Hale, George Tobias, and Reginald Gardiner, and the love interest was provided by Brenda Marshall (booked later).

The only gaping hole in the cast was the leading man. That vacancy was filled in early July when Jack Warner persuaded Jimmy Cagney that he "would be combatting Nazism by undertaking the role" of bush pilot Brian MacLean. Less for patriotic and more for nepotistic reasons (Warner agreed to hire Cagney's brother, William, as an associate producer), Jimmy took the part.

The *Captains of the Clouds* entourage of about eighty technicians and production staff, as well as half a million dollars worth of colour cinematography equipment, got to the United States–Canada border on July 12, 1941. Detailed Customs and Immigration checks, including the expected delay over Sol Polito's Italian citizenship, stalled the entire process. Then, when the Warners crew found out that they were to be housed in a tent city at Uplands, they threatened a walkout. Alternative arrangements—transforming a mess hall, some officers' quarters, and a hangar into crew accommodation—defused that problem. By July 15, the stars were safely checked into Ottawa's Château Laurier hotel and shooting was set to begin.

First up were the scenes depicting the arrival of the bush pilots—Cagney, Hale, Tobias, and Gardiner—at Uplands to enlist in the RCAF. This scene marked the first of many occasions when the British Commonwealth Air Training Plan nearly stole the spotlight.

MacLean (Cagney) and his buddies—Tiny Murphy (Hale), Blimp LeBec (Tobias), and Scrounger Harris (Gardiner)—rumble their bush planes right into the middle of the day's training at Uplands. They leap from their cockpits (rather like Tyrone Power at Trenton) ready to take on the Luftwaffe, only to be confronted by the first of eight RCAF airmen given roles in the film, Warrant Officer J.C. Sprott. He tells them, "The place to apply for the air force is the nearest recruiting centre. So I think you'd better take your aircraft off this tarmac."

"Why can't we park 'em here?" asks Cagney, smiling.

Turning to his second in command, Sprott delivers the coup de grâce. "If these aircraft are not removed in five minutes, put these men under arrest for trespassing on government property."

Not the least bit dismayed or dissuaded from their mission, the bush pilots take their case to the station's chief flying instructor, played by the film's technical adviser and script consultant, F/L Owen Cathcart-Jones, who delivers the same disappointing verdict that so many real RCAF pilot applicants had to swallow.

"I realize that you're all anxious to get overseas," begins Cathcart-Jones as the chief flying instructor. "If you didn't want that, we wouldn't want you in the RCAF. And you are wanted, gentlemen!

"Your experience will be invaluable in training the young men who are physically capable of taking a 7G dive without blacking out, who can retain consciousness after a tight turn at 400 miles an hour. I'm offering you a chance to take the Service Training course for instructors—a chance to become a vital part of the Commonwealth Air Training Plan."

Everything at No. 2 SFTS Uplands, from daily routine orders to flight training, came to a complete standstill on the morning of July 16. Michael Curtiz's cameras were ready to roll on one of the most ambitious scenes of the movie: the Wings Parade. The scene would depict an actual SFTS class—Course 29—being paraded in front of parked Harvards and Ansons on the Uplands tarmac, saluted by an honour guard of fifty buglers and a full RCAF band, and then presented with RCAF graduation wings by Air Marshal Billy Bishop himself.

The very first airman to receive his RCAF wings on film that July day was LAC Tom Wallnutt, who believed that he was featured "partly because I graduated in the first half of my class, but also because I was six feet tall, stood straight, marched well, and looked the part."

In the film, Bishop asks Wallnutt where he is from.

"Yukon Territory, sir," Wallnutt replies. (He had been working in placer gold mining in the north.)

"You've come a long way," Bishop remarks, as he pins wings to Wallnutt's chest (it took six takes to get this right).

"Yes, sir," says Wallnutt (who didn't miss his cue once).

"I suppose you're anxious to make it an even longer way, overseas," Bishop comments.

"Yes, sir."

"Good luck to you, boy," Bishop concludes. They shake hands. Wallnutt turns smartly and marches back into line.

Wallnutt graduated with special distinction, was assigned to Trenton, and then became a flying instructor. His dream, like that of the hero in *Captains*, to become a fighter pilot in the skies over Britain, was never realized. He flew 3,000 hours as an instructor and won the Air Force Cross for his service to the BCATP.

LAC Art Badland was in Course 29. He remembered the two predictions Chief Flying Instructor G. Everett Wilson had made when he arrived two months before, that "at least one of you will be killed before the class graduates," but that in the end most would graduate. He was right on both counts; one of Badland's fellow students was killed in a Harvard crash, but Badland survived training to receive his wings from Billy Bishop, not once but several times before the *Captains* cameras.

Bishop's speech to the graduates also had to be filmed repeatedly, which prompted Warners executive Camm Ship to comment that "he did it splendidly without much time to learn it. It was all the more remarkable because we had to take the shots of the same thing several times over, and he has been better than our professional actors." Ship exaggerated, as most movie PR types should, but Bishop's speech did prove to be one of the highlights of the film. What further complicated the speech and the choreographing of several hundred Royal Canadian and Royal Australian Air Force airmen, officers, and ground crew in front of the camera was the arrival of an unexpected airborne visitor over the Wings Parade.

"Our script," Wallis later wrote, "called for a plane flown by Cagney to perform stunts over the ceremony, showing the character's contempt for officialdom, which later changed to patriotism."

"We were the backdrop to the scene," remembered Jim Coyne from The Pas, Manitoba. He was used to bush planes buzzing about but not to Hollywood cameras and a director who "made us go through quite a bit of practice. We were the junior course, due to get our wings at the next graduation. We didn't know what the hell was going on. Then this [Norseman] aircraft came sweeping in from behind us."

"Timing the famous stunt pilot, Paul Mantz, as he flew over Air Marshal Bishop giving his speech to the ranks was extremely difficult," Wallis continued. "On our first day of work, the plane flew in on schedule, but the air marshal was late. . . . Next day, the weather was good, but Mantz developed engine trouble . . .

"A week dragged by. Every morning, hundreds of badly needed airmen had to be pulled from active duty to form their lineup for the picture. The air marshal, who was very busy, had to re-emerge and give his speech while Paul Mantz looped-the-loop and performed other stunts. But rain, technical mishaps, and problems of every kind continued to dog us"—including an unexpected vice-regal visit.

On the sixth day at Uplands, the station got word of an impending visit from His Excellency the Earl of Athlone, the governor general of Canada, and an entourage comprising Lady Byng of Vimy, Her Royal Highness the Princess Alice, Lady May Abel Smith, and Sir Shuldham Redfern. Filming ground to a halt as the station brass organized a ceremony at which His Excellency accepted an RCAF flag from Warner Brothers on behalf of the station. The guests watched some of the proceedings, engaged in some small talk with director Michael Curtiz, posed for pictures with Air Marshal Bishop and the movie stars, and then departed.

When it became clear that the mechanical, atmospheric, and human elements could not be coordinated for the sequence, Curtiz decided to concentrate on the parade and Billy Bishop's speech and to simulate the Norseman buzzing the Wings Parade. However, as Bishop's son, Arthur, later recorded, "The trouble was there were no aircraft to look at—only a stagehand holding a red flag running along an elevated ramp at a height above eye level. . . . The scene had to be shot over and over, until at the end of the warm day, the exasperated Curtiz exclaimed, 'This is the last take positively if I have to take an airplane up myself.'"

"We finally had to piece together fragments of film footage from the many days of shooting in order to achieve a finished result," Hal

Wallis concluded. "In the picture, however, it looks as if the whole sequence was shot at high noon in optimum sunny conditions."

Between takes at Uplands the Warners cast and crew enjoyed themselves in a city abuzz with Hollywood fever. The press chased Dennis Morgan as he viewed Ottawa from a Rideau Canal tour boat. A mob on Sparks Street forced Alan Hale into a specialty shop where he bought an expensive dog leash as thanks for the proprietor's sheltering him from the throng of people. Jimmy Cagney heaped praise on the city of Ottawa and the Uplands instructors and trainees for their professionalism on camera; they reciprocated with a birthday gift—a silver identification tag with the engraving "Flying Officer James Cagney, Captain of the Clouds, 1941."

To wrap up the Ottawa phase of the shooting schedule, Joe Clark's RCAF public relations team and the Warners promotional flacks dreamt up a Red Cross fund-raiser. More than 2,000 Ottawans jammed the stands at Lansdowne Park to cheer the "Hollywood Stars" and a team of Uplands instructors and staff in five innings of baseball. The Hollywood Captains of the Clouds defeated the RCAF captains of the clouds by a score of 5-to-4.

With the Wings Parade in the can, the moviemakers began shooting B-Roll footage, or background visuals that would be intercut with the scenes depicting Dennis Morgan training Cagney to be a BCATP flying instructor. By editing together the dramatic sequences with general activity at the air force stations, Warners hoped to make their product appear authentic. Plans called for BCATP aircraft to be filmed taxiing on the tarmac at Uplands and Trenton, taking off, landing, practising aerobatics, and flying in formation. If the RCAF had been concerned about lost man-hours to this point, *Captains'* greatest influence on the progress of training was about to be felt, when BCATP instructors from across southern Ontario gathered for briefing sessions at Trenton and Uplands to learn how to fly in front of the camera.

"Each morning they assembled us in this room with a big board on the wall," Fred Macdonell said. He and nine other instructors had flown in from No. 6 SFTS Dunnville and No. 1 SFTS Camp Borden with a squadron of Yales just to participate in formation flying, "but it still took them three or four days to film it."

Charlie Konvalinka, then an instructor at Trenton CFS, attended those early morning pre-production meetings conducted by what he called "the movie merchants." Hollywood stunt pilot Paul Mantz would map out the day's filming with model airplanes stuck on sticks; he'd push them into holes on the peg board and demonstrate the aerobatic or formation manoeuvre he expected. None of the training aircraft had radio communication, so the instructors either memorized the sequences or made notes on clipboards.

"We flew a lot of hours for the filming in a concentrated way," Konvalinka said. "We were up as many as three hours at a crack. That's getting right up to the limits of a Harvard's endurance—and our endurance. Our average separation in formation flying would be three to six feet, but this was for the movies, so we tucked it in pretty tight. Murray Stroud was my formation leader; I flew number two position; and Joel Aldred was in number three position."

Joel Aldred was a deputy flight commander at Trenton in the summer of 1941. Most vivid in his memory of the *Captains* filming were "the purple jackets and yellow pants that some of the movie people wore." He also said that not many hours of his formation flying were ever officially logged, because "the air force didn't want the amount of gas we were using on record."

However off-the-record all this flying might be, it involved just about everybody on the station. Len Schryer was a student instructor at Trenton that summer week and found himself "taxiing Harvards in a giant circle on the tarmac, with the aircraft being filmed as they went by the camera. It gave the illusion of hundreds of aircraft" coming and going at the station. Trenton examining instructor Russ Bannock claimed it was no illusion, because "one day we had close to a hundred aircraft up flying in formation over the aerodrome."

Meanwhile, off in a corner of the airfield was a young AC2 doing guard duty. Tom Hawkins remembered the commotion and rumours of movie star sightings, but what caught his attention most was "the multi-engine [Stinson Trimotor] aircraft with a great hole in the side of it; it was this enormous camera ship."

"They tried to set up aerial shooting times to take advantage of atmospheric conditions," Konvalinka said. "It's pretty dull to shoot all this against a plain blue sky. It might be a better day to fly, but it doesn't make as dramatic a shot as it does to have nice puffy clouds up there. So they'd arrange the shooting around their choice of conditions. And that meant if we were going to be flying for three hours, we'd either take our students up before or after the filming. We put in a lot of hours in a day. This was extracurricular duty, and it was duty."

In typical Hollywood fashion, the B-Roll camera crew looked for the most spectacular way to do things. One morning at the peg board in the Trenton briefing room, Paul Mantz lined up fifteen miniature Fleets on sticks as the assembled BCATP instructors looked on with great interest.

"You guys are going to take off, line-abreast at the camera," Mantz said.

"We don't do things like that," was the instructors' reply.

"You know it. We know it, but . . ." Mantz encouraged them to give it a try, even though most RCAF flyers usually didn't learn formation take-offs until operational training school, if at all.

Out on the grass airfield, Mantz's crew positioned the camera on a flatbed truck and directed the instructors to taxi out and line up the Fleets, fifteen abreast in front of them. As soon as the pilots saw where the truck was, all activity ceased. One of the instructors got down from his cockpit and explained, "You guys are gonna have to move back."

"Nonsense," the crew said. "It'll make a great shot from here."

Under any other conditions, the instructors would have shut down the entire exercise, but they decided if the camera crew wanted the aircraft to bear down on them from that short a distance, well, it was okay with them. So the fifteen Fleets powered back up and began their formation take-off run at the camera. Konvalinka has a vivid picture in his memory of "everybody on the truck having to get out of the way in a real hurry. It was a full-fledged retreat, more like a rout, with people flying in every direction. It was really funny."

Throughout July, August, and September 1941, as BCATP instructors juggled movie flying with training flights in a war against time, Cagney's Brian MacLean continued his war against the King's Regulations. Warner Brothers cameras captured both Hollywood's and the RCAF's versions of the BCATP in action: a full-dress parade at Manning Depot at the CNE in Toronto; a dramatic dive-bombing sequence at No. 6 Bombing and Gunnery School near Mountain View, Ontario; and simulated training flights involving Fleets, Yales, Harvards, Ansons, Fairey Battles, and scores of "on-duty" instructors.

None of the instructors was paid for his extra time and effort. Of course, there would be no movie credits for the individual instructors whose precision aerobatics and tight formation flying helped stitch together Norman Reilly Raine's Hollywood version of life in the BCATP. Compensation came from the enjoyment of scattering a cinematography crew with a line of charging Fleets, or demonstrating a dogfight with a dozen Harvards diving past Paul Mantz's Stinson camera ship at 5,000 feet. And on more than one occasion, when Warner Brothers' business manager bought a round of milkshakes in the station canteen, one or two lucky instructors got not only a shake, but a tip too—the change from a twenty-dollar bill. It wasn't much. It never got logged. But it provided some reward for service above and beyond the call of duty.

As the RCAF's Joe Clark and Owen Cathcart-Jones attended to the details of the film's final scenes—ferrying Hudson bombers across the Atlantic—Michael Curtiz and the bulk of the *Captains* crew moved to North Bay, Ontario. This would be their headquarters for filming the bush piloting scenes for the first half of the movie.

The ten days that followed turned out to be the toughest of the production. Apart from the first day when the skies were clear, it rained nearly every day. Lightning struck a reloading shed and it burned to the ground. It was so late in the season that some of the leaves began turning to their fall colours, throwing the scene continuity off. Then, the neighbourhood wildlife got into the act. During an early rehearsal with some Husky dogs, one bit Dennis Morgan on the hand. Beavers flooded the road to the filming site so badly that crew cars got mired repeatedly and a bus en route to the day's shoot skidded off a steep road and three crew members were injured.

Things went off the rails in front of the camera too. Various pilots at the controls of Jimmy Cagney's Norseman had problems negotiating pontoon landings on Trout Lake; one sequence required nine landing attempts before the camera got an acceptable take. On another set-down the Norseman suffered so much pontoon and elevator damage that a replacement aircraft had to be flown up from Toronto.

On the ground, Jimmy Cagney decided he would be his own double. During a scene in which a seaplane propeller knocks him into the water, his fall was so realistic that he suffered a concussion. However, two North Bay stand-ins gave Michael Curtiz and his camera seamless, trouble-free performances. Ted Roy doubled for Dennis Morgan in several scenes and, as the North Bay *Daily Nugget* reported, "doubling for Brenda Marshall, spunky Mildred 'Middy' Morland stood nonchalantly atop a haystack . . . while a plane flown by famous Hollywood stunt flyer, Frank Clarke, dove down upon her . . . and at full throttle, pulled out of its dive . . . missing Middy and the haystack by inches."

North Bayites lapped it up. Everywhere the stars went, their northern Ontario fans were sure to follow, from the airport to the lobby of the Empire Hotel to the shores of Trout Lake, where there was a daily traffic jam to get a glimpse of Cagney, Morgan, and Marshall at work. The crowds harassed the stars so mercilessly that Warners relocated the visitors to remote cabins near the fictional Lac Vert Trading Post shooting site. The stars were forced to use homing pigeons to carry messages to the outside world. Even as special effects wizard Byron Haskin waited for a break in the weather to shoot the final North Bay area scenes—a breath-taking bush plane dogfight sequence—the roads to Trout Lake were clogged by cars full of tourists and locals eager to see the backwoods air show.

Meanwhile, the fight for public attention had begun in earnest in Ottawa and Hollywood. Joe Clark and the RCAF Directorate of Public Relations, who had invested financially and politically in *Captains*, found themselves in a promotional battle with 20th Century Fox. Fox's *A Yank in the R.A.F.* was set for release in September and threatened to upstage Warners' *Captains of the Clouds*. Things grew tense when Fox requested an RCAF band to join in the hoopla planned at the New York City premiere of *Yank* and at a photo session of RCAF airmen knitting a sweater for Betty Grable, the female lead in their picture. Clark conferred with Hal Wallis, who registered a "strong protest against the RCAF lending itself for promotion of any picture other than *Captains of the Clouds*."

Clark had Chubby Power yank the RCAF band from *Yank* and began considering a barrage of *Captains* promotional ideas from the Warners publicity machine. Among them was a transcontinental train junket of stars and press people travelling from Hollywood to Ottawa and promoting *Captains* all the way; the commemorative naming of a BCATP aerodrome as "Cagney Field"; a syndicated exclusive article of anecdotes about the movie by Billy Bishop; advertisements tying Hiram Walker and Canada Dry to the film; a version of the *Captains of the Clouds* title song performed and recorded by big band stars Guy Lombardo, Tommy Dorsey, Benny Goodman, and/or Paul Whiteman; an appearance by Billy Bishop on the radio programs "We, the People" and "Information Please"; and the donation by Lockheed of a Hudson bomber named "Captains of the Clouds" to the Canadian war effort. In all, Charles Einfield, who was Warner Brothers' director of publicity and advertising, sent Joe Clark a dozen pages of suggested publicity stunts, culminating in a celebrity-packed evening at the Waldorf Astoria Hotel in New York, where both President Roosevelt and Prime Minister King would introduce *Captains* to the gala gathering and, by domestic and short-wave radio, the world.

The escalation of the war—the Japanese attack on Pearl Harbor took place as *Captains* was being edited for release—forced Warner Brothers to scale down plans for the premiere evening, on February 12, 1942. Instead of Roosevelt, Harry Warner, by that time a United

States Army Air Corps major, and veteran broadcaster Lowell Thomas emceed the evening, and King was represented by the new Canadian deputy minister for air, Sydney de Carteret, and Air Marshal Lloyd Breadner. Warners did, however, win the game of one-upmanship with 20th Century Fox, when the same RCAF Central Band and Precision Drill Team that Fox had wanted for their *Yank in the R.A.F.* premiere rolled into New York for *Captains*. The day before the gala, all 195 members of the crack musical and parade contingent marched to the Waldorf from Grand Central Station with New Yorkers cheering every step of the way.

The day of the premiere (not coincidentally, Abraham Lincoln's birthday), the airmen paraded to the Eternal Light in Madison Square, received inspection from Air Marshal Bishop and Mayor Fiorello LaGuardia, posed with Brenda Marshall at the Waldorf, and then marched up "the Great White Way" to Times Square, where they put on a public performance in front of Warners' 2,758-seat Strand Theatre. As the RCAF band played "God Save the King" and Metropolitan Opera soprano Lucy Munroe sang "The Star Spangled Banner," *Captains* prints that had been specially dispatched by RCAF Ferry Command premiered in Cairo, London, Melbourne, Vancouver, Ottawa, and Toronto.

All that remained for Joe Clark and Hal Wallis was to await the verdict of the press. The *New York Times* called the movie "stoutly heroic and exceedingly masculine" and said that "the scenes of RCAF training are impressive and dignified." In typically cryptic fashion *Variety* called the film a "socko air adventure with timely patriotic appeal." The rave in the New York *Herald-Tribune* said "the flying scenes are breath-taking and will leave you limp with suspense." The Toronto *Daily Star* headlined its review "Canada's heroes of the air, flying headlong to victory, are the heroes too of 'Captains of the Clouds'"; while in North Bay, raves were hardly necessary, as the Capital Theatre enjoyed a city record—7,000 paying customers in the first three days of *Captains* screenings.

On the frontlines of the British Commonwealth Air Training Plan, the reviews were mixed. Instructor Russ Bannock, who saw the movie in a special showing at Trenton, said, "We were all quite impressed." Fellow instructor Joel Aldred saw that screening and remembered "applauding my friends [in the movie] and booing the enemy." Art Badland's graduating course was immortalized in the movie, but what he cherished most was a photograph of himself with his wings, standing beside Jimmy Cagney.

One member of the junior course that had acted as window-dressing for the Wings Parade scene, Jim Coyne, later flew Whirlwinds* on ops and "roared with laughter when I saw *Captains* in England." When Charlie Konvalinka and his instructor colleagues attended the Ottawa premiere, they realized that most of their aerobatic flying had ended up on the cutting room floor; but Konvalinka also remembered the Warners people telling him to "keep watching Warner Brothers movies and you'll see every foot of stuff we took." Konvalinka was convinced that he and his Harvard squadron diving through the clouds over Trenton in August 1941 were the Japanese zeros attacking Marines in the South Pacific in Warner Brothers' 1942 war picture *Wings for the Eagle*.

Because of the extra feet of aerobatic film, the artistic acclaim, the box office profits, and the general goodwill accompanying their first major location shoot, Warner Brothers were thrilled. They even hinted that a *Captains* sequel was in the works. To cap it all off, the picture earned two Academy Award nominations, for Best Colour Cinematography and Best Interior Decorating.

Awards and critical raves, however, were not really the object of the exercise. Joe Clark and the RCAF had put the BCATP in the movies not for Oscars or boffo box office, but to give the RCAF's plan a public boost and to validate the unofficial campaign to recruit American pilots for the RCAF and the BCATP. After the bombing

---

* The Westland Whirlwind fighter, the RAF's first single-seat, twin-engined, cannon-armed fighter, was a contemporary of the Spitfire. Capable of flying faster than the Spitfire at ground level, with better all-round vision than the Spitfire and with heavier armament, Whirlwind fighters were flown by pilots of No. 263 and No. 137 Squadrons, but were then withdrawn from service in 1943.

of Pearl Harbor in December 1941, however, the tide of American pilots shifted to the other direction, and RCAF recruiting offices across Canada recorded a decline in enlistment in the two weeks following the movie premiere.

Ultimately, Joe Clark, who later called this enterprise "the greatest undertaking of my career," felt disappointed. Perhaps he expected Canadian public opinion to come on side in as little time as he and Warners had taken to produce a feature film. Fortunately for Clark, the air force, and the Allies, the core of the BCATP had not been the object of widespread public criticism in late 1940. The reportedly $3-million Hollywood movie had not affected the plan's daily progress either way. At its centre, the real "captains of the clouds"—the BCATP instructors—were still hard at work training real heroes.

As Chubby Power, minister of national defence, had said at the inception of his Directorate of Public Relations: "The plan is proceeding; the work is progressing . . . we are not yet out of the woods . . . [but] those of us who are closely associated with the plan . . . believe it will win through [as] Canada's most important contribution to the common effort and ultimate victory. We are determined that it shall be."

(ABOVE LEFT) For twenty-one years, barnstormer Walt Leavens and his Pitcairn Autogiro were a fixture in the skies over Quebec, Ontario, and the Prairies. He spent more than 1,200 hours hauling banners, spraying trees and crops, and inviting passengers to "See Your Town From the Air" for a penny a pound. One of Walt Leavens's passengers in June 1934 was later BCATP instructor and fighter pilot Cap Foster.

(ABOVE RIGHT) Intended to show the British colours and "bind the Empire together," the rigid dirigible R100 visited Toronto during morning rush hour on Monday, August 11, 1930. As thousands stopped to watch, the ship passed the Royal York Hotel.

(RIGHT) The recruiting poster depicted the adventuresome aspect of RCAF service in wartime. But the mature-looking fighter pilot was misleading. Most air force recruits, even after training, were eighteen or nineteen years old.

Buried under 750,000 blueprints and 33,000 drawings of hangars, drill halls, and barracks blocks, in May 1940 the Directorate of Works and Buildings staff in Ottawa determined the look and layout of BCATP training stations and of Canada's postwar airports for years to come.

(LEFT) The livestock and produce had barely left the CNE's Coliseum in the fall of 1939, when the new recruits took up temporary residence. This was Manning Depot.

(RIGHT) Morning ablutions in the former livestock quarters began each day of parade drill, clean-up, kitchen duty, inoculations, and PT—the air force's way of moulding recruits in its own image.

(RIGHT) To even the keenest Aircraftman 2nd Class, marching drill seemed a long way from the air war over Europe. However, the parade sergeant scolded recruits: "How in the hell do you guys ever expect to fly aircraft in formation when you can't even walk in a parade?"

(BELOW) It didn't matter—blazing sun or chilling cold—marching was mandatory.

(ABOVE) Run by civilian air clubs, EFTS stations like the one at St. Catharines fostered an informal atmosphere among instructors, evident in the way the instructors posed for this group shot in winter 1941: Eric Johnston, Keith Patman, Jack Connelly, A. K. Patterson, Al Bennett, Earl Detenbeck, Bob Brumigin, Bruce Woods, Lloyd Hyman, Ernie MacDonald, Hap Bollar, Ben Messenger, Bill Scott, and Bruce "Banty" Pallett. Many of their friendships continued for half a century.

(RIGHT) Al Stirton, another early instructor at No. 9 EFTS St. Catharines. This was about as official as EFTS instructors were allowed to look in 1941. Note the "StC FTS" insignia, designed by the school, not the air force.

"Can you imagine landing in this stuff?" St. Catharines EFTS instructor Eric Johnston claims, "you couldn't even taxi the Fleets without somebody pushing the wings. This was February 1941. The air field was just a farm field. That's how fast we had to get things going in the BCATP."

The original cadre of civilian instructors at No. 7 EFTS Windsor in summer 1940. Back row: Frank Vines, Les Crook, Gus Bennett, Ted Vasser, Bob Eaton, George Stewart, Tom Calladine, Arnold Warren. Seated: Craig Ainslie, Brick Bradford, Al Lewis, Abner Hiltz, Ferguson, Paul Hovey, K. B. Wilson.

(LEFT) A few seconds before this Fleet Finch crashed (left), instructor Bob Eaton and his student, Mac Bryon, were in an unrecoverable flat inverted spin near No. 7 EFTS Windsor, Ontario. Bryon bailed out at 2,300 feet, Eaton at 50 feet.

(RIGHT) EFTS student Ross Truemner's proudest moment: he has just successfully completed his first solo in a Tiger Moth at No. 19 EFTS Virden, Manitoba, in 1941.

The strongly American flavour of the BCATP was most evident at the Bombing and Gunnery Schools and Air Observer Schools. Of the ten staff pilots and two managers depicted here at No. 1 AOS Malton c1940, seven are American. Third from right in back is American Danny Duggan, second from left in front is manager Babe Woollett, next to manager Peter Troup, American Chuck Banfe, and Duke Schiller.

Within four months of being driven from their homeland and across the English Channel in April 1940, Royal Norwegian Air Force trainees were crossing the channel from their new barracks on the Toronto waterfront to Toronto Island for pilot instruction. Note Toronto Maple Leaf baseball stadium and Tip Top Tailors behind.

Most St. Thomas Technical School students never saw a functional aircraft in one piece until they graduated and were assigned to a BCATP station or overseas. Riggers (ABOVE) and fitters (BELOW) learned their ground crew trades on bits and pieces of non-operational aircraft sent to the school.

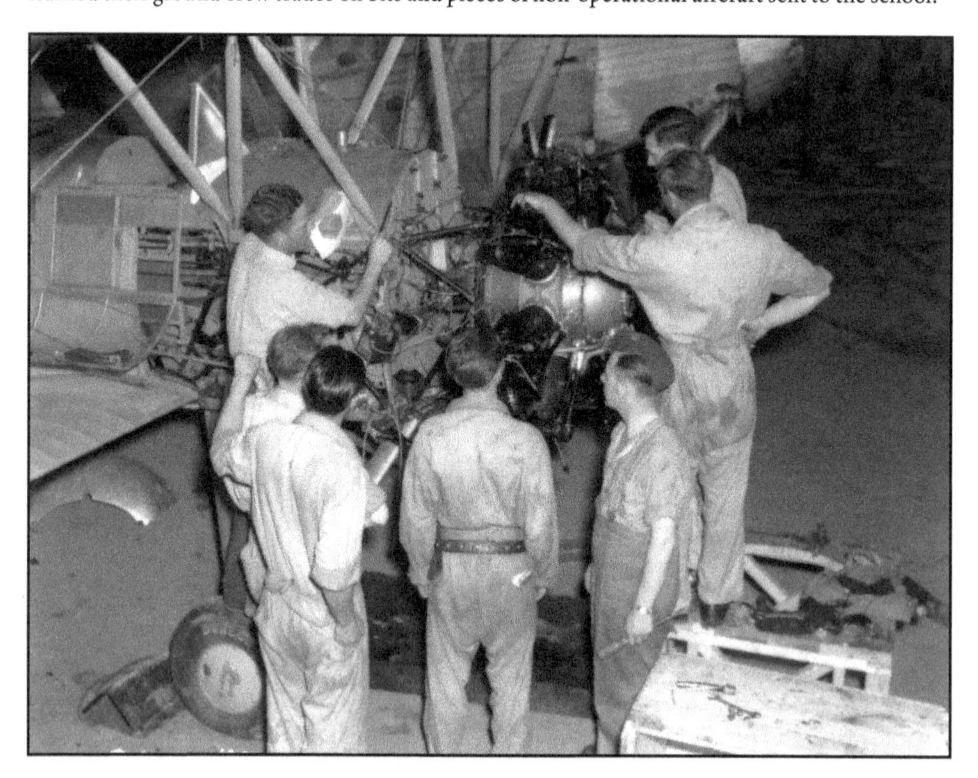

(ABOVE) Air gunnery students took practical training in turrets like this one at No. 7 Bombing and Gunnery School at Paulson, Manitoba. Some instructors also improved their students' marksmanship by having them practice on a skeet shooting range.

(LEFT) In the air, the B&GS student took target practice with a Vickers "K" gun mounted in a Fairey Battle. "They smelled of oil," remembers gunner Ted Relf. "There was so much oil running down the fuselage of the Battle that it could actually make you sick. The smell was terrible."

(RIGHT) Fairey Battles were the workhorses at Jarvis B&G School in 1941. The lead Battle towed a drogue (airborne target) on about 100 feet of line (right). A gunnery student in the rear cockpit of the second Battle opened fire with about 200 rounds of tracer ammunition per exercise. The goal of the student was a 4 percent hit rate. The goal of the staff pilot towing the drogue was not to get hit by beginner students.

(LEFT) A star of the BCATP, Air Marshal Billy Bishop chats between takes with the star of *Captains of the Clouds*, James Cagney. Director Michael Curtiz is apparently unimpressed, or preoccupied by the endless delays during the filming at Uplands.

(BELOW) The little things made the big scenes. The famous wings presentation filmed at Uplands in July 1941 required precision timing, calm delivery of lines, and for Air Marshal Billy Bishop, a small platform underfoot to help him pin wings on tall LACs like Tom Wallnutt.

(LEFT) It took a recruit about ten months to earn his RCAF wings in the BCATP. Jimmy Cagney got his the easy way — sewn on his tunic by a member of the air force Women's Auxiliary. The seamstress was so starstruck she jabbed the needle into her finger.

(ABOVE) In this climactic scene from *Captains*, Billy Bishop finishes his rousing speech to the assembled graduating class just as disgruntled ex-bush pilot Brian MacLean (James Cagney) and his buddy Tiny Murphy (Alan Hale) buzz the airfield. MacLean shouts from his cockpit: "Oh Billy, Billy, don't pay any attention to us." Seconds later, Murphy passes out doing illegal aerobatics and crashes.

(RIGHT) Instructor Charlie Konvalinka took part in the filming of *Captains*, and wondered about Hollywood's idea of heroes. "Were we heroes? In military terms, if you got a medal for it, you're probably in a place that you didn't want to be and got out of it . . . I don't think we were heroes. We were competent professionals. We produced a fine product in the air crews that came out of Canada. But circuits and bumps wasn't the glamour stuff."

(LEFT) The original plans for the premiere of *Captains* in New York called for President Roosevelt and Prime Minister King to introduce the film to the world on short-wave radio. Instead, on opening night, February 12, 1942, the RCAF Central Band and Precision Drill Team performed in front of Warner's Strand Theatre at Times Square to kick off the festivities.

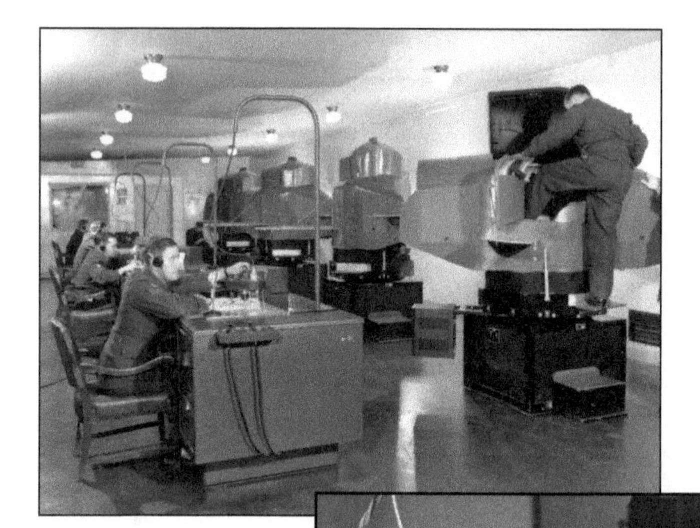

(LEFT) The Link flight simulator (like those at No. 19 EFTS Virden, Manitoba) weeded out potential pilots from those who didn't have the hand-eye-foot coordination for the job. When fitted with a hood, the Link accurately simulated instrument (or blind) flying conditions, needed for combat flying in cloud or at night.

(RIGHT) The only woman instructor in the BCATP, Margaret Littlewood, shown at her Link Trainer desk 1943–44. "Some of the pilots felt that female touch was a bit more exacting to the air signals when applied to the Link," she says. "Link instructors had to be exact. Any mistakes would cause confusion and the poor pilot would be twisting all over the place."

(LEFT) BCATP instructors churned out more than 20,000 wireless radio operators from schools at Montreal, Guelph, Winnipeg, and Calgary. This course at Montreal was lucky to have enough Morse code equipment for every trainee. Some early classes made do with blackboard mock-ups until the real thing arrived.

As this formation of Harvards passed over the Parliament Buildings in Ottawa, so did Air Vice Marshal F. S. McGill in an Oxford. McGill took the photo, landed at No. 2 SFTS Uplands, and received an inquiring telephone call from the Prime Minister.

Strafing exercises were among the joint manoeuvres conducted between the army base at Barriefield and the air force station at Trenton, Ontario. On June 20, 1945, a Harvard simulated a strafing run over an army truck convoy near Kingston. The captain in command of the army unit leapt onto the cab of a transport truck to direct the defence of the convoy. The Harvard passed over the truck, struck him, and killed him. Then the Harvard crashed, killing the pilot.

The August 30, 1944, burial of New Zealand LAC Noel Wood. He crashed during a low-level Harvard roll over a farm near Uxbridge, Ontario. Two graves away is British LAC Smith, who crashed while "shooting up" a ferry boat on Lake Erie in 1943. Both were SFTS students at Dunnville, Ontario.

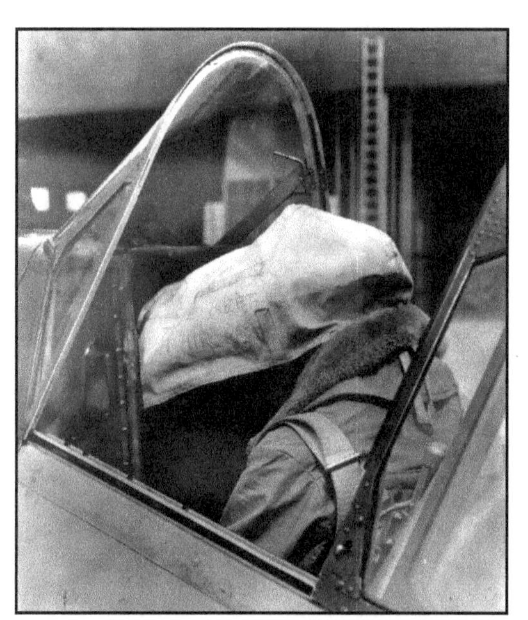

(ABOVE LEFT) "Flying under the hood," recalls pilot trainee Wally Ford, "taught you to believe your instruments. You could be upside down and swear you're right side up. The moment you say 'I don't believe my instruments' is the moment you're in deep trouble." (ABOVE RIGHT) Charley Fox and his fellow instructors at No. 6 SFTS Dunnville trained more than 2,500 pilots. Unlike many instructors, Fox got his chance overseas. His No. 412 Squadron commander, D. H. Dover, wrote: "F/Lt Fox can only be assessed as an exceptional fighter pilot."

(LEFT) Like low-flying over the German POW camp near Port Colborne, Ontario, or under the Jacques Cartier Bridge at Montreal, flying formation over the Canadian Rockies was an irresistible treat. These three Anson Is are from No. 7 SFTS Fort Macleod, Alberta.

(RIGHT) This is all that was left when Anson 8266 from No. 16 SFTS Hagersville went into an unexpected dive from 250 feet, on January 6, 1943. Before he and his students were killed, instructor John Caskie must have shut off the ignition on his two engines in an attempt to reduce the threat of explosion. The engines did not burn.

(ABOVE LEFT) The Avro Anson was not only the classroom for pilot trainees, but also provided enough room behind the cockpit for air observer students—E. M. Romilly, RCAF; W. H. Betts, RAAF; and J. A. Mahoud, RAF—who trained at Rivers, Manitoba, in June 1941. (ABOVE RIGHT) Norm Harrison claims, "I couldn't take my eyes off those wings"—although he did long enough for this publicity photograph in an Anson, taken in December 1943.

(LEFT) The largest BCATP location was Trenton, which housed Central Flying School, No. 1 Flying Instructors School, No. 1 Composite Training School, and a Reselection Centre for washed-out air crew. Its 3,000 air force personnel and 500 civilian employees outnumbered the air force personnel in the entire RCAF at the beginning of the war.

(RIGHT) Before becoming a decorated Mosquito pilot overseas, Russ Bannock (here at No. 3 FIS Arnprior in January 1943) logged several thousand hours as a BCATP instructor. "Overseas, a pilot who completed a tour got an immediate DFC, but the fellow who slogged through 2,000 hours of instruction in Canada and turned out a lot of first-class pilots didn't automatically get a decoration. Instructors didn't get the recognition they deserved."

(BELOW) Looks like a bit of trick flying by instructor Maury Dillingham, but it's the result of a forced landing in a field near Trenton in November 1941. "Just as the Finch rolled to a stop, it hit a ditch buried in snow. The tail came up and the Finch nosed over completely." The forced landing was necessary because a ground crewman had forgotten to recap the gas tank—during aerobatics, Dillingham and his student had inadvertently emptied their tank of fuel.

(LEFT) Opening Day, March 5, 1941, at No. 10 SFTS. For the civilians of Dauphin, Manitoba, the arrival of the BCATP meant a very real sense of contributing to the war effort.

(RIGHT) Taking sun-shots for these New Zealand air observers at Central Navigation School (Rivers, Manitoba) looks casual enough. And "conditions for star recognition were perfect in the west," remembers navigator Alan Tustin, "but when December came along, early morning routine included lighting the woodstove in the classroom so that we could write without mitts by 8 a.m."

(ABOVE LEFT) "We pulled into Winnipeg about 6 a.m.," remembers RAF pilot trainee John Campsie. "To our astonishment, the station concourse was full of ladies from the city's volunteer services waiting to welcome us. A band was playing popular dance tunes of the day, and before you could say 'May I have the pleasure' some of the airmen and younger ladies had started to dance."

(ABOVE RIGHT) When Campsie received his wings and was told he had to stay in Canada as a BCATP instructor, he felt "a long way from everything that really mattered. Of course, what we were doing did matter when you stopped to think about it."

(LEFT) Most of the nearly 200,000 graduates of the BCATP eventually became guests in the hotels of Bournemouth, England, on their way to the front.

(RIGHT) The Spitfire smile at Kenley, summer 1943. It's hard to say whether Cap Foster was happiest about his first tour of victories, or about having escaped his two years of BCATP instructing for a chance to fly on ops.

May 6, 1945: Danish underground representative Torkille presents former BCATP instructor Eric Johnston with a hastily wrapped gift and the flag of the Resistance at Aalborg. With Johnston are his navigator Chuck Hall, flight engineer Jock Horn, and WAG Norm Matheson. The Halifax IX's engine is still running, keeping the gun turret operational—just in case.

8

YELLOW PERILS

Aerial bombs exploded over the Niagara River late on the morning of November 1, 1941.

They were a sign not of war but of celebration. Although Canada was entering its third year of the war against Germany, the United States, across the river, was still neutral and this was the day of the opening of the Rainbow Bridge, an arch of steel and concrete connecting the twin cities of Niagara Falls, Ontario, and Niagara Falls, New York. It was to date the most modern structure to span the gorge and link the two nations.

One of the bombs that exploded that morning scattered American and Canadian flags, which landed on River Road on the Canadian side, where youngsters scuffled to retrieve them. A few minutes later, the special inaugural car drove slowly from the American to the Canadian side, signalling that the Rainbow Bridge was officially open for traffic. However, the bridge had received something of an unofficial christening earlier that spring.

"I had always had a fascination for bridges," Cap Foster said. "There was a little bridge on the Grand River [in southwestern Ontario] and there were a couple of spans. I used to look at them and think, 'I think I can get under that.' Finally, I flew down one day. I took a couple of passes at it, but I eventually chickened out."

By spring 1941, the young flyer from Grimsby, Ontario, had become a bold but proficient pilot. He was, he thought, well on his way to combat flying in Europe. Although he had had problems with his first solos in the Fleet Finch back at No. 3 EFTS London, Ontario, Foster had excelled on Harvards at No. 2 SFTS Uplands, and he had scored well on his wings test, graduating (and receiving his wings from Billy Bishop) in November 1940. However, because his was the second course in the BCATP, only five graduates were posted overseas to combat duty. As Foster put it, "The rest of us were sentenced to serve as flying instructors at one of the many new flying training schools being opened across Canada." The RCAF was so desperate for advanced flying instructors that they didn't bother sending Foster through the usual Central Flying School instructor's course. Nor did he receive a commission.

Nevertheless, by April 1941 his instructor's credentials at No. 6 SFTS Dunnville were impressive. As a sergeant pilot, Foster was handling a higher than average student ratio, flying as many as eight instructional missions a day and another four at night, and logging more than a hundred flying hours a month. He had learned how to push himself and the Harvards he flew to the limit.

"I was particularly fortunate in having Sergeant Cap Foster as my flying instructor throughout my course," wrote Victoria-born trainee Bill Olmstead. "His teaching and dare-devil flying fashioned my style of flying . . . [His] aerobatics prepared me to become as comfortable upside down or in other strange attitudes as I was flying straight and level."

"I taught students like Bill by demonstration," Foster said. "That was my technique as an instructor. Because I hadn't had the instructor's course, I didn't have the patter. They handed me the patter book, told me to learn it. I attempted to read it but ended up saying, 'To hell with this. I'll *show* them how to fly.' So I instructed strictly by gut feeling. I'd tell them how to do it, and if they couldn't do it, I'd show them."

Cap Foster's teaching methods obviously had an influence on LAC Bill Olmstead. Their friendship and respect for each other's flying skill prompted them to try out stunts. When circumstances put them in separate aircraft in the air together, they'd do complicated aerobatics, fly at extremely low levels, tail-chase each other, and fly under telephone wires. One day Foster went into a slow roll about 500 feet off the ground, and as he put the Harvard on its back, he looked down to discover another Harvard directly beneath him slow-rolling at 200 feet. It was Olmstead. On another day in mid-April 1941, as Bill Olmstead neared the end of his service training, the two took off sharing a two-seater Harvard on what was logged as an instrument flight. They headed northeast from Dunnville and soon found themselves over the off-limits airspace of the Niagara River gorge on a low-level approach to the Rainbow Bridge.

"I did these things only with selected students, like Bill," Foster said. "There wasn't much to it. . . . We actually looped the bridge. It wasn't a proper loop. We went screaming under with all the speed we could gather in the Harvard. Then we went up, in an inverted climb, so that we went well out and would have lots of time to peel down for the second pass. It was almost like an egg-shaped loop."

"The feat was even more amazing," Olmstead pointed out, "since there was a net hanging under the bridge."

Foster suddenly realized "that they were still doing construction on the bridge, so we had to extend the dive down under the net."

All Olmstead remembered at the bottom of the loop was that Foster's flight path "left very little room between the net and the angry gorge waters." Then he climbed back into the clouds above Niagara and was gone before anyone could record the Harvard's registration markings.

Bill Olmstead went on to become a BCATP instructor too, and later chalked up a colourful wartime RCAF career, flying fighter sorties in three invasions in Sicily, Italy, and Normandy. Cap Foster, for the moment, went back to instructing.

As hectic as Cap Foster's days were in the air, George Barrett's nights in the hangars were even busier. With his brand-new RCAF uniform (courtesy of Billy Bishop's public relations inspection at the St. Thomas Technical School), Barrett had graduated as a group "A" fitter (air engine mechanic) in fall 1940. His first posting was to the recently opened Service Flying Training School at Dunnville to maintain their Harvard trainers.

When Barrett arrived at No. 6 SFTS it was little more than "a sea of mud." The first barracks blocks listed at one end, and when he washed his hands with soap in a lavatory basin, the sulphur in the water turned the basin jet black. And there were the long hours. Barrett worked twelve days, had forty-eight hours off, and then worked another twelve days. His daily responsibility was "to have all the Harvards with engines running, out on the flight line at dawn. I think we had about thirty aircraft. It seemed like we had a million of them."

Nonetheless, each Harvard engine received as much attention in the hangar as did an airman in the station hospital. Off came the cowling and panels. In went skilled hands to check for oil leaks, frayed electrical conduits, and faulty pressure or drain tubes. Sometimes the engine's push rods would fill up with oil and make the valves clatter; a good fitter could hear that and repair it in time for the next day's training flights. The air engine mechanic's reward for a night's work was to hear the Harvard's 600-horsepower, nine-cylinder Pratt and Whitney engine turning over normally. George Barrett called it "a sound as recognizable as an aria from an Italian opera, or a church pipe organ. It's distinctive. Nothing sounds like a Harvard."

Another of Barrett's hangar patients was an aircraft he described as "brain damaged"—the Yale. A single-engine product of the North American Aviation factory in California, the Yale looked very much like the Harvard (the most obvious difference was its non-retractable undercarriage). The RCAF came by the Yales by accident. During the early days of the war, the French armed forces ordered 230 Yales; about a hundred of them were being shipped when France fell in 1940 and they were re-routed to the BCATP. Yales helped early SFTS pilots in the transition from primary trainers (Finches and Tiger Moths) to advanced Harvards. However, the Yales presented more problems than expected.

"Yales were a minor version of the Harvard," said Art Harrison, a flying instructor who worked with George Barrett at Dunnville. "The undercarriage didn't fold up like the Harvard and the aircraft rattled like a tin can. It made a hell of a lot of noise, particularly when you did spins; you'd think the whole thing was coming apart."

In addition, the Yale's controls were "all backwards." In order to increase fuel flow (and therefore speed), a pilot had to pull back on the throttle, the exact opposite to the Harvard. The mixture control was pushed forward to enrich the mixture, also the opposite to the Harvard.

"But what made life really interesting," said Chuck McCausland (who was a student pilot and later an instructor at Dunnville), "was that the Yale's instruments were all in metric for the French air force. I would do my circuit and come in for a landing, and instead of being at 2,500 feet, I was reading the metric altitude as imperial altitude [i.e., 2,500 metres], so there was no way I was going to touch down anywhere near the runway. I'd have to go around and do it again."

Between September 1940 and October 1943, twenty-four of the 117 Yales delivered to the RCAF had crashed. Six of the Yales at No. 6 Dunnville were involved in fatal accidents.

The Harvard trainer was the most important single-engine training aircraft in the plan, in quantity, if not in quality. It was the workhorse of advanced flight training. During the lifespan of the BCATP, nearly 2,000 Harvards were delivered to the RCAF from North American Aviation of Inglewood, California, and later from Noorduyn Aviation at Cartierville near Montreal. With the help of thousands of fitters and riggers including George Barrett, Harvards gained a wide reputation for durability and serviceability.

Eventually, there would be 100 Harvards stationed at No. 6 SFTS Dunnville, each with its distinctive "trainer yellow" fuselage, perspex coupe top canopy, black anti-glare nose cowling, retractable undercarriage, and characteristic engine roar. Rarely were fewer than ninety of them in the air on any given day. The Harvard did, however, possess a less commendable but equally consistent trait. It was a killer.

The Harvard's reputation as a "yellow peril" was the last thing on Jack Harris's mind when he arrived at No. 6 SFTS Dunnville training station as a student. Jack had left home in Humber Bay, west of Toronto, to join the air force in summer 1940. After a stint at the CNE Manning Depot and guard duty at St.-Hubert, near Montreal, Jack had gone on to No. 1 ITS in Toronto (which at that point included altitude tests in a decompression chamber at the Banting Institute), and No. 7 EFTS Windsor. But it was at Dunnville that he learned what flight training was all about.

It was December 1940 when "we walked up through all the mud and crap. And here was a hangar full of brand-new yellow Harvards worth $45,000 apiece. They were absolutely beautiful, spanking new, sparkling machines. We looked at them and said, 'There's no way that this aircraft could ever kill anybody.' The week we arrived, a kid never recovered from a power spin and crashed in full view of everybody at the station."

The fatality Jack Harris and his course witnessed on December 14 was Dunnville's first, and the first of forty-seven airmen killed in accidents at No. 6 SFTS. Twenty-five were pilot trainees; eighteen were pilot instructors. In thirty fatal accidents recorded at Dunnville, twenty-six Harvards were written off. Five crashes involved mid-air collisions and eleven resulted from unauthorized low-level flying or aerobatics.

Properly supervised low-level flying and aerobatics (loops, rolls, spins, and so on) were integral to military flying. Graduates of EFTS had to be able to taxi, take off, climb, fly straight and level, bank, descend, and land without difficulty. They had also been taught aerobatics, spins and recoveries, low-level flying, instrument flying, and night flying, and how to navigate over the countryside. What they were expected to learn at SFTS was how to transfer these skills to more powerful and sophisticated aircraft.

When EFTS training ended, students went in one of two directions. Those recommended for bomber, coastal, or transport operations moved on to twin-engine SFTSs to fly Ansons, Cranes, or Oxfords. Potential fighter pilots were posted to SFTSs for training with Harvards. Unlike the civilian-run elementary schools, the RCAF ran the service schools, so each school consisted of three wings (or sections): a headquarters or administrative wing; a maintenance wing with servicing, salvage, and repair facilities; and a training wing.

By 1940, the training wing consisted of 168 students (expanded to

240 in 1942) in six training flights. Every three weeks the school accepted another intake of about sixty pupils for a course lasting from ten to sixteen weeks.* As the new pupils arrived before the senior course had finished its final tests, there were usually four courses in the school, three in training and one in testing. At the end of the course, the senior students would graduate with a Wings Parade. Each instructor was responsible for no fewer than four and sometimes as many as eight students at a time. The SFTS syllabus, compared to that of EFTS, was more complicated and more demanding on both student and instructor.

Later, when he went back to Dunnville as an instructor from May 1941 to February 1944, Jack Harris likened the flight training in a Harvard to learning to play the piano. "You can learn to play one simple tune on a piano. And for twenty years that's the only tune you ever play, so that when people hear you play that tune, they think you're a marvellous pianist. Flying an airplane is exactly the same. You can learn to take off and land it. You can learn to spin it and do a roll or two. The extent of your flying is not dissimilar to commercial flying. The truth is, though, you don't know anything about flying airplanes.

"Most of us who survived decided that if you were going to fly an airplane, you'd better bloody well be proficient at it. You'd better have stalled that airplane at every conceivable attitude, every conceivable power-setting. You do it right-side-up, upside down. Do everything at night that you could do in the daytime. As a consequence, whenever you ran into a problem, which we all did, at least you'd have half a chance to deal with it."

---

* Course length at SFTS fluctuated throughout the war, depending on the demand for pilots at the front. When the Battle of Britain was raging in the summer of 1940, the BCATP reduced the course from sixteen to fourteen weeks and again to ten weeks that October. In 1942, when the plan was renegotiated to accommodate Arthur Harris's Bomber Command offensive, extra instrument flying and night flying time were added to the course and it was extended to sixteen weeks. In the last year of the war, when there was a surplus of trained pilots, SFTS might be extended as wings graduates awaited a posting. And, of course, poor weather conditions might extend the time of service training.

In the words of another instructor, Stan Castle: "It was our job to take the stress out of our students' flying, make them fly relaxed, help them make love to the airplane, so to speak."

At SFTS the training aircraft were more sophisticated, faster, and more powerful than those at EFTS. And with the greater speed and horsepower of an Anson or a Harvard, a pilot had less time to react, the margin of error was increased, and the line between life and death more critical.

"Before we could fly the Harvard," Charlie Purcell remembered, "we had to pass what my instructor called a blindfold test." Purcell received his service flying instruction from southwestern Ontario native Pat McLean, who had been among the first BCATP graduates and had been posted to Dunnville, where he taught from 1941 to 1944. It was McLean's job to make students such as Purcell make sense of the instrument panel of black-faced dials and toggle switches, and to make him comfortable with the handles, wheels, and levers that protruded from every surface of the cockpit. "Pat would say, 'Show me your right rudder control,' and you'd have to reach in there and touch it. 'Show me your trim controls,' and you'd do that. 'Throttle . . . this . . . that . . .' You were blindfolded. As soon as we passed this test, then we would make our first flight."

Pat McLean understood that it was essential that his students know the Harvard cockpit intimately and that they believe their instruments. Some months before, when he was a trainee at Central Flying School, McLean's class had assembled at Mountain View auxiliary field near Trenton. He recalled how soupy and dark the air was that night. He recalled his uncertainty too—should he keep his eyes on his instruments and trust their readings in the dark or look outside the Harvard to get his bearings? Denny Young, one of McLean's classmates, took off in the Harvard in front of him. It is not known whether he failed to believe his instruments or whether he got disoriented inside his darkened cockpit, but Young lost control. McLean remembers "watching him taking off. I watched his lights—his starboard light and his port light. I saw him go down like a stone. And I saw a huge ball of fire. It was his first night solo."

Instructor Charlie Krause nearly paid a similar price. Krause, like McLean, had scored high when he graduated from SFTS and was put through CFS to be an instructor. He arrived at Dunnville in 1942. Among the regular duties performed by station instructors was the pre-solo check-out. When an instructor felt his student was ready to solo, he'd get another instructor to go up with the student to make sure.

"I remember one night I was checking out one of Bob Black's students," Krause explained. "The student pilot was an officer; he had already done a tour, won a DFC as an air gunner, and was now going through to become a pilot. Bob said he was a pretty good pilot. So I wasn't really watching that closely. Now, after you take off, you're supposed to fly straight until you're at about 700 feet. Then you do a climbing turn." However, the Harvard sometimes had a tendency to "drift off." If uncorrected, a wing would drop, then the nose, and finally the aircraft would pick up speed and spiral into the ground. This tendency was hard to detect at night.

"Well, my God, I don't know what I was doing, but I wasn't paying attention. I looked down. We're not doing a climbing turn at all. We had sixty degrees of bank on and we were going down! I took over and got it straight. I could see the runway lights through the leaves in the trees—through the fucking *trees!*"

Despite this near miss, Charlie Krause ended up doing a lot of night flying. After a couple of years instructing in Harvards at Dunnville, he was posted overseas—he was halfway across the Atlantic on D-Day, 1944—and went to the Operational Training Unit in Shropshire in the Midlands, "where you learn to use your aircraft as a weapon." After a couple of circuits and bumps at OTU flying Mosquitoes, he was taught to dive-bomb and strafe in the dark and spent the rest of the war flying night sorties into Europe.

Flying a Harvard at night was a nightmare for some pilots, exciting for others. Instructor John Clinton remembered the night one of his Harvard students "suddenly looked to his right and saw his exhaust system shooting flame. He thought the aircraft was on fire, pulled back his coupe top, undid his safety harness, stood up, saluted, and dove over the side [to parachute to safety]. There wasn't a thing wrong with the Harvard."

As a student pilot, Jeff Mellon enjoyed night flying and loved to gain lots of altitude over Hamilton at night, throw his Harvard into a spin, and watch the city lights whirl around his cockpit as he descended. Stan Castle described the nighttime sensation of guiding his Harvard through a gentle 360-degree roll with the moon lined up in his sights as "pure sex."

This delight in flying never left many airmen. Instructor Pat McLean recollected climbing into the clouds in the daytime to play an exhilarating game of follow-the-leader with another Harvard instructor; in the course of their descent, they would roll over the tops of the churning thunderheads, dive through holes, and chase each other all the way down.

Some students found the Harvard a difficult airplane to master. Unless a pilot was prepared for it, as the Harvard's tail lifted off the ground on take-off, the torque (the tendency of the aircraft to rotate around the propeller shaft) often pulled the aircraft to one side. The earliest Harvard Is became notorious for their stalls, particularly when an inexperienced pilot levelled off for a landing too high and lost his air speed too soon before touching the ground. In these cases, the Harvard would often stall and flip over to the right.

The Harvard was also difficult to steer on the ground, with its huge radial engine sitting out at the front of its nose section and its steep body angle—high at the nose and low at the tail. The aircraft had a high centre of gravity, so that if a pilot didn't land straight and level, he was likely to swerve and ground-loop. If he applied too much brake, he could nose over on to the propeller. Moreover, as with other single-engined aircraft before the development of the tricycle undercarriage, neither the instructor nor the student could see directly in front of the aircraft when it was on the ground.

Bill McCauley, who instructed at No. 2 SFTS Uplands, referred to Harvards as "tail draggers." McCauley, who before the war had been an orchestra musician at Toronto's Royal York Hotel in the winter and at the Banff Springs Hotel in the summer, had signed up for air crew in November 1940. The air force assigned him to play in RCAF bands, and it was 1943 before he remustered as a pilot, received his training, and became a service flying instructor teaching on Harvards at Uplands. McCauley remembers that the tail-dragging idiosyncrasy of Harvards sometimes baffled even experienced pilots. "One time a fellow instructor brought his Harvard off the runway, turned in, and didn't see another aircraft there. His propeller chewed the other Harvard through the tail, right up to the back seat where the instructor sat." Miraculously, he wasn't hurt.

One spring day in 1943 at Dunnville, two Harvards took off from the station in formation. In the lead was Pilot Officer Bill Bouton, sitting in the rear cockpit of the Harvard, with student pilot Bill Hill in the front. In the second Harvard were student pilot Harold Becker in the front cockpit and instructor Jim Buchanan in the rear.

"As soon as we were in the air," Buchanan recalled, "I gave Becker control. He was one of those guys that even fifty hours before he gets his wings, I feel comfortable flying with. So we're on the wing. He has control and is hanging in there beautifully."

Once the two Harvards reached about a thousand feet, the practice of formation manoeuvring began. There were various positions. The aircraft could fly "line astern" (one behind the other), "line abreast" (side by side), or "vic" (one ahead and the other slightly behind in an echelon starboard or echelon port position). Instructor Bouton and student Hill stayed in the lead and instructor Buchanan and student Becker moved to echelon port.

"Cross under," Buchanan told Becker through the gosport tube. Becker dropped down from his wing position, left of the lead Harvard, and crossed underneath to take up the same position on the starboard wing of the lead aircraft.

"Cross back," Buchanan ordered. Becker manoeuvred back to his original position.

Then Buchanan said, "Cross over."

"Sir, that's not permissible," answered Becker, citing station rules for formation flying. But when Buchanan repeated the order, Becker throttled up to cross on top of the other Harvard. As he moved to cross over, Becker lost sight of the Harvard beneath him and instinctively leaned forward to improve his view. That slight movement nudged the control stick forward, which pushed the nose down, and drove his propeller toward the dual cockpits of the Harvard beneath.

In the lead Harvard, now directly below Becker and Buchanan, student pilot Bill Hill was in control and looking for his wing mate. "I looked around to the left with the intention of clearing my area," Hill said later. "When I turned my head back to the front, I leaned forward slightly. And at that instant I felt the prop of the aircraft above hit the straps behind me."

"Suddenly I see a lot of debris coming up on the leading edge of our wing," said Buchanan, who realized quickly that the prop of his Harvard was now chewing through the perspex canopy of the Harvard below. He took control from Becker, but when he "yanked back on the stick, the tail wheel of my airplane hit instructor Bouton on the back of the head and knocked him unconscious. I saw Bouton's Harvard spinning out of control, and that's when I thought, 'I'm only fifty miles from the border. I could cross the border and disappear back to the States.'"

Even with a shattered coupe top, Bill Hill managed to recover from the spin and landed back at the field without flaps, touching down at 124 miles per hour. Ground crews took axes to the rest of the canopy to remove Hill and Bouton from the cockpits. At the station hospital, Hill was found to have three gashes on his back. The Harvard's propeller had ripped apart the canopy, cut through his parachute straps, and sliced through his jacket, but it had barely cut into his back, which required only a few stitches.

Buchanan's better judgement told him to head for Dunnville airfield too. When he pulled up alongside the damaged aircraft, Bouton was conscious again and came up swinging and swearing at Buchanan. Eventually he calmed down enough to feel thankful that he was able to celebrate that day, his birthday, in one piece. Buchanan felt guilty about the whole incident. His flight commander, Larry Walker (at nineteen, believed to be the youngest flight commander in the

RCAF), said, "We all knew they were good flyers. So the air force gave them a bit of a break when it came to discipline." After an investigation Buchanan received only a "red endorsement" (a black mark) on his record, and was allowed to continue instructing.

If the idiosyncrasies of the Harvard trainer didn't always kill the novice airman, they managed to keep him humble. On the other hand, maintaining a healthy respect for the Harvard's power and limitations offered the pilot—whether student or instructor—a vivid simulation of fighter aircraft flying and considerable satisfaction.

When Dunnville instructor Jack Harris paired off with fellow instructor Charlie Spurgeon to do Harvard formation flying, "instead of changing positions the normal way—by going underneath the other plane—we used to roll over the top of the other plane and come to rest in position on the other side. And if you had some smart-ass instructor around, one that you had to bring into line, two of us would get him in between our Harvards and we'd bang his wingtips—one guy lifting up his right wing, then the other guy lifting up his left."

At some point all pilots engaged in crossovers in formation, inverted spins, tail chasing, whip-stalls, mock dogfights, or low-level flying. Some of these practices were high jinks. Some were written into the syllabus as flight training in "unusual positions." All were part of the learning process, or as Jack Harris described it, "becoming a whole pilot." Every military flyer had to feel absolutely confident and in control in the cockpit, and some of them did this by testing the limits of their aircraft and of their own courage. On occasion, a pilot went too far and tried something foolish and dangerous. To combat this urge, one station CO routinely assembled his instructor staff and stood before them with a revolver in his hand to say: "If you really want to commit suicide, go off by yourself and use this. But don't take a kid with you and don't use one of His Majesty's aircraft."

That didn't stop some instructors or students from playing games in the Harvards. At night, one of the service instructors from No. 6 SFTS Dunnville, Bob Black, took great delight in flying his Harvard, with a single landing light on, headlong towards an oncoming freight train. The engineer, thinking he was on a collision course with another train, would screech to a halt as Black swooped off into the night. Dick Ross, who came back from an overseas posting on Spitfires to instruct on Harvards at No. 35 SFTS North Battleford, once flew a simulated low-level attack on a railway pumper car. All he remembers as he roared back up into the clouds was the sight of two railway workers diving into the ditch beside the tracks.

There was a time and a place for every training manoeuvre. There were zones adjacent to service flying schools where low-level flying was authorized. Flying over these flat and open spaces helped give students a sense of their speed in relation to the ground and sharpened their control of the aircraft down "on the deck." Everywhere else was off limits for ground-level flying. But prohibited areas were usually very attractive to some daredevils.

Instructors at southwestern Ontario service flying stations often made illegal low-level passes over the German POW camp near Port Colborne to scare the inmates. Every day the prisoners dug trenches in the bog there, retrieving peat for local farmers. In the eyes of instructor Ted Arnold, who had travelled from Argentina to join the RCAF only to be waylaid from combat to become an instructor, "we couldn't shoot the Germans up in real life, so we decided we'd better 'shoot them up' by flying low over the bog.

"One day, Wiley Stone, an instructor friend from Texas, was flying formation with me. Well, we went down low over the bog where the Germans were digging. But they were fed up with this, so this one chap threw his spade up at us. Wiley was flying so low that it hit his wing. It made a hell of a dent. The crazy Texan's excuse was that he'd hit a flock of ducks."

This incident made Harvard pilots think twice about "shooting up" the POW camp, but it didn't deter some low-level flying addicts. Because he had logged so many hours in them, Charlie Konvalinka was something of an expert on Harvards. He had flown them in freezing prairie conditions and in maritime fog. Konvalinka had even done the production tests on the first Canadian-built Harvard IIs coming off the assembly line at the Noorduyn factory in Cartierville, Quebec. Konvalinka was so keen on Harvards that one day when he was chatting to a group of his fellow instructors at No. 8 SFTS Moncton he claimed, "this airplane will do anything."

"How is it flying inverted?" asked one colleague.

"Piece of cake," Konvalinka bragged.

They wouldn't believe him.

"You know that valley at Sussex," said Konvalinka, referring to the Kennebecasis River valley in south-central New Brunswick. "I'll fly a Harvard through the entire valley upside down!"

Nobody believed him. But bets were made. When demonstration day arrived, an entire flight of instructors flew to the valley to watch Konvalinka fly it upside down in a Harvard.

"As I got closer to the valley," Konvalinka said, "it began to look longer and longer. However, I was committed. I put her over the edge of the valley, rolled her over, and started through. I wanted to be going as fast as possible to get through as quickly as possible. It was more than a mile long.

"Remember, the Harvard does not have a pressure carburetor and the engine doesn't take kindly to being flown that long upside down. I had a wobble stick on the left-hand side that allowed me to keep pumping fuel into the engine. Well, I was pumping pretty vigorously and flying at about 700 feet off the bottom of the valley. I made it. I've been told that there are people in that valley who still say, 'Do you remember that goofy air force guy that went through here upside down?'"

The second full year of the Second World War, 1941, had dramatically shaped the RCAF and its now expanding British Commonwealth Air Training Plan. The war became a world conflict when the Japanese unleashed Plan Z, the surprise attack on the United States' Pacific Fleet stationed in Hawaii, on December 7, 1941. In addition to the fighter, dive-bomb, and torpedo attack on Pearl Harbor, the Japanese objective was to seize the Dutch East Indies, Malaya, and

Singapore, as well as the American forward positions on the islands of Guam, Wake, and Midway. On December 8, the United States and Britain declared war on Japan, and on December 11, Germany and Italy declared war on the United States.

These developments dealt a potentially crippling blow to the BCATP. After Pearl Harbor, American airmen wanting to enter the conflict were free to join their own armed forces, and the 6,129 American air crew serving in the RCAF were free to return home to serve. Nearly 2,000 put in for transfers.

The effects of the migration of these Americans rippled through the plan. At No. 7 EFTS Windsor, eight pilots resigned and returned to the United States immediately. LAC Bill Walker from Regina remembered arriving at No. 11 SFTS Yorkton, Saskatchewan, on December 6 "and waking up in our bunks the next morning, when we heard the news about Pearl Harbor. We had two Americans in our flight. They had just arrived too. By the end of the day they had vanished. They were posted as deserters at Yorkton, but nobody ever went looking for them."

In May 1942, a special train left Washington on a cross-Canada mission to retrieve American air crew. One Trenton instructor grappled with the decision but eventually got aboard, "entering one end of the train as an RCAF flight lieutenant and coming out the other end as a captain in the United States Army Air Force." The American recruiting train stayed a week at Trenton, and when it pulled out, Russ Bannock recalled, "the RCAF had lost a third of its pilots and a third of its instructors."

Meanwhile, although the United Kingdom had weathered major bombing attacks on Plymouth in January 1941, Clydebank (near Glasgow) in March, and Coventry in April, after the massive assault against London on the night of May 10, 1941, the Blitz ended. All available Luftwaffe strength was thereafter redirected to join the invasion of Russia. Hitler's Operation Barbarossa ultimately changed the BCATP too.

RAF priorities were also shifting from an emphasis on fighter aircraft and pilots to a demand for bombers and bomber air crew. In

February the RAF had introduced its four-engine Stirling bomber during an attack on oil storage tanks at Rotterdam. Later that month the twin-engine Manchester bomber made its debut in a raid on Brest. In March another heavy bomber, the four-engine Handley Page Halifax, on which many BCATP graduates would serve, first saw action. Six Halifaxes led a raid on Le Havre, but one was accidentally shot down by an RAF night fighter on its return flight.

The British Air Ministry drew up a list of forty-three German cities as Bomber Command targets. The required strength: 4,000 bombers. However, if the results of the November 7, 1941, raid on Berlin were any indication—21 of 169 Allied aircraft were lost—the war's consumption of bombers and air crew promised to be heavy. Churchill temporarily reduced Bomber Command activity over the European mainland.

In February 1942, several events confirmed the new thrust of the European air war. First, a new heavy bomber—the Lancaster—was put into service. (Eventually 7,300 Lancasters would become the backbone of Bomber Command's night bombing campaign.) Second, Bomber Command introduced a new navigational device, known as GEE, by which radio signals broadcast from England guided crews to and from target areas. Finally, Air Marshal Arthur Harris was appointed head of Bomber Command. Harris was convinced that only relentless bombing could bring Germany to its knees and win the war.

Canada's massive air training plan had to shift gears to meet the new air war agenda. During 1940 and 1941 Harvards were plentiful, but Ansons were not. (As the Phony War ended in Europe, so did the supply of Ansons from Britain to Canada.) Pilots at service flying level trained more frequently on single-engine aircraft. However, with the end of the Blitz and the new emphasis on Bomber Command, more EFTS graduating pilots were channelled to twin-engine training. By 1942, the plan's deficiency in twin-engine trainers was corrected when Canadian-built Avro Ansons began rolling off the assembly line at de Havilland.

The Anson, or "Annie" as it was affectionately known, proved to be the twin-engine workhorse of the BCATP. By the middle of the war, twenty of the twenty-nine SFTSs were training advanced-level pilots on Ansons. In all, the RCAF used more than 4,000 Ansons during the Second World War.

Like the Harvard, the Annie in Canada was painted the standard training colour—bright yellow. But that's where the similarity ended. The Annie was a more forgiving aircraft than the Harvard. Many of the more than 20,000 pilots who received their wings flying the Anson claimed that if you just pointed it in the right direction, it would fly itself. The Anson had plenty of flexibility; it trained pilots, air observers (navigators), and wireless operators; it ferried air crew, civilians, and supplies around the country; and since it had been designed as a reconnaissance bomber in Britain, it could be outfitted with bomb racks for bombing practice. With its cockpit surrounded by perspex (to give pilots and navigators an unobstructed view) it was also dubbed "the flying greenhouse." The one thing the Anson could not do was aerobatics.

In the last weeks of December 1942, training was not going well at No. 16 SFTS Hagersville in southwestern Ontario. The winter weather in that part of the country had been consistently bad. Flying days had been few. And the course of students due to graduate on February 5, 1943, had fallen behind in flying hours. Instruction was so delayed that the station CO had cancelled all Christmas leave. For many of the Americans on the course, it didn't really matter. But for a number of Canadians, whose homes were within driving distance of Hagersville, the lost leave was particularly disappointing.

LAC Norm Shrive came from Hamilton, an hour's drive from Hagersville. He had lived all of his twenty-one years in the industrial city at the western end of Lake Ontario. As a kid, infatuated with aviation and with names such as Lindbergh, Earhart, Turner, Doolittle, and Post, young Norm Shrive had become a fixture at the Hamilton Airport. The Gipsy Moths, Avro Avians, and Fairchild 71s on the airfield fed his imagination, and at home he often donned his father's First World War leather flying coat and aviator's helmet (with one ear pad shot off) and pretended he was flying an airplane.

For Shrive, as for many other southern Ontario youngsters, 1934 had been a watershed year. In July, the RAF uncrated five Hawker Furys at Hamilton Airport for a series of demonstration flights over eastern Canada. Not only had he watched spellbound as the Furys conducted formation aerobatics but he had also managed to get the autographs of the five RAF pilots who flew them. Norm Shrive felt he was destined for the air force. During the Battle of Britain, Shrive's mother forbade him to join up, so he took a job in Hamilton at National Steel Car, producing anti-aircraft shells. But with encouragement from his father, Frank (who was instructing at No. 10 EFTS Mount Hope), he enlisted in 1941 and started the long road, he thought, to winning his wings and glory in the skies over Europe.

"A couple of weeks before Christmas 1942," Shrive recalled, "I had been able to go to Hamilton with a fellow student named Steelman, an American. He had gone to a shop to buy a sweater for his girlfriend back in the States. But because training was so far behind he wasn't able to take it home to her.

"My instructor was a fellow Hamiltonian, a pilot officer named John Caskie. He was very quiet, good looking, a decent sort of guy. And whenever we used to get up in an Anson, if the opportunity came up, we'd fly over the city; he'd circle a certain spot, and sure enough, out would come his wife from their little house and she'd wave a tea towel at us.

"On this particular day [January 6, 1943], Caskie was just going to take up two of his four students—Steelman and Jones. The normal procedure when you took up two students was one would do the takeoff and fly for a while, then he would move to the back of the left seat as the other did the flying. The Anson was a big airplane, so sometimes the instructor would also take up a third student to sit in the back and do map reading.

"That day, Caskie said to me, 'Shrive, get your map and a parachute pack and go out to such-and-such an Anson.' But they didn't have enough parachute packs to cover everybody that day and I couldn't find one. 'Come on anyway,' said Caskie. 'No one will know.' It was illegal to go up without a parachute, but I took my map and got in the airplane. We were just taxiing out and I guess Caskie didn't want to get into trouble, so he stopped the Anson, turned to me, and said, 'Maybe you better not. You'd better get out. When I get back, I'll take you up.'

"I jumped out and walked back to the flight room a couple of hundred yards away. After about an hour, I went up to the flight desk and asked, 'Sir, is Pilot Officer Caskie back yet?'

"'No, no, just go and sit down.' An hour and a half went by. No sign of Caskie. Two hours . . . I knew there was trouble.

"It turned out that the three of them were up near Guelph, over a village called Crieff. There was a low-flying area up there and they had come down, belting along at about 160 knots, and when the aircraft pulled out, the starboard wing just folded. They went straight in and burned. I felt really sad. Steelman was a good friend. And I liked Caskie; he had a new bride and a baby son. The luck of the draw—I missed that trip."

A training crash that killed an instructor and two trainees prompted a post mortem. As the airmen's bodies were removed and returned to their families for burial, the newly formed Accidents Investigation Branch* of the RCAF descended on the site to go over the wreckage in search of the cause. In spite of the charred condition of the aircraft, investigators found a crack in the main spar of the Anson's starboard wing—a crack that had been there before the crash.

Station authorities did not blame the manufacturer. They suspected that the Anson had been improperly piloted just before Caskie's flight. They were probably right. Later that winter, Hagersville instructor Ross Truemner may have discovered the truth. "On the graduation night of the senior course, one of my four students

---

* An Accidents Investigation Branch was formed at RCAF headquarters on March 1, 1942, to investigate all service flying accidents in Canada and to compile data for the promotion of safety in flying.

approached me and said, 'Sir, I have to tell you something. I looped the airplane that lost its wing.'"

The switch from a single-engine trainer aircraft to a twin-engine Cessna Crane, Airspeed Oxford, or Avro Anson was quite a challenge for the student. The aircraft was much heavier, its controls more sophisticated, and its two engines more powerful than anything they had experienced. The cockpit, or cabin, also had two of everything—two oil pressure gauges, two oil temperature gauges, two tachometers, and a pair of cylinder-head temperature gauges, as well as dual control columns. Take-off procedure was more complicated and cumbersome.

To simplify the process, instructors taught their students to memorize codes to be spoken aloud as the pilot went about certain activities in the cockpit. Student Murray Peden, who trained on Cranes at No. 10 SFTS Dauphin, Manitoba, recalled that he learned to "chant magic alphabetical incantations," such as H-T-M-P-F-F-C-G-S-I, which reminded a pilot to check hydraulics, trim, mixture, pitch, flaps, fuel, carburetor heat, gas, switches, and instruments before take-off.

Another innovation in a service aircraft such as the Harvard, Anson, or Crane was the retractable undercarriage. In preparation for a landing, the student now had to remember to lower his landing gear. Some stations put observers out on the runways; if a descending aircraft got below 500 feet without putting its wheels down, the observer fired a red flare from a Very pistol to alert the pilot. The aircraft's registration letters were then reported to the chief flying instructor, who called the student up on the carpet. Punishment ranged from writing a thousand times: "I must not approach to land with undercarriage retracted," to rolling an aircraft wheel around the perimeter of the airport.

A long walk around the airfield fence might correct a memory lapse about lowering the undercarriage, but making a smooth landing, or "greasing it on the runway," was definitely an art. As a kid growing up in Edmonton, Wilf Sutherland saw his fair share of perfect landings. The great bush pilots of the day—Wop May, Punch Dickins, and Grant McConachie—regularly greased bush planes on Edmonton's Blatchford Field, or seaplanes on Cooking Lake southeast of the city. A little of their skill must have rubbed off on Sutherland, because when he began instructing at No. 10 SFTS Dauphin in 1942, he was known for his smooth landings. He said jokingly, "When my students asked, 'When are we going to land?' I'd say, 'Get out.' And they'd say, 'My God, we're down.'

"The trick to landing," Sutherland explained, "was in depth perception. You're never looking down, but straight ahead. It's your peripheral vision of things, especially at night—the flare pots you can see all the way down—and as you come in and round out, all of a sudden they become one line.

"I always thought it was a terrible thing when an instructor took over the controls too quickly. I'd let the student come in and round out. But I remember sitting—talk about white-knuckle flyers—with my feet on the boards, saying to myself, 'Back, back, back.' Sometimes I had to say 'Back!' aloud. But it was good to let the kid go as far as he could, hoping he would see that he wasn't rounding out enough, and when he'd start to pull back a little, I'd let out a sigh of relief.

"If he learned to do that once, the next time he'd probably be better. But if the kid's coming in to land a bit too high and the instructor immediately says, 'I have control, I'll land this thing—you were way too high. Let's go round and try again,' rather than let the kid realize his mistake, that's no good. As long as the instructor doesn't leave it so long that he's going to damage the aircraft or wipe himself and the student out."

Ansons, Oxfords, and Cranes were built for basic flying—takeoffs, straight and level flying, climbing, diving, steep turns, and landings—not high-performance aerobatics. These aircraft were airborne classrooms for future bomber pilots, whose jobs in Bomber Command would one day be to fly multi-engine Halifaxes or Lancasters to a particular target and back. Learning to manoeuvre quickly to elude German fighters or anti-aircraft gunfire was part of the training syllabus, but flicks, rolls, and loops were not.

Although flying an Anson upside down was not part of regular training at twin-engine schools, recovery from "unusual positions" certainly was. This was covered in step 19 of the Sequence of Instruction—instrument flying. At night, in cloud, or in any poor-visibility situation, military pilots had to be able to fly without visual reference to the landscape by employing only the instruments in the cockpit.

From the First World War on, RAF pilots at Central Flying School in England had been taught to "fly by feeling." They were taught to rely on the sensations of flying, such as the force of gravity or the wind on their cheeks, to correct an aircraft in flight. However, the moment a novice pilot went into cloud or became disoriented, he risked ending up in a spin, sometimes an unrecoverable spin. That changed in 1930, when RAF officer Patrick Johnson reported to CFS commander Basil Embry about the principles of "*pilotage sans visibilité*" being taught at the Farman School outside Paris. Flying blind using only a magnetic compass, an airspeed indicator, an altimeter, and a needle-and-ball or turn-and-side-slip indicator (and, on service aircraft, an artificial horizon) became mandatory. It was accomplished by placing a canvas hood over the pilot's head that allowed him to see only the instrument panel as he flew. "Going under the hood" became a standard method of training and testing military flyers. That's how trainee Tom Hawkins accidentally looped his Anson.

Until that time, the high point in Tom's air force career had been seeing the *Captains of the Clouds* crew filming aerobatic sequences while he was on guard duty at Trenton in 1941. He considered himself fortunate to be in pilot training at all. His high marks in mathematics put him in line for training as an air observer (navigator), but on Selection Day at ITS, he asked for pilot training and got it. During elementary training he was sick twice in a Tiger Moth and was warned if it happened a third time he would be washed out. But he hung on, and in the winter of 1942 he was at No. 5 SFTS at Brantford. There his instructor took him up in an Anson to learn sequence number 19: "instrument flying" while in "unusual positions."

"I was supposed to close my eyes until the instructor gave me control," Hawkins recalled. "So he put it into what I thought felt like a steep dive. However, there's a lag in the Annie's instruments. You pull the nose up and it's a one-two-three count before your altitude shows a change, and the climb-and-glide indicator was slow because it works on a differential between the actual pressure and the pressure where you started. So the instruments were all behind the fact.

"I could have sworn we were going down. We weren't. We were going almost straight up. I pulled the control column back and there we were, as the saying goes, upside down at 8,000 feet with nothing on the clock but the maker's name. That was the first time I'd ever been up to 8,000 feet in an Anson.

"Because of the heavy engines, the nose dropped. We didn't spin. But we ended up in a spiral dive, going down like hell. By the time the two of us got it under control, we'd hit 270 miles an hour. (I think the top speed in an Anson is about 170.) Memories were flashing through my mind like crazy. I thought we were going in. Anyway, we pulled out at 800 feet—from 8,000 to 800 in nothing flat. We had cracked a main spar on the one side. The engine was throwing all kinds of oil. So we aimed straight for home."

LAC Hawkins seemed to have nine lives. Shortly before graduating from No. 5 SFTS Brantford, he asked to go to Toronto, saying that he was supposed to be an usher at his sister's wedding there. (It was actually his wife's sister's wedding.) The station obligingly sent Hawkins and Sergeant Pilot Beal on a cross-country to the Toronto Island Airport in an Anson I, the version that needed compressed air for its brakes to function. Halfway there, one of the Anson's engines failed. And by the time they reached Toronto Island, the compressed-air gauge showed zero, so they were also without brakes.

"One engine. No brakes. And we had to land on Toronto Island where the runways weren't very long. If you undershoot, you're in the water; if you overshoot, you're in the water. I let Beal do the landing, and he did a darn good job of it. He side-slipped the Anson, came in a little high and lost height with a side-slip, and stopped it without running off the end. It made my trip to the Island Airport memorable. There was just enough time for me to get onto the mainland for the wedding."

While engine failures were tough for students, they were "definitely sweaty palms time for instructors," Bob Hesketh recalled. Hesketh had trained with Tom Hawkins's brother Ed in 1944. The two had become close friends during training, but at the end of SFTS, Bob Hesketh got a commission while his friend Ed Hawkins got sergeant stripes. Hawkins became a staff pilot at No. 4 B&GS in Fingal, Ontario. Not long after, he was up in an Anson with another sergeant pilot, who inexplicably fired a Very pistol inside the cabin; the Anson went down in flames and both pilots were killed. Meanwhile, Bob Hesketh graduated from Trenton CFS and went on to instruct at No. 9 SFTS Centralia.

"We had this drill on take-off," Hesketh said. "You would get to about 150 feet and cut a switch and hope the student reacted quickly. The proper reaction was full opposite rudder from the failed engine, pour on the power with the remaining engine, and try to get around again. Full opposite rudder would offset the power loss on the one side and keep the aircraft from yawing to that side. You just prayed the student's knee-jerk reaction would be correct."

This procedure was often followed with the pupil under the hood, so he couldn't see which engine had been cut. During take-off the remaining engine would be on full power. If the pupil decided to come back to the airfield, he had to turn in the direction of the good engine. If he went the other way, the combined lift of the raised wing and the engine at full power would flip the aircraft over and it would spin in.

One student at No. 9 SFTS Centralia "used the wrong rudder one time. The Anson did a right-angle turn across the runway and was headed straight for a barn on the other side." Only a quick recovery by the instructor, Eric Haynes, saved the day.

An instructor's quick thinking also saved the lives of the crew of an Anson in the skies over No. 16 SFTS Hagersville. The twenty-sixth item in the Sequence of Instruction was formation flying. All BCATP students—single- and twin-engine pilots—required a certain number of hours flying in formation with other aircraft. Towards the end of one course, a twenty-three-year-old instructor from Edmonton made arrangements for students in two other Ansons to fly in formation with him. As the student pilot in the lead Anson levelled off, the instructor caught sight of an Anson coming in on the right side much too fast. The instructor told his student, "I have control," just as the wing of the onrushing Anson smashed into the instructor's aircraft. The impact tore the wing off the other Anson; it flipped over and fell, killing its students. The instructor had to struggle at the controls to bring his own crippled Anson home.

That was the closest Max Ward came to death during the Second World War. Much as he wanted to be posted overseas, his teaching skills kept him in the BCATP. After the war he went on to fly in the bush of northern Alberta and to establish Canada's third international airline, Wardair.

Tragedies like the mid-air collision that Max Ward survived still didn't deter some pilots from taking risks during formation flying. Centralia instructor Bob Hesketh was sitting in the right-hand seat one day as his student, flying on the port wing of a lead Anson, nearly put the starboard wing through the lead Anson's cabin door.

LAC Fred Lundell, who had passed all the necessary pilot tests at No. 24 EFTS Abbotsford, British Columbia, remembered that at No. 7 SFTS Macleod, Alberta, the real test was surviving formation practice with "Mad Australian Gussie Grimmer, who thought formation flying meant touching wingtips. We drew straws to see who would have to risk touching tips, or death, with grinning Gussie."

The best formation flyers ran the greatest risk. The lead pilot was responsible for the safety of the formation, so he scanned the air space ahead. Flying to port or starboard of the lead, or following him in single file, the trick was to stay nearly glued to the leader. The wingman's concentration was riveted on the aircraft leading the formation.

Cy Roberts always took flying seriously, from the day in 1932 he stowed away on a ten-seater Ford Tri-Motor for a ride over Calgary, to his RCAF instructing days during the war at No. 12 SFTS Brandon. Roberts and his instructor colleagues often flew their twin-engine Cessna Crane trainers in close formation. Roberts believed "when you formated, you formated close, and you were proud of that, because you fly in the other guy's cockpit. I have come up behind an airplane, line astern, and rolled the tail wheel of his airplane on the nose of mine."

If flying in tight formation was intense and risky, and flying under a bridge was risky and prohibited, instructors Dick Ross and J.J. Hill really tempted fate. Hill had come up from the United States to fly in the RCAF and Ross was a New Brunswicker who had been overseas briefly on Spitfires. In 1943 they were both instructing at No. 13 SFTS St.-Hubert, outside Montreal. One fall day, a 200-foot ceiling and fog on the St. Lawrence River nearly washed out flying for the day. It was a day for instructor flying only, so Hill and Ross flipped a coin to see who would fly the lead Harvard and who would be wingman to fly formation—under the Jacques Cartier Bridge.

"Hill won the toss," Dick Ross said. "So he got to lead and I had to formate. First he takes off. Then I take off. Then I join up with him, formating on his port side and right down we go, just off the water. Of course, flying in formation, I can't take my eyes off Hill, because I was tucked in pretty close, only a foot or so away, and I've got to watch him all the time. He's doing the looking around.

"Wasn't long before I could sense the bridge coming. Then, under we go. But just as we get past it, all of a sudden, up he goes into the overcast in nothing flat. He pulled up so fast that he startled me.

"Right in front of me, coming out of the mist, is the bow of a ship on its way out to sea. I was so close to it, I could see the waves breaking away from the bow, the rivets on it, and the Roman numeral markings up the bow, all way the hell above me. I'm only ten feet off the water. So I pour the coal to it and pull the stick back. And here's the foremast and the crew of the ship looking at me. I was close enough to read the ranks of the guys on the bridge. I go screaming over the front part of the bow and up into the overcast. J.J. knew. He could make it, so as far as he was concerned, if he could make it, I could make it."

Two BCATP students were passengers the day Hill and Ross challenged the Jacques Cartier Bridge in their Harvards. Neither said a word throughout the whole escapade. Both were sworn to secrecy after it.*

What Ross and Hill did was wrong. Ross admits it. They had conducted unauthorized low-flying and probably unauthorized low-level aerobatics. They had also endangered the lives of the two students they had with them. Some might argue (although Ross doesn't) that their run under the Jacques Cartier Bridge showed initiative, aggressiveness, and bravado—positive qualities necessary in the fighter pilots of an air force at war. Others would criticize their stunt as a vain and unnecessary demonstration of foolhardy flying that endangered property and lives.

Had their escapade been noticed by anyone other than the crew of a merchant vessel on its way out to sea, and had their aircraft numbers been recorded, Hill and Ross might well have been court-martialled and tossed out of the RCAF. So might Cap Foster and Bill Olmstead for looping the Rainbow Bridge. Or Jim Buchanan for allowing his student to cross over in formation. Or Jack Harris and Charlie Spurgeon for wing-tapping. Or Bob Black for playing chicken with a train

---

* It wasn't uncommon for instructors or LACs to be punished or thrown out of the air force for "shooting up the farm." It happened to George Flinders. Stationed at No. 14 SFTS Aylmer in southwestern Ontario, Flinders took off one day in March 1943 on a Harvard cross-country flight that just happened to pass over New Toronto, where his wife of three days was staying. He piloted the Harvard down over the house to the amusement of his relatives, but to the consternation of a manager at the CIL paint plant nearby; he reported Flinders's numbers and the young pilot was court-martialled. "After the trial, they marched me out in front of the entire station. No belt. No hat. They read me my sentence—sixty days—and sent me to a detention centre at Manning Depot in Toronto. Then they relegated me to control tower duties and standing at the end of runways to signal pilots with flare guns. They made an example of me." Fortunately, Flinders was later allowed to remuster for air crew training and eventually he became a flight engineer in Bomber Command.

engineer at night. Or Wiley Stone for "shooting up" the German POW camp. Or Charlie Konvalinka for flying a Harvard inverted up the Kennebecasis River valley. But they weren't, perhaps because they were lucky, perhaps because each of them on every other training flight was conscientious, loyal to his country and the Allied cause, and otherwise entirely committed to the task of teaching his students the safe way to fly.

Instructors were human, after all. They were young (eighteen to twenty-one years old on average) and therefore sometimes careless. For many, this was the first real paying job of their lives—three square meals, a bed, and a pay cheque. They were eager to prove their worth to their peers, to their superiors, and to themselves. Arguably, unauthorized flying was not the way to win approval. But they were also flying around the clock building an air force. They lived with the constant responsibility of shepherding half a dozen other young men at a time through danger, and they received little credit for doing so. They had to know the difference between taking control of the aircraft away from a student too soon, before he could learn from his mistake, and taking control too late to be able to prevent an accident, which one instructor called the difference between "the quick and the dead."

They tested others, but rarely tested themselves. Often they experienced boredom. Day and night, course after course, one training school after another, they filled students' heads with patter, routine, and sequences. And when they had shaped a handful of sprog airmen into capable pilots, their protégés graduated and there was yet another group of novices to teach from scratch. "Flying instructing," said one who experienced it, "was very important work, but it was not glamorous, and that perhaps was the trouble. Life in the BCATP was made up more of hard work and dogged application than death-defying feats and mortal peril," so some instructors broke the monotony by legitimate tail-chasing and aerobatics, while others flew under bridges and pulled illegal stunts as a temporary antidote.

The culmination of SFTS training was a series of wings tests. Written tests in navigation, aircraft recognition, bomb-aiming, and armament had to be taken, and in the air the leading aircraftman had to demonstrate proficiency in basic flying (including side-slipping, spin recovery, and precautionary landing), as well as advanced skills in instrument flying (flying under the hood), air navigation, cross-country flying, and formation flying. Then came the wait—usually several days—before pilot graduates' names were posted and arrangements for the graduation announced.

Getting your wings—described by one instructor as holding "the Holy Grail"—could be a ceremony full of pomp. Certainly the graduation of Course 29 at No. 2 SFTS Uplands during the filming of *Captains of the Clouds* was memorable, as Air Marshal Billy Bishop pinned the wings on the graduating airmen. However, Bishop didn't perform the duty just for Hollywood cameras—Cap Foster received his wings from Bishop too. Jeff Mellon received his wings the day that Billy Bishop presented wings to his son Arthur Bishop at Uplands; also in that graduating class were Nick Nylands (later one of America's most decorated bomber pilots) and Peter Lehman (who received a DFC for his fifty-eight flights over Germany).*

Wing Commander R.H. Waterhouse took the opportunity of a Wings Parade at No. 5 SFTS Brantford to warn the graduates, "In the future, there will be no instructor to correct your faults. You will have to look after yourselves and you will be flying heavier and faster planes . . . I hope you will enlarge upon the glory of the Royal Canadian Air Force. I wish you goodbye, good hunting, and good luck." As he completed his speech, the wings recipients from Britain, the United States, France, and Canada received an appropriate salute: a formation of Harvards did a low-level pass over the airfield.

By contrast, Stan Castle's Wings Parade was a rather hasty, informal affair. "Typically, they'd get the course together for a class picture.

---

* Peter Lehman was the son of Herbert H. Lehman, the American financier, diplomat, and governor of New York State for ten years. Lehman trained with the RCAF, later transferred to the USAAF, and won a DFC. He had intended to present the medal to his father on his birthday in March 1944, but was killed on a training flight when his Thunderbolt fighter crashed near his English base.

But the air force was in such a hurry to move pilots through the system that they didn't take our photograph. They had a small band, all in their tartans. Friends and family were supposed to be there, except that coming to the ceremony my family and girlfriend got stuck at a railway crossing, and Castle being early in the alphabet, when they got there, I'd already done my trick."

Like his first solo, or his wedding day, the Wings Parade—or some image of that graduation day—was usually etched on an airman's memory. At No. 3 SFTS Calgary, Pat McLean remembered "the great moment" when he received his wings from Group Captain (later Air Commodore) A.D. Ross, as well as the celebration at Calgary's famous downtown hotel, the Palliser, dubbed "the Paralyzer" by visiting airmen.

A few days before his graduation, Joel Aldred and three of his classmates crossed the Ontario–Quebec border to party in Hull, got into a brawl at a nightclub, and were hauled up before the CO. There was no danger Aldred would fail, he was top of his class, but the CO went through the motions of "admonishing us at some length with a grin on his face."

Max Ward recalled being part of a huge Wings Parade at No. 15 SFTS Claresholm, Alberta, where a course of sixty-two pilots graduated "all ready to go off and win the war." Bob Hesketh's Wings Parade was in March at No. 36 SFTS Penhold, Alberta. Despite the bitter prairie cold and being so far from home, he has warm memories of his wings presentation; his wings were pinned on by the daughter of a family that had befriended many visiting airmen. After graduating from No. 6 SFTS Dunnville, John Clinton asked his girlfriend to sew his new wings onto his uniform; then the two of them dashed off to the Brant Inn and danced to big band music all night.

The moment Bill Lennox received his wings at No. 5 SFTS Brantford was bittersweet; he had just learned that his younger brother, piloting a Halifax over Dortmund on a Pathfinder mission, had been shot down and was missing. A nearly fatal Anson crash at Brantford delayed Harvey Timberlake's Wings Parade, but his wings plus a commission as pilot officer "made me feel like a millionaire." Tom Hawkins got his wings at Brantford too, and remembered it as "the proudest moment of my life."

"I couldn't take my eyes off those wings," Norm Harrison said. His wings ceremony and elevation in rank to pilot officer took place in December 1943 at No. 17 SFTS in Souris, Manitoba. In a small prairie community in the middle of winter there wasn't much of an audience, so a group of his course-mates got an allowance to go to Winnipeg to purchase their officers' uniforms.

"On our way to Winnipeg, we said, 'The first guy to salute us once we've got our new uniforms, we'll buy him dinner and a drink.' So we go into the Hudson's Bay Company store as LACs and we come out as commissioned officers. There were three of us walking down the street. Imagine, I'm the shortest at six-foot-one; the other two are six-foot-five. That's pretty imposing with all this brass and the flat hat.

"Along comes this army corporal, and of course, right like that, he salutes. So we salute and wheel right around to corner him. We told him, 'We promised the first guy that salutes us we're going to buy him dinner and a drink.' 'Oh no, sir, no, no,' he says. The poor guy was so frightened. That's what I remember most about getting my wings. We went home on the train, had a great Christmas and got ready for our posting overseas."

Norm Harrison never did get an overseas posting. Nor did Stan Castle or Max Ward. Nor did Pat McLean or Bob Hesketh or Bill Lennox, Harvey Timberlake, or Tom Hawkins. Even though they graduated near the top of their SFTS courses and felt ready for operational duty, the BCATP still needed instructors, not heroes. Harrison flew more than a thousand hours instructing at Centralia and for the Fleet Air Arm at No. 31 SFTS Kingston. Castle began the war as a mechanic, remustered to air crew, and was posted to several elementary schools instructing for the duration. Ward instructed at Moncton and Hagersville and was demobilized in 1945 with 2,800 hours in the air. McLean served for four and a half years and more than 2,000 hours as an instructor at Dunnville. Hesketh and Lennox both went to instructors' school and taught at Centralia until 1945. Timberlake served at three stations from 1942 to 1945, instructing twenty-eight full-course pilots. Of the forty-nine men who graduated at Tom Hawkins's Wings Parade, forty-eight were made instructors; Hawkins taught right to the end of the war.

Jeff Mellon, Joel Aldred, and Cap Foster would eventually win that coveted overseas posting and return with decorations. But they first had to weather the frustration of not being immediately allowed to fight in Europe, North Africa, or the Pacific. For now, their military flying would be restricted to Anson and Harvard trainers. Their service would be to the BCATP and Training Command. Their victories would not be kills but the repetitious work of keeping course after course of nervous flyers alive from first solo to wings test. Any acknowledgement of their role would be lost in the race to get air crew to the front and into the Allied air war.

9

TOO VALUABLE TO RISK

EVEN THOUGH the news from overseas in 1941 and 1942 was discouraging, the war did not preclude all celebrations. On the home front in Canada, there was still room in people's lives to attend a school convocation, dance to the music of Mart Kenney or Trump Davidson, or even celebrate a wedding in the family (although wartime rationing meant not throwing rice over the bride and groom). Imperial and national holidays certainly didn't fade away either; in fact, civilian and military officials took full advantage of events such as Queen Victoria's birthday and civic holidays to demonstrate that Canadians were "keeping the home fires burning."

On occasions like these, the Patriotic Salvage Corps ran drives for metals, rags, paper, bones, rubber, and glass to be recycled into war supplies. The IODE promoted the sale of Victory Bonds and War Savings Stamps. The Wartime Prices and Trade Board hired Toronto broadcaster Kate Aitken to encourage Canadians to remodel and recycle clothes and household furnishings. Red Cross volunteers invited the families of prisoners of war to assemble ditty bags and to write letters of no more than twenty-five words to their loved ones. Meanwhile, the air force sent war heroes—including Billy Bishop and, later, Buzz Beurling—across the country to visit cities and towns and BCATP stations to boost morale.

On July 1, 1942, the city of Windsor staged its annual Dominion Day celebrations—the seventy-fifth anniversary of the founding of Canada—in Jackson Park. The official program included a civic parade and a military review with precision drill by servicemen and speeches by high-ranking army, navy, and air force officers. It certainly did not include a fly-past by two Fleet Finches from the Elementary Flying Training School at Windsor.

"There must have been five or ten thousand people in attendance," Brick Bradford recalled. Because he had been among the first to enlist in the RCAF with a private, a commercial, and an instructor's licence, Bradford had been whisked off to Trenton's Central Flying School to become an instructor right at the beginning of the war; he had then been posted on indefinite leave without pay to the civilian EFTS at Windsor to teach other recruits how to fly. He'd been there for just under two years. Similarly, the RCAF had snapped up Frank Vines when he enlisted, sent him off to Trenton, and posted him to Windsor; he had put in two years as well. However, instructing was losing its lustre, and Bradford and Vines were getting impatient for a posting overseas to the battle front.

As Frank Vines puts it, "After six months of instructing, I thought anybody could do it—and wished they had. It was just the monotony of it. You'd just get a guy to where you thought he could fly and you'd lose him. Then you started all over again with another bunch of new students."

"So Frank and I got in a couple of Fleets," Bradford continued, "and flew low formation over the Dominion Day event. We did a slow roll and a couple of loops down over the park." Vines and Bradford figured this exhibition was the quickest way to express their frustration with the system and a surefire way to get them shipped out of Windsor and off to Britain.

"Of course we got called up on the carpet. Ab Hiltz, the CO, and Al Lewis, the chief flying instructor, told we us were bad boys, that we were liable to be charged or court-martialled and thrown out of the air force. And we kept saying we were just drawing attention to the fact that we wanted to go overseas and nobody was listening to us."

Fortunately, neither Bradford nor Vines was disciplined beyond a tongue-lashing and two weeks of additional night duty. Their exhibition over Jackson Park had made its point. Accomplished flyers who had volunteered early, gone to Trenton to learn military instructing, and then taught scores of recruits to fly were being overlooked. Like most of the others who had joined up, they had dreamed of flying Spitfires and Wellingtons in combat. Their experience, however, worked against their wishes. Later, because of Bradford's and Vines's stunt, the air force instituted a plan to move some of the original instructors on, but not before many capable pilots suffered from the indifference of the system.

By 1942, the British Commonwealth Air Training Plan needed to be overhauled and updated. Events in Europe had shifted the emphasis of the air war from dogfights to carpet bombing; fewer fighter pilots were required, but Arthur Harris's Bomber Command desperately needed air crew. The entry of the United States into the war had also brought American military production and manpower to centre stage.

The agreement that had created the BCATP was due to expire on March 31, 1943, and Prime Minister Mackenzie King was eager to extend the plan, to involve the Americans, and to press his "Canadianization" of the plan with the British. At the same time, Britain wanted to keep any review of the BCATP strictly in the Commonwealth family.

On April 15, King took the opportunity to press his case for a review of the BCATP while dining with President Roosevelt in Washington. The next morning, a joint communiqué announced "a conference in which all of the United Nations with air training programmes will be invited to participate," which left little room for the British to refuse. The conference was convened on May 19 in Ottawa. However, the revamping of the plan remained very much in the hands of the original signatories—Britain, Canada, Australia, and New Zealand.

The termination date for phase one of the BCATP would be moved up to June 30, 1942. The second phase would carry joint air training from July 1, 1942, to March 31, 1945, at a cost of $1.446 billion. The United Kingdom accepted responsibility for 40 percent of the training capacity of the combined training organization. The quotas from each country for each air crew position were recalculated to reflect the plan's projected output: Australia and New Zealand would provide 4,753 trainees annually, Canada 34,600 a year, or about half the plan's projected yearly intake of 68,419 air crew. Unlike the lengthy wrangling over the inception of the plan in 1939, most issues were settled quickly and amicably (the exception being a policy for granting commissions). The most significant internal change involved the composition of air crews for Bomber Command. The introduction of medium and heavy bombers dictated that future crews would consist of a pilot, a navigator (previously the air observer who had been responsible for navigating and bomb dropping), a wireless operator/air-gunner, an air-gunner without wireless training, and a new member of the crew, the bomb-aimer (or air bomber).*

These new air crew functions and the increased quotas put more pressure on the RCAF. Air observer schools would have to be expanded. More bombing and gunnery schools were needed. New courses would have to be organized for navigators and bomb-aimers. More staff pilots would be needed to fly crews on training missions. However, the system had already produced more for less and in less time than anyone had expected. In 1942, the BCATP graduated 27,778 air crew, almost double the 1941 output of 14,182.

Naturally, rising output expectations meant an increased demand for instructors. And at the rate Bomber Command was going through

---

* The flight engineer function was added when the Avro Lancasters were introduced; the BCATP began training flight engineers per se at Aylmer, Ontario, in July 1944. Previously, as Elmer Keating pointed out, "I went to St. Thomas Technical School in the first flight engineers' course in fall 1943. We studied instruments, engines, and had an air frame course, but because there wasn't sufficient Lancaster and Halifax equipment on hand there, we finished our training with a three-month course overseas in Wales, at St. Athan, the biggest station in the British Isles."

pilots—bombing missions over Europe now involved as many as a thousand aircraft a night—Trenton's production of instructors at Flying Instructor School* had to scramble to keep up.

At EFTS and SFTS, the trainees looked up to their instructors with respect and even awe. But once they got their wings, trainees lost their sense of the mystique of instructing. Most of them hoped to avoid going to FIS and instructing on Harvards and Ansons; as BCATP graduate Carl Puterbough explained (he later became a bomber pilot, completed thirty-six missions, and won a DFC): "I wanted to fly *real* airplanes."

However, no one listened when flyers asked not to be streamed into instructor school. When his CO congratulated him during his wings ceremony, Harvey Timberlake already knew he was being posted to Trenton and complained, "But what can you do as an instructor?" His CO reassured him that he'd be doing "a hell of a lot." Timberlake did indeed do a lot: as a service flying instructor he got twenty-eight full course pilots through to Wings Parade on single- and twin-engine aircraft and logged 1,650 hours, not one of them beyond the shores of Canada.

There were more dramatic ways of expressing dissatisfaction with air force policy and procedure. Some of Timberlake's colleagues vented their frustration by purposely wrecking aircraft. One RCAF fighter pilot claimed that the ticket out of instructing was insubordination—causing such trouble at a station by brawling or smashing up a barracks latrine or, worse, dating the CO's daughter.

Like Vines and Bradford, Bob Eaton had instructed at Windsor right from the beginning. He was a capable and selfless instructor; in 1940, while trying to pull a Fleet Finch out of an inverted spin, he made certain that his student bailed out to safety before he himself jumped. But he hated instructing, remembered colleague Gus

---

* Central Flying School (CFS) in Trenton made the BCATP instructors' training program official when the Flying Instructor School (FIS) was formed on August 3, 1942. Eventually, there were other FISs at Vulcan, Alberta, and Arnprior, Ontario.

Bennett, and "didn't hesitate to tell the chief flying instructor or the supervisory officer that he didn't like it, that he wasn't good for his pupils. The CO finally posted him out to Bombing and Gunnery School" to tow drogues (airborne targets) for air-gunnery practice. This dreary task was viewed by most pilots as a fate worse than death.

After graduation in 1941 from Dunnville, Cap Foster's star student Bill Olmstead joined the parade of disappointed wings graduates to Trenton to become an instructor. That autumn he went out west to No. 31 EFTS in De Winton, Alberta, to teach elementary students, but he felt that his potential on Spitfires was being wasted in the cockpit of a Tiger Moth trainer. He requested an interview with his station commander. When Olmstead finally got a few minutes with the station's chief flying instructor, he complained, only to be curtly informed that his pilot abilities were below average. "In front of [the CFI's] horrified eyes, I tore the instructor's certificate out of my logbook, destroyed it, and dropped the pieces on his desk." As punishment for his outburst, Olmstead was posted to No. 1 B&GS Jarvis, on the shores of Lake Erie, to fly bomb-aimers and air-gunners as they learned their trade.

To his credit, Olmstead turned the demotion into a positive experience. He flew every kind of aircraft he could get his hands on, improved his navigational skills, and accumulated valuable experience in the air. He later wrote that the flying knowledge he gained as an instructor, "may not have been appreciated at the time, but it later allowed me to fly [on ops] with never a glance at my cockpit instruments. Many more pilots would have survived had they gone through a similar learning experience."

Former RCAF instructor Bill Walker agreed. As a bomber pilot with No. 77 RAF Squadron, 4 Group, flying Halifax IIIs from Full Sutton, Yorkshire, in the latter stages of the war, Walker completed thirty-five operational flights and earned a DFC. When he was repatriated to Canada and discharged in 1945, he returned to civilian life and enjoyed a successful career as an actor and broadcaster (as the on-air spokesman for the Ford Motor Company). He admitted he might not have survived had it not been for the instructors' courses he grudgingly endured at Trenton and the year of instructing he put up with at No. 3 SFTS Calgary.

Walker got off to a rocky start in the air force. On his eighteenth birthday he enlisted in his home town of Regina, Saskatchewan, "figuring I'd be in uniform the next day," and was immediately sent on leave without pay. When he was finally called up, the following July, his boss at CKRM Radio in Regina was not pleased. Walker coped well at Manning Depot in Brandon and ITS back in Regina, but at No. 19 EFTS Virden, Manitoba, soloing on the Tiger Moth didn't come easily. Most LACs, including his good friend Vic Rouse, had soloed after eight hours, but Walker flew fifteen hours dual without going solo.

"They called Vic and me over to the officers' mess one night," Walker said. "We had a little comedy act called 'The Microphone Maniacs.' We did jokes and a couple of routines. One was an Indianapolis car race. Vic did the commentary and I did the sound effects of the cars. We made the cars different nationalities. The German car was [sound of a Bronx cheer]. Then we'd say, 'There's the Italian car going backwards as usual . . .' We had another routine about a German U-boat commander sinking the wrong ship. And that went over well. We thought we were hysterical.

"The officers were having a party that night, and Vic and I did our routine. It was a smash hit. The chief flying instructor, who was feeling pretty good, told us how wonderful we were. And he says, 'If you boys ever have any trouble with your flying, you come and see me.' And I said, 'Sir, I'm gonna see you right now.' I swear that night of entertaining resulted in my becoming a pilot and not a navigator."

Rouse and Walker entertained at No. 11 SFTS in Yorkton, Saskatchewan, too. They got their wings in March 1942 and received tele-grams informing them that they were commissioned pilot officers and would be posted overseas. They had two weeks' leave. But at the last minute, both of them were removed from the overseas draft and told they were going to Trenton to become instructors. As Walker said, "The first thing the air force told us was, 'If you try to fail this course, we'll send you somewhere you'll never be seen again, so you'd better take this course and be good boys.' So I did. I went to Trenton. Thank God I didn't go overseas then. I only had 180 hours. By the time I went overseas a year later, I had over a thousand hours and I knew something about flying."

Proof of the experience that Walker needed in the cockpit before "going overseas to save our country" came after his first category test at Trenton. The squadron leader wrote: "C average. Needs practice on aerobatics, approaches, and landings." Walker was flabbergasted. "What's left?" he wondered. "I was being sent out to be an instructor and I needed practice on aerobatics, approaches, and landings."

A posting to Trenton and not Britain may have been a disappointment and a blow to a military flyer's pride, but it had its perks. For most, a posting to Flying Instructor School meant a step up in the world. There was usually a commission attached and that meant an officer's uniform, a flat-top hat, being saluted, and getting billeted and fed in the officers' mess, where a batman made your bed and kept your shoes shined.

Pilot Officer John Evans, whose family members had pooled all their cash—eighty-five cents—on a spring day in 1931 so that he could take his first aeroplane ride with a barnstormer over the Niagara peninsula, will never forget his first payday at Trenton. "We were only paid once a month," Evans wrote. "At the end of February [1941] I stepped up to the paymaster, saluted, and received my first pay as an officer. He paid me in fifty-dollar bills. Three of them plus a twenty and a ten—$180. Wow! It was heady stuff.

"So far, the war had done nothing but provide me with marvellous opportunities. I had my first drink of hard liquor—a gin collins at one of the mess parties—met some fine fellows, who, like myself, were being groomed to teach flying, met some lovely local girls—and lost my virginity."

As part of their grooming, all instructor trainees at FIS were quickly introduced to the patter book. The small red cloth-covered book, about half an inch thick, became the instructor's constant companion. It covered every flying sequence a military flying instructor would need to teach—take-offs, landings, precautionary landings, aerobatics, the works. It was the instructor trainee's job to memorize it. It was a bit like studying a part in a play—learning the lines by heart and repeating them constantly. Once committed to memory, the patter could then take on what Pat McLean calls "your own personality." Long before he introduced his pre-flight cockpit blindfold test at No. 6 SFTS Dunnville, McLean remembered pacing back and forth in the Trenton hangars reciting aloud each sequence from the red patter book when he was a student instructor.

"On take-off, we pull the airplane onto the centre of the runway. We put the nose on a certain object at the end of the runway. We push the throttle on slowly. At the same time we're easing forward on the control stick. At a certain speed we ease the stick back. At this time we've pushed the throttle on full, and we climb . . ."

Reciting the sequences from the patter book verbatim, however, was not the real trick to instructing. What mattered was coordinating the patter with flying manoeuvres. Each time an FIS trainee went up with his instructor, the trainee had to "shoot patter" through the gosport tube as he flew the aircraft. He talked as he took off. He talked through straight and level flying. He pattered his way through aerobatics, instrument flying, and recovery from unusual positions. Everything he had learned at EFTS and SFTS he relearned at Trenton, explaining each step aloud as he went.

Pat McLean revelled in this new phase of flying. Learning the patter, experimenting with it, and giving it his own spin was a challenge. Others, such as Bill Walker and Hadley Armstrong, hated it. Armstrong had been so impressed by the derring-do of his EFTS instructor, Moss Burbidge, who had repaired his Tiger Moth trainer in flight, that he found routine instruction monotonous. "Getting up there and throwing out words, not really knowing what all the words meant," bored him. What did attract him about Trenton, however, was the variety of aircraft on the field—in particular a Northrop dive-bomber. His curiosity nearly killed him.

"They sent me off on a cross-country flight," Armstrong recalled. "I took a small deviation from my planned route to come to Port

Hope. My girlfriend was visiting her mother there at Trinity College School. I got up to about 10,000 feet. Here I was in a dive-bomber, even though nobody had told me much about dive-bombing, but I rolled over and went straight down.

"I guess I was doing about 340 or 350 mph, and I thought maybe I'd better start getting out of this. But there was no way I could pull it out—I was going too fast. And the lower I got to the ground the harder it was, until finally I stood on the pedals, pulled with both hands and my whole body, and started to come out of the dive. On the way down, bits and pieces kept flying off the airplane. Everybody on the football field thought I was disintegrating. They started to scatter like mad. I finally panned out [just above the field]. But then, right in front of me was the school bell tower. And here I was going at 350 mph. So I lifted a wing, missed the bell tower, and went out over Lake Ontario. I was one very happy young man."

In contrast to the boredom that Armstrong felt at Trenton, Joel Aldred took on the challenge of Central Flying School eagerly. Graduating at the head of his class at No. 2 SFTS Uplands in early 1941, Aldred was one of eleven posted to Trenton. He felt he would get his chance overseas one day, but until then he would be the best at whatever he did. In April, after two months of training at CFS, he already had a B Category rating and became a CFS instructor. Aldred still hoped to go on ops at some point, but the way he saw it, "to be kept at Central Flying School and to be part of the Air Training Plan, teaching students from all over the world, gave me a real sense of pride. If I did well and showed them how well I could perform, they might send me over."

A perfectionist, Aldred made a point of finding and memorizing the instruction manual for every aircraft on the Trenton flight line. A disciplinarian, he tolerated no clowning around in his ground school classes. A cautious flyer (something he had learned from his own elementary instructor at No. 2 EFTS Fort William, Ontario), Aldred would say to his students, "We want to keep the luck factor to a minimum. That means we're going to have the most knowledge we can, tucked away in our heads. And the more knowledge we have, the less likely we are to get into trouble."

After a year at Trenton, Flight Lieutenant Joel Aldred was assigned to travel the country as part of No. 2 Visiting Flight. Each Visiting Flight consisted of a handful of senior Trenton instructors who visited BCATP stations to maintain RCAF training standards. On Visiting Flight duty, Aldred tested and categorized instructors with the same directness and attention to detail he had shown at Trenton; but even Aldred's cautiousness couldn't have prepared him for the test he administered to an RAF student pilot in Lethbridge, Alberta, in 1942.

"He just couldn't seem to land airplanes," Aldred said. "We were flying a twin-engine Oxford at about 5,000 feet. I had put him under the hood to practise a little bit of single-engine flying. He didn't handle that very well. So we were headed back to the airport, when I had an attack of appendicitis at about 2,000 feet.

"I was sitting on the right side and didn't want him to know, but I could feel a cold sweat breaking out all over me. So I said to him, 'I just want you to carry on. I'm going to put my head down and pay no attention to you. You tell me when you're on your final approach.'

"Soon he said to me, 'Sir, I think I'm levelling out a little high.' I looked, and sure enough he was at about fifty feet. We would have gone in tail down. I took over and landed the airplane. I got out but couldn't walk from the airplane, so they carried me and took me to the Lethbridge Hospital. This kid was scared to death. He said afterwards, 'I'm really glad I didn't know you were sick.'"

Partly because of that experience, and partly because he travelled the country in No. 2 Visiting Flight, Aldred earned quite a reputation for himself. Norm Shrive, who had received his wings and gone to Trenton, remembered Aldred very well. When he was first posted as an instructor to No. 16 SFTS, Shrive was put through a check-out test by the tall, slim, red-headed Aldred, now squadron commander at Hagersville. As the two walked out on the flight line to an Anson, climbed in, and buckled up, Aldred announced in his resonant voice:

"You're very lucky, you know. You happen to be flying with the best goddam pilot on this station."

Aldred's wingmate in the formation filming for *Captains of the Clouds*, Charlie Konvalinka, explained that he and Aldred used to argue over which of them was the better pilot. Konvalinka remembers that "there was one instructor at Trenton who had a convertible. Each day, he'd drive over to the flight line from the mess. Aldred would sit up in the back of the car like visiting royalty and the minute the car came through the gate he'd shout out: 'Let the flying commence! Aldred is here!'"

The instructor staff at Trenton station had a marked American flavour by the middle of the war. Some FIS students had been recruited by the Clayton Knight Committee. Others, such as former barnstormer Maury Dillingham, had simply walked across the border at Niagara Falls because, as he said, "I wanted to fly bigger aircraft and I wanted to get into the war." Dillingham was not alone. Of his twenty-two classmates in the service course at Camp Borden in 1940, twenty were Americans. The two Canadians were immediately dubbed "the foreigners."

For Dillingham, Trenton was the thrill of a lifetime. There were trainer and operational aircraft of every shape and size and the most remarkable airfield he had ever seen—no control tower, no runways, just a big sod field, which in the wintertime "became like one big skating rink—you wouldn't believe it, but we weren't skidding all over. There was more traction on the ice than one might believe, and during the time I was there, we didn't have a single accident." He did have one near miss, however.

One winter day, Dillingham was instructing in a Fleet, when his student alerted him to the dwindling gas supply. When the engine cut out, Maury picked out an open area for a forced landing and (still giving his student the patter) brought the Finch down on a snow-covered field. Just as the Finch rolled to a stop, it hit a ditch buried in snow. The tail came up and the Finch nosed over completely. The mystery of the lost fuel was traced to a ground crewman, who had failed to recap the gas tank; during their aerobatic exercises, Dillingham and his student had inadvertently emptied their tank of all its fuel.

Six of Maury Dillingham's Camp Borden classmates were posted with him to Trenton's Central Flying School that same autumn. Among them was a stocky, broad-shouldered American flyer named Harold E. Dahl. Both Dillingham and Dahl had come to Canada with military training under their belts. During the Depression they both had enlisted in the United States Army Air Corps, Dillingham in air/ground photography, Dahl as a student pilot. But that's where the similarity of their experience ended. When the fair-haired Dahl, whom everyone knew as "Whitey," arrived in Canada in 1940 to enlist in the RCAF, he was already one of the most famous aviators of the era.

Dahl had enlisted in the USAAF in 1931 and trained at Randolph and Kelly Fields in Texas, beginning active duty in 1934. During the air mail emergency of 1934, when a strike shut down the American postal system, army pilots took over air mail flights. Second Lieutenant Dahl flew the first run of army-carried mail into Atlanta, Georgia. His conviction of a felony in 1936 forced him out of the army, but not out of flying. That year he ferried aircraft from California to Mexico for shipment to the Spanish Republicans, who were under attack from Franco's rebel Nationalist forces. Spain's civil war was an inviting testing ground for the world's military machinery and for a generation of fighter pilots eager to prove themselves and to taste glory in combat.

In December 1936, Whitey Dahl became a soldier of fortune. With signed contracts and immigration papers from the Spanish embassy in Mexico, Dahl (Hernando Diaz Evans on his Spanish passport) booked passage from Veracruz to France en route to Spain. On board ship with Whitey was his new bride (his second wife), Edith Rogers, a violinist and showgirl who was hoping to find work in France.

In Spain, Dahl and a handful of other American freelance pilots advanced quickly from bomber squadrons to fighters. They were assigned to La Escuadrilla (Squadron) La Calle and flight-checked on the Russian-built Polikarpov biplane (the Chato—Spanish for "snub nose") and the Polikarpov monoplane (the Mosca, or "fly"). Their commander, Andrés García La Calle, commented that Dahl was "more aggressive" than other American mercenaries. With good reason. Whitey's salary was $1,500 a month, with a $1,000 bonus for each Franco pilot he shot down. However, the Nationalist air force, flying German Messerschmitts and Italian Fiats, outnumbered and outgunned Whitey Dahl and the Republican flyers. And although he earned several bonuses, Whitey was also shot down twice, the second time over Nationalist-occupied territory. He was imprisoned at Salamanca in July 1937.

In October, Dahl was tried by a military court, found guilty of "rebellion against Franco's regime," and sentenced to death by firing squad. The international press was suddenly attracted to the American pilot's plight when Edith (who was living in Cannes) wrote a letter to General Franco himself, begging for clemency for her husband. She explained that Dahl had no political allegiance in the civil war and that he had merely joined the Republican air force because there was no work for pilots in America. She claimed, "We have been married only eight months. . . . He flew only to get money for me. . . . I was an actress for several years, but now I have found my happiness. Don't destroy it." A photograph of Edith in evening dress accompanied the letter.

Franco apparently replied that he would issue a reprieve; the return letter included the sign-off "*que besa sus pies*" (who kisses your feet). Dahl was spared from the firing squad, but he remained a captive in Spain until February 1940, nearly a year after Franco had secured victory over the Republicans. Meanwhile, Edith's career skyrocketed; she soon became known on the French nightclub circuit as "the woman who melted Franco's heart." In fact, Franco had never seen her letter, nor the picture, and had had nothing to do with Dahl's stay of execution. The Generalissimo's staff officers had handed the photograph around and, according to the New York *Daily News*, had passed judgement, written the response promising mercy, and attached the romantic closing.

When Dahl finally returned to America, everybody but Edith seemed eager to meet him. Walter Winchell interviewed him. Even Hollywood was keen; later that year, Paramount released *Arise, My Love*, an anti-isolationist comedy starring Ray Milland and Claudette Colbert, loosely based on the life and love of Whitey and Edith Dahl.* Meanwhile, Edith was too busy milking her newfound notoriety to care much about Whitey any more; in his turn he announced that their marriage in Mexico had been neither legal nor binding. He then made his way across the border to Canada to put his military flying talents back to work.

It took a number of attempts and several refusals for Dahl to get into the RCAF. Early in spring 1940, Dahl arrived at the home field of the London Flying Club in southwestern Ontario. It was just before the inauguration of the BCATP, when fuel rationing all but closed down civilian airfields. A young flying student named Florence Elliott was earning sixty dollars a month plus half an hour's flying time a week by working as the club's secretary. She remembered when this "gentleman from the South, with a lovely voice and courteous manners—something rare at the flying club," arrived to build up his hours for an instructor's licence.

Elliott was thrilled to meet an aviation hero. During spells of bad weather when flying was washed out, Dahl would sit and talk with her as she logged flying times, paid bills, and typed letters. Finally, Dahl's application to the RCAF was accepted and he went off to Camp Borden for service training on Yales in September 1940. That's when he met up with fellow American Maury Dillingham and with a Torontonian who had just earned his commercial pilot's licence. Roger Wilson remembered that "Whitey's skill as a pilot could not

---

* *Arise, My Love* was co-written by Benjamin Glazer and John S. Toldy, who won the Oscar for Best Original Story. When Glazer took the podium to accept the award, in February 1941, he informed the Academy guests assembled at the Biltmore Hotel in Los Angeles that his collaborator, John S. Toldy, was really a pseudonym for someone then in Nazi Germany; Glazer claimed he couldn't risk jeopardizing his partner's life by divulging his true identity. Toldy's real identity was never revealed.

be questioned at anytime. He was an extremely capable pilot. You could sense his professional demeanour right away. He was a knowledgeable and skilful pilot. . . . Yet he never boasted, but was rather modest about his flying exploits."

Wilson, Dahl, Dillingham, and three others were posted to Trenton's Central Flying School to become instructors in the BCATP. They learned their instructing patter in open-cockpit Fleet Finches, got twin-engine experience in Lockheed 10As, and logged night flights in Harvards. Finally, all three were posted to instruct in Ansons at No. 8 SFTS Moncton, New Brunswick. Wilson remembers Dahl's fun-loving nature—leading expeditions to Cape Tormentine for oysters on his day off; dodging station rules to bring young women onto station property; or taking unauthorized personnel, such as erks (ground crew), up for rides. But what struck Wilson as odd was that "the air force didn't really use Whitey's combat experience to best advantage in the training plan. They needed pilots who could be taught to teach other pilots. And that's what they did with us. His operational skills were never used."

After Moncton, the air force split up the original Camp Borden group. Roger Wilson went to conversion training at Picton, Ontario, and then on to operations, flying Spitfires with No. 421 Squadron from Kenley and Tangmere. Maury Dillingham was repatriated to the United States in 1942 and eventually flew B-17s, leading No. 547 Squadron of the 384th Bomb Group until he was shot down in December 1943. He spent eighteen months in a German POW camp.

Meanwhile, Whitey Dahl was transferred back to Trenton and an unexpected twist in his life.

Soon after his posting back to Central Flying School, he met Eleanor Bone, daughter of former Belleville mayor Jamieson Bone. The Bone family spent their summers at a cottage on the Bay of Quinte on Lake Ontario. Eleanor and her sister frequented the tennis courts at an adjoining country club. On an early summer day in 1941, the two met a number of young men and women in the clubhouse and invited the group back to the cottage for a swim. Eleanor introduced herself to one of the young men and asked his name.

"Dahl," he said, "D-a-h-l."

Eleanor thought a moment and remembered the newspaper stories she'd read. "You were in the Spanish civil war. Your wife sent her photograph to Franco," she began.

"She wasn't my wife," Dahl said.

He told her that he was now an instructor at the nearby Trenton air force station. As they talked, she realized that his time in Salamanca had taken its toll physically, but that in spite of it all he had a wonderful sense of humour. Eleanor taught him how to play tennis. He invited her out to dine and dance. He sent her roses.

"One of the ways he used to court me," Eleanor admitted, "was by doing aerobatics over the cottage. I'd go out and watch while he took all the leaves off the tree tops. He would do slow rolls and he'd take the thing straight up as far as it would go and then bunt the aircraft. He didn't know it, but his commanding officer, Joe Stephenson, lived in a nearby cottage. Joe gave him hell for using His Majesty's fuel and airplanes to show off, but he also said, 'I've never seen aerobatics like it in my life.'"

On July 26, 1941, six weeks after their first meeting on the Bay of Quinte, Whitey Dahl married Eleanor Bone at St. Andrew's Church in Belleville. Like many married instructors at Trenton, they lived off the station. Dahl put in long days, instructing from early morning till late at night. Sometimes Eleanor would drive to nearby Mountain View airfield to watch her husband and the other American instructors (nicknamed "the Royal Texas Air Force") teach trainees how to instruct night flying.

By all accounts Whitey Dahl was a superb pilot instructor who never had a student wash out. He offered his students and his colleagues at Trenton something few instructors had—accounts of actual aerial combat. He could draw on his operational experience in Spain to show, not just tell, his students about dogfighting, dive-bombing, and strafing. Whitey had bombed gunpowder factories on the Jarama River, strafed troops on the road to Madrid, and engaged German fighter pilots in the air over the Battle of Brunete.

Like Joel Aldred, Whitey Dahl became part of a Visiting Flight, travelling the country categorizing instructors, administering check-out tests, and helping to maintain a high level of instruction in the BCATP. Still, the frustration of being sidetracked into an instructing career when there was an air war in Europe began to eat at his pride. Long before December 7, 1941, he grew impatient with Roosevelt's reluctance to enter the war. By now he was thirty-two and not considered in his prime for operational duty. He was also upset by the death of one of his students.

As she became more acquainted with the BCATP instructor's life, Eleanor grew more fearful that a student pilot would one day freeze at the controls and Dahl would "die in a flaming crash. I'd hear the sirens in the distance at the station and worry. Then Whitey would come home and say, 'We lost another one.' Sometimes he'd scream out at night in his nightmares. Then one night, one of his best students took off and flew right into a bunch of trees and was killed. He had to call on the family and tell his wife. He was really shaken over that. I don't think people realize the contribution those men made in the flying training program."

Whitey Dahl eventually left instructing. Soon after the United States came into the war, he joined Atfero, the Atlantic Ferry Organization (later Ferry Command), ferrying Baltimores and Dakotas from Belém, Brazil, across the south Atlantic to Ascension Island and on to Egypt. He never flew in combat again. At the war's end he was court-martialled by the RCAF for allegedly selling parts from air force aircraft in South America. In 1956, Whitey was killed in an Arctic plane crash. He had logged some 12,000 hours in the air, many of them instructing.

Whitey Dahl wasn't the only American celebrity to come to Trenton during the war. For morale-boosting purposes the station invited singer Kate Smith, who put on a show there in June 1942. On Halloween night that year it was radio star Jean Dickenson's turn. By far the most heralded American visitors, however, were the 100 members of the United States Army Air Force Band. According to the editor of *Contact* magazine at the time, Flight Sergeant Bill Sargent, on May 9, 1944, five DC-3s set down at Trenton on a "mission to promote goodwill and comradeship between the U.S. and Canada." Within its ranks the band had former members of the New York and Philadelphia symphony orchestras, as well as big band musicians who had performed with Glenn Miller, the Dorsey Brothers, and Charlie Spivak. The USAAF Band performed three times that day—at the Sports Hangar in the afternoon, at No. 6 Repair Depot at five o'clock, and at a Victory Dance for 2,500 spectators in the Sports Hangar that evening.

Some of the best musical performances Trenton air crew ever heard, however, were unscheduled ones. In December 1941, Ross Truemner, with his pilot officer's ring newly sewn on his sleeve, arrived at Trenton to become an instructor. Truemner brought his saxophone with him; he had taught himself to play when he was fifteen and had organized his own Blue Baron band, which played dates in southern Ontario in the 1930s. Occasionally at Trenton he would pull out his sax at a bar or play duets with a fellow instructor trainee, Jack Creeper. At one of those impromptu evening jam sessions in the station library, a tall, handsome pilot, with perfectly parted blond hair, appeared in the doorway.

"Hey, Truemner, can I borrow your sax?" he asked. It was another CFS instructor trainee, a fellow by the name of Buff Estes. Truemner had gone up with Estes when the two of them were brushing up on their patter in a Cessna Crane earlier that month.

"Sure," replied Truemner as he passed the sax to Estes. When Estes started to play, a crowd gathered to listen. Estes complemented Creeper's piano playing beautifully. They harmonized and passed solos back and forth.

When Estes finally took a break, Truemner said, "You know, what you're playing sounds an awful lot like a counter melody I used to hear Benny Goodman play on the radio."

"It should," said Buff off-handedly. "I played with Benny for a couple of years."

Born in 1918 in Missouri, Sterling Buford Estes took up the alto saxophone when he was five years old. By the time he was fourteen, he had toured the United States twice as sax soloist. Orchestra leader Lawrence Welk discovered Estes and hired him; but good musicians' reputations travel fast and Benny Goodman soon attracted Estes and hired him on his seventeenth birthday. Performing as Benny's third alto, Estes took the time to memorize every solo Benny played on clarinet. Goodman must have acknowledged the young sax player's talents, because he allowed Estes to front for him occasionally when he wasn't up to it himself. Estes left the band in 1940 when Goodman's recurring back troubles forced him to lay off his musicians temporarily. Somewhere along the way, between musical engagements, Buff Estes also learned to fly, and by 1941 he had crossed the border to become an instructor at Trenton.

Several air force bandsmen who had been posted to Trenton recalled the energy that Buff Estes imparted to the station's musical functions. From the moment he had enlisted, Bill McCauley's skill as a trombone player had kept him out of the cockpit and serving his country in various RCAF bands. Finally, in 1943, he was trained for air crew duties and posted to Trenton to become an instructor. McCauley enjoyed rehearsing in the station's fourteen-piece band under Estes's leadership; he remembered that Estes played "those Benny Goodman solos so well, he could do them in his sleep."

In the sax section was Bill Hill, another RCAF journeyman musician. As a teenager, Hill had supplemented his factory wages by playing his sax in a dance band twice a week. In 1939 he enrolled at the Boston Conservatory of Music and moonlighted with pianist Sabby Lewis's orchestra, along with Tote Tanner (formerly in the band of Earl Fatha Hines) and vocalist Marie Hawkins, who later married Nat King Cole.* When he came home to Waterloo, Ontario, for the

---

* Bill Hill was one of the few white musicians in Boston's black musicians' union. In fact, when a theatre manager in Barre, Vermont, realized that Sabby Lewis had two "fayes" (white musicians) in his band, Hill was forced to colour his face black three times a day when the band performed.

summer, Hill enlisted in the RCAF and found himself posted as an air force bandsman to Ottawa and then Trenton, "where I felt most fortunate to be on the same bandstand with Buff Estes. He never stopped practising. He'd call a one o'clock rehearsal every Thursday, but we'd arrive there and Estes would have been there since noon, blowing his heart out."

Buff Estes was as passionate about flying as he was about playing sax. Students claimed he was "methodical"—"a perfectionist" with an "exacting" manner in the cockpit. Gus Bennett (who was originally a civilian instructor at No. 7 EFTS Windsor, but later got his RCAF wings and was posted to Trenton FIS) remembered Estes as "a good pilot, a good party man, a good drinker, a good musician, so therefore a good air force type." No matter how good an air force type Buff Estes was, however, there would be no overseas posting for him.

Complaints about the frustration of being stuck in an instructing job were common. "The courses usually arrived on a Sunday evening," Russ Bannock explained, "and you would hear a lot of grumbling going on. Trenton was considered a prestige posting, but these fellows had their hearts set on going on operations and flying combat aircraft. Out of a class of fifty wings graduates, the top ten usually went to instructor school. They had the qualifications—the personality, temperament, and communication skills.

"Some made it quite clear that they didn't want to do it and everything that we tried to teach them they would ham up intentionally. But we made it equally clear that if they didn't make the grade, they weren't going overseas on ops, but would be posted as staff pilots to bombing and gunnery schools to tow drogues with people shooting at them."

Civilian instructor Al Stirton was also pretty frustrated. He had taken the initiative in 1938 to invest $150 at the Moose Jaw Flying Club to get his pilot's licence and had made the commitment to King and country by answering a telegram from the minister of national defence to enlist in 1939. He had succeeded in getting scores of novice military pilots off the ground in Fleet Finch trainer aircraft and safely back down. He had coaxed them to solo and advanced them to service training school and beyond. Yet two years later, he was still at the same job at No. 9 EFTS St. Catharines, still instructing a new course of recruits every eight weeks, still waiting for a chance to go on ops.

"About September 1942," Stirton recalled, "a notice was posted that any civilian instructors who wished to remuster back into the air force could do so and would receive their SFTS training and RCAF wings with a posting of their choice. Three of us put our names down immediately. We left the next day with no farewell ceremony, no handshakes or thanks from the higher-ups, not even a goodbye, go to hell, or anything.

"We were sent off to Lachine, Quebec, for a four-week course in drill and air force rules and regulations. We were issued RCAF sergeants' uniforms, no wings, and took the regular drill and marching that we had missed two years earlier. We had ITS ground school with Morse code, Aldis lamp, and flag signals. We received the same treatment the new recruits received with no recognition of our years of service."

Among the remusters at Lachine was Banty Pallett, one of the original twelve instructors at No. 9 EFTS St. Catharines. He'd had his fill of schooling, both as a student at Barker Field getting his commercial licence in 1938 and as a civilian instructor helping the first entrants to the BCATP get over the fear of soloing, spinning, and night flying. Now in 1942, he was being treated like a rookie again.

One day, he was sitting at the back of a classroom listening to an RCAF ground school instructor pontificate about the importance of compensating for engine torque and the gyroscopic effect as the tail of the airplane rises on take-off. Banty decided he'd had enough.

"Bullshit!" he said loudly.

Silence in the room.

"You just tell them to look at the shit house on the horizon," Banty continued. "Keep your feet moving. Keep the nose of the airplane on the shit house. Keep it straight. And they'll be fine."

Next day there was a sign on the daily routine orders bulletin board: "Ex-Elementary Instructors need not attend Ground School."

Pallett never did get posted on ops even though he was allowed to skip ITS ground school. He had to go through regular SFTS training at Dunnville, then he was shipped off to Flight Instructor School at No. 3 FIS Arnprior, then he was sent back to EFTS instructing at St. Catharines and Oshawa until the end of 1944, when he was discharged.

Al Stirton considered himself more fortunate. He had to put in another year of training at Dunnville to get his wings and at Charlottetown, P.E.I., learning astro-navigation, but then he got his overseas posting to fly Sunderland flying boats on anti-submarine patrols with No. 423 RCAF Squadron in Northern Ireland. In 1945 the RCAF discharged him a week before he was due to receive a promotion to squadron leader.

Success at getting a posting away from EFTS or CFS or a Visiting Flight was not necessarily a ticket overseas. The same year of Frank Vines's and Brick Bradford's performance over Jackson Park in Windsor, one of their colleagues, Gus Bennett, got his release from No. 7 EFTS Windsor. He was the first civilian EFTS instructor from Windsor to go through for his RCAF wings.

After graduation in June 1943 from No. 6 SFTS Dunnville, Bennett instructed for a year at FIS and then his posting to a Transport Command training course came through. As soon as he had completed that he was asked to instruct in Transport Command—first at Rockcliffe, then at Moncton, and finally at No. 34 Operational Training Unit, Pennfield Ridge, New Brunswick. Even when he got overseas, his lengthy and spotless instructor's record plagued him. Shortly after VE Day, when Bennett was flying supply aircraft into Europe with No. 435 Transport Squadron, his wing commander approached him.

"Flight Lieutenant Bennett, I'd like to know if you'd do some instructing for us."

"Sir, I'd just like to stay with my squadron," Bennett replied.

"You sure?"

"I've been instructing most of my career," Bennett explained. "I'd like to stay."

Two weeks later, Bennett was posted to London as a training officer with No. 120 Transport Wing and was given the job of organizing an airline training scheme for aircraft and pilots throughout England and the continent. "I never did get out of instructing," Bennett said regretfully.

A number of RCAF air crew also got trapped in instructing. John Bigham spent most of the war instructing wireless courses. The air force shuffled him through half a dozen stations between Ontario and the Atlantic coast. It wasn't until he was back at Manning Depot for his discharge at the end of the war that he discovered why he had never been rewarded with an overseas posting. The records stated: "This man is considered too valuable as an instructor to send overseas."

Six months into his instructing career at No. 16 SFTS Hagersville, Norm Shrive presented his case for an overseas posting to his commanding officer; the CO listened, but told him, "You forget one thing. All you instructors forget it. You've been here six months. I have good reports on you. You're a good instructor. And we need good instructors. Come back in another six months." Condemned by praise. Good instructors were sentenced to fight the war on the home front.

Rusty Rutherford suffered the same sort of fate. Recruited in 1940 as "officer material" in Toronto, he had been sent to the new navigation school in the rural Manitoba community of Rivers. He didn't stay there long. The air force needed qualified navigators overseas (Rutherford felt sure that's where he was headed) and the BCATP needed qualified navigation instructors even more desperately than it needed navigators on ops. But what really hurried him on his way was that "a polio epidemic had broken out in Manitoba and they were going to close the Manitoba border, so the air force got us the hell out of the province two days early.

"I never graduated. I was suddenly a navigation instructor. I was sent down to No. 9 AOS St.-Jean, Quebec, where I was immediately put in charge of a class of about twenty sergeant airmen to be trained as navigators. I just started teaching them what I knew about navigation." His success as an instructor sealed his fate until he escaped to Transport Command by pouncing on a vacancy he spotted at No. 6

OTU Comox, on Vancouver Island. Along the way—teaching basic navigation to ITS students and troubleshooting at several air observer schools—Rutherford got "stuck in instructing." He became indispensable. And because of it, there were times he detested the very idea of sharing his knowledge with student navigators.

In May 1942, what Rutherford had once called the "boondock" at Rivers, Manitoba, was rechristened Central Navigation School. Alterations to the BCATP and the composition of bomber crews meant the phasing out of the air observer category and the emergence of highly trained navigators. What Air Ministry officials in Britain and RCAF authorities in Canada rarely admitted was that during the first Bomber Command push in 1941 and 1942, Allied bombers were not hitting their marks. Despite the claims by most returning crews that they had obliterated the targets, aerial photography showed otherwise. As Air Marshal Arthur Harris explained, "The navigator had more than enough to do . . . to get the aircraft within a few miles of the target, especially when making the run-up. . . . Apart from all the other difficulties . . . the work he had done as a navigator left him no time to get his eyes conditioned to the darkness, which he would have to do before trying to spot the aiming point." This was the rationale for the creation of the new crew member—the bomb-aimer—and the retraining of the former air observer into a full-time navigator, unencumbered by other duties.

No. 1 Central Navigation School took on this task. Once again, the cream of the crop of CNS graduates were held back from operational postings and sent to swell the ranks of the BCATP corps of instructors. As Pilot Officer Jack Kelshall described it, "the very unpleasant truth . . . is that instead of finding opportunities to perform glorious feats of arms and heroic deeds, you will find instead a tremendous amount of dreary, monotonous, boring work."

The son of a solicitor and member of the Trinidad Legislative Council, Kelshall had gone to school in Port-of-Spain and trained as a solicitor. When war broke out he travelled to Canada, enlisted in the RCAF, and received his wings at No. 6 SFTS Dunnville. However, his strengths as an instrument and cross-country flyer channelled him into navigation instruction. By the middle of the war, he had become both a leading instructor and a leader of men. His ground school lectures on navigation syllabus were succinct and articulate; his lectures about morale and duty were inspiring. They showed his students not only what they were doing but why they were doing it. At a course completion that year, Jack delivered the graduation speech. Most of his audience was not going overseas to fight but was staying in Canada to instruct.

"In one of the instructor's courses here recently," Kelshall explained, "one of the students showed himself to be a most able and intelligent lad. He got excellent marks all through . . . and was gifted with the ability to express himself. Obviously a man well fitted to instruct. On graduation, he was asked to assume the duties of an instructor here at No. 1 CNS. He refused. He went so far as to say that if he was posted here he would refuse to lecture. His reason? Rivers was too isolated. He wanted to be posted to a service school near a big city. Less work, easier access to pretty girls, dances, parties, bars. Since it would have been useless to post him to as important a job as that of an instructor at CNS against his will, he succeeded in having his way. His was a glaring example of the type of attitude which is losing this war for us.

"On those of you who are going to become instructors, a tremendous responsibility rests. This is because the extreme importance of the job you are to do is inversely proportional to the inducements and encouragements which will help you to do it thoroughly. You must realize the importance of the work. The success of the war rests directly on the fighting efficiency and mental attitude of the men in our services . . .

"If you make the effort to arouse in each of the boys you will have in your charge the determination to do his level best, the conviction that no sacrifice is too great—if you see that each one of them gets the very best training that it is in your power to give—then you are fighting against the Reich in the most powerful and the most effective way there is . . .

"The difference between an operational flyer and an instructor can be the equivalent to that between a single rifleman and a Bren gunner—if the instructor makes it so. The operational flyer can fight with only his own brain, his own hands. The instructor can fight with the brains and hands of all the hundreds he influences and teaches. To do so, however, needs a tremendous expenditure of energy—a tremendous driving power.

"In your work as instructors you will have none of the excitement of combat, you will have no hope or expectation of pretty little ribbons to pin under your wings. You will have no bright prospect of quick promotion or triumphal tours through Hollywood and New York. Nobody is ever going to throw ticker tape on you. The unswerving driving energy needed to do a good job as an instructor must come from within you yourselves . . .

"It is not easy. It is not attractive. But, gentlemen, if you do a good job of instructing, the reward, though not material in nature, is very great. It lies in the knowledge that in this the greatest and most critical conflict in the history of the world between the forces of right and wrong, you have been entrusted with a difficult and important job . . . that you have been worthy of the trust . . . and that you have done your part to the limit of your ability. It is worth it, gentlemen. Good luck to you all."

10

TO THE EDGE OF THE WORLD

At three o'clock on the morning of August 19, 1942, the 179 landing craft of an amphibious attack force, code-named Jubilee, plied their way southward through the lightly swelling seas of the English Channel. The night was starry and peaceful. In the darkness ahead of them lay the pebbled beaches of Dieppe, a town on the north coast of France. Aboard the craft were members of six Canadian regiments, about 5,000 men, preparing for their first experience of combat. The "reconnaissance in force" raid on Dieppe was designed to test the defences of Hitler's occupying forces and the ability of the Allies to launch a large-scale invasion against his *Festung Europa* (Fortress Europe).

The Dieppe raid was also launched to ease political tensions among the Allies. President Roosevelt and his chiefs of staff—just eight months into the American involvement in the war—wanted an action against French soil to relieve German pressure on the Russians. Prime Minister Churchill and his Cabinet Defence Committee discussed the need for another surprise raid like Operation Chariot, which had destroyed the Normandie Dock at St.-Nazaire in June 1942. And Prime Minister Mackenzie King felt pressure from his own Department of National Defence to "have our army put into action somewhere at once."

Dieppe was a disaster. In the hours that followed the first landings just before dawn, only the battle-hardened British commandos (assisting the main assault) achieved their objective—knocking out German artillery batteries near Varengeville and Berneval. Elsewhere, troops of the 2nd Canadian Infantry Division landed on the Dieppe esplanade at Puys and Pourville, but met such stiff resistance that none of their objectives was achieved. About 600 defending German soldiers were killed. More than 900 Canadian soldiers died and 1,300 were taken prisoner; their war had lasted only nine hours.

In accounts of the Dieppe fiasco, little, if any, attention has been paid to the fighting that took place over the heads of the doomed amphibious assault. Three-quarters of an hour before dawn, hundreds of fighter aircraft assembled on the airfields that had become famous during the Battle of Britain. At Biggin Hill, Tangmere, Hornchurch, Kenley, Duxford, and Debden in the south of England, fighter pilots of the RAF, the Royal New Zealand Air Force, the United States Army Air Force, and the Royal Canadian Air Force took off into the pre-dawn sky. This would be Fighter Command's first opportunity since the Battle of Britain in 1940 to meet the Luftwaffe in strength on their side of the Channel. The pilots' orders were to provide air cover for Operation Jubilee at Dieppe; but as Air Vice-Marshal Trafford Leigh-Mallory later reported, "There, in fact, developed one of the greatest air battles of the war."

Allied commanders had about 800 aircraft at their disposal. The Luftwaffe could muster only 360 from across northern France. Six RCAF fighter and two army cooperation squadrons joined the attack, providing air cover (strafing German gun positions, laying smoke screens, and engaging German fighters), escorting bomber formations, and conducting reconnaissance over the approaches to the battle zone.

Scores of BCATP graduates took part. Dick Reeves, a graduate of No. 12 SFTS Brandon, attacked a shoreline lighthouse being used as an observation post for German artillery. Identical twins Bruce and Douglas Warren, who had received their wings at No. 34 SFTS Medicine Hat in 1941, flew together over Dieppe; as members of the same flight of Spitfires in No. 165 RAF Squadron they kept tabs on each other by whistling over the radio. Torontonian Don Morrison, who had earned his wings at No. 10 SFTS Dauphin, flew two sorties in a Spitfire with No. 401 RCAF Squadron over Dieppe—one escorting B-17s on a bombing mission to Abbeville, the second against Focke-Wulf 190s over the beaches. As a flight commander with No. 416 RCAF Squadron, Lloyd Chadburn, who had graduated from No. 2 SFTS Uplands, helped down three 190s and four Junker 88s. Meanwhile, a former instructor from Uplands, George Hill, flew four sorties that day with No. 403 RCAF Squadron, destroying one 190 and damaging another.

The air battle intensified so quickly that the Luftwaffe was forced to call up aircraft reinforcements from stations across occupied France, Holland, and Belgium. As the futile beach attack continued into daylight, CBC Radio war correspondent Bob Bowman looked up from his position aboard a tank landing craft and recorded that "planes were coming out of the skies like leaves tumbling down in autumn."

British Air Ministry officials recorded ninety-one German aircraft destroyed. Of those, the RCAF claimed ten enemy aircraft destroyed, four probables, and twenty-two damaged, while its losses were put at thirteen aircraft and ten pilots.

One group of fighter pilots is credited with more than its share of scores against the Luftwaffe over Dieppe. The graduates of Little Norway—flying as two Royal Norwegian Air Force squadrons in the RAF—downed sixteen German aircraft. Making up just 5 percent of Allied air strength in the fight, the Norwegian graduates of the BCATP in Canada inflicted 15 percent of the losses sustained by the Luftwaffe that day.

The night before the Dieppe raid, Jim Askew, a young Aircraftman 2nd Class, arrived at a holding unit in Brighton, on the south coast of England. Recently dispatched from the Air Crew Reception Centre at Regents Park in North London, Askew had been waiting for a posting to Initial Training Wing (the equivalent of Initial Training School in Canada). However, on August 12, he and a number of other RAF cadets were sent to Brighton to take a crash course in Morse code. On the evening of August 18, he was awake, working to increase his code sending and receiving speed up to four words a minute. At about five o'clock, "for reasons not explained to us, we were confined to barracks. As we were billeted in the Hotel Metropole with a room overlooking the sea, we all had a clear view of the Channel and of the many boats" heading towards the French coast and the Dieppe raid.

Like the Canadians making their way across the Channel that night, Jim Askew had been itching to get into the action since 1939. Born during the First World War (just before his father went off to fight with the British Expeditionary Force in France, where he won the Military Medal), Askew grew up in a military atmosphere, where his father "brought up [my brother and me] as if we were on parade at all times." On his eighteenth birthday, he announced his intention of joining the army. His mother would have none of it, so he took a job as a draughtsman with Plessey Co. instead, where he fell in love with flying.

"In January 1939," Askew recalled, "I accompanied my superior, George Da Costa, to Hornchurch Aerodrome to install a self-starter in a Spitfire. Up until then, all aircraft were started by swinging the prop, but of course this consumed valuable time, which might mean the difference between life and death in war. So a number of engineers had been working on the problem; one was George Da Costa. . . . I was thrilled to take part in this installation.

"When we arrived at the aircraft, there were two pilots to assist in starting. They introduced themselves as Flight Lieutenant Peter Townsend and Flying Officer Bob Stanford-Tuck [both were later to become well-known aces during the Battle of Britain]. . . . It was at that moment that I decided I should be a pilot . . . and in May 1939 I went along to the [Royal Air Force] recruiting office in Romford."

It took two years of repeated applications and persistence on his part, but the RAF finally called up Jim Askew and made him an AC2. After his stint at the holding unit at Brighton in August 1942, he was sent to air crew camp at Ludlow in September, to ITW in October, and to EFTS training at Desford, where he soloed in a Tiger Moth in February 1943. Eventually he went to the air crew holding unit at Heaton Park for selection, and finally to Liverpool harbour and embarkation aboard the *Nieuw Amsterdam*, where he was "herded into lower decks . . . and allocated a hammock . . .

"Sometime during the night she slipped anchor and quietly left. . . . From the day we left Liverpool we saw nothing, not a ship or aircraft for the whole six days, until, on the morning of the sixth day, a Sunderland came out to greet us. That afternoon we slipped into the harbour at Halifax, Nova Scotia, Canada."

Askew's knowledge of Canada was limited to Niagara Falls, Nelson Eddy, and Jeanette MacDonald. He knew nothing about the IODE, Colonist cars, or prairie winters. But during his first weeks in Canada, each would play a part in his new career in a new country. After a brief stay at Moncton in early 1943, Askew and seventy of his RAF mates were ordered to pack up, issued with blankets, and loaded aboard trains of Colonist cars. In the 1880s, these cars with their wooden-slatted seats, pull-down bunks, and wood-burning kitchen stoves had been used to transport immigrants to the Canadian west. In the cold winter weather, the blankets were indispensable. Ladies from local IODE chapters provided hot coffee and food when the shivering cadets temporarily detrained at Montreal, Sudbury, and Winnipeg.

Five days of rattling around inside the train, without showers and with three men squashed into a space intended for one person to sleep, tested the mettle of the cadets. But the food—bacon and eggs, white bread, and pitchers of fresh milk—made some feel "guilty of betraying our families back in tighten-your-belts Britain."

At the end of the line was Caron, a small farming community two CPR stops west of Moose Jaw, Saskatchewan. Its tiny airfield and No. 33 EFTS station would be the RAF students' first home away from home in Canada.

Another RAF cadet who had left Britain and travelled to Caron earlier that winter was Doug Lomas. Because he had his sergeant's stripes, Lomas was charged with the responsibility of ensuring that of 120 RAF cadets loaded aboard the train in Moncton, sixty were dropped off at No. 26 EFTS Neepawa, Manitoba, and the other sixty at Caron. Fortunately for Lomas's air force career, "we didn't lose anybody. I sent a cable home to Britain; when my mother read it, instead of Caron, it read Karam, and the only Karam in the world was in Russia!

"We thought we had dropped off the edge of the world. Caron is right in the middle of the prairie. There was one little hut with a pot-bellied stove and one railwayman there. It wasn't big enough for sixty guys. And it was cold. I went in and asked, 'Where's the airport?' The railwayman said, 'It's a few miles up the road. They know you're coming, don't worry. They'll send a couple of coaches.' So we sat around for a couple of hours; then they finally took us into camp. It was two o'clock in the morning by the time we finally got into barracks. I wondered what the hell I'd let myself in for."

RAF cadet Michael Foster, who had arrived in Halifax aboard the Dutch ship *Volendam* the previous winter, recalled his first impressions of Caron as "three grain elevators and a Chinese laundry alongside the CPR, but precious little else. Weather was the chief enemy. Forty and fifty degrees below zero temperatures were recorded. Flying was cancelled only when a student pilot in the uncovered rear cockpit [of a Tiger Moth] came down with the tell-tale white [frostbitten] tips to his ears or nose. By April, they had provided cockpit covers for all Tiger Moths. At first, only the instructors in the front cockpit were protected."

LAC Askew survived the cold his first winter at Caron. It was the spring environment that took him by surprise. One of the few pastimes enjoyed by British trainees on the prairies was a game of European football, or soccer. With so many BCATP schools being created for the RAF across Manitoba, Saskatchewan, and Alberta in 1942, inter-school matches began. At one of these impromptu games, Jim Askew encountered a gopher hole and wrenched his knee, tearing his cartilage and forcing him to give up flying for six weeks. Still, he trained in Caron's Cornells long enough that his instructor, RAF Flying Officer Kelly, reported: "You have sometimes some difficulty in getting a point, but when you've got it, you really have it. . . . You seem to have the patience to stick it out . . . I think you would be a good instructor . . . you would give your pupils a chance."

Jim Askew lived up to Kelly's expectations. His knee mended sufficiently to allow him to join the military marching contingent in that year's Calgary Stampede parade. Later that July he was "hurled into the sky" in his first Harvard at No. 37 SFTS Calgary and by November 1943 he had passed his wings test, been issued a white arm band (signifying his officer's commission), and been dispatched to Trenton to become an RAF instructor in the BCATP.

It wasn't until he had been posted to No. 31 SFTS Kingston (a service flying training school for British Fleet Air Arm students) and had met his first student that he realized he was no longer a student himself. Until then, as a student, Askew had been able to rely on an instructor to watch over his take-offs, help him recover from spins, or correct his mistakes while instrument flying. Now he, Pilot Officer Jim Askew, had to be the reliable one. He would have to judge how far he could let a student go before taking control and correcting a mistake. He was responsible for another man's life.

"As I sat down at a table across from Acting Leading Airman McLeod on the morning of February 3, 1944," Askew said, "I don't know who was more scared, him or me. He was the first pupil I'd had. Fortunately, he did not know this. We talked of a number of things: why and when he decided to fly . . . where he had trained . . . I tried to get to know him and to give him some idea of what kind of person I was.

"When I discovered he was nineteen, it shook me to realize that I was an old man of twenty-six. He was still a boy. . . . We spent an hour and fifteen minutes in the air. I demonstrated what this [Harvard] aeroplane could do, without making him uncomfortable or sick. This is the pattern I followed . . . I was as patient as I possibly could be." He was living up to Flying Officer Kelly's prediction that he would give his pupils a chance.

The last thing in the world that John Campsie wanted was to become a flying instructor. Throughout his service training at No. 33 SFTS

Carberry, Manitoba, his course of about sixty RAF cadets had been told that those who graduated with the highest marks could have the first choice of available postings—whether fighter, bomber, or coastal duty. That knowledge had been a wonderful incentive to work hard and score well in flying and ground school study. However, even though Campsie graduated near the top of his class, and received his wings and his commission as a pilot officer, he was promptly sent on instructor training.

Like Jim Askew's, Campsie's family had a strong connection with the armed forces. His father had been a second lieutenant in the Black Watch during the First World War and had won the Military Cross on the Somme. After the war, Alexander Campsie completed his theological training, became a naval chaplain, and was sent to Malta as Church of Scotland chaplain to the Mediterranean fleet. John was born there, in Valletta. Malta was alive with RAF and Fleet Air Arm aircraft in the 1920s. It was a perfect place for the chaplain's son to watch flying displays of Bristol Bulldogs, or to watch Fairey Swordfish ("Stringbags") take off from the Royal Navy carriers *Hermes*, *Eagle*, and *Courageous*.

The family returned to England in the 1930s, and John Campsie was studying classics at Oxford University when the war broke out. Oxford had a combined army, navy, and air force recruiting office. He went into each office in turn. The navy told him to come back Tuesday. The army didn't seem to be in any hurry either. The air force signed him up right away, although he wasn't called up until summer 1941.

He was first posted to a holding area at St. John's Wood in London, and then to Initial Training Wing at Scarborough, where he studied navigation, armaments, wireless telegraphy, and aircraft recognition and endured constant parade drilling.

It was the beginning of 1942 before he did his first elementary flying in Miles Magisters, soloing after about eight hours. On one of his first flights, LAC Campsie was also given his first taste of aerobatics, from "a Polish pilot who had been in the Battle of Britain. They were just giving him a rest as an instructor. Of course, he was bored silly by instructing. He was one of these chaps who was never happy flying straight and level. In the course of the lesson, while demonstrating recovery from spins, he decided to spin down through a cloud. I suppose he knew where the ground was. I certainly didn't. When we came out of the dive, we were fifty feet above a golf course. I suppose he liked scaring pupils. He scared me."

Campsie was sent to Canada aboard the Polish troopship *Batory* in spring 1942. His course of BCATP students travelled west by rail during the early prairie summer, when "the heat made it necessary to keep the windows of the coaches open for ventilation, with the result that everything inside, including ourselves, was soon coated with soot from the smoke poured out by the locomotive. Facilities for washing, shaving, and other matters of personal hygiene were, to say the least, limited.

"We left Montreal's Windsor Station at ten o'clock in the evening. And I think it must have been two and a half days later, we pulled into Winnipeg about 9 a.m. To our astonishment, the station concourse was full of ladies from the city's volunteer services waiting to welcome us with coffee, candy, fruit, and magazines. . . . A band was playing popular dance tunes of the day, and before you could say 'May I have the pleasure . . .' some of the airmen and the younger ladies had started to dance. . . . If you can imagine what it must have been like for a young woman to go through this performance at nine o'clock in the morning with some stranger who had been shut up for nearly three days in a hot, sooty train with only the most meagre of facilities for washing and shaving . . . you will have some idea of what the gallant young ladies of Winnipeg endured as part of their contribution to the war effort."

The RAF station at Assiniboia, Saskatchewan, became LAC Campsie's home for far longer than he anticipated. He did his elementary training there at No. 34 EFTS during the summer of 1942 and then his service training at No. 33 SFTS Carberry, Manitoba, where he received his wings in December. He was then posted to No. 3 FIS at Arnprior to become an instructor, and in February 1943, he was shipped back to the prairies "to do my year's tour of duty as an instructor at Assiniboia, where I had done my own elementary flying training.

"No one I knew wanted to be an instructor," Campsie admitted. "All the way through, we all regarded it as a fate worse than death. I rather fancied myself as a night fighter. We felt we'd been betrayed. We all wanted to be heroes, and you couldn't be a hero as a flying instructor."

As things turned out, Campsie eventually flew Seafire fighters in the Fleet Air Arm, to which he transferred on his return to England.

Like most instructors, however, Flying Officer Campsie gave course after course of students the essentials for survival. He reminded them not to keep their eyes glued to the instruments but to scan the skies constantly; he showed them how to keep their cool through spins, stalls, forced landings, engine failures, and instrument flying; he taught them to fly carefully, without taking stupid risks. As Campsie put it, "When you got on ops there would be enough dangerous things to do without having to invent dangerous things before you got there."

Nonetheless, some aspects of flying on the Canadian prairies defied the usual precautions. Whenever a student training on the prairies realized he was lost, the practical (although not official) method of finding his way home was to drop below the clouds and search for a town or village (in those days no more than nine miles in any direction); he could identify it by spotting the name displayed atop one of its grain elevators, and plot his way home. Campsie tells the story of a pupil who got lost on a solo cross-country and had to make a forced landing in a farmer's field.

"Why didn't you look for an elevator with the name on top?" his instructor asked.

"I tried," was the answer. "But it didn't work. Did you know that every town around here is called Ogilvie? And the damn place isn't even on the map!"*

---

* The Ogilvie name, of course, was common on grain elevators across Saskatchewan as one of the West's largest grain storage and distribution companies.

Prairie conditions afforded some opportunities for unique flying experiences. Top speed in a Tiger Moth might be eighty-five or ninety miles an hour, with an equally low stall speed of about forty miles an hour. John Campsie recalled that on one occasion when the wind was high, he and fellow instructors got "a formation up above the field, flew at forty-five mph into the wind, and from the ground the whole formation was seen moving slowly backwards."

Other conditions special to prairie flying were not nearly as harmless as a strong head wind blowing across the Assiniboia airfield. Even as an experienced instructor, Archie Pennie discovered that flying in Western Canada always held devilish surprises. Like Campsie, LAC Pennie had found himself in one of the selected RAF drafts for overseas posting to the BCATP in Canada and had been transported in a Colonist car west to No. 32 EFTS at Bowden, within view of the Rocky Mountain foothills of western Alberta. He received his wings at No. 37 SFTS Calgary, went to FIS, and then began training some of the 2,500 RAF students posted to Assiniboia for elementary pilot training between 1942 and 1944.

Yet, as capable a flyer and instructor as he was, nothing Archie Pennie learned in elementary, service, or instructor school could have prepared him for the November night he and a student were nearly killed when their Fairchild Cornell trainer collided with a flock of migrating Canada geese. Nor could it have prepared any of the Assiniboia staff and students for the unique training conditions created by a bitterly cold prairie winter. In December 1943, instructor Pennie made two ominous entries in his logbook; they were identical and read: "Instructor and pupil killed when wing came off."

Experience told the Assiniboia staff that the wing separations were probably due to the instructor catching a wingtip while low flying or performing an illegal flick roll. But word spread that other Cornells had been involved in similar accidents. And Training Command quickly forbade all aerobatics in Cornells while the matter was being investigated.

"For my sins," Pennie wrote, "at the same time I was on night flying instruction. We had our own aircraft, which were never flown by day and consequently were never subjected to violent or disturbing manoeuvres. We assumed that these planes were above suspicion and flew them happily.

"Personally, I had no fears or qualms about the aircraft . . . and we persuaded the night pupils to accept this philosophy and pressed on regardless through that crisp cold prairie night air. . . . Within a week, all theories about the failures were shattered when an aircraft, in straight and level flight, shed a wing on the circuit and crashed within the airfield boundary.

"This tragedy resulted in the immediate grounding of all Canadian-built Cornells. Investigation revealed that the glue used in the box spar [securing the wing to the fuselage] had been affected by the dry cold and had caused the joints to separate. All aircraft were affected. . . . What sent chills down my spine was that planes of the night flight had been just as seriously affected as the others."

From then on, all Cornell aircraft were assembled using resin-based glues, which were better adapted to the severe dry cold of the BCATP's prairie stations. However, the incidents at Assiniboia were further evidence that the system would never be perfect. Preventable accidents would continue to plague the plan and kill its instructors and students. In some ways, things hadn't changed since fall 1940 when a design flaw in the Fleet Finch caused a crash that killed instructor Stormy Fairweather and LAC Axler at No. 7 EFTS Windsor. After three years of operation, the air training plan, its aircraft, and the air environment were just as life-threatening to those training Allied air crew on the supposedly safe home front as they had been when the war began.

Prairie weather didn't always kill those who ventured out in it. Sometimes it just scared them to death. Westerly winds gusting from the Rockies generally prevented flying after noon at No. 2 FIS Pearce, Alberta; while strong winds blew up so quickly at No. 26 EFTS Neepawa, Manitoba, that they often caught students up in the air; so, as Len Schryer recalled, "all hands scrambled out to the airstrip as a student was landing to . . . reach up, grab his wing tips, and literally hold his airplane on the ground" as he came in.

An Anson returning to Rivers, Manitoba, after a navigation flight in summer 1941 looked as if it had come through anti-aircraft flak; the gashes and pockmarks across its wings and fuselage were the result of an encounter with a prairie hail storm. In the winter of 1942–43, instructors at Carberry suddenly faced a rash of wheels-up belly landings; it was soon discovered that hydraulic fluid in their Anson fleet's landing gear was good only to thirty-five degrees below zero; at 10,000 feet the temperature outside the cabin was eighty degrees below zero. Another winter at No. 17 SFTS Souris, Manitoba, it snowed so heavily that "on the windward side of the control tower, snow drifted up forty feet, so it was level with the control tower. The station was closed for a week."

Winter elements never ceased to surprise the more than 50,000 Royal Air Force airmen who came to Canada as instructors or students in the BCATP. In fall 1940, Flying Officer Jack Meadows was instructing on Harvards at No. 15 SFTS at Kidlington, just outside Oxford. He was twenty-one and with the air war in Europe intensifying, he fully expected an operational posting at any moment. Instead, he was shipped overseas with other RAF instructors, first to Carberry and then on to establish No. 7 SFTS Macleod, Alberta. Meadows and several of his colleagues flew the first Ansons into Macleod to begin the first twin-engine courses there. That first winter, he discovered the difficulty of flying Ansons in sub-zero temperatures.

"On one flight," he wrote, "I was shaken by an enormous bang behind me. One of the large perspex windows had cracked explosively in the cold. I noted it in my logbook, only to add some time afterwards, 'At a later date such an occurrence was so frequent as not to be worthy of mention.' Holes were drilled at each end of each crack to stop it spreading. . . . Soon the otherwise delightful greenhouses of the Anson fuselages resembled draughty colanders, to the further discomfort of the inhabitants."

Kenneth McDonald recalled "flying hot and cold in Ansons," on hot and cold airfields. Trained in the RAF, McDonald was posted to Canada before the war. He conducted navigation tests for a year at Camp Borden, but then was sent to Portage la Prairie, Manitoba, to help launch No. 7 AOS. As chief supervisory officer, McDonald recalled "my first flight into Portage was in a de Havilland Dragonfly . . . when the field was still frozen. My second was with [station chief pilot] Scotty Moir, delivering an Anson after the thaw when the field was gumbo. Scotty put on full flap, held it with power on, just above the stall, [then] side-slipped off the last 100 feet and landed on the hangar apron."

After reassuring his mother back in Britain that he hadn't been banished to Karam in Russia, RAF cadet Doug Lomas settled into his EFTS training at Caron, Saskatchewan, during fall 1942 and then advanced to No. 33 SFTS Carberry in 1943. That spring, just before receiving his wings and his commission and leaving for a navigation course in Ontario, the prairies gave him one more experience to remember. It was a hot, dry, typically windy day across Manitoba. Lomas was piloting an Anson when "we got a call that there was a dust storm building. We were told to get back and land, and to get the aircraft into hangars, because dust storms are just murder on airplanes, filling up carburetors and everything.

"We could see it coming. That dust storm must have gone up as high as 10,000 feet. It was just a solid bank. You couldn't see through it. It was just like a wall of night coming, brown night. Naturally, we wanted to know what it was all about, so we flew up to it, then turned tail. It must have been travelling at forty or fifty knots. We had spent too much time looking at it. By the time we got back to Carberry, it was closing in. We had to outrun it to Winnipeg, where we landed at Stevenson airfield. The dust was everywhere. Even though we were inside the aircraft, we got dust in our hair, in our teeth. It was inescapable."

Doug Lomas later returned to his native England, where he extended his RAF career as an instructor, working on an experimental project at No. 21 FTS Snitterfield, taking students from grading directly to service training on Harvards, then on to jets, flying through the worst fog and cloud in the world; but in all his flying, he says, "I never experienced anything like that dust storm."

Similar forces of prairie nature caught up with service flying trainee Don Suthers. LAC Suthers's early wartime record included guard duty in 1941 at the St. Thomas Technical Training School, where he had to keep several hundred fellow students in quarantine during a diphtheria epidemic. He also endured the dreaded "Harvard Step Test," a physical endurance exam in which the trainee would step up onto a chair and down again continuously for five minutes. Later (as a B&GS staff pilot), Suthers survived the explosion of a practice bomb in the bomb bay of his Anson. But by far the most hair-raising experience he lived through was at No. 10 SFTS Dauphin, Manitoba, the day his instructor was giving him an instrument test in a Harvard.

"I was under the hood," Suthers explained. "I loved this and got to be pretty good at it. My instructor, Curly Ford, must have gone to sleep or something, because suddenly the stick was jerked from my hand . . .

"Ford barked out, 'I have control,' and my [instrument flying] hood snapped open. . . . It took me some time to figure out what was happening. We were inside a thunderhead. . . . The instruments began to go crazy. . . . The artificial horizon indicated we were in a steep dive, but the altimeter was winding up like a top, indicating we were climbing at several hundred feet a minute. We were flipped over on our backs. The Harvard was pointing down in a dive. But we were ascending. . . . We finally broke out of the cloud at about 9,000 feet and recovered. . . . No textbook could have impressed the lesson any more clearly—that very strong updrafts are found inside thunderhead clouds."

By late 1942, Canadian centres—from the smallest on the western great plains to the largest along the St. Lawrence and the Great Lakes—were beginning to look like a mini League of Nations. The streets of Toronto had been home for the refugee airmen of the Royal Norwegian Air Force since summer 1940; but the "Little Norway" training station had outgrown its facilities on Toronto Island, and the entire operation had been transplanted to Muskoka Airport outside

Gravenhurst, Ontario, with living quarters re-established on 430 acres of nearby farmland, dubbed Vesle Skaugum (after Crown Prince Olav's residence in Norway). Meanwhile, General Charles de Gaulle had proposed a similar training centre for the Free French. Even though Quebec was French-speaking, Canada had no facilities to instruct pilots in French. So when the Free French began to arrive in 1942, they joined other European air crew trainees—Czechoslovakians, Poles, Dutch, and Belgians—at the RAF schools across the country. Most foreign airmen wore some insignia identifying their nationality within the RAF and RCAF, but they all joined a vast throng of Commonwealth and Allied trainees preparing for the climax in the air war that was fast approaching.

Some of the new arrivals were (or later became) celebrities. Actor Robert Coote, already renowned in the 1930s for his Shakespearean roles in England and his musical performances in Australia and later remembered as Colonel Pickering in the Broadway production of *My Fair Lady*, came to Canada to join the RCAF. The air force put his theatrical talents to work; by 1941 he was producing the RCAF "Blackouts"—musical revues performed by air force personnel for air force audiences around the world.

No. 37 SFTS Calgary became the wartime home of another RAF trainee, Arthur Hailey. His flair for the dramatic was evident even in the BCATP; just before a weekend leave, Flight Sergeant Hailey went to special unauthorized lengths to prepare a unique gift for his date. "The idea," Hailey explained, "was to photograph her house from the air. I lay on the floor of the aircraft while someone flew the airplane for me. Some wag in the photographic department painted a pair of hearts and an arrow on the photograph and added the caption: 'Sgt. Hailey—Target for Tonight.'" In 1947 Hailey left the RAF as a flight lieutenant, immigrated to Canada, and began a successful writing career with a CBC television drama, "Flight into Danger." This was followed by a string of best-selling novels, including *The Final Diagnosis*, *Hotel*, and *Airport*.

Even though he was shipped to Canada late in the war, Oxford drama student Richard Burton came to Winnipeg's No. 5 AOS to become an RAF navigator in 1944. Burton's air force career in Canada was highlighted more by what he did on leave than by how he performed in his course, including participation in "barrack-room and public house brawls," and a 2,000-mile hitchhike from Winnipeg to New York on two dollars' worth of air force pay.

On Empire Day, May 23, 1942, the 35,000-ton troopship *Argentina* put to sea from the port of Melbourne, Australia. On board were several hundred airmen of the Royal Australian Air Force, including a twenty-three-year-old pilot trainee who had been born in Papua New Guinea. LAC L.J. "Ren" Henderson had been attending a lecture at the Melbourne showgrounds when his course was quickly bussed to the harbour for embarkation. Henderson barely had time to pack his gear and wire his girlfriend that he was headed for service flying training in either South Africa or Canada.

The first few days at sea were idyllic. The Australian airmen played poker, enjoyed the former luxury liner's fine cuisine, and were allowed to take their cameras up on deck to take photos of Stewart Island (New Zealand). Henderson and his cabinmates even charged fellow airmen a fee to see their state room, where, they had been told, Carmen Miranda had stayed on her first trip from Brazil. (Cabin 40 was normally the bridal suite, with a peacetime price tag of $2,000 return for the New York-Buenos Aires run.)

But the *Argentina* did not leave the war completely behind. On his second day out of Melbourne, Henderson was posted to gun crew on a four-inch ack-ack gun. Soon after they had cleared the Panama Canal, the *Argentina*'s guns fired on a U-boat in the Gulf of Mexico, and the troopship's captain took a grave risk by stopping in dead calm seas to take on the lone survivor of a torpedoed tanker.

By June 20, Ren Henderson and his fellow Australians were safely ashore in New York and bound for BCATP service training in Canada. At No. 6 SFTS Dunnville, far from the Japanese air attacks on Darwin and an entire ocean away from the Battle of the Coral Sea, Henderson began the final phase of his pilot training, en route (he thought) to the front in Britain or in the South Pacific.

Right from the beginning, BCATP instructors found they had their hands full when teaching the Australians. Unlike most American and Canadian trainees, most Australians had never driven a car before. It put them at a definite disadvantage. Driving gave a trainee a knowledge of distance, a sense of speed, and the basics of hand-eye coordination in a cockpit. As a result, the Australians were particularly vulnerable on take-offs and landings. As LAC Henderson put it, "Flying an aeroplane was the first time I had ever been in control of a wheeled vehicle, for God's sake. On my familiarization flight [in a Harvard], there was the noise and the power. It was exhilarating. But it was scary."

Dunnville instructor Bill Benbow, himself from New South Wales, described his Australian students' landings as "controlled collisions with the ground." One of Benbow's colleagues at No. 6 SFTS, Pat McLean, recalled the dilemma of teaching landings to one of his Australian students, LAC Simms, one day at Dunnville's auxiliary field in Welland, Ontario. McLean took Simms through circuits, "and every time we'd land, he'd run off the runway. He would have ground-looped the Harvard if I didn't catch the thing.

"I finally said to him. 'Do you think you can fly this aircraft better alone?'

"'Yes, sir,' he said.

"So I got out and went to the middle of the field, sat on my parachute, and away he went. A nice take-off, beautiful circuit, beautiful approach, touch down. He went down the runway about 100 yards and away he goes, ground-looping with dust and stones flying. But he didn't do any damage to the airplane. He came around and I walked up and said, 'That wasn't too bad.' He was as white as a sheet.

"We went back to the aerodrome. I checked him out solo there in circuit traffic. I went to the flight room, got a Coke, sauntered out, and thought, 'Oh God, I've sent him out for an hour of circuits and landings.' I expected to hear the crash truck. He did the circuits, came back within an hour, and the crash trucks didn't go out.

"He wrote me from Africa. He'd done two tours. He turned out to be a hell of a pilot."

Another Dunnville instructor, Charley Fox, also had to use unorthodox methods with an Australian student. Towards the end of his instructing days at No. 6 SFTS, Fox encountered an Australian who had gone past the required number of hours to go solo in a Harvard and was about to be washed out. He had all the necessary skills in the air; his take-offs, circuits, and manoeuvres were all fine, "but coming in to land, he gets on the runway and starts sawing on the rudder pedals, and that's just asking for trouble, because you're going to get the tail wheel out of the groove and it'll swing you into a ground loop.

"He did it once, twice. So I took him back in and I said, 'I think there's something the matter with the tail wheel.' I said that I would check with the corporal of maintenance. So I went to the corporal and said to him, 'I want you to come, inspect that aircraft, and tell my student there's something wrong with the tail wheel.'

"So he did. I told the student, 'You're okay. It's the aircraft that's faulty. I'm sending you up solo.' And I must admit, I stood outside watching him, not sure what was going to happen. Well, he did another circuit, made his approach, and greased it on the runway perfectly. Giving him a little confidence was all it took."

Most Australians and New Zealanders needed very little confidence-building. Charlie Konvalinka claimed that neither nationality of pilot "knew the meaning of fear," and Dick Ross remembered their "unique bravado and desire" to train and then get on with the job of winning the war. For that reason when a course of Australians was told to wash the barracks at No. 4 SFTS Saskatoon, to a man they refused, saying, "We didn't come here to scrub floors. We came here to fly." They won that stand-off.

They didn't always get their way. In fall 1943, Australian trainees at the RAF Operational Training Unit in Pennfield Ridge, New Brunswick, watched in horror as one of their crews was killed in a twin-engine Ventura that crashed at the airfield. The Australians refused to fly any other Venturas, claiming they were death traps. Robert Fowler, a Canadian trainee at the station, watched as "the chief flying instructor, an RAF squadron leader with a DFC and Bar, who had done a tour on Blenheims and another on Mosquitoes, got everyone out on the airfield. . . . We watched him fail and feather an engine on take-off, and after a couple of low passes and tight turns, he landed in front of the crowd with the engine still shut down. He then got out, walked over to our group for a chat. And the Aussies then went back to work." The CFI knew their language; only bravado greater than theirs could move the Australians.

Few trainees had as much pride as the Australians and New Zealanders in their role in defending the Empire. Few outdid them in their off-duty antics either. Their post-graduation celebrations, including wild "Maori war chants," were notorious, and sometimes lasted a week or more. Recognizing that the Australians knew how to enjoy themselves, some station COs responded by making the wet canteen off limits until after graduation, while others, like the manager of No. 1 AOS at Malton, Ontario, erected a special marquee for their off-duty festivities. Manager Babe Woollett's contention was that "these boys were eventually going to go over, and if necessary give their lives or take the greatest risk, so I wanted them to have the best."

"I remember when the first Australian course graduated," Woollett said. "Well-educated chaps and the right stuff. I had got them a special marquee at Malton because I knew they liked their beer. So, after their Wings Parade, they came up and invited me to their dinner at the Royal York Hotel as one of their honoured guests. We all sat at the head table and these fellows got up and made speeches. I tell you they were junior Churchills, they inspired you so much. They had been at the hotel for two or three days and they had pinched a duck from a Chinese restaurant and they had it swimming around in a bath at the Royal York. At the end of the evening, they presented me with this duck. It went back to the station. We called it Donald. And for a long time afterward, Donald marched around the station after the troops and waddled after me. I never forgot those Australians."

Allied air crew trainees and instructors left an indelible mark on Canada and vice versa. Some BCATP stations or, as some communities called them, "pilot factories" breathed new life into towns hard hit by a decade of depression. When the prospect arose for placing a training station at Yorkton, Saskatchewan, the local paper, the *Enterprise*, predicted "it will bring about 1,000 men here with an average pay of about $100 a month. . . . Airmen have clothing to buy, suits to be cleaned, shoes to be purchased, yes, and shoes to shine. They will frequent restaurants and hotels, and in a nut-shell will leave $100,000 a month with Yorkton business institutions. . . . Yorkton will be in for one of the greatest booms in its long history." The boom, while financially stimulating, created a pressing demand for housing. In 1941, Yorkton experienced the biggest house-building year of its history.

A hundred miles to the west, at Dafoe, Saskatchewan, the BCATP had erected No. 5 B&GS on an alkaline lake; aside from the town's granaries, garages, and a few shacks on streets named after the Dionne quintuplets, there was little living accommodation. Newlywed Eileen Topham arrived with her husband, Bill, an engineering officer, at Dafoe in July 1942. Their new home in "Boomtown," outside the front gates of the station, was a converted granary, measuring twelve by sixteen feet.

"The first winter was a bit grim," Eileen wrote. "Several times my face was frostbitten when the temperature dropped to minus fifty-two degrees Fahrenheit. It was no wonder that fruit and vegetables had to be wrapped in blankets or coats to keep them from freezing. . . . The second winter was better as the landlord added a second layer of boards on the floor. I sat up all night reading by the Aladdin lamp many times with my feet in the oven, when my husband was on night shift. All the other wives were in the same boat and we took it in stride. No one had room to entertain, so we had progressive dinners—appetizers at one house, main course at another, and dessert at another—all carried their own plates and cutlery."

Meanwhile, in return for the butter, eggs, and unpasteurized milk delivered on wagon or sleigh, the trainees, instructors, and staff used their forty-eight-hour leaves to join the threshing crews and help prairie farmers bring in the harvest. In Saskatchewan it was wheat. In the Annapolis Valley it was apples.

In March 1942, the 500 RAF officers and men aboard the *Orbita* disembarked at Halifax. Their mission, code-named Giggle Sprat, was to establish No. 36 RAF Operational Training Unit at Greenwood, Nova Scotia. Awaiting them on the railway platform at Greenwood were barrels and barrels of fresh apples, which "to people coming from wartime England, where fresh fruit was almost nonexistent . . . brought on visions of bellyaches from overeating—visions that in many cases were realized."

In addition to fresh fruit, the communities of the valley provided the airmen at Greenwood with dances, curtains for the station hospital, books for a library, a tea room with cards and darts, and food boxes to send home to their wives in England. Vernon McLeod, an RCAF instructor stationed at No. 36 OTU, wrote that "in absorbing this influx . . . the inhabitants of the Annapolis Valley . . . were not shattered by it. They did not resist nor fight it, but rather opened their arms and took the visitors into their homes, their shops and their hearts. Their ways changed only slightly, but the way of the visitors changed much more. The friendly conquerors were conquered by friendliness."

The meshing of non-Canadian and Canadian cultures was not always complete. With the exception of the station's annual track meet involving all personnel, the RAF airmen pursued their favourite sports—cricket, soccer, and boxing—while the local population enjoyed hockey, baseball, and curling. The British couldn't understand country and western music. There were also differences in cuts of meat (but there *was* meat, which, after all, was unavailable back home). Some imported traditions were doggedly followed by the expatriate airmen. To the disgust of Hadley Armstrong, when he arrived with a Visiting Flight, "the RAF stations had tea at 11 a.m. and tea at 4 p.m., come hell or high water, and I had to sit on my ass during those two periods, while the students, the instructors, and the CO had tea."

Inevitably, the young airmen met and befriended women in the community or those working on the station. Charlotte Tyerman's entire family was connected with the armed forces. Her brother was in the army, her sisters were in the Women's Division of the air force, and at sixteen she took a job "in the airmen's mess at Central Navigation School in Rivers [Manitoba], feeding 1500 men a day. I remember the cook fried ninety dozen eggs one morning. Each of us was assigned to a certain part of the meal. One day I was helping the cook make the coffee and he was putting some white stuff in the coffee. He said with a smile, 'It's payday and we can't afford to have you girls all getting pregnant.' It was saltpetre." In spite of the cook's efforts, she eventually married one of the station's radio operators, Ken Anderson. At least two women radio operators—Jackie Gaudette at No. 9 AOS St.-Jean, Quebec, and Anne-Marie Couchman at No. 1 AOS Malton, Ontario—met their future husbands while working alongside them or communicating with them by wireless.

At No. 1 Training Command headquarters in downtown Toronto, Betty Ross worked as a stenographer processing fatality statistics in the BCATP. Her mother, Mrs. E.H. Ross, the doyenne of the local IODE chapter, regularly staged buffets and dances for airmen from overseas. At one of those hospitality gatherings, Betty met RAF pilot Ernest Shadbolt, who was training at No. 1 EFTS Malton. The Rosses became his proxy family and opened their home to him. By the time "Shad" had completed EFTS, moved on to Uplands, earned his wings, and been posted back to England, he and Betty had made plans to marry after the war. On the ship home he wrote her about how the stay in Canada had affected him. He vowed to return. They were engaged by cable when he arrived home at St. Albans, near London. But their vows were never fulfilled. Shad was killed in action over the English Channel.

Many other Canadians took the BCATP airmen into their lives and into their hearts. Hostess Club and IODE tea dances fostered romances. Blind dates led to engagements, and many visiting airmen eventually married and settled in the communities that were their temporary wartime homes. From the moment he left Melbourne through his early training, Ren Henderson wrote faithfully to his girlfriend back home. However, on the day he arrived at Dunnville for his SFTS training, a volunteer from the community arranged for several airmen—including Ren—to attend a dance. At the dance he met the woman he would later marry.

The friendships between local families and BCATP instructors or trainees were usually lasting. Christine Paterson worked as a passenger agent in the Trans-Canada Airlines office at Windsor airport. With all the activity across the airfield at No. 7 EFTS, she soon met the civilian instructors at the station. And because her sister and brother-in-law—the Boyers—had a large house with very little furniture, their home (with its hardwood dining-room floor) became a regular location for parties and sing-songs among civilians and instructors for as long as the elementary training station operated in Windsor. Many Canadian households offered visiting airmen a home away from home in a similar fashion.

At the end of 1943, LAC E.T. "Jock" Evans celebrated his nineteenth birthday en route to Canada. He had lied about his age in 1941 when he joined the New Zealand Territorial Forces, but after two years, his signal and wireless experience in the army made him prime air force material. He had taken EFTS training at home and was sent to Canada—first to Manning Depot at Edmonton and then to No. 6 SFTS Dunnville. Evans was one of just over 7,000 New Zealand air crew trainees in the pipeline to BCATP stations in Canada.

Jock Evans entered Course 104 at Dunnville in spring 1944 and began training with an instructor who had served a tour in Britain. Flight Lieutenant Brady moved Evans quickly through familiarization, basic aerobatics, and instrument flying. Before long, Brady was teaching his student evasive tactics and high-speed stalls. Evans's course was at capacity—sixty students from Canada, Britain, Australia, and New Zealand. Instructors were flying almost around the clock.

For the Dunnville station these were times of both excitement and tension. That spring a former air gunner—Jimmy Kerr—with a DFM and more than thirty operations to his credit, graduated as a pilot officer. Later fifty-seven graduates of Course 96 formed part of a parade into Toronto's Maple Leaf Gardens for a ceremonial march past Air Marshal Robert Leckie; they were then met by entertainer Gracie Fields. However, in three separate crashes, several of Evans's course-mates were killed.

At about 3:30 on March 12, 1944, the afternoon's flying was well under way at Dunnville. Several Harvards were going through final cockpit checks for take-off. One contained two Australians. LAC L.O. Stokes was about to demonstrate an instrument take-off for his instructor, Sergeant D.G. Stranger. The aircraft left the ground, climbed to about 400 feet, rolled over, spiralled in, and crashed on the runway. Stokes got free of the burning aircraft. Stranger might not have, had it not been for veteran instructor Pat McLean and Australian student LAC N.F. Wolgast, who saw the crash as they each taxied for take-off; the two immediately rushed towards the crash and pulled Stranger unconscious from the burning wreckage. McLean received the Order of the British Empire and Wolgast the British Empire Medal for the rescue.

During those pressure-filled days, Jock Evans and several of his New Zealand course-mates at Dunnville accepted a long-standing invitation from a farm family in the small rural community of Uxbridge. Just east of the town on Reach Street, Pearl Webster and her two daughters, Marjorie and Helen, operated a 100-acre farm growing grain and some small livestock. It was Marjorie's fiancé, Graham Kerr (another BCATP airman by that time back home in New Zealand), who had recommended that Evans and his mates call on the Websters.

"We contacted them," Evans remembered, "and were invited to Uxbridge where we spent many pleasant weekend leaves. They became our family; in fact Mrs. Webster was Mom to at least half a dozen of us during our time at Dunnville. . . . We had great times—hiking around the countryside, boating on Lake Scugog, and entertaining ourselves around an old player piano."

Tagging along with Jock Evans on a number of the weekend leaves to Uxbridge were fellow New Zealanders Wally Hutton, Len Ryder, Murray Sanderson, Alick Loveridge, and Noel Wood. They used to accompany the Webster family to church, attend dances, and as Ryder put it "act the goat," by dressing up and masquerading to create their own fun. The nineteen-year-old Wood, soft-spoken and handsome, particularly enjoyed himself, riding the Websters' horse

Beauty and posing for photographs. For Marjorie, waiting for the war to end so she could be married to her New Zealand fiancé, and for Helen, on summer holiday, the airmen's visits filled the time with laughter "to replace the sad times of losing our father the previous fall." At the end of each leave Mrs. Webster cooked a huge meal for the airmen, providing what for them was a haven away from the tensions of SFTS training.

Back at Dunnville the training of Course 104 raced on through the summer of 1944. The war overseas was intensifying. Allied fortunes were reversing. Rommel had been repulsed at El Alamein in North Africa in 1942. The Russians had held at Stalingrad in 1943. Atlantic victory was near; Admiral Dönitz had withdrawn his U-boat fleet from the North Atlantic. Sicily had been liberated and the drive to Rome was complete by June 1944. More important to airmen from the South Pacific, Guadalcanal and much of the Solomon Islands had been secured from the Japanese in early August, and the push towards the Philippines was under way.

On a Saturday late in August, Noel Wood and Alick Loveridge each took off from Dunnville on a solo cross-country flight. Noel's navigational exercise was to last five and a half hours. His flight plan included a refuelling stop at B&GS Mountain View, a second leg to Camp Borden, and a third home to Dunnville. En route to Camp Borden, however, LAC Wood made a detour. Less than a half dozen miles south of his intended route from Mountain View to Camp Borden was Uxbridge and the Webster farm; the few minutes he would spend over Uxbridge could easily be made up by increasing his speed on into Borden.

"It was a beautiful, bright sunny day," recalled Helen Webster (now Helen Barnett).

"I had just come home from work," Marjorie added.

"It was just after lunch," Helen continued. "Whenever we heard airplanes, we would always run out to see where they were and what kind they were. This day, we ran out to see two Harvard airplanes circling with their canopies back. Noel came down out of the circle. We could see it was him."

"I ran out across the road to get a better view," Marjorie said, "because we had trees around the house."

At that moment, Noel's Harvard suddenly roared out of the southern sky. He had dropped his Harvard to tree-top level and began a simulated strafing run over the house. Then with the Webster girls waving madly back, the young pilot put the Harvard into a slow victory roll over the barn. He never completed the roll. The Harvard's nose dropped. It lost height and ploughed into the hill north of the barn. The Harvard's fuselage careered up the hill another 150 feet.

"There was a loud thump," Marjorie said, "and dust flying everywhere. The engine came flying off because we found it separate from the rest of the plane. We tore off like rabbits, and I got up on the wing."

"We pulled him out," explained Helen, who burned her leg on the Harvard's hot exhaust pipe pulling Wood out of the cockpit. "Someone got a truck, put a mattress in it to lay him on, because there was no ambulance in those days. We took him into town to Dr. Wilson's place, but his head was badly injured. I waited until the RCAF ambulance arrived from Oshawa. The fellows used to say that Noel always took chances when he was flying."

Noel Wood died during surgery at the Manning Depot hospital in Toronto later that afternoon.

The next day RCAF officials cordoned off the area, interrogated the Webster family, removed the wreckage, and recorded their findings.

"Court of Inquiry or Investigating Officer's Report:

"Cause: Unauthorized low flying.

"Conclusions of A.I.B.: Deliberate unauthorized aerobatics at a low altitude.

"Recommendations: Nil."

Noel Wood's remains were not returned to New Zealand. Few foreign trainees' ever were. The Dunnville station staff and his New Zealand course-mates assembled for a military funeral. Rifles were fired in salute. The bugler played the Last Post in tribute. Three civilians—Mrs. Pearl Webster and her two daughters from Uxbridge—

witnessed the burial. The rest of the New Zealanders went back to Uxbridge one more time on leave, but were soon posted overseas.

"All overseas trainees at some point found a Canadian 'home,'" Jock Evans wrote later. "Local people treated us with great kindness and many lifelong friendships grew from these visits. It was very tragic that Noel Wood lost his life on the very spot which he also considered home."

One other person attended the funeral of LAC Noel Wood—a Dunnville instructor. For some reason he brought a camera and snapped a picture of the funeral ceremony.

Like Wood, and his buddies from New Zealand, Ted Arnold had travelled thousands of miles—from Argentina—to train in the air force and get into the war. As an AC2 in Manning Depot at Lachine, Quebec, Arnold was chosen to take precision drill marching (and was once pelted with rocks by anti-English rioters during a performance in Trois-Rivières). At SFTS he had seen several of his classmates killed in accidents. He went on to instructor school at Trenton and trained with Whitey Dahl, "the best pilot I ever flew with in my life." As an instructor Arnold survived a flight with a student who froze at the controls and endured being called "Pop" and "Oldtimer" because he was among the oldest of the staff instructors at Dunnville. He had put in a year of instructing at Dunnville by then.

At one time or another that spring and summer, Ted Arnold had instructed and tested most of that New Zealand group—Course 104. He had given Len Ryder his ten-hour instrument test, Murray Sanderson his wings instrument test, and Jock Evans his final formation test. Later he would watch as they received their wings and got their operational postings. They would all be going overseas except Noel Wood.

Wood had tried a victory roll over a barn and died without ever having fired a shot in combat. Like Wood, Ted Arnold never got overseas. He would survive, instructing right through until January 1945, but never fight in the air war that was the raison d'être of the plan.

11

THE SURVIVAL DIVIDEND

By 1943, when the British Commonwealth Air Training Plan was one year into its new mandate, the war was a long way from being won. However, the battle of training *was* being won.

The manufacture of the plan's training aircraft was one indication of success. Canada's aircraft manufacturing production reached record highs. Thanks principally to Munitions and Supply Minister C.D. Howe and the Crown corporation he formed, Federal Aircraft Limited, by June 1, 1943, 1,850 twin-engine Ansons were flying; that was 350 more than had been targeted. Canadian assembly lines at de Havilland and Fleet Aircraft had produced 2,360 elementary trainers; and other manufacturers had turned out 3,578 advanced trainers and 2,076 service aircraft. A grand total of 8,014 aircraft had been built by an industry which had been virtually non-existent before the war.

Meanwhile, the air crew quotas signed into effect on July 1, 1942, by the original Commonwealth countries—Britain, Canada, Australia, and New Zealand—were being surpassed. In January 1943, for example, the plan graduated 1,574 airmen; in October of that year, the plan graduated an all-time monthly high of 5,157 fully qualified air crew graduates. Instructors and trainees were flying more than a million miles a day in the BCATP. By the end of the year, Canada's massive air training scheme had produced almost 75,000 pilots, navigators, wireless radio operators, air-gunners, and bomb-aimers for the Allied war effort.

The remarkable strides made by Canada's more than 100 training facilities and its war munitions factories were not going unnoticed. Joseph Goebbels, Hitler's propaganda minister, recorded in his diary in March 1943, "It drives one mad to think that some Canadian boor, who probably can't even find Europe on the globe, flies here from a country glutted with natural resources, which his people don't know how to exploit, to bombard a continent with a crowded population."

More favourable reviews were forthcoming from the White House, where President Roosevelt planned to send a message of goodwill to his friend Prime Minister King on the third anniversary of the BCATP. In his search for the best words with which to congratulate King, Roosevelt sought the help of his staff, and they turned to the Canadian embassy. The second-in-command at the Canadian legation was former University of Toronto professor and football coach Lester B. Pearson, who was asked if he "would be kind enough to do a draft of the message for the President. I did. So on 1 January 1943, the Prime Minister of Canada received a very impressive letter lauding Canada as the 'aerodrome of democracy' drafted by me but signed by the President of the United States."

As the plan reached its peak of air crew production in May 1943, a twenty-three-year-old flying instructor at No. 6 SFTS Dunnville, Ontario, received the posting he had dreamed about for two years: "No. 1 Operational Training Unit, Bagotville, Quebec." Instructor and recently promoted Flight Lieutenant Charley Fox was finally going to escape his training duties and get his chance to fight overseas.

Fox had applied for service in the air force in spring 1940, and had worked for Walker's, a southwestern Ontario department store chain, until he was called in the autumn. He survived scarlet fever at EFTS; but in February 1941 made it to SFTS, where an RCAF flying officer showed him aerobatics in a Yale, giving him the only case of nausea in the air he would ever experience.

Fox graduated in midsummer 1941; it was so hot at the wings ceremony that seven of his fellow graduates in the parade fainted. When he received his commission, Fox was certain he was headed overseas. However, nearly two years of service as a flying instructor lay ahead of him, and it was not until May 1943 that he was finally dispatched to Bagotville for operational training.

Operational Training Units (OTUs) had not always been part of the BCATP training process. Before 1939 they had not been necessary: RAF pilots-in-training had simply gone directly from advanced training to operational (combat) squadrons. This was possible because there were only minor differences between training and operational aircraft. For example, an RAF trainee who had learned to fly in the standard training Avro Tutor in the early 1930s could easily make the jump to the cockpit of the RAF's commonest fighter, the Gloster Gauntlet. However, the introduction of the Hawker Hurricane—the first eight-gun fighter monoplane—in 1937 required a more deliberate conversion process. Thus, the RAF introduced the intermediate training stage or operational training unit in 1940. In 1941 and 1942, six OTUs were transplanted to Canada—there were two in Nova Scotia, at Debert and Greenwood, one at Pennfield Ridge, New Brunswick, two in British Columbia, at Boundary Bay on the mainland and at Patricia Bay (later moved to Comox) on Vancouver Island, and one at Bagotville, Quebec.

"I commenced training at Bagotville on May 18, 1943," Fox recalled. "It was a large station by then, with a Norseman there for search and rescue, and twelve Hurricanes and Harvards for battle formation training. First they checked you out on Hurricanes, doing air firing of its guns for the first time. I had never fired any guns until OTU. You also practised evasive manoeuvres and formation take-offs."

Shortly after Fox made his first solo Hurricane flight on May 27, he was involved in a mid-air collision. On June 1, Fox led a formation of three Harvards to practise stern attacks. That same morning, a section of Hurricanes left the Bagotville station for attack practice. It was a general rule, however, that if Harvards and Hurricanes met in the skies, they were to steer clear of each other because of the vast speed differential—180 mph versus 325 mph respectively.

"That morning, I was leading my section of Harvards back to Bagotville station, when the Hurricanes, who were up in the sun, made a simulated attack on us. I picked them up and called for a break to port. So the three of us broke to the left.

"But Flying Officer Buckley [the lead pilot of the Hurricane formation] dove down below me and pulled up. He must have blacked out on the climb back up, and he hit the underside of my Harvard directly on the engine and tore it off completely; everything in front of the firewall forward was gone."

Buckley's left wing and left tailplane were torn off in the collision, and his Hurricane spun out of control and crashed; he was killed. Meanwhile, Fox's Harvard, still right side up, flopped about the sky as he tried to regain control. His head had hit the instrument panel, and with the blood pouring down his brow he could see out of only one eye.

During his months as a BCATP trainee and then his two years as an RCAF instructor, Fox had become intimately familiar with sequence 17 of the instruction syllabus—the forced landing. During this simulated crash landing drill, the pilot throttles back on the aircraft's engine so that it is just ticking over. The pilot must quickly pick out an emergency landing site, then "dead stick" the aircraft (manoeuvre it without power) down to the site. In practice sessions, the pilot brings the aircraft down to within a hundred feet of landing and then throttles the engine up and flies away.

On one such forced landing drill, back at No. 6 SFTS Dunnville, Fox had a fellow instructor in the front cockpit, Harold Jewitt. In the final seconds of Fox's approach to an emergency site on Hamilton Mountain, Jewitt (as a prank) cut the magnetos so that Fox couldn't restart the engine. Fox had no choice but to dead stick the Harvard all the way down to a safe landing.

That experience with Jewitt back in the winter of 1942 as well as his ingrained reflex to try to save one of "the King's precious training aircraft" crossed Fox's mind after the mid-air collision with the Hurricane. But it quickly became clear that saving the Harvard was impossible. He had to bail out. Even a safe parachute landing was not assured. At first Fox couldn't find the D-ring to pop the chute. When the red-and-white canopy finally unfurled at about 300 feet, he faced a rough landing in dense evergreen bush and rocks. Despite his bloodied eye and badly banged right arm, he survived. Two French-Canadian farmers found him and brought him out of the bush later that day. Nevertheless, Charley Fox credits his 1,400 hours as an instructor (and, grudgingly, Harold Jewitt's unexpected prank) for his cool-headedness that day.

Fox used these same skills on ops. When he arrived overseas and progressed to flying Spitfire fighter aircraft later in 1943, the ex-instructor joined George "Buzz" Beurling's A Flight in No. 412 Fighter Squadron. Fox then flew bomber escort, daylight sweeps, dive-bombing, and low-level attacks over Europe.

Among his 222 operational sorties was a sweep mission on December 22, 1944. Fox was returning to Volkel, Holland, when he realized he couldn't get his Spitfire undercarriage down. He managed to make a perfect wheels-up forced landing on the airfield grass. The landing was so smooth and damage so light that ten days later the Spitfire was back in action.

His final operational forced landing occurred on a weather reconnaissance flight, his last official sortie with the 2nd Tactical Air Force, on January 18, 1945. During the flight across the Rhine from Holland, his Spitfire was hit by 88mm anti-aircraft shrapnel from ground batteries. Once again, Fox resorted to emergency landing procedure, brought the damaged Spitfire back from German-occupied airspace, and safely crash-landed in a farm field near Eindhoven.

However, Fox's skill was not limited to weathering forced landings. On July 17, 1944, Charley Fox's flight log indicates that he led a flight of four Spitfires on an armed reconnaissance sortie. Fox explained that during the seventy-five-minute flight, he spotted a German military staff car speeding along the Livarot Road (an avenue dotted with tall pine trees on the German side of the Normandy front). Fox went down and strafed the car at tree-top level, hit it, and drove it off the road. Intelligence reported later that day that Field Marshal Erwin Rommel had been severely injured in an attack on his staff car along the Livarot Road.

Charley Fox completed his tour of 222 sorties (double the normal ops tour) with a DFC and Bar and an RCAF flight-lieutenancy to his credit, but he points to his 1,954 hours in the air, most as a BCATP instructor, as the key to his survival and success.

The objective of any instructor in the BCATP was to bring his student back alive—from his first solo or from his last wings test. Commonwealth training statistics are proof of the instructors' success. Midway through the First World War, the Royal Flying Corps in Canada flew 200 hours for every fatality recorded. By October 1918 it had improved to 5,800 hours. During the first year of the BCATP the number of hours flown per fatality was 11,156, and by the end of the Second World War it was 22,388 hours per fatality. If, in addition, a BCATP-instructed student survived one or more operational tours, so much the better. No instructor could guarantee a safe return from a combat sortie. But he did guarantee to instill the right attitude for flying competently and safely.

Windsor EFTS instructor Gus Bennett asserted that in flight instruction "from the Wright Brothers to the Royal Flying Corps to the early days of RCAF training at Camp Borden and Trenton, safety is the whole thing. Safety for the individual, safety for the aircraft, and the care and concern not to take chances but to organize and carry out your work so that you always had a margin. Never let yourself get into a situation where you don't have a little bit of leeway.

"That was consistent all the way through. Make sure you don't fall into any of the traps: doing aerobatics too low, not coming out of spins properly, pulling up too abruptly and creating high-speed stalls. The guy who knew how to operate his airplane properly had a much better chance of going through the necessary jinks of evading an enemy fighter or working his way through flak fields."

Veteran instructor Joel Aldred described it as "keeping the luck factor to an absolute minimum." He instilled it in his students both at Flying Instructor School and on Visiting Flight missions across Canada. And he carried that attitude from the cockpits of trainer Harvards and Ansons to the flight deck of the Lancasters he flew with No. 431 "Iroquois" Squadron in 1944 and 1945.

From his Yorkshire location, the most northerly bomber station in the United Kingdom, Aldred flew sixteen operational flights. Each one was serious business. He never let his crew chat or joke during a mission, insisting that "they'd only address me if we had trouble, if we had an engine on fire that I couldn't see. Otherwise we didn't talk, so we could pay attention to what our job is, scan the skies, fly the airplane right, conserve our gas, and work together quietly like bank robbers. You don't say a thing. You just do the job." Aldred returned to Canada with a DFC.

Disciplined instruction paid Herb Liebman a healthy dividend even before he left the BCATP for an overseas posting with Transport Command. LAC Liebman remembered each of his instructors building his sense of confidence and pride, by "drumming procedure into your mind." For at least one fellow student on Liebman's course in Davidson, the discipline didn't work; he challenged a bridge on the South Saskatchewan River and the bridge won.* But for Liebman, the repetition of safe flying practices worked, particularly during a landing at No. 10 SFTS Dauphin in 1943.

"We were flying Cessna Cranes," Liebman recalled. "They were fabric-covered, twin-engine, reasonably fast, and difficult to land; they tended to float. I had about a month's training—about sixty or seventy hours on them. I was coming back from a solo cross-country. Two aircraft were approaching the station, mine and another one. We were coming from the same direction but at different heights.

---

* Hardie Gray recalled the incident as well: "It was my first familiarization flight at No. 23 EFTS Davidson, Saskatchewan. My instructor [P/O Richards] and I were lead plane in a VIC formation. We were flying so low that we had to pull up to clear several haystacks. Then we saw the crash site. This poor chap had tried to fly under a bridge on the Saskatchewan River; he didn't make it. The debris was scattered all over the island."

"The fellow in the booth that was giving us flashing lights for landing or not landing at the end of the runway was apparently not paying attention, and we collided one on top of the other fifty feet above the runway. We were always taught in an emergency like this to burn off all the fuel in the engines. Well, the moment we hit, without thinking I 'leaned out' the mixture—gave it full throttle, burned everything out, and then switched off the engines. The other guy must have done the same, because neither his aircraft nor mine caught fire. We were lucky. The Cranes were complete wrecks, but neither of us was hurt at all.

"Lean out the mixture. Full throttle. Cut the switches. It was just automatic"—and it saved his life. Herb Liebman went overseas flying Dakotas with No. 437 Transport Squadron in 1944. He never had another collision, and flew missions during the Battle of the Bulge and the Allied push into Holland, always flying "by rote."

The repetition of training exercises, flying by rote, and verbal abuse from short-fused instructors (such as the tongue-lashing he got from an EFTS instructor when he ground-looped a Fleet Finch) annoyed George Bain when he was a BCATP trainee. He learned more from the example of others. He remembered sitting tensely in the second cockpit of a Harvard during a night flight while his SFTS instructor confidently brought the trainer down through a dense Ottawa Valley fog to a perfect landing at Uplands station. Moments like these "instilled in me a sense of caution or carefulness."

By the time Bain had crossed the Atlantic, done his OTU training, and been posted to combat duty, "Bomber" Harris was stepping up the Bomber Command offensive against German cities, and the first solely Canadian bomber group, No. 6 Group, was being inaugurated. In January 1943 Bain's No. 424 RCAF Squadron joined No. 6 Group at Topcliffe, Yorkshire. He flew thirty-four operations—sixteen over Europe and eighteen from North Africa—piloting Wellington X bombers.

After his tour of combat duty in 1943, Bain even flew some hair-raising missions in Britain for the J. Arthur Rank film company; they were shooting *Signed with Their Honour*, a propaganda movie about the life and times of three RAF squadrons of Gloster Gladiator fighter pilots. Bain piloted the Wellington II camera airplane through some dicey action sequences. But the experience that unnerved him was a very different flying assignment.

"I was posted to instruct at an OTU," Bain said. "We did bombing exercises, cross-country exercises with Wellington crews. You would fly to a bombing point, drop mock bombs there, and come back to base. Mostly I sat there to make sure the pilot got his courses right and then got us back in one piece. I hated it. I was always a lot more confident in me than I was in anyone else. I kept thinking, 'Jesus Christ, my life's in this guy's hands.' I felt I was a captive of this guy who I'd never met before. I'm not a very good second driver."

Veteran pilot George Bain had suddenly witnessed pilot training from the other side of the fence. In fact, he admits he was perhaps as shrill and curt with British OTU students as his own elementary instructor had been with him back at No. 13 EFTS St. Eugene, Ontario, in 1941.

By autumn 1942, Cap Foster had had enough of the BCATP. The young RCAF pilot who had looped the Rainbow Bridge at Niagara Falls out of frustration with the system was told he was in line for a position on a Visiting Flight.

"No way," Foster says. "I joined the RCAF for the sole purpose of getting the chance to fight, not for the purpose of teaching others, who, upon graduation, were sent directly overseas. I was going overseas if I had to swim over!"

Soon after he received his A Category instructor status from Training Command headquarters, Cap learned that his prayers had been answered. In October, he travelled to Halifax and boarded the *Queen Elizabeth* with 24,000 other troops bound for Britain.

Whether they travelled on the 85,000-ton *Queen Elizabeth* or the tiny New Zealand coastal boat *Materoa*, which had previously hauled mutton to South America, airmen found the eastbound transatlantic voyage an adventure. Their memories of these days confined to a ship's hold or deck are vivid. Some sailed through storms that either made them violently seasick or had them chasing their meals across the table. Others recall the money won and lost at poker and craps. Most remember sharing accommodation with thousands of other servicemen, as well as British civilians returning home after the Blitz, or, in one case, a group of short people employed in the American aircraft industry because they could work in small, confining spaces inside aircraft. Everyone remembered the constant, but rarely discussed, threat of a U-boat torpedo attack.

The threat was real. In April 1943, the Danish ship *Amerika* had set sail from Halifax with fifty-three BCATP airmen in the ship's company. Among them was Scott McCloskey, who had graduated in 1940, served three years as an instructor at Trenton, and finally been given his ops posting overseas. On his embarkation leave in March, he had married his sweetheart and written home, "I've wanted this posting for so long now, that I want to get over there and have a crack at it."

"On April 22," explained his sister Rita McCloskey Carey, "they ran into heavy weather and the ship was torpedoed and sank, only sixteen airmen surviving. Scotty was not among them."

When the *Queen Elizabeth* left Halifax for Gourock, Scotland, in October 1942, Cap Foster heard stories that the eastbound convoy just ahead of them had been badly beaten up by U-boats. Despite the sense of tension, he settled in to the rhythm of eating twice a day in the dining halls, which served troops around the clock, and waiting for a chance to sit out on the promenade deck.

"A day or so before we got to Britain," Foster said, "we were sitting on deck chairs listening to Lord Haw Haw on the radio.* He suddenly announced, 'We have just sunk the *Queen Elizabeth*!' And as he spoke, the ship made a sharp turn. When it made these kinds of turns, it apparently listed as much as twenty-seven degrees to one side. Well, this evasive action literally threw us out of the deck chairs and sprawling across the deck."

* Lord Haw Haw, a.k.a. William Joyce, was a former member of the British Union of Fascists who offered his services to the Nazis at the beginning of the war and who became the Nazis' chief English-language broadcaster.

Cap Foster was among the first BCATP flying instructors to receive an overseas posting, cross the Atlantic, and reach No. 3 Personnel Reception Centre in Bournemouth, the resort town on Britain's south coast. There he joined hundreds of BCATP-trained air crew who were awaiting postings to OTUs. In Bournemouth, the airmen were billeted at homes and in what RCAF air gunner Ted Relf called "the millionaire suites," Bournemouth's finest resort hotels—the Highcliffe, the Bath, the Regent, the White Hermitage, and the Empress.

During these days of suspended animation, Flight Lieutenant Foster, as did all Commonwealth airmen, carried out daily routine orders for parade and guard duty. He learned about food rationing and figured out how to shop with pounds, shillings, and pence at Bobby's, Bournemouth's downtown department store. During his off-duty hours, he went to English tea dances, visited British public houses, and drank room-temperature beer. The Canadians even started their own black-out tradition; they followed English girls in the streets at night and shone flashlights on their legs in search of the best pair.

"Travelling about in the black-outs at night took some getting used to," John Evans remembered. Like so many BCATP instructors arriving in Bournemouth, Evans had joined up early, scored well on his wings test, gone to Central Flying School, and instructed at SFTSs in Calgary and Hagersville. Then in late 1943 he boarded the *Aquitainia* and joined the pool of ex-instructors in Bournemouth awaiting a posting. To break up the boredom, "I remember going to one of the hospitality dances that were put on once a week. I danced once or twice with girls who were there trying to be hospitable to us Canadians. One young lady spent her days helping build Spitfires in a local plant and volunteered a couple of times a month to attend these duty dances, fending off endless hordes of amorously inclined Canadian airmen."

"We were dancing one night," recalled former Bournemouth resident Madge Janes Trull. "Suddenly the sirens started to go off and all these Canadians dived under the tables for shelter. We knew jolly well the table wasn't going to do much. I guess we were pretty blasé about it."

Madge later joined the Wrens (Women's Royal Naval Service) at Portsmouth and went through rigorous psychological and security testing at Mill Hill to become a code-breaker in Churchill's "Ultra-secret" service. When she came home on leave to her family's house in Alum Chine (the most westerly of the deep gullies that ran down to the beaches at Bournemouth), she used to relax at the seaside pavilion where Edmond Hockridge and his band regularly performed. But with so many airmen billeted in Bournemouth, the city became a frequent target for bombs.

On the premise that it was expedient to disable an air force sitting on the ground before facing it in the air, packs of Messerschmitts and Focke-Wulf fighter and bomber aircraft would routinely swoop in low off the English Channel, slip under the protective scan of coastal radar, and bomb the square downtown, or strafe the promenade below the seaside cliffs, where airmen strolled down the zig-zag pathway to the beaches. German hit-and-run raids killed scores of civilians and air crew. Early in 1943, a single German bomb gutted Bobby's department store. During that summer another low-flying German bomber scored a direct hit on the Metropole Hotel, killing thirty airmen.

"We were an easy target for enemy intruders," agreed bomb-aimer John Neal. A native of Verdun, Quebec, who had been employed as a machinist apprentice with the Canadian National Railway when he enlisted, Neal seemed to lead a charmed life. At No. 1 B&GS Jarvis, Ontario, five of his course-mates were killed in a Bolingbroke crash. With his graduate's bomb-aimer wing newly sewn to the breast of his tunic, he fell ill and was unable to ship out of Halifax with seventy-five fellow airmen in April 1943; that ship was torpedoed and sank, killing two-thirds of the air crew aboard. Neal safely crossed the Atlantic the next month.

"One sunny day, in Bournemouth," Neal recalled, "we were walking through a park in the centre of town. Three Messerschmitts came in low overhead, spitting gunfire into the park. We scattered behind park benches to avoid the bullets. This was our first indication that those chaps just across the channel were really serious about killing us."

At OTU, Neal's Halifax bomber survived a faulty automatic pilot and a direct hit from a lightning bolt. The following spring, John Neal joined No. 419 "Moose" Squadron for his twelfth operation, filling in for a bomb-aimer who was ill. The target was Laon, in northern France, which "would normally have been a milk run, a fast in and out trip. But this night we were to be the target, instead of the railway yards." By 11:30 that night, April 22, 1944, Neal's Halifax had been shot out of the sky and he was parachuting to earth. He spent six months evading the Germans in occupied France.

When Cap Foster finally got a posting to train on his beloved Spitfires, his struggle to escape his instructor's past was not over. The flight he was assigned to was commanded by a sergeant pilot, and "because most of us ex-instructors were flight lieutenants, we were not received with open arms when we joined our respective squadrons. As a matter of fact, we were met with a certain amount of hostility and told that our previous flying experience didn't cut any ice there. We were sprog pilots with a hell of a lot to learn before we would be of any value to the squadron."

Cap Foster learned fast, and went on to win a DFC for his more than 200 combat sorties on Spitfires over Europe. On the first trip of his second tour alone, he became separated from his squadron, found a squadron of Messerschmitt 109s, knocked two out of the air, and was tailing a third when "the hair on the back of my neck stood right out like a porcupine. I knew something was wrong. I hadn't seen or heard anything and just looked back to see a 109 behind me. I jogged immediately, but he hit the top of my engine. My cockpit filled with smoke. My windscreen was covered in oil. Unable to see, I went into a steep dive, went into the clouds, lost my pursuer, and headed for home. I stayed with the aircraft as long as I could, then bailed out on our side of the battle lines."

Foster claimed that fate and a sixth sense saved him. Pilots who knew him, including his one-time student Bill Olmstead and a fellow instructor at Dunnville, Charley Fox, were inclined to credit Foster's razor-sharp reflexes, extraordinary aerobatic skills, and the thousands of hours he had logged as an instructor in the BCATP as his more likely salvation.

The very nature of instructing—countless hours in the second seat of a Fleet, Harvard, or Anson—gave flyers like Foster a sense of ease at the controls. First World War ace Billy Bishop is said to have accumulated 172 hours in the air by the time of the Armistice in 1918. Most BCATP pilots had that many hours at graduation.

When he received his pilot's brevet at No. 11 SFTS Yorkton in March 1942, Pilot Officer Bill Walker had 192 flying hours. After a year of instructing at No. 3 SFTS Calgary he was posted overseas with nearly 1,000 hours in his log. He hated instructing, but he realized that "a lot of flying is reacting to a situation that is unforeseen. If you've flown enough hours, there's not much you haven't seen. One night we had a runaway propeller and our Halifax nearly went over on its back, but I managed because no panic came into it, given all the hours I'd had in the seat."

On a winter morning in 1944 former BCATP instructor John Trull's 1,400 hours in the cockpit paid him a survival dividend. Trull had been on ops for only six weeks. For the previous three years, he had instructed on Tiger Moths at No. 32 EFTS Bowden and on Harvards at No. 14 SFTS Aylmer in the BCATP. On Sunday, February 20, however, he was flying one of the first Spitfire IXb fighters assigned to his No. 403 "Wolf" Squadron at Kenley. The new Spits were equipped with a thirty-gallon auxiliary fuel tank (attached to the belly of the fighter). The tank could be jettisoned when it was empty.

"Our squadron was going out to pick up a bunch of Fortresses coming back from a bombing mission over Germany," Trull remembered. "There was solid cloud cover at about 2,000 feet. So we were being guided to and from the rendezvous with the Fortresses above the clouds by radar. By the time I figured we were over Belgium, my jettison tank ran out of gas. But when I switched over to my regular tank, nothing happened. I'll never forget that desperate bloody feeling.

"I kept trying to switch over. Nothing. I got down to about 10,000 feet and started to think about what I was going to do. Instructions were to bail out and let your plane crash. But I had a horrible feeling that I was above a dangerous spot. So I thought I'd better look and see what was below me. I shoved the nose straight down, got up all the gliding speed I could, started to pull up at about 4,000 feet and broke clouds at about 2,000 feet. Sure enough, there was a German aerodrome right below me. So I pulled up into the clouds again, glided quite a few miles and came down in a field, putting the Spit on its belly, not far from Wiers." The Spitfire's on-board fuel line had been blocked by an air-lock.

Trull's log entry for February 20, 1944, reads, "Missing. My damned kite up and quit on me. Took five and a half months to get home from German-occupied Belgium." He credits his instructing experience, and the time he had to think his predicament through on the way down from 27,000 feet, for saving his life.

After his unauthorized low-flying "shoot up" of the Dominion Day festivities at Jackson Park in Windsor in 1942, instructor Frank Vines finally escaped his instructing job at No. 7 EFTS Windsor. He arrived in Bournemouth early in 1943 with nearly 2,000 hours' flying time in his logbook. By midnight June 5, 1944, Vines had been checked out on Dakotas and was flying paratroops over Caen to begin the D-Day landings in Normandy.

"It was pitch black as we dropped the paratroops about twelve miles inland," Vines said. "But then the Allies were bombarding the coast with battle cruisers and battleships. It was like watching lightning below us; these bloody great guns were going off.

"The Royal Navy were pretty touchy, shooting at anything that flew over. And we got shot up. A 20mm shell went right through the can area and blew it apart. Nobody was hurt.

"Then, just after I dropped the paratroops, we pulled up. But with all the weight gone from the back, the airplane was wanting to go down. (A cable was damaged and the airplane was permanently trimmed in a nose-down attitude.) The route we were supposed to use coming out of France was to head out over Holland and come home that way, which was going to take us another ninety minutes. So we just went straight back across the Channel, over all the ships. We were hanging on for dear life, but we managed to get back.

"I think my instructor experience helped me adjust to these situations, in which I might otherwise have been killed."

Although many instructors found that their training prepared them well for combat, a few airmen believed that instructors were a liability on ops. Former Dunnville instructor Ken Summerville recalled that "it wasn't always the best idea to send instructors over as fighter pilots, because they flew too well.

"The reason was that when I taught a student to give me a rate one turn to the left, or a medium turn to the right, I wanted to see that ball and that needle absolutely perfect. So much rudder. So much stick. Otherwise the airplane would be slipping and sliding on the turn. I wanted to teach them safety when they're learning to fly. To an instructor that's second nature. He just automatically does things perfectly.

"Now when you get overseas, with Jerry on your tail, you don't want to turn perfectly. You want to be slipping and sliding, dropping flaps, doing anything at all to get the hell away. The one thing you don't want to do is to fly perfectly. Unfortunately, when they sent some instructors overseas, they didn't last very long."*

Max Ward admitted he wouldn't have lasted on ops for that very reason. While he could never get along with air force protocol, procedure, and discipline, he had always believed in flying by the book. When a student pilot crashed into Ward's lead Anson during a formation practice over Hagersville, his precise response—calmly taking control from his student co-pilot and bringing his Anson down safely—almost certainly saved their lives.

---

* Former instructor and fighter pilot Cap Foster recalled that when he arrived at an Operational Training Unit, he was sent up on a practice dogfight with a cautious Norwegian OTU pilot who insisted on banking his fighter airplane in a gentle rate-one turn. Foster, however, would whip his fighter over and be on his opponent's tail in seconds. The Norwegian was shot down on his first operational sortie.

"I instructed students to fly precisely from day one," Ward said. "Ball in the centre. No slipping or sliding. Fly the airplane properly. If it wasn't precise, then I felt I'd blown it. I felt uncomfortable. So I instructed them incorrectly from the standpoint of military operations." Later he sensed that may have been the reason he was never sent overseas and that "I would have been a dead ringer over there, not worth a damn overseas on ops."

All sorts of lessons from BCATP instructors came in handy on ops, often quite unexpectedly. Even precision flying, thought by some airmen to be of no use in combat situations, occasionally saved the day.

Jackie Rae was at first reluctant to recognize the value of his BCATP training. Rae was self-motivated, fiercely independent, and something of a maverick. Born into a show business family, he learned to read by memorizing song lyrics. After high school in Toronto, he produced radio shows for the Metropolitan Advertising Agency. His boldness was evident even on the day he enlisted. At the recruitment centre he was being interviewed by an RCAF corporal. On the desk between them sat two stacks of files—one pile marked "West," the other "East."

"What does that mean?" asked Rae, pointing to the piles.

"The fellows in the West pile live in the East," explained the corporal. "We want them away from their families. So we send them to train in the West. And the fellows from the West, we bring them to the East to train."

Rae nodded. Then when the corporal left the room, Rae, who wanted to stay close to his Toronto family, found his file in the West pile and quickly moved it to the East pile, "so I trained at the Eglinton Hunt Club ITS in Toronto, at EFTS Sky Harbour in Goderich, and at Camp Borden [near Barrie, Ontario], never more than 150 miles from home."

In Rae's mind, his BCATP training did nothing more than "teach me precision flying, how to fly the plane safely and accurately, not how to dogfight. It was at OTU on Hurricanes in England where the survival training really started. That's where the instructors had flown in the Battle of Britain. That's where I learned how to be rough with an airplane. They made it very clear that the precision flying days [of EFTS and SFTS in Canada] were over. Now I learned how to be aggressive, how to turn the airplane inside out."

Rae remembered his "terrible baptism" which took place on August 19, 1942. Flying with Lloyd Chadburn's No. 416 Squadron, Rae and his fellow Spitfire pilots flew four sweeps over Dieppe, dogfighting with Messerschmitts and chasing Junkers bombers away from the Canadians trying to establish a beachhead. Rae's squadron shot down eleven Luftwaffe aircraft without a single casualty. In the heat of air combat he recalled "spinning away from a pursuer to get out of trouble. They would think you were hit, because you were spinning away. You had to know how to recover quickly, though—opposite rudder to stop the spin, column forward and open the throttle." Spinning and spin recovery were part of sequence 10 of elementary training he had taken at No. 12 EFTS Goderich.

Later, during the massive daylight bombing raids of the war, Rae's squadron escorted American B-17 Flying Fortress bombers from Britain over to the continent. Typically, ten squadrons (about 120) Spitfires would meet 200 B-17s from stations all over Britain at a rendezvous point over the English Channel.

"One time," said Rae, remembering an escort operation, "our squadron of twelve Spits took off and immediately went into cloud. We were flying with three groups of four, line astern. I remember being tucked in very tightly in formation. We went into cloud at 3,000 and stayed in tight formation. I never lost sight of the next Spitfire, though I was perspiring like mad till we came out of the cloud at 26,000 feet.

"That's where you needed precision flying," Rae admitted. "So the precision flying from Service Flying Training School was the basis of knowing how to fly tightly and accurately. The only fellow flying on instruments is the leader. Everybody else is formating on him." Instrument flying was, of course, part of the EFTS syllabus, and formation flying was a basic flying skill Rae learned at No. 1 SFTS Camp Borden.

Pilot Officer Jackie Rae received his Distinguished Flying Cross in 1943 at Buckingham Palace. At nineteen years of age and still as cocky as the day he had switched files at the Toronto recruiting centre, Rae claimed that "it didn't mean a thing" and wondered outwardly, "Why are we bothering with this?" However, when at last he stood before King George VI to receive his DFC and then was introduced to Queen Elizabeth, "I was absolutely petrified, and was the ramrod airman when the moment arrived."

Jackie Rae survived his tour on Spitfires and his day at Buckingham Palace and came home from active service with his DFC, the Air Crew Europe Star, the Defence of Great Britain medal, and the Victory Medal. Because of his bravery—and his precision flying—he lived to return to his first love, show business, producing radio programs for the CBC, grandstand shows for the Canadian National Exhibition, television shows in the United Kingdom, and eventually appearances and recordings as leader of the Spitfire Band.

In the early days of the BCATP, when the air crew jobs of wireless radio operator and air-gunner were the responsibility of a single airman, called a wireless/air-gunner (WAG), a young recruit from Beaverton, Ontario, named Walter Loucks enlisted in Toronto. In 1941–42, he trained at No. 4 Wireless School in Guelph, Ontario, at No. 7 B&GS in Paulson, Manitoba, at No. 2 AOS in Edmonton, and at No. 32 OTU Patricia Bay before getting his operational posting.

Overseas, Loucks survived the crash of a Halifax on a conversion course at Dishforth, a bail-out over the French coast, and the aborted take-off of a fully gassed, fully bomb-loaded Halifax. On a Lancaster mission to Hamburg, WAG Loucks remembers they had just dropped their bomb load when "flak hit our transmitter. It exploded with a big flash right in my face. All the lights went out and we lost all electrical and voice communication.

"I knew the circuit breakers were to my right. That's when the voice of my instructor came back to me: the placement of each breaker, which breaker was which. By running my hands over them in the dark, I found that every one was in its proper place. However, my instructor had said that the main circuit breaker would never go. Turned out it was the only one that *had* gone. But that was a real thriller, that trip."

Pilot Officer Malcolm Davies also recalled his BCATP ground school instructors and his "intensive training in navigation." In August 1941, during his stint with No. 31 General Reconnaissance School (RAF) at Charlottetown, P.E.I., Davies perfected his dead reckoning and astro-nav techniques to plot dozens of flights on the ground and in the air over the Gulf of St. Lawrence. The idea was to be able to navigate in an emergency. He needed those skills in 1942, while flying with No. 612 Squadron, Coastal Command.

"I was flying as captain over the North Sea," Davies remembered. "It was minimum visibility and terrible weather with a trainee crew. My navigator became so airsick that he was unable to carry on. Even though a year had passed since my hands-on navigating in the air, I found I was able to take over and, with my second pilot at the controls, navigate us safely back to Cranwell base. I put it down to incessant drills in navigation.

"Those ground school instructors played an important role during the war and they probably received even less kudos than the flying instructors."

Perhaps out of respect for what his own instructors had given him, Davies later accepted a posting as instructor, first as a flying instructor on Wellington bombers at Haverfordwest in Wales and then as a navigation instructor at his former ground school in Charlottetown in Canada.

Jim Peat joked about the "flying ass-hole" air observer's crest he was awarded at Central Navigation School in Rivers, Manitoba, early in 1941. But he acknowledged the former army telegrapher (a First World War arm signalman) who helped him brush up his Morse code at No. 1 AOS Malton and the "excellent astro-nav training" he received at Rivers. "In a day when there was no radar on ops, we used to navigate by dead reckoning and star shots. My sextant gave me the necessary sightings, otherwise we would have been guessing—and lost." Peat was later seconded to the RAF Observer OTU at Wigtown, Scotland, where he instructed the first Canadian observers to train overseas. In 1943 he returned to Canada to serve as assistant chief instructor at No. 5 AOS in Winnipeg.

Lessons had become ingrained in BCATP hangars too. The daily and nightly routine of keeping fleets of training aircraft safely airborne over stations from Patricia Bay, Vancouver Island, to Debert, Nova Scotia, was a priceless asset to the war effort when some of those same ground crews were transferred to the operational airfields of Middleton St. George, Leeming, Skipton-on-Swale, Topcliffe, and Linton-on-Ouse for No. 6 RCAF Bomber Group.

Back in Canada the unofficial motto of the six BCATP repair depots across the country was "Ubendum Wemendum." Engineer Officer Bill Dunphy had endured his share of treks into the backwoods to retrieve airmen killed in training accidents and to salvage the wrecks. Once he was posted to Middleton St. George, Dunphy's experience at BCATP stations came into play regularly as he and his crews were called upon to "get approximately eighty Lancasters or Halifaxes away to their targets every night."

Also posted to Middleton St. George and No. 6 Group's 419 "Moose" Squadron was instrument technician Larry Mann.* Even though he joined the RCAF in Toronto in August 1941, he wasn't called up until December 8; and they called him "a patriot for joining the air force the day after Pearl Harbor." He chose to learn instruments (servicing air speed indicators, artificial horizons, altimeters, and fuel gauges) simply because "at St. Thomas Technical School there were hundreds of guys in class for air-frame mechanic courses, hundreds in aero-engine mechanics, but only fifteen for instruments. I liked the small class."

Mann was not impressed with the school, or the instruction, or the instructors. And life as an instrument tester at No. 3 SFTS

---

* Canadian-born Hollywood actor Larry Mann is known in performing circles today as Larry D. Mann.

Calgary was not hectic. Still, what he learned in the BCATP served him and the aircraft of "Moose" Squadron well.

"I guess I developed work habits that paid off," Mann said. "No one ever showed me exactly what to do. It was all in the book. And I have no memory of anyone ever taking me out to an aircraft and saying, 'This is how you should look for stress along a piece of aluminum from vibrations to the point that it's going to crack.'

"I used to take sandpaper and sand my fingers, so that when I ran my fingers along the metal and felt anything but smoothness, I knew there was a stress fracture there. And I taught myself never to go into an aircraft to do an inspection or an installation without a mouthful of chewing gum. When you screw an instrument into a hole, unscrew it, and put it back in a second time, the hole gets a bit bigger, and to make a tight fit again I found that chewing gum works fine when it hardens." Later, when Bomber Command needed someone to instruct Halifax bomb-aimers on their new Course Setting Bomb Sights, Mann was posted to an OTU to do the job.

While not a matter of life and death, a wad of well worked-over chewing gum to ensure that a reinstalled instrument would stay put was a handy bit of improvisation. Other tricks of the trade played a more crucial role in surviving. Whenever he practised aerobatics as a Harvard instructor at Dunnville, Charley Fox used to go into a steep turn, flip around in the other direction, and turn the aircraft upside down; he called it "sliding downhill." He used the same manoeuvre chasing a Focke-Wulf 190 and shot it down by putting the Spitfire into the same upside-down attitude.

Another technique was called for when bomber aircraft were "coned," or pinpointed in converging searchlights over a target area. The pilot often responded by quickly manoeuvring the Lancaster or Halifax into a twisting, rolling dive; this dangerous corkscrew action often allowed the bomber to level out at a lower altitude, sometimes eluding the searchlights and deadly anti-aircraft fire.

On his fourth mission over Kiel, Regina-born bomber pilot Erik Nielsen encountered what he called a "veritable hail of flak." Nielsen's

Lancaster was well back in the stream of bombers that night, and when he reached the target and unloaded his 22,000 pounds of bombs, the German ground batteries coned his airplane. "In seconds there was the drum beat of shrapnel pounding into us," he wrote, "piercing the aircraft skin and causing serious damage. We had to get out of that cone fast . . .

"I decided to try a hazardous manoeuvre I had heard more experienced pilots talk about. Having lowered both wheels and flaps, I throttled off all power and simultaneously raised the flaps and wheels. The aircraft dropped like a stone. The stresses on the aircraft were considerable; rivets popped and a metal panel on the starboard wing ripped off. We were out of the cone, but we were losing altitude at an alarming rate," from 23,000 feet to 10,000 feet.

Despite encountering a Heinkel 110 fighter, losing two engines (including one that powered the aircraft's generators and therefore the navigator's electric equipment), Nielsen's crew managed to limp home on the two remaining engines and the navigator's dead reckoning calculations. They landed at their No. 101 RAF Squadron station at Ludford Magna so late that most of their mess mates thought they had been downed.

"We had had our baptism of fire and survived," concluded Nielsen, "We survived because the long days, weeks, and months of training came to our aid when we needed it most." Nielsen's training helped him outlive a full tour of thirty-three operations. He went on to survive and thrive on thirty years of public life (from 1957 to 1987) as the MP for Yukon in the Canadian House of Commons.

Jeff Mellon accumulated three years' worth of military flying between the time the RCAF called him up in August 1941 and March 1944. He piled up instructing hours at Uplands, Dunnville, St. Catharines, Goderich, and Centralia (in one month at Centralia he logged more than 130 hours). Yet his logbooks full of instructor's hours did eventually pay off in 1944, when he was finally posted overseas to train on the Spitfire XIV, "considered the number-one fighting aircraft of its day.

"I was totally confident. I didn't have many hours on the Spitfire, but I had a lot of flying time. I knew how to get out of a mess. I knew a lot about flying. Hours of flying experience helped you spot certain things that indicated you had more experience than the other guy. When you see a German aircraft going into combat with an auxiliary fuel tank still in place, well, that means he is an inexperienced pilot. You can take liberties with him that you might not with others. This guy is admitting right off the bat that he is out of control, that he doesn't know how to fly his airplane. Trying to dogfight with a big gas tank in place like that cuts down his manoeuvrability."

Ex-instructor Frank Montgomery also believed that "the whole thing about flying is time." Since 1937, when he had painted houses and picked rocks from farmers' fields around Saskatoon to finance his flying lessons, Montgomery had been logging plenty of flying time. An early instructor in the BCATP, he had flown single- and twin-engine elementary and service aircraft. He had taught pilots on the Canadian prairies and run the Conversion Training School at Trenton. By 1944, when he went overseas to fly two-man Mosquitoes with No. 418 "Cat's Eye" Squadron in the 2nd Tactical Air Force, he had logged more than 2,000 hours. He eventually completed a tour of forty-five missions.

"One night we went to Groeningen, in northern Holland," Montgomery recalled. "Just as we got there, they coned us with searchlights. So we turned and ran for it. But we turned right, not left. Everybody turns left. They assumed you would turn left. It's easier to turn an aircraft left because of the propeller. So we turned right, dove, and got away. That was the beauty of the time you put in instructing."

Designed as a fast bomber, the twin-engine Mosquito was originally intended to fly a daylight bombing run to Berlin and back without serious opposition. At sea level its top speed was 385 miles per hour. It could carry four 500-pound bombs. It was armed with four cannons mounted underneath the aircraft and four .303 machine guns in its nose. Its speed and manoeuvrability soon hurried the Mosquito into a greater role as fighter-bomber, assigned to make low-level night strikes against German airfields. This "intruder" role included "Flower Missions," providing cover over German night-fighter airfields along the routes that Allied bombers were travelling to a target.

By the time Russ Bannock commanded No. 418 Squadron, virtually all his Mosquito pilots were former flying instructors, including Bannock himself. None had fewer than 1,000 to 2,000 hours of experience back home in the BCATP. Each could devote his full attention to the operation at hand without having to worry about flying the Mosquito. And because night-intruding was usually carried out by a single aircraft attacking each airfield, the Mosquito crew worked alone, relying on the combined experience of the pilot and navigator to accomplish the mission. Among Bannock's fellow Mosquito pilots were: Don McFadyen, who in 1941 became the first BCATP graduate to get an A2 instructor's category and instructed at Summerside and Trenton CFS and as part of a Visiting Flight before going overseas to win a DFC; Charlie Krause, who had spent two years and 1,400 hours instructing at Dunnville; Larry Walker, who had logged 1,650 hours by the time he left instructing duties at Dunnville in 1944; and John Evans, who had instructed at Calgary and Hagersville before going overseas to join No. 418 to participate in "Flower" operations beginning in February and March 1944.

"Typical of one of these 'Flower' operations was my own experience on June 10, 1944," Bannock described. "It was immediately after D-Day. The bombers were attacking railway yards south of Paris. I was assigned a known Luftwaffe night-fighter airfield called Bourges Avord, about 100 miles south of Paris. About midnight I attacked a Messerschmitt Bf-110 as it landed. It exploded just as he touched down. Then the whole airfield was like the CNE—coloured lights coming up at me from all directions. We did a tight 180-degree turn at 100 feet.

"I had turned so tight, though, that the Mosquito actually flicked on me. But having had all that instructing experience, I instinctively let go. The thing you mustn't do in a high-speed stall when it flicks over is to attempt to correct it with aileron. If you do that, it will just whip right around. Instead, I just let go and let it unstall itself, and carried on the other way. I chalk it up to instructing experience."

A contemporary of Russ Bannock's in No. 418 Squadron was navigator Dave McIntosh. Born in the small Quebec village of Stanstead near the Vermont border, McIntosh dreamed of becoming a journalist. By the 1930s he was taking courses in political science and English (taught by poet E.J. Pratt) at the University of Toronto. When the war broke out he began pilot training, but he spun a Link trainer at ITS and was sent to Malton's No. 1 AOS.

"My chief course instructor was a man named L.S. Wismer," McIntosh remembered. "He was very patient and methodical and knew how to lodge this dead reckoning, map reading, and celestial navigation stuff into our heads. And we had this great textbook called *Air Navigation* by Weems, an American army flyer."

In Britain in April 1943, McIntosh was crewed up at the OTU for No. 418 Mosquito Squadron with a former BCATP instructor from San Francisco, Sidney Seid, a pilot McIntosh described as "a Jewish Billy Bishop [intent on] killing as many Germans as possible."

Between Seid's extraordinary low-level flying ability and McIntosh's navigation they chalked up forty-one trips on Mosquitoes, and were credited with nine aircraft destroyed on the ground. They both received DFCs. McIntosh credits his success and survival to Seid's flying hours (as an instructor), a lot of luck, and his navigational techniques. McIntosh used to nick off intervals on a long pencil, one per minute. With their Mosquito flying at 240 mph, every nick represented four miles. This method gave McIntosh his time and distance against the map.

"With the map reading I had learned from Wismer, I could go anywhere. Flying over Ontario at night, beyond the cities where it was totally dark, your pinpoints were roads, rivers, and lakes. Of course, with Europe blacked out this practice really helped.

"One night we flew into Poland and timed it so we arrived at the first airfield we were going to attack at dawn. I remember tracing a route along the bends and turns of the Elbe River with my pencil and my map-reading.

"We got so good at this, we once went all the way back into Stargard on the Polish-German border and interrupted Sunday morning church parade. There they all were, drawn up for parade. We'd come all the way across Germany. They had no idea we were there. With this low-level navigation you could go anywhere. . . . When I think of it now, Wismer's instruction was behind it all."

McIntosh and Seid were both back home in North America by Christmas 1944. McIntosh's DFC citation said that he had shown "great skill and determination in navigating his pilot to the target and back." The air force encouraged him to instruct and he said, "I tried to teach some navigators at Greenwood, Nova Scotia," but he soon gave up and resigned the instructing to the L.S. Wismers of the world.

Many Allied combat flyers also cite their instrument flying experience as a key to their survival on ops. Indeed, several describe training "under the hood" at Service Flying Training School as their "life insurance policy" overseas.

At first glance, flying on instruments in the second cockpit of a Harvard, or the left-hand seat of a twin-engine Anson, may not seem at all like piloting an eighteen-ton Lancaster in a 1,000-bomber raid to Berlin, until one realizes that en route to the target in Germany there were no lights. In effect, the pilot was flying blind. Collisions with friendly aircraft were common, some said as high as 10 percent of the aircraft losses on a raid.

"When you took off in a bomber at night," remembered former Dunnville instructor Fred Macdonell, "everything was blacked out. No lights on the ground. No lights in the air. Barely enough subdued light in the cockpit to see your instruments. The navigator was in a little compartment behind; there was a curtain all around; he had a little light for his logs, that's all. You knew there were aircraft all around you in the same raid. You knew before you took off what height you'd be bombing from.

"Then all of a sudden you would feel the aircraft go and you knew you were in somebody's stream. As wide as you opened your eyes you couldn't see anything in front of you at all. You felt the flutter, the turbulence, and you knew there was an aircraft there.

"At night we went as individual units. My navigator was doing all the calculating. We weren't allowed to use radios at night. You would hear and feel the flak bursting around you. It wasn't unusual to come over the target, say at 18,000 feet, and all of a sudden be able to see in front of you, because over the target, with flames and fire below, there would be a certain amount of light. And you would see the outline of another aircraft opening its bomb doors, ready to drop its bombs.

"After you went over your target, you usually went straight on for about sixty seconds, then came down to a different height and a much faster speed. But you wouldn't see anything in the night until you got back over the aerodrome again in Britain. Then you would hear all the others landing. Then there would be lights on the runway and we could use our radios.

"I wasn't really nervous. I had flown over 2,000 hours and plenty on instruments. I had a job to do—get those bombs dropped and get out of there as fast as possible."

The same kind of instrument experience was essential when flying in clouds. Clouds were often a refuge for bomber and fighter pilots being pursued by fighters. On the other hand, flying in clouds could confuse an operational pilot the same way they did trainees on the Canadian prairies or along the Great Lakes. Rock-solid skill on instruments was something instructor Willy Clymer insisted upon when he came back from an overseas tour on Spitfires early in 1943.

"My instrument flying was not very good when I first went overseas," Clymer said. Even at Initial Training School, he admitted he never had an aptitude for mathematics, and despite his strong aerobatic skills, Clymer ignored his instructors' attempts to improve his tests under the hood. Clymer went overseas in January 1942, learned to fly Spitfires at Grangemouth OTU in Scotland, and then joined a fighter squadron on convoy patrol over the Irish Sea.

"One day we got scrambled to go after a German who was going up and down the Irish Sea. We had to climb up through about 20,000 feet of cloud. Just solid. I was in good formation with my leader, Lloyd Hunt. I clung to his wing all the way up. When we got up above this cloud, they told us the German had been shot down over Ireland and to return to the station. So down we came. Lloyd was going like hell. Eventually, I lost him in the clouds. So I pulled away, so I wouldn't hit him. Course, I was upside down. And everything toppled. The instruments were flopping all over, and in a Spitfire things happen so fast.

"I was coming straight down. Then the IFF [the Identification, Friend or Foe radio*] blew up, went blam! right behind my head. Luckily I came out of the dive, didn't hit the sea, and got back. But I should have paid attention to my instruments."

Clymer's tour ended during the North Africa campaign in November 1942. A burst of ground fire came through the instrument panel of his Spitfire, went through his shoulder, and brought him down at Medjez el Bab, Tunisia. Fortunately, he managed to scramble back to nearby Allied lines. The next year, back in Canada as an instructor in the BCATP, Clymer found he could share much of his combat flying knowledge with his students. But above all, he insisted that they "rely on those instruments for those times you're by yourself in cloud."

That's how former EFTS instructor Brick Bradford survived a Spitfire flight deep into China. In June 1944, Bradford took off from his No. 681 Squadron station at Calcutta. His destination in Japanese-occupied China was a bridge crossing the Salween River. Intelligence wanted to know if the Japanese were using the bridge as a supply route to the Burma Road. Bradford made one fuel stop near the front in northeastern India, then set out in search of the bridge. When he had found it, photographed it, and left it behind, Bradford realized his Spitfire was at the limit of its range.

---

* The IFF, or Identification, Friend or Foe device, was similar to a modern transponder and constantly transmitted a coded signal so that British radar could track the airplane's flight path. The signal identified Allied aircraft; if it wasn't on and operating, an aircraft stood a good chance of being mistaken for a German aircraft and of being shot down by Allied fire.

The route back to the fuel stop was now blocked by a vast storm front. He couldn't afford the extra fuel to climb over it, so he chose to fly through it at about 22,000 feet, where the Spitfire "got all iced up flying through the weather. I lost my airspeed, my vertical speed, and my altimeter. My horizon toppled. And in the turbulence even my compass was spinning around.

"For the better part of an hour, going through thunderstorms, snow, and icing, you might say I was down to zero instruments, except for the slip-and-skid (or turn-and-bank) indicator. I used that and the sound of the slipstream going by the aircraft to climb through this weather."

When Bradford's Spitfire finally broke out of the cloud, he was at 42,000 feet, flying between two towering thunderstorms. His fuel gauge showed thirty gallons of fuel left. And he was well past his fuel stop. He had no choice but to make a long descent to his home station at Calcutta. When he landed, his fuel tanks registered empty. He had been in the air three hours and forty-five minutes. The photographs he had taken revealed that the Japanese had rebuilt the previously bombed-out bridge and had re-established supply lines. Thanks to Bradford's blind flying, a mission to destroy the bridge again was accomplished a few days later; "but," Bradford added, "I'm sure anybody with a couple of hundred hours could never have made it through that weather."

Flying in cloud nearly killed Australian Ren Henderson. After being initiated into the BCATP by the Canadian winter of 1942, Henderson received his wings later that year at Dunnville. He endured six months' instructing at Camp Borden, then was posted to OTU at Bagotville, and finally went overseas. In May 1944, Henderson was flying alone in cloud over Dieppe and, he said, "I did something almost fatal. I didn't believe my instruments.

"I went into a spin. I had no idea of the altitude of the cloud base. But having done a little more of this stuff as an instructor than normal, I was fortunate enough to do a spin recovery in the cloud on instruments. And when I broke cloud, there was less than a thousand feet of clearance.

"If I hadn't come out when I did, I would have been killed. No one would have known any different. It was just plain stupidity. I would have paid the price with my life. But I was lucky. I got away with it."

If Henderson had crashed that day, he would have missed perhaps the most exhilarating experience of his wartime career. A month after his near miss at Dieppe was D-Day. On the evening of June 6, ex-instructor Henderson was up over the same French coast escorting the gliders that carried paratroops of the British 6th Airborne Division to Normandy.

"The glider stream was forty-six miles long," Henderson said, "with 460 gliders and tow planes. We had probably twelve or fourteen squadrons. We picked up the glider stream at a place called Littlehampton on the south coast of England. You had a specific rendezvous; if you were two minutes late you could be thirty miles out of position. But we picked them up at 8:30 and stayed with the stream, patrolling it.

"It was an incredible sight. There were something like 8,000 vessels of every description, all headed in one direction, across the Channel. We could have bailed out anywhere between the south coast of England and the coast of France, and where you landed, you couldn't have been any more than 300 yards from a ship. There'll never be another sight like it."

When Henderson got back to his home station at Newchurch, he stole the bulletin of the day's activities as a memento. It described the "Operations for 6/6/44 by Newchurch Squadrons," and commended No. 56 Squadron including the twelve aircraft pilots, F/O Henderson among them, for providing "close escort for Albemarles towing Horsa gliders to the beach head."

"The whole scene was rather like a lurid cover of the *Boys Own Paper* depicting war in a hundred years' time," he said. "The sky was a mass of aircraft, bombs dropping, hundreds of barges landing, ships firing at the shore, and gliders landing. The squadron escorted the tugs home after the gliders had been released and landed safely at 22.25 hrs, a trip of 2 hrs 35 mins."

Across the bottom of Henderson's souvenir bulletin, a warning read: "The above information is secret and may not be discussed off camp or communicated to anyone."

In the days and months of war that followed D-Day, Allied airmen on ops compared notes on their flights. Officially they were debriefed to determine whether targets were achieved, whether scores could be confirmed, which crews were lost, and how others limped home. Pilots' logs showed nothing but the bare facts of an operation—details of departure, destination, and flight duration. Diaries told much of the rest of the personal story. Yet many air crew just retreated to their Nissen hut bunks and kept what they had seen and heard in the skies to themselves.

There was some "hangar flying" though—conversations in the officers' mess, at the NAAFI van that sold sticky buns and tea, and on the flight lines where the ground crews and combat crews prepared for their next sortie. Airmen talked about yesterday's heroes and tomorrow's targets. They speculated about what the thinking was at Bomber and Fighter Command. They dreamed out loud about what they would do after the war. And while some probably talked about the good or bad state of the war effort, it's not likely they talked much about how much of the war's outcome had been determined by the plan that had trained them.

12

THEY GOT NO GONGS

During the first week of May 1945, pilot Eric Johnston flew his final operational missions. He had flown Halifax bombers for most of his thirty-five trips, so when his squadron got its orders for May 6, to attack a German ship on Skagerrak—the strait of water between Denmark and Sweden—he expected a fairly routine flight. Not that these ops were a cakewalk. In fact, as many as five crews a week had been lost during what would turn out to be the last month of the war.

The war in Europe was finally coming to an end. On February 4, 1945, Churchill, Roosevelt, and Stalin held a conference in Yalta to discuss the liberation of German-occupied Europe, the Allied occupation of Germany, and the creation of a United Nations organization. In the weeks that followed, German resistance on the ground crumbled. The British, Canadians, and Americans crossed the Rhine in March and, with the Russians, surrounded Berlin in April. The Germans surrendered Italy on April 29. On May 4, General Bernard Law Montgomery accepted the surrender of German forces in Holland, Denmark, and northwest Germany.

Eric Johnston had waited a long time to share in a little of the glory that the Allied air forces were enjoying in early 1945. In 1939, the eighteen-year-old Johnston had been "a Sunday afternoon pilot," building up his hours and hanging around legendary barnstormers like Walt Leavens and Len Trippe. Unlike other private pilots with their sights set on the RCAF, all Eric Johnston wanted was "to build up my hours and land a job flying for Trans-Canada Airlines. Then we started hearing these wonderful rumours about this plan the government was setting up, where you could pick up a couple of hundred hours flying by instructing."

A couple of hundred hours of instructing turned into several thousand. Johnston enlisted in the RCAF, joined a program with Leavens Brothers at Barker Field to increase his flying time, and took an instructor's course at Trenton. Early in 1941 the air force put him on indefinite leave without pay and sent him to No. 9 EFTS St. Catharines to replace one of the two instructors—Whitaker and Wellington—who had been killed in a mock dogfight over the station the previous October.

For the next two years, Johnston settled into the role of elementary instructor. He lived on the fourth floor of the Lincoln Hotel in downtown St. Catharines, but his time was consumed by flying—sometimes a hundred hours a month. He introduced scores of jittery LACs to aerobatics and the airsickness bag. He coaxed them to solo in Fleets and then to fly cross-country on their own. He hated to wash anyone out. Every eight weeks he graduated another three or four trainees on their way to SFTS, Wings Parade, and ops.

Johnston had his share of close calls. One winter day when the weather closed in, there was an extremely low ceiling and icing conditions, so trainees were grounded. Instructor Johnston took a student up in spite of the weather, "because I kept thinking about all those hours I would need before the war ended, so that I could get into Trans-Canada Airlines."

Above the overcast the flying was fine, but on the descent through the clouds the Fleet's wings iced, its carburetor clogged, and the engine died. When he broke through the ceiling, Johnston found himself just above the high-tension electrical wires over Niagara Falls, Ontario. It was too late to bail out. His only hope was to land the Fleet in a stretch of open residential backyards nearby. He glided beneath the wires, just avoiding the tree-tops of an orchard, and brought the airplane down in one piece. They had to take the Fleet apart to remove it from its forced landing site.

On another occasion, Johnston took a student for some low-flying practice along the beach of Lake Ontario "perhaps about twenty-five feet off the deck, as we whizzed past the enemy—a civilian. Just as we passed him, he hurled a fair-sized rock at us with very admirable aim; it went right through a rondell on the side of the fuselage behind the wing." No damage was done, but it could have been serious. "My wife and I often laugh at what she would have told the kids: 'Father was shot down while in the service by a guy with a rock.'

"Instructors were always saying that we all wanted to go overseas and be heroes," Johnston said. In September 1942, the air force released some of the senior instructors at St. Catharines—Banty Pallett, Al Stirton, and Keith Patman—to train for their wings and try for overseas postings. Six months later, the air force invited more instructors to move on to wings and operational training. Johnston was surprised when his signature was one of only two applying. "All my fellow instructors discovered their wives were pregnant and their dog was having pups and all sorts of important reasons why they didn't want to go overseas. I was still angling for Trans-Canada and figured I needed experience on four-engine aircraft."

In late 1944, with 5,000 hours of flying logged, Johnston waited in Bournemouth for a posting. There he heard that an RAF Halifax crew at St. David, in Wales, was in need of a pilot. The CO, a former BCATP instructor from Rhodesia, checked him out on a Halifax and he got the posting. Thirty-odd operational flights later, Johnston was flying with No. 502 RAF Squadron on anti-shipping missions from the Isle of Lewis in northern Scotland.

On May 6, 1945, he received the order to proceed to Skagerrak. Although Denmark had capitulated, some German forces were apparently trying to consolidate what manpower and armaments were left by shipping supplies from Norway via Skagerrak to the Kiel Canal back into Germany. Allied Intelligence had also heard about a sloop that was going to make a dash from the Kiel Canal through the straits to the open sea. Rumour had it that Hitler and Goebbels were aboard.

(It was later learned that Hitler had committed suicide on April 30, Goebbels on May 1.)

Johnston and two other Halifaxes took off at 4 a.m. in search of the sloop. But after several passes over the straits, all they encountered was some German shipping. They engaged the convoy, dropped their bombs, and turned for home. However, Johnston's crew discovered their Halifax had been hit—oil was pouring out of one of its engines.

"All the previous day and night," Johnston said, "we had been hearing these reports from Denmark that the Germans had surrendered there. As we flew around in search of the shipping, we could hear American pilots talking to each other about getting down into Copenhagen [which had been surrendered to British troops on May 5]. We decided that with the leaking engine we had the perfect excuse to get down to these parties in Copenhagen. I got permission from our base in Scotland to land at Copenhagen, but when we got there it was all closed in with fog."

Johnston then flew his Halifax up the Danish peninsula to the aerodrome at Aalborg, which he assumed had been liberated during the surrender of Denmark on May 2. He got clearance from his Scottish base and in a display of bravado "went screaming up the main street of the town just over the streetlights. After attracting the town's attention this way, we circled the airport. I got the green light from the tower, landed, taxied up to the control tower, and was just going to shut off the engines when I looked around. I couldn't see one single American airplane. We were the only Allies that had arrived there. I thought, 'What if the Germans have been instructed to shoot it out to the last man?'

"My reaction was to keep the starboard outer engine going so we could at least shoot it out with them from the mid-upper turret and die a glorious death or something. But the German commandant wheeled out in his big Daimler, with his beautiful uniform and his adjutant in the front seat.

"My engineer, Jock Horn, could speak German. He said, 'They're surrendering the airport.' And here is Johnston, with the sleeve out of his shirt at the elbow, unshaved, looking like a bum.

"Then, like the Keystone Kops smashing through the fence at the far side of the aerodrome, came about ten cars speeding across the runway, bouncing up in the air, with people all hanging off the running boards. This was the Danish Underground coming out to greet us."

For the next twelve hours, Johnston and his Halifax crew experienced one of the strangest days of their lives. They were driven down the main street before hundreds of ecstatic Danish citizens, fêted at the Phoenix Hotel as the guests of honour, and given a tour of the former Gestapo headquarters and the cell block where German SS prisoners were now being held. Johnston was presented with the flag of the Danish Underground fighters and was hailed as the conquering hero of Aalborg. The following morning, May 7, 1945, as the Germans signed an unconditional surrender to the Allies at Reims, France, Johnston rounded up his six-man crew, returned to the Aalborg airport to find his Halifax repaired, and took off for Scotland.

The next day was May 8—VE (Victory in Europe) Day.

Three months later, after his return to Canada on August 11, an emotional reunion with his wife, and an honourable discharge from the RCAF, Eric Johnston gathered up his logbooks, put on his uniform, and went to Trans-Canada Airlines. He did not have any significant war decorations—no "gongs" as they were called—but neither did his record show any endorsements, or black marks.

At that time, the chief pilot at Trans-Canada was an old friend of Johnston's, another pilot who had learned to fly with the Leavens Brothers outfit in the 1930s. He had flown for Ferry Command. Seeing a familiar face, Johnston figured his lifelong dream was about to be realized.

"I'm here," Johnston said proudly. "I've come to get a job."

The TCA chief pilot looked at Johnston for a moment. Then he said, "We don't want any more of you air force pilots. We don't like the kind of experience you have. If we change our course, I'll let you know."

This was Johnston's reward for the 5,000 hours he had flown, the students he had taught, the combat he had survived, the air war he had helped to win. No acknowledgement. No gongs. No job.

Medals had an odd effect on the airmen who won them. When a flyer received one—a Distinguished Flying Cross, a Distinguished Service Order, or a Bar—he understandably felt tremendous pride. So did his comrades in arms and his family. But most recipients were modest about the honour. They acknowledged that it symbolized simply carrying out orders in the line of duty. Nevertheless, any decoration worn by airmen generally announced to all who saw it that the wearer had gone to war, had served willingly, and had demonstrated commitment and bravery to the cause.

It was no disgrace not to win a medal of bravery. But an airman who had served in Canada and therefore did not receive an overseas service medal often suffered a certain amount of embarrassment, frustration, and even grief.

In the course of two years of instructing at St. Catharines, Pendleton, and Windsor, Stan Castle calculated that he turned out fifty new pilots for "the war machine." He flew 1,400 hours. He survived (and helped his students survive) numerous brushes with death in Tiger Moths, Harvards, Cornells, Cranes, Ansons, and Fleets. After the war he met up with an old air force friend at an RCAF function in Toronto.

"Hiya, Betts," Castle called out.

After greetings were exchanged, Betts asked why Castle didn't have any gongs or even the Canada flash on his shoulder—something only those who went overseas received. Castle explained that he had instructed throughout the war.

Betts was unimpressed. "I did thirty trips. Every one can be your last."

Castle didn't say another word to him. He respected, even envied his friend's experience, but thought, "I didn't elect to be a flying instructor. He didn't elect to go overseas with Bomber Command. You went where you were told. I felt forlorn that he'd rejected me."

Elementary instructor Gus Bennett flew neither Lancaster raids nor Spitfire sorties. But he was probably in the air longer than an entire squadron of bomber or fighter pilots. And the more you flew in training aircraft, the more you ran the risk of being killed by an inexperienced student. His career in EFTS and FIS instructing included countless forced landing drills. None was, as some operational pilots would say, "a piece of cake." After one forced landing in a muddy field, on take-off a large clod of mud from the wheel of his Fleet flew into the propeller and broke off a third of one of the blades; the single engine nearly tore itself apart before Bennett brought the Fleet and its petrified student down safely.

"I'm not bitter at not getting any gongs," Bennett said. But since he instructed at elementary level in Windsor, CFS level in Trenton, and at Transport OTU in Britain, "it would have been nice if we could have been recognized in some way for a tour of duty, for a year or two years of instructing. We put our lives on the line. We all did."

Many BCATP instructors had flown five to ten times as long as bomber and fighter pilots. Although they quickly point out that flying in combat situations was more stressful and heroic, as Ren Henderson (an Australian who had both instructed and flown operations) put it: "There's nothing a pilot could have done on ops that would have been any more dangerous than sitting in the back seat while some jackass is trying to land an aircraft thirty feet above the snow. That's dicey stuff."

Nevertheless instructors were often treated like lesser servicemen. Many people considered an overseas posting superior to an instructional posting and therefore the flying ability of an instructor inferior to that of an ops flyer. The feeling was that "dashing heroes were needed overseas; steady, safe, and studious types were needed as instructors." Some civilians even believed that instructors were evaders, cowards, or "zombies" (those who had refused to serve).

It took Bill McCauley half the war to escape his first air force assignment in the RCAF band, playing at the funerals of airmen killed in training. When he finally got his wings he was sent to FIS at Trenton and then to Uplands to instruct, "which was considered a second-class job. Everybody wanted to find out what they could do in an actual situation, not practising," McCauley lamented. "I wanted to have a whack at it. There was a certain pride to going overseas, and if you didn't go overseas, what you did didn't count for much."

During his three years instructing in the BCATP, Wess McIntosh flew more than 3,000 hours, earned his A Category instructor's rating, and took up more than 200 students. His CO sent in a recommendation that McIntosh receive the Air Force Cross, but it was turned down.

Even when an instructor received some recognition for his efforts, it was done in a backhanded way. Bruce "Banty" Pallett used to kid his friends that the reason he never got overseas was that he was a coward. He often said he was fortunate that "I never had a shot fired at me . . . just students trying to kill me in the training circuit." He instructed at No. 9 EFTS from 1940 to 1943, and when he finally won his wings, he was sent back to instructing at elementary schools in St. Catharines and Oshawa, Ontario. After the war he received the Air Force Cross.

The citation read: "This officer has been employed as an elementary flying instructor for almost three years. His devotion through hundreds of hours of instructional time has been outstanding. His keen sense of humour, marked determination and organizing ability, as well as his outstanding abilities as a pilot and instructor, have been a splendid example and inspiration to all." The AFC was mailed to Pallett from Trenton. It arrived at his home in Dixie, Ontario—in spring 1949.

At one time a rumour circulated among the BCATP schools that the air force was planning to award medals to acknowledge instructors who had accumulated a thousand hours in Training Command. Tom Hawkins had 2,200 hours, and his frustration at not getting an overseas posting was temporarily eased when he heard this. He had got his wings in June 1942, when the plan was in greatest need of instructors; forty-eight out of his graduating class of forty-nine were kept back from overseas duty to become instructors.

Of course the rumour of an instructor's medal turned out to be just that. Hawkins instructed from August 1942 until August 1945 and went through the mixed emotions of helping to close down No. 13 EFTS at St. Eugene, Ontario, the school where he'd spent most of the war years. When he realized he was never going to get official recognition, he consoled himself with memories of the more than fifty students he helped go solo, and took satisfaction in knowing he was among the best in his occupation.

"In instructing," Hawkins said, "you had to let the student go as far as possible to recognize he was doing something wrong. You had to let him go so he could learn. Then, if he didn't recognize his mistake, you had to take over before things really went wrong. No one can teach you that. You learn by experience.

"One time a student was landing a Fleet Finch. He had control. I was in the back cockpit. There was a hell of a strong cross-wind from the left. The student tried to touch down for a three-point landing, but with the wind gusting it got away on him. The wind got underneath and we were headed for the mud. I had let his landing get to a point where there was going to be a disaster.

"Well, I banged on full throttle and full stick back. We ended up vertical with both right wingtips in the mud. We pivoted and ended up level, going back parallel to the runway downwind with some air speed. I tried to get it airborne.

"What saved us was that at the end of the field there was a twenty-foot gully with a little stream at the bottom. We hopped into this twenty feet of air space, and that enabled the Fleet to pick up enough speed to stay fully airborne. We staggered into the air again and came around and I made the landing. It was stupidity on my part for allowing the student to try a tail-down three-point landing in that strong wind. We got away with it. And I learned." For Hawkins, the reward for service was simply the sense of lessons learned and a job well done.

Hadley Armstrong did get the AFC for his three years of instructing, but a more personal form of recognition upstaged his medal.

"During the two years I instructed at Fort Macleod, Alberta, I taught one class of Aussies," Armstrong recalled. "One day before I left the station, this fellow came into the flight office and introduced himself. He was a group captain. Turned out he had been my student. I asked him what the hell had happened.

"'Everybody else was killed on the squadron,' he said. 'You wake up in the morning and there's two of you left. One becomes squadron commander, the other flight commander. Next morning someone else is gone, so the squadron commander goes up to wing commander and the flight commander goes up to squadron commander.' Early in the war when they were all getting killed, that's the way promotions went.

"And he thanked me for the instruction I'd given him. That meant more to me than any medal."

Not everyone regretted missing the experience of ops. As with so many RCAF instructors, the desire to fly an airplane—any airplane—as often as he could was Bill Frost's incentive to join the air force. Once into the RCAF training stream, Frost became an SFTS instructor and was quite happy teaching young pilots how to fly Harvards at Moncton, Kingston, and Weyburn. As for operations, Frost said, "I looked on what I did as a job. It wasn't a patriotic gesture. Some instructors wanted to be shooting types, cowboys. They wanted to go over and have a whack at some of the fighting. I signed up to go wherever they wanted to send me. I had no regrets at not going overseas."

Ross Truemner had no desire to go on ops either. But for him, instructing became a passion, not just a job. When he graduated at the top of his class at No. 10 SFTS Dauphin in October 1941, he was given an immediate commission and, based on his course standing, sent to Trenton's Central Flying School, not to Fighter Command. Some of his fellow graduates even called Truemner down for wanting to instruct rather than to fight. "I didn't have a burning desire to get over and get shot at. Now maybe that's cowardice. But I knew two or three instructors who saved my bacon. I just wanted to return the favour." So, for the better part of three years, principally at Hagersville, Truemner did his part by giving scores of BCATP trainees the confidence and competence to become capable operations pilots, often employing the "ground briefing" method his own EFTS instructor had used to help him get up solo. Truemner was awarded the Air Force Cross in large part for his dedication in Training Command.

Other pilots found few rewards of any kind in instructing. Wilf Sutherland and Cy Roberts referred to their instructing assignments as "the kiss of death." Sutherland came from Edmonton, Roberts from Calgary, and both taught service flying at Manitoba stations—Brandon and Dauphin respectively. Although they came to love twin-engine Cranes and Ansons, neither joined the air force with any other intention than "to go through to be a fighter or bomber pilot. That was the whole raison d'être," Sutherland insisted. "You weren't supposed to sit back in Canada in some two-by-four sandlot teaching some damn sprog to fly.

"Most of the fellows we graduated, they generally got awarded the DFC, because it was good distinguished flying to survive an operational tour. They earned it. But a lot of us could have bought it many times on training. I would have liked to see a little more recognition for instructors."

Rarely, if ever, in the six years of the Second World War and the British Commonwealth Air Training Plan was an instructor referred to as a hero. The idea makes most BCATP veterans extremely uncomfortable. They insist that instructing was not dangerous when compared to piloting a bomber with the responsibility of a crew and bomb load aboard, surviving flak, fighter engagement, and the treacherous trip home. They add that the training aircraft were always in good flying condition and that if an instructor had to crash-land, it was always in friendly territory.

"Anybody could have done it," Hadley Armstrong said. "We were the right age at the right time and we were willing. But what we did was routine. We really weren't heroic." He even wondered, "How many of our students who went on ops died because of what we didn't teach them? Nobody will ever know."

Armstrong was one of only 427 RCAF airmen who received the Air Force Cross. In contrast, 4,021 received the Distinguished Flying Cross; 515 won the Distinguished Flying Medal; and 2,197 were Mentioned in Dispatches. Air force records also show that by the end of the war the RCAF had suffered more than 13,000 operational casualties and more than 3,000 training fatalities.

Despite the lower numbers of training deaths, Stan Castle, who witnessed the deaths of fellow instructors and students during his service in the BCATP, comments, "An instructor killed in a crash at the hands of an inexperienced student or because of internal damage done to the airplane an hour before is just as dead as if he were shot on ops."

However, the statistics processed at No. 1 Training Command headquarters and the awards for valour determined at the Air Ministry could never recognize all the remarkable deeds done by all its air crew, least of all those who served 3,000 miles from the front lines. The day-to-day heroism in the daily routines of BCATP students and instructors is not recorded officially, although it is remembered by the flyers who participated in the plan.

During his two and an half years of instructing on Fleet Finches and Tiger Moths at No. 12 EFTS Goderich, civilian instructor Harold Lancaster remembered "flying our backsides off." Harold was the youngest of seven boys raised on a farm in southwestern Ontario; four of his brothers enlisted in the RCAF, and two were killed—one overseas and the other in a training accident. Harold had expected to go overseas but was chosen by the air force to instruct. He logged nearly 1,500 hours as a flying instructor at Sky Harbour airfield in Goderich.

It was probably not recorded in any other place but the station's mechanical fault reports, but one winter day in 1943, during three morning instructional flights, Lancaster survived three engine failures on the same Tiger Moth. The first happened during aerobatics practice when the Tiger's carburetor iced up; Lancaster brought the aircraft down safely in a farmer's field. Later the same morning, the incident was repeated, and he glided the Tiger Moth safely back to the station.

"So I went up a third time," said Lancaster with a laugh, "thinking, to hell with it, this isn't going to stop me. We went up as far as we dared doing aerobatics. She iced up and stalled again. This time I just set her up on her nose, put her into a steep dive, and finally she started ticking over. We got back in, but all three stalls happened the same morning."

Lancaster's EFTS student that day might have described his instructor as nothing less than heroic and deserving of some reward—if only the operational posting he wanted. But unlike most of his students, Lancaster was kept on at Goderich until July 1944. When he finally got overseas, it was too late to realize his dream of flying fighter sorties. Lancaster trained on Spitfires but never flew an operational mission. The war in Europe ended May 8, so he volunteered to serve on Transport Command in the Pacific. But as he was en route "across the pond" back to Canada, the Allies bombed Hiroshima and Nagasaki, and he never got to Transport Command either.

If BCATP flying instructors received no recognition from the air force fraternity, those who flew as staff pilots must have experienced the equivalent of solitary confinement. Airmen such as bush pilot Duke Schiller, former aeromechanic Johnny Brown, and even de Havilland plant worker Fred Hotson and chief test pilot Ralph Spradbrow became the workhorses of the Air Observer Schools, Wireless Schools, and Bombing and Gunnery Schools. Sometimes referred to as "taxi pilots" or "air chauffeurs," these airmen logged as many hours as the overworked flying instructors—up to 1,000 hours a year. They wore civilian flying gear, were on the payroll of the civilian schools, and piloted Ansons full of trainees learning various airborne trades. Staff pilots flew simulated bombing runs for the bomb-aimer students, cross-country flights for wireless trainees, and night flights for air observers (later navigators).

"Heroism" was the way RAF student navigator Bill Davies described what a staff pilot did on one of his training trips in 1943. Born in Liverpool, Davies grew up with an aptitude for mathematics and attended Leicester University. He enlisted in the RAF in 1941, sailed for Halifax on the *Queen Elizabeth* in December 1942, and was posted to No. 5 RAF Flying Training School in Florida, where he was nearly washed out of the service for having a conversation with a black waiter in the dining hall. When he earned his observer's brevet he was posted to No. 33 Air Navigation School at Mount Hope, just outside Hamilton, Ontario.

"On November 12, 1943, we took off from base at Mount Hope at 0900 hours," Davies wrote. "The pilot flying the Anson was Flight Sergeant [Frank] Boyd. Our scheduled navigation trip was St. Marys to Caledonia and back to base.

"After leaving St. Marys, we ran into a very heavy snowstorm and we became hopelessly lost. F/Sgt Boyd wasn't the slightest bit concerned as he growled to me, 'Let's go down to ground level and see if we can find a railway line.' Sure enough, down at almost nought feet, we found our line, and following it only several feet above the track, we quite suddenly encountered a railway station. I vividly recall looking *up* and seeing the huge sign sitting on the platform of the station reading 'Caledonia.'"

Davies eventually flew over Europe on Pathfinder missions. The Pathfinder Force flew, generally at dangerously low altitudes, in advance of a bomber stream to locate and set flares around a bombing target. After surviving forty PFF missions, Davies still said, "Heroes such as the unflappable F/Sgt Boyd deserve a huge pat on the back."

A wireless/air-gunner student and two navigator trainees count their blessings that staff pilot Alan Wingate was at the controls during a training flight in fall 1943. The year before, Wingate had come from Toronto with his private pilot's licence to No. 9 AOS in St.-Jean, Quebec. He was hired as a Pilot Under Instruction and trained in Ansons and at the AOS ground school to earn staff pilot status. His baptism of fire occurred on his very first familiarization flight, when the Anson's cockpit emergency hatch blew off in mid-air. Wingate kept flying as if nothing had happened.

But the bit of flying he did on a night exercise in September 1943 neither he nor his crew of three trainees forgot.

"I experienced a starboard engine failure over the Quebec town of Wakefield up the Gatineau River about fifteen miles north of Ottawa," Wingate wrote. "This necessitated a single-engine emergency let-down through a thin overcast and an approach to join the Ottawa Uplands Airport circuit . . .

"My WAG's efforts to contact the Uplands tower were futile. Undetected, I mixed in with the students flying Harvards on night training. I continued around with them and on to the final leg of the circuit, received a green light, and continued in for an uneventful landing. My aeroplane was still undetected as a stranger until I turned off the runway and then was unable to taxi with only the one engine . . .

"The only ill effect of the episode was that my leg ached from keeping full left rudder on, flying the aircraft straight with the port engine throttled up to hold our height until we got over Uplands." Although he got little praise for the single-engine landing, Wingate was quick to credit his training "because the night emergency due to the engine failure caused me no anxiety or panic. It was just a routine procedure, and none of the crew inquired whether they should prepare to jump."

John Bertram's crew panicked once and nearly did bail out on a night flight that got into trouble. Bertram had graduated from the BCATP in July 1943 and become a staff pilot for No. 10 AOS at Chatham, New Brunswick. Bertram, his two student navigators, and a wireless operator were flying home from a training session "when one engine started shaking and emitting flames. The crew were getting ready to jump. This made the plane tail heavy as I had shut off the defective engine and had slowed to single-engine speed.

"Having spent many hours in the Link trainer practising navigation, I was familiar with all the radio range signals in the area. I asked the wireless operator to get Moncton range. He gave me Charlottetown in error. However, I got him to correct it and we finally made it to Moncton.

"But it was near midnight. No lights on. And it was raining. Beside the pilot seat was a Very pistol. We shot off two flares. A light appeared. And a safe landing was made. But it was an experience for the trainees and yours truly!"

Heroism could express itself in hundreds of unspectacular ways. Cheerfully enduring the tedium of instructing was one. When AOS managers Peter Troup and Babe Woollett were hiring Americans in the early years of the war, they looked for personality as well as flying ability. Woollett made it clear that "these pilots lent themselves magnificently to the plan, because they were very patient and pleasant with the students. In those days we didn't have a lot of rules and regulations for them. I just let them have their head to do the job."

Another quiet form of heroism, according to Woollett, was the determination to get the job done under difficult conditions. This was particularly important at the beginning of the war, when there was so little time to get the civilian operations working to capacity. As a result, Woollett gave his AOS station maintenance staff and ground crews—more than 2,500 men and women—plenty of autonomy. Among those who shone under these conditions was Woollett's former operations manager at Dominion Skyways Ltd. in Rouyn/Noranda.

Joe Lucas came to No. 1 AOS at Malton with Woollett as his chief engineer. In the backwoods of Quebec, Lucas had performed miracles retrieving aircraft wrecks and getting them operational again. At the civilian AOS, he was required to keep scores of twin-engine aircraft flying around the clock. For his resourcefulness and ingenuity Woollett called Lucas "an unsung hero."

"We had Anson Is and we found ourselves running out of valve springs and valve guides," Woollett said. "Joe couldn't get supplies because they were all being sunk on shipping coming from England to Canada. So, he simply analyzed the material he needed, took it down to a bed spring manufacturing outfit, and had them make valve springs for the Ansons."

Shortly thereafter, James Duncan, a dollar-a-year-man who was deputy minister for air, visited the station with RAF Group Captain Maxwell, a strictly-by-the-book officer. When Maxwell spotted the bed springs, he asked what Lucas and his crew were doing. Woollett explained Lucas's source for the valve springs.

"Have you had any accidents?" Maxwell asked.

"Not even a forced landing," Woollett replied. "We know we're using the wrong materials, but we've got to keep them flying."

Duncan asked, "What's your state of serviceability?"

"Eighty-five percent," Woollett answered.

Duncan turned to Maxwell. "When we were at Borden last week, they had only five percent of their Ansons serviceable."

"But sir, these people are using the wrong material," Maxwell retorted.

"Bugger the material," exploded Duncan. "If Mr. Woollett and Mr. Lucas agree, I suggest you send your top maintenance men down here tomorrow and learn how to do it the wrong way."

The shy, red-headed Lucas obliged, shared his knowledge, and improved the availability of Ansons to the training regimen, not only at AOSs but at SFTSs across the system. Later, Woollett moved with Lucas to No. 9 AOS St.-Jean, and promoted the engineer to assistant general manager. At the peak of the plan's productivity, Lucas was handling everything at the eastern AOSs—from fire protection to plumbing problems—with only 3 percent of his staff drawn from those fit for military duty. Lucas was fulfilling the original mandate of civilian involvement in the plan and lifting the burden of training from the RCAF fighting force. As Babe Woollett said, "Many people were highly decorated for far less than this great Canadian."

A further form of heroism was shown by a flyer who contributed to the war effort in spite of discrimination and lack of experience. The fact that No. 2 AOS in Edmonton hired instructor Littlewood at all was remarkable, but the event received little acknowledgement beyond the station staff.

Instructor Littlewood was a woman.

RCAF wartime regulations prevented women from front-line duty and from instructing. Margaret Littlewood could have gone overseas where flyers such as Canadian Marion Orr were hired by British Overseas Airways to ferry aircraft for the Air Transport Auxiliary from factories to stations in the United Kingdom. She could have joined the Women's Division in Canada. Ever since an Order-in-Council on July 2, 1941, had created the Canadian Women's Auxiliary Air Force (renamed the Women's Division, RCAF, in 1942), the air force had recruited women to "release to heavier duties those members of the RCAF employed in administrative, clerical and other comparable types of service employment." In other words, women would be allowed to work as clerks, cooks, equipment assistants, fabric workers, hospital assistants, motor transport drivers, and telephone operators, but not as instructors.

Margaret Littlewood took a different route. The only child of an Eaton's window display worker and his wife, Margaret grew up a tomboy on Wolfrey Avenue in Toronto. Her habit of attending football games with her father and climbing trees made her more comfortable among the neighbourhood boys than the girls. She completed a high school commercial course and planned to become a secretary. Then she met Marion Gillies, whose father, Fred, ran Gillies Flying Service, and the two girls got hooked on flying.

"I had never been in a plane before when Mr. Gillies gave me my first airplane ride," Littlewood said. "Being an instructor, he let me take the controls. It was a Piper Cub monoplane. It was great, marvellous. I liked the take-offs and landings, but I couldn't get over standing still up there, as it were. The higher we got, the more the cars looked like little toys. I was even more fascinated with the horizon. It was as if there was no end to it."

In 1938 Margaret Littlewood got her private licence and Marion Gillies went to Trenton for her instructor's licence. Littlewood quit her job in Eaton's mail order department and started working in the Gillies Flying Service office at Barker Field. But in the first year of the war, gas rationing forced the civilian flying schools at Barker Field to shut down, leaving Littlewood unemployed.

"It was so disappointing," she recalled. "I had worked so hard memorizing this book for my instructor's licence. I thought it was all going down the drain, when one of my students said, 'Marg, why don't you try and get into Link training in the Air Observer Schools?' So I wrote a letter to each of the ten Air Observer Schools in the BCATP."

All ten schools responded. The first nine turned Littlewood down. The tenth was No. 2 AOS Edmonton, where the manager was former bush pilot Wop May. In the first week of January 1943, he telephoned her in Toronto.

"I'm losing my chief instructor in the Link room," May explained.

"How soon can you be out here? Can you get here by February?"

"I guess so," Littlewood said.

"Good. I'll see that your ticket for the train is at Union Station."

That was it. Partly because Wop May's reputation was almost larger than life in the aviation fraternity, and partly because it was a civilian-operated station, housing both an AOS and an EFTS, May could do pretty well whatever he wished. When he lost a Link instructor to Canadian Pacific Airlines, he decided to fill the vacancy the best way he knew how. Edmonton had a new teacher in the Link room and the BCATP had its first woman instructor.

Cutting through the red tape of military bureaucracy was only the beginning of Margaret Littlewood's adventure in the BCATP. On the first day she was introduced to the rest of the instructing staff, who greeted her with mixed reactions. That same day a notice was posted in all flight hangars—stiff penalties would be exacted for anyone not taking his scheduled hour of Link training. Her first day on the job, Littlewood realized the dilemma she faced. Some students would resent a woman instructor. Others would rebel against the tedium of Link practice whoever taught them. But worst of all, as she entered the Link room for the first time, she realized that she had bluffed her way into the job. She had never even seen a Link trainer before that day, much less instructed on one.

"But I went in," Littlewood remembered. "The Links were operating at the time. Students were in them. And Wop left me there. I learned from the desk, by watching the recorder and working with the students in the Links. The Link was small, but soon I was at home in them, because it was like the small airplanes we had flown back in Toronto, with a few instruments in front of you. And that was the importance of them—learning blind flying."

There were plenty of wisecracks about Littlewood; she heard herself called "hatchet face" and "the dame with size twelve shoes." Some students at the station whined, "Why do we have to get the only woman?" Yet in time Littlewood's exceptional teaching skills and her down-to-earth personality won the station over. She came to be respected not only by the EFTS trainees she taught, but also by the experienced pilots, who were expected to put in their Link time—pilots such as Grant McConachie, North Saul, and Hollick Kenyon (in 1929, Richard Byrd's navigator to the South Pole and during the war the check pilot for Canadian Pacific Airlines). From February 1943 to May 1944, instructor Littlewood trained nearly 150 pilots in simulated spins, following radio signals, and blind flying in the Link trainers at Edmonton.

Perhaps her greatest challenge in the Link room was former bush pilot Vic Fox. "I'll always remember when Vic walked in for the first time," Littlewood said. "He had a beard and a Siwash sweater. You could hardly see his face for hair. I knew CPA had told him he had to take Link. But I thought, 'He'll never listen to me.' I got nervous because he was such an experienced pilot.

"But it got so eventually Vic would phone ahead and say, 'Is Marg on? I'd like to have my lesson with her.' That was the nicest compliment. But the greatest satisfaction of my work was knowing every time I gave the signals and pointed out a mistake to the boys, that it might save their lives when they got lost coming home in bad weather."

For many BCATP instructors, the reward for service was simply that they survived the war. Of the fifty-six pilots in his course graduating from No. 5 SFTS Brantford in October 1941, Harvey Timberlake was one of only eleven who were still alive in 1945. Several went to Coastal Command, Timberlake and four or five others became instructors, and the rest went overseas. The latter group suffered the greatest losses.

Timberlake never forgot that, and he never complained about getting no gongs. He counted his blessings that he had survived. And yet, because he had been a service flying instructor for nearly three years at Moncton, Weyburn, and Hagersville, "I felt that we had contributed tremendously. Not under the duress of fire, but our work wasn't a lunch-bucket job either.

"I put twenty-eight full-course pilots through on twins or singles. And yet we were looked on as chickens. They said that operational pilots got shot out of the sky, while we just fell out of the sky."

Like Eric Johnston, Timberlake took his BCATP credentials to a commercial airline after he had been demobilized. Trans-Canada Airlines turned him down, using the rationale that "if you'd gone over and done what operational pilots had for their country, you would have had experience under more detrimental conditions. And you would be better in the cockpit with eighty people behind you."

There was a further setback a few years later. Because of a mechanical fault in an Anson I that he was flying during his SFTS training in December 1941, Timberlake had crashed and suffered lacerations and internal injuries. At the time, the air force asked him to quit with 100 percent pension. He refused and completed his tour in Training Command. After the war he began suffering dizzy spells and severe headaches, but he couldn't prove that they were related to his accident. His medical expenses were never covered by an air force pension.

Others were deprived of benefits too. In his earliest days with the Camp Borden ground crews, George Barrett found the pace exhilarating but physically draining. While they were maintaining aircraft, Barrett and his fellow erks (ground crewmen) were busy enlarging the station. Materials were in such short supply in 1940 that crews resorted to taking the crates that had contained the Fairey Battles shipped over from Britain and turning them into storage buildings. As Barrett worked to prepare one of these crates to be moved by crane, the crane hook struck him on the head and knocked him unconscious. The blow was so severe he couldn't remember the accident. Barrett moved on to Dunnville, where the pace was just as frenetic. Then one weekend on leave, he lay down and slept three days straight.

He was taken to Christie Street hospital in Toronto, run through a battery of tests and psychological examinations, and released back to Dunnville, where "the first thing I knew I was handed a discharge certificate and $35 to replace all the clothes I had worn out in the first three months of service. That was it. It was May 1941 and I was finished. I applied for a pension and didn't get it. But that was the air force. Most things in the military do not exist. It didn't happen, therefore it doesn't exist."

Wireless instructor Henry Gordon also fell outside the air force safety net. After a year of intense training activity in the BCATP—

helping to establish No. 2 Wireless School at Calgary, launching No. 3 Wireless School in Winnipeg, and training perhaps 200 WAGs, Gordon fell ill and was given a medical discharge. Air force doctors claimed that he was developing ulcers and that a remedial diet would be too difficult for the RCAF to accommodate. Gordon couldn't prove that his illness was related to his tour in Training Command and so did not receive any air force pension.

"We were kind of a non-entity," Ab Bowman complained. After enlisting in Toronto in 1941, the twenty-one-year-old airman had unpleasant memories of his training—the horrible food rations during his guard duty posting to the RAF-run No. 31 Air Navigation School at Port Albert, Ontario, and the accidents that killed two close friends who instructed at Mount Hope and Aylmer. But tougher still was the treatment he received after four years of instructing in the BCATP. "I was not entitled to Department of Veterans Affairs coverage for illness or any pension benefits because I had never been offshore." After age sixty-five, of course, all veterans enjoyed Canada Pension, but Bowman was not eligible for benefits before then. If he had been overseas, he could have enjoyed benefits such as having the DVA take care of snow removal and grass cutting at his home. But because he was a non-operational RCAF pilot instructor he was entitled to none of this recompense or peace of mind.

Meanwhile, Harold Jackson, who had logged 3,000 hours instructing at Dunnville, Aylmer, and Kingston between 1942 and 1945, applied to the Royal Canadian Legion for dental coverage after the war. Like other instructors, he received no air force postwar benefits because "we didn't serve beyond the borders of Canada." Former instructor Norm Shrive, who spent the war instructing at Hagersville station, pointed out that generally civil service jobs were not available to former instructors. "When you join the air force, you volunteer automatically for service anywhere in the world. It wasn't your choice that you were kept to be an instructor. But we were denied some of the benefits that the overseas guys got. It made us bitter."

This double standard—one for operational air crew and another for airmen at home—left many BCATP instructors baffled and angry.

When RCAF airmen were demobbed and paid, instructor Stan Castle had a hard time swallowing the rationale for service pay—operational air crew were paid $7.50 for every month of service, plus $7.50 per month overseas, while instructors were paid the basic $7.50 only.

Len Schryer couldn't understand why, after more than four years and several thousand hours of instructing at Stanley, Nova Scotia, and Virden, Manitoba, and three other stations in between, he should be displaced from the Trans-Canada pilot application list by operational pilots; certainly they were experienced flyers, but so was he.

After serving in the RCAF for most of the war, Al Stirton came home just in time to bring in the 1945 harvest. Stirton had instructed for 1,800 hours at No. 9 EFTS St. Catharines. Overseas he had flown 231 hours on Sunderlands and 457 hours on Cansos. Like Eric Johnston, Stirton paid a visit to the Edmonton offices of Canadian Pacific Airlines later that year and proudly displayed his 3,000 hours of accident-free flying time.

"Air force pilots are a dime a dozen," he was told. "CPA prefers bomber pilots between twenty-two and twenty-five years of age."

Stirton was twenty-nine. And though he did receive the standard service recognition and was "satisfied with what I did," one of the country's hardest working elementary instructors in the BCATP got no gongs and got no acknowledgement for his years of service in the training of a victorious air force. "We didn't win the war by ourselves," Al Stirton admitted, "but it could not have been won without us."

In late 1944, when it became apparent that he was going to finish his RCAF career as an instructor at No. 19 SFTS Vulcan, Alberta, Wilf Sutherland inquired about pilot positions with Trans-Canada Airlines. He was told that those jobs were reserved for overseas pilots.*

---

* This fact is borne out by a Southam news story published in the High River *Herald* on February 22, 1945. H. Reginald Hardy reported that while "overseas service is not essential for any person to qualify for a pilot's certificate of any class . . . it is a fact, however, that in employing pilots, the Trans Canada Air Lines and commercial firms generally will give preference to men with overseas service . . . as the needs of these men are of paramount importance."

Sutherland's displeasure over the ruling was apparently common among instructors, because Trenton's chief flying instructor, V.M. Terry, dispatched a memorandum to the Department of National Defence entitled "Recommendations Re: Instructor Discrimination." In part it said:

> At the present time, with the Training Plan being reduced, some instructors have already been released from the Air Force, and are faced with the problem of rehabilitation.
>
> It is felt that there is considerable public and even official misunderstanding of their contribution to the war effort. [It] arises from the fact that probably 95% of the instructors being released from service have not had a tour of operations, and results in discrimination, which appears to be unjustified. If this policy of discrimination is permitted to continue, it will work a definite hardship on a large group of men who have served patiently and conscientiously through long periods of instruction duties.
>
> Discrimination adversely affecting the instructor takes the following forms:
>
> (a) Only Service personnel who have been overseas can qualify for a Civil Service Post;
> (b) Trans-Canada Airways [sic] will not employ pilots who have not completed a tour of operations;
> (c) Instructors are barred from Transport Commands where they might get the necessary experience to qualify for commercial airlines work;
> (d) At present Commercial Pilots' Licences cannot be procured by an ex-service pilot unless he has already contracted to fly for a commercial company—but such contract can scarcely be procured without overseas experience, as long as the present discrimination exists . . .

It is strongly recommended that:

(a) An immediate effort be made to clarify in the public and official mind the importance and value of the flying instructor's services;
(b) An attempt be made to alter the official restrictions which prevent the flying instructor from competing for Civil Service employment;
(c) That he be given every opportunity to receive training and to enter fair competition for commercial flying employment;
(d) That Air Force Headquarters officially recognize an eighteen month's tour of flying instructional duties as equivalent to one tour of operations, insofar as rehabilitation is concerned and that rehabilitation agencies be advised of such recognition;
(e) That individual instructors receive some official recognition or citation for each tour of instructional duties.

(Signed) V.M. Terry, W/C, No. 1 CFS, Trenton, Ontario.

The letter was apparently ignored, because none of its recommendations was implemented, which further frustrated instructors seeking some acknowledgement for the air force they had trained, some equality with those who had gone overseas while they stayed in Canada, and equal opportunity in the peacetime workplace. Sutherland was disheartened, because even though he had not "been closer to the war than Summerside, P.E.I., I would like to have gone overseas, but I had no choice."

Bill Topham made a choice. In September 1942, after Topham had served a short time as engineer officer at No. 5 B&GS at Dafoe, Saskatchewan, his school received a call for volunteers for overseas postings. He had been married only a few months, and he felt torn between duty and emotion. That night he agonized over the decision, but wrote his wife the next day, "I gave my name in. I would not have joined up if I was afraid to give up a few comforts. We will never win the war sitting on our fannies. The sooner it is over, the sooner we will be settled." His application was never accepted, and he served four years in the BCATP instead.

RCAF bandsman Allan Wigby also served at home, although he had volunteered for overseas service. His frustration was exacerbated by his homefront posting because as an RCAF band trumpeter he was constantly called upon to perform the Last Post at funerals of airmen killed in training. Eventually, he became one of many who needed counselling by the air force over the way he felt. He concluded that many problems could have been avoided "if they had only sent airmen over, even for one day, on operations!"

Navigation instructor Desmond "Doc" Crossley got his one day on ops. Crossley had just completed his MSc in silviculture, his daughter had just been born, and he was working at Indian Head, Saskatchewan, supervising the planting of shelter-belts, when he enlisted in 1940. The air force misinterpreted his science degree to mean strength in mathematics, and he was immediately streamed into Air Observer School. After a time as instructor at Central Navigation School in Rivers, Manitoba, and at No. 2 AOS in Edmonton, Crossley began applying for a posting to Ferry Command. It never came through.

However, when he spent a year at War Staff College in England later in the war, he "wangled his way onto one Lancaster bomber mission." That was all. It may have been enough. He was soon back in Canada at No. 4 Training Command Headquarters in Calgary and then as station commander at No. 2 AOS Edmonton into 1945.

In four and a half years as a wireless instructor in the plan, Paddy Sellars never once got the opportunity to go on ops. Yet few instructors taught, examined, and graded as many BCATP graduates as Sellars did. In two years with No. 4 Wireless School at the Ontario Agricultural College in Guelph, Sellars dealt with twelve courses (each of 120 men) a year. In other words, Sellars had a hand in training 2,880 wireless trainees—teaching them Morse code, the RAF rainbow radio set, aircraft recognition, and skeet shooting. Not surprisingly, after months of repetition and grinding out graduates, Sellars began applying to remuster as air crew. He tried every six months beginning as early as 1940.

In June 1944, Flying Officer W.C. Sellars and fellow instructor Bob Mooney received a letter from F.J. Goldsmith, the air officer commanding No. 2 Training Command; it said that the two "can not be released from the Signals Branch at the present time. Their applications for air crew training are not concurred in by this headquarters. May they be so advised."

Throughout the war, Sellars felt a sense of guilt, sending course after course of nineteen- and twenty-year-old WAGs to the front while not going himself. Statistics showed that one in three would die in combat. In comparatively comfortable surroundings and with much higher odds for survival, Sellars stayed behind forever wishing for an ops posting, "wanting to share the risk."

Then, a month before the war ended, Sellars and a Norseman crew took off for Brig Harbour Island along the coast of Labrador. The operation was to allow Sellars to recalibrate the direction finding equipment (used for locating German U-boats in the north Atlantic) as well as to fly out a sick airman. On the way back, the Norseman went down in an ice storm ninety miles short of the Goose Bay station. As a result of the night spent exposed to the blizzard, Sellars suffered frostbite that later required surgery. Because Newfoundland and Labrador were not yet part of Canada, the mission was considered an overseas trip and Sellars later received an overseas bar citation. Because of his injuries, Sellars said, "I felt exonerated. I felt that I had shared something with the boys. I'd gone overseas too. In a way I had a war wound."

When their war was over, operational airmen and some instructors ended up back at Manning Depot, where it had all begun. Air crew demobilization and discharge usually took place in those huge livestock palaces in Lachine, Toronto, Brandon, or Edmonton. It didn't take long. Papers were processed. Service pay doled out.

For Bob Hesketh, who had joined up in Toronto in 1942, trained during 1943, and then instructed until 1945 at No. 9 SFTS Centralia, Ontario, departure from the air force was without ceremony or fuss. He had received a letter that said, "due to the current surplus of air crew, we are in the process of winding down the air training plan." By late January he had received his documentation for discharge, been processed back at Manning Depot in Toronto, and was a civilian again. With that, he left his air force career behind, and landed a job as a city hall court reporter with the *Toronto Telegram*, "because I had read Shakespeare and could type." Hesketh later went on to a successful Toronto broadcasting career. Rarely did he even mention his three years' service in the BCATP.

Even long after the war, Hesketh avoided air force and pilot association gatherings, because on the rare occasions he attended, inevitably after lunch and a few drinks, the discussion would get around to wartime experiences. Someone would ask him what and where he flew. When he told them, "Ansons in the air training plan," they would usually turn away because all they wanted to hear were ops stories—stories of fighter and bomber trips, close calls over Germany, and DFCs and bars won. In contrast to their tales of derring-do, his instructing seemed dull and unexciting. Eventually he avoided talking about his air force career entirely.

Then one day on a routine medical check-up at Sunnybrook Hospital in Toronto, Hesketh chatted with the young physician examining him. The subject of his wartime service came up. "I was in the RCAF. I was a pilot," Hesketh said.

"Oh. Were you one of those guys who rained death and destruction on those innocent people of Germany?" said the doctor.

"No," Hesketh said. "I was an instructor."

Hesketh was at first angered by the young doctor's remark. No, he hadn't been on Bomber Command over Germany, but if he'd had the chance to go, he would have. It was the first time Hesketh had encountered anyone in Canada with a negative attitude about what the RCAF had achieved during the war. But for the first time since the war, Hesketh felt proud at what he *had* contributed, proud that he had trained some of those pilots who flew over Germany. It had taken fifty years, but suddenly his work instructing air force pilots at Centralia meant something. For the first time he sensed satisfaction that his work in the British Commonwealth Air Training Plan had been important and necessary and had contributed to the outcome of the war.

About 1943, an anonymous piece of poetry appeared in the national RCAF magazine, *Wings*, edited in Ottawa by direct entry officer Gerry Anglin; in Bill Sargent's *Contact*, the station newspaper at Trenton; and in countless BCATP station circulars. It was called "The Flying Instructor's Lament," and its sentiment was universally understood among instructors.

"What did you do in the last war, Daddy?
How did you help us to win?"
"Circuits and bumps and turns, laddy,
And how to get out of a spin.

Woe and alack and misery me,
I trundle around in the sky,
And instead of machine-gunning Nazis
I'm teaching young hopefuls to fly.

Thus is my service rewarded,
My years of experience paid,
Never a Hun have I followed right down,
Nor ever gone out on a raid.

They don't even let us go crazy,
We have to be safe and sedate.
So it's nix on inverted approaches
They stir up the C.F.I.'s hate.

For it's oh, such a naughty example,
And what will the A.O.C. think?
But we never get posted to fighters
We just get a spell on the Link.

So it's circuits and bumps from morning 'til noon,
And instrument flying 'til tea.

Hold 'er off, give her bank, put your undercart down,
You're skidding, you're slipping, you see.

And as soon as you finish with one course,
Like a flash, up another one bobs,
And there's four more to show 'round the cockpit,
And four more to try out the knobs.

But sometimes we read in the papers
Of the deeds that our students have done,
And we're proud to have been their beginnings
And shown them the way to the sun.

So, if you find the money and turn out the planes,
We'll give all we know to the men,
'Til they cluster the sky with their triumphs
And burn out the Beast from his den."

Few records in the archival institutions of Canada exist as a testament to the instructors' contribution to the plan and the war effort.

The costs are fully documented: Canada contributed $1,617 million, the United Kingdom $216 million, Australia $65 million, and New Zealand $48 million. BCATP statisticians also record that the plan trained 72,835 RCAF airmen, 42,110 RAF airmen (including about 2,000 Free French, 900 Czechs, 677 Norwegians, 448 Poles, and about 800 Belgian and Dutch air crew), 5,296 Royal Navy Fleet Air Arm personnel, 9,606 Royal Australian Air Force, and 7,002 Royal New Zealand Air Force personnel. The plan also graduated between 40,000 and 45,000 ground crew tradesmen. The total production of the BCATP approaches 200,000 airmen.

Unfortunately, though, no figures exist of the number of instructors in the plan, although some figures at Trenton's Central Flying School reveal that as of January 31, 1945, the school had received 5,890 instructor candidates, of whom about 4,700 graduated. Department of National Defence records show that 856 air crew students died in training accidents. And although the total number of fatalities among officers and other ranks (men and Women's Division) in RCAF training was approximately 3,000 (including pre-operational training outside Canada and training fatalities in Britain), nowhere is there a record of the total number of instructors who died in the service of the plan.

Their contribution did not go unnoticed by a grateful Winston Churchill, who thanked the men and women of the BCATP, saying, "Throughout these great movements of men and material, the instructors and ground crews, though no less eager than their comrades for a share of the fighting, have faithfully performed their hard and unspectacular duties. They remained far removed from the excitement of battle; but their devoted and patient work will not be forgotten as playing a vital part in our victory."

In February 1944, the signatories of the British Commonwealth Air Training Plan under the Balfour-Power Agreement began to reduce the number of trainees and staff at the plan's 107 stations across Canada. By June, when the training pipeline was already clogged with too many qualified air crew, the RCAF stopped recruiting airmen and ground personnel. That October, BCATP training schools began closing.

When No. 38 SFTS at Estevan, Saskatchewan, shut down in February 1944, the departing 406 RAF airmen were bussed through a bitterly cold evening to the train station, where lights had been strung to brighten up the send-off. Each man was presented with gifts of cigarettes and fruit and a copy of the local Estevan *Mercury* newspaper. The town band played in the depot waiting room. Then, about 500 townspeople gathered to honk their car horns, shout goodbyes, and wave as the train pulled away into the darkness.

A month after VE Day in May 1945, the station commander at No. 8 OTU at Greenwood, Nova Scotia, publicly congratulated the last graduating class of Mosquito pilots and then had them fly many of the intruder aircraft into storage. At No. 31 SFTS in Kingston, RAF instructor Jim Askew sadly remembers "that some of the pupils, who were almost finished their course in August 1945, were not allowed to [graduate and receive their wings]. All flying ceased on August 28, when everything was shut down and we were told to prepare to be returned to Britain." Askew had instructed in Canada from February 1944 to August 1945. During that period, except for three weeks of leave, he had flown an average of four hours a day and taken about 125 pilots to wings standard. Then in October 1945, without having had an opportunity to fight for his native England, Askew set sail aboard the *Île de France* for home. The former instructor was asked to consider staying in the RAF; but, adding insult to the injury of not getting an ops posting back in Britain, he was put in charge of releasing personnel—counselling airmen being demobilized from the service.

Former air force men and women from the Second World War generally agree that the BCATP contributed to the ultimate Allied victory. Assessments of the plan, from those who were trained in it, range from "it was a necessary evil" to "it was magnificent in concept and execution." Some, when pressed, will go so far as to say the war could not have been won without it. Historians praise the foresight of Vincent Massey and Stanley Bruce for suggesting the idea. They credit Mackenzie King for making the plan a Commonwealth priority and for insisting on its being "Canadian" in name and in application. They applaud the Royal Canadian Air Force, which had barely 4,000 personnel and 270 aircraft in 1939, for spearheading the plan's implementation so that by the war's end it had become the world's third most powerful air force.

Historians also salute Canadian business and labour for translating stacks of government blueprints into workable, practical air force stations where the training could be done. They pay tribute to patriotic entrepreneurs—the dollar-a-year men such as C.D. Howe—for transforming a country's peacetime manufacturing into a world power in aircraft production (with companies such as de Havilland, Fleet, and Noorduyn). Occasionally, they recognize the civilian aviation managers such as Babe Woollett and Peter Troup, who applied their business acumen to run many BCATP schools, thus reducing the drain of valuable air force personnel away from the fighting. And they even acknowledge the role played by a ragtag string of air clubs, pulled together by Murton Seymour into a network of flying schools that helped a generation of pilots get from first solo through elementary flying and ready for service flying training and their wings.

The legacy of Canada's monumental air training scheme is both obvious and invisible. Just five years after the Second World War ended, the war between North and South Korea broke out. Former BCATP trainees and ops air crew were quickly mobilized for Canada's support of United Nations forces in the conflict.

Another tangible and long-lasting benefit from the plan was the rejuvenation of private flying clubs in Canada. Twenty-two of them had provided the foundation of the BCATP's elementary training system. As recompense, when hostilities ceased, the Canadian government helped rebuild their peacetime enterprises by supplying aircraft, panel trucks, fire trucks, Link trainers, refuelling tenders, and cash. Some BCATP instructors, excluded from airline pilot jobs, found gainful employment with the aero clubs—instructing, of course.

The BCATP left an indelible impression on places such as the province of Saskatchewan. The Air Cadet movement blossomed there. And even after the war, the RCAF enlistment rate in Saskatchewan as a percentage of voluntary army enlistments was higher than in any other province, only fractionally short of 50 percent. But the influence on ordinary citizens in those prairie communities is summed up in an editorial in the Weyburn *Review*: "People in Weyburn who a few months ago found it difficult to sleep because of the unfamiliar drone of training planes overhead, are like the child accustomed to be rocked to sleep—they now find it difficult to get to sleep without the familiar purr of engines in the sky."

Transcontinental and transatlantic aviation benefitted from the trail-blazing done by BCATP air crew. Graduates who previously crewed Bomber and Fighter Command, Coastal Command, Ferry

Command, and Home War Establishment aircraft staffed the growing business of long-distance commercial aviation. By May 1944, pilots and air crew had flown 15,000 transatlantic missions; they had sustained less than half of one percent losses throughout the war, despite the radio silence required to avoid German detection. BCATP air crew had also helped pioneer methods of controlling flight using radar, radio beam, and meteorology. Their combined experience enhanced the efficacy and safety of Canada's air mail, cargo, and passenger carriers.

The BCATP provided a reservoir of highly skilled air and ground crew for the country's passenger carriers, even if they chose to hire operational pilots rather than former instructors. The ten smaller commercial carriers of Canadian Pacific Airways that had handled the training of air observers in the plan became the national passenger carrier CPA. Meanwhile, Trans-Canada's passenger transport by the war's end was eight times greater than in 1939, while its staff had increased six times over.

When former BCATP instructor Max Ward returned home to Edmonton after the war, he founded Wardair, a bush-flying operation into the Canadian North. Ward hired former operational and instructor pilots, but found he preferred "not the stick-handlers, but those cautious pilots who could go out and handle both the weather and an airplane and get safely back." Former instructors were among his most reliable staff pilots.

The achievement of the air training scheme is recorded, to varying degrees, in a number of Canadian communities. In Brandon, Manitoba, a museum was established in 1981 to commemorate the BCATP. At an airstrip in the middle of a corn field near Tillsonburg, Ontario, an organization known as the Canadian Harvard Aircraft Association rebuilds Harvards, trains young pilots to fly them, and each year celebrates the contribution of the aircraft and their instructors to the Second World War. Scores of other Harvard hulks, salvaged from National Defence surplus after the war, are perched on pedestals in town parks all across the country. Most are little more than bird nests and neglected wartime relics, and rarely is there any acknowledgement of the airmen who trained an air force in them between 1939 and 1945.

Headstones of BCATP airmen also dot the countryside. Few if any commemorate individual deeds or the collective distinction the plan gave the wartime campaign. The graves of air crew who died in the plan bear air force insignia, a name, a service number, an engraved cross, and the date of death. These stark and simple stones are the only remembrance of instructors such as EFTS instructor Stormy Fairweather at Windsor, naval air instructor Finn Strand Kjos at Little Norway, and SFTS instructor John Caskie at Hagersville; they died in the line of duty just as the thousands of bomber, fighter, ferry, and coastal pilots and air crew did. But there was little attention paid to those killed in action this side of the ocean.

The airman who trained in the plan and went overseas to fight earned his wings, "got a bellyful of war," and came home with gongs. Many of the friends he made in wartime were lost over there, and some received posthumous medals and citations. But those who died in the plan got nothing but death. Whether he died in a Halifax over Hamburg or an Anson over Hagersville, an airman was just as dead and just as much a tribute to the air force, his family, and the ultimate victory. He was just as loyal, just as courageous, just as young, and just as prepared to do glorious deeds as the ops airman who did. But in the end the instructor killed on the job rarely got any credit. "Dulce et decorum est pro patria mori" (it is glorious for a man to die in the defence of his country), but there was no glory in the British Commonwealth Air Training Plan.

In 1949, as a token of their appreciation to Canada, the nations participating in the BCATP presented the RCAF station at Trenton with a set of memorial gates. The national crests of the four contributing countries were mounted in the wrought-iron lattice, and the RCAF crest surmounted the gates. The impressive entrance faced on the parzade square, where nine years before—on October 24, 1940—the first class of BCATP observers had received their wings.

In accepting the memorial gates for Canadians, Prime Minister Louis St. Laurent said, "We are today dedicating an enduring monument to the vision of those who conceived the air training plan, to the energy of those who organized it and to the trained airmen from its schools who fought and won victory in the air."

When the speeches concluded, Princess Elizabeth and others attending passed through the memorial gates and read an epitaph engraved in the adjoining limestone walls:

Their shoulders held the sky suspended;
They stood, and earth's foundations stay.

Heroes in wartime were those who did great deeds and who were admired for them. Heroes in the air war between 1939 and 1945 received gongs for great bravery and daring in the service of their country. Mentioned in Dispatches, Air Force Crosses, and Air Force Medals were the rare rewards for outstanding performance in the BCATP. But none of the instructors in the plan ever thought himself a hero. Airmen who became instructors did what they were ordered to do and what the job demanded. Sometimes ordinary people were called upon to do extraordinary things, but they never called it heroism.

Charlie Konvalinka met a hero in the BCATP. The man wasn't a commanding officer, although Konvalinka served under good officers. He wasn't a fellow instructor. He wasn't even, when Konvalinka met him, a pilot. He was a trainee. Konvalinka met him in Moncton, when he was a flight commander at No. 8 Service Flying Training School. As a flight commander, Konvalinka wasn't supposed to have direct contact with students; he oversaw other instructors rather than instructing students himself.

However, when one of the instructors in his command came to Konvalinka with a "hand-off"—a student who for some reason had been unable to achieve the required level of pilot proficiency, in this case to go solo in a Harvard within the required number of hours—Konvalinka was forced to deal with him personally. In other words, the student was down to his very last chance. It was a matter of going solo quickly or being washed out.

That's when Flight Commander Konvalinka met Leading Aircraftman Mooers from Newfoundland. He was a short, stocky man, quiet, even dour, and carrying a great deal bottled up inside him. Konvalinka didn't know why, but Mooers's demeanour got to him. And the flight commander did something he wouldn't normally have done. He took him up to test the trainee himself. During an hour-long check-out, Mooers seemed ill at ease at the controls and did his best to kill both himself and his flight commander.

"I don't think you've got it," said Konvalinka when they returned to the airfield. "You've demonstrated conclusively that this isn't for you. But I'm going to have the squadron commander take you up to see what he thinks."

It was about noon at the Moncton station. Konvalinka told Mooers to take a lunch break and to come back immediately thereafter for another test flight with Squadron Commander Marty Fraser.

When Konvalinka returned to the flight line with his superior officer and checked in with the duty pilot to sign out a Harvard, he spotted Mooers's name on the time sheet. Mooers had waited in line for the first available Harvard, and when one had been refuelled and the duty pilot made it available, he had signed it out. He had never soloed before.

When Fraser arrived, Konvalinka told him the news.

"I guess we'd better go up to the tower," Fraser said, "and find out where he's going to crash."

In the tower, the two officers apprehensively took out field glasses and scanned the circuit for Mooers's Harvard. Konvalinka remembered the Harvard's numbers and soon spotted the aircraft about to re-enter the flow of traffic on final approach to land. "He hasn't killed himself so far," he said.

Unfortunately for Mooers, the winds that normally blew up and down the main Moncton runways had shifted, and he would have to bring his Harvard down in a strong cross-wind. The tower crew watched breathlessly as the young flyer let down into the circuit, flew down wind, and put his undercarriage down. Konvalinka remembered watching the approach and expecting the worst.

But Mooers made a nearly perfect landing and managed to keep the Harvard straight in the cross-wind. He brought it down without the slightest hesitation.

The squadron commander turned to Konvalinka. "He's your problem now," Fraser said. "You'll have to decide what to do with him."

Konvalinka went down on the flight line and waited as Mooers taxied the Harvard in and climbed out. The two men walked together across the tarmac and into the hangar.

"What made you do it?" Konvalinka asked.

"I don't care what happens to me now," Mooers said. "I had to do it because I knew I could. I know that all I showed you this morning was awful flying. But I knew I had to do it."

There was a long pause as the LAC and his flight commander entered the hangar. In the moments that passed Konvalinka weighed his options. He could wash Mooers out then and there, except that, ultimately, he had successfully soloed. And Fraser's delegation of the decision to Konvalinka suggested that Mooers might prove to be a talent in the rough. Konvalinka recalled his own introduction to the Harvard; it had not been a picture of grace either—on his first take-off he had wiped out several runway markers before his instructor took control and got the Harvard safely airborne. Konvalinka recognized in Mooers the same passion to fly, win his wings, and contribute to the war effort that he had felt when he joined up. After all, as an instructor wasn't that his job—to nurture talent, encourage enthusiasm, and make a capable pilot out of a raw recruit?

"I'm not supposed to have a student," Konvalinka finally said to Mooers. "But from now on, you're my student. We're going to get you your wings, or it'll kill us both."

Konvalinka succeeded. Teaching Mooers aerobatics, night flying, instrument flying, and formation work took every ounce of Konvalinka's perseverance as a person, tolerance as a commanding officer, and experience as an instructor. Often Mooers scared Konvalinka half to death. Mooers was, as he had been the day he soloed, unpredictable but determined. Admitted Konvalinka, "I saw something in his temperament and in his determination; instinctively I sensed we were blood brothers."

In the end Mooers proved to be competent. He learned all nineteen of his flying sequences, took his wings test—not from Konvalinka, but another testing instructor—and got his wings. Not long after, Mooers got his overseas posting on Spitfires.

That autumn, Konvalinka heard about his maverick student. Word came by the grapevine. Someone had seen on one of those green-coloured dispatch sheets from overseas that Mooers had been killed. Whether he was killed in action or a casualty of a training accident, Konvalinka never knew. Mooers had become just another wartime statistic.

So Charlie Konvalinka—who had joined the air force because he loved to fly; who was taught, learned to teach, and then taught others; who had trained himself to be every inch a professional and taught young men how to survive; who had served his country, like hundreds of other instructors, by helping to build the third most powerful air force in the world and then was called a coward for it—in turn paid Mooers, his young student, and all the determined air crew trainees like him, the ultimate tribute.

"Mooers wanted to fly, to be a pilot," Konvalinka said, "and he was prepared to put his life on the line in order to do it. He got his wings, and then somewhere over there it ended. He was the bravest man I ever knew. As far as I'm concerned, this guy was a genuine hero."

With or without gongs it took a hero to know a hero.

Notes

The number at left is the page number on which the cited information appears. Unless otherwise indicated, quotations from participants in the BCATP are taken from taped interviews. These are listed in the section "Sources."

CHAPTER ONE – CALLING CARDS FOR HITLER

page

6 "the nearly 150,000 qualified navigators": F.J. Hatch, *The Aerodrome of Democracy: Canada and the British Commonwealth Air Training Plan, 1939-1945* (Ottawa: Directorate of History, Department of National Defence, 1983), p. 206.

7 "expend about $2 billion in the training": ibid., p. 199.

7 "third of a million sorties": Martin Middlebrook and Chris Everitt, *The Bomber Command War Diaries: An Operational Reference Book, 1939-1945* (New York: Penguin, 1985), p. 11.

7 "more than a thousand victories": Dan McCaffery, *Air Aces* (Toronto: Lorimer, 1990), p. 2.

7 "possibly the decisive factor": Winston Churchill, quoted in Jack Meadows, "A Decisive Factor," *Aeroplane Monthly*, February 1989, p. 98.

8 "sent 2,500 pilots . . . in the First World War": S.F. Wise, *Canadian Airmen and the First World War: The Official History of the Royal Canadian Air Force*, Vol. I (Toronto: University of Toronto Press, 1981), pp. 119-20.

8 "ten . . . air aces were Canadian": James Eayrs, *In Defence of Canada: From the Great War to the Great Depression*, Part I (Toronto: University of Toronto Press, 1964), p. 185.

8 "pilot training . . . at two flying schools": Peter C. Conrad, *Training for Victory* (Saskatoon: Western Producer Prairie Books, 1989), p. 1.

8 "some camera equipment donated by the British government": S.P. Cromie, "RCAF Attains Mature Might," *Canadian Aviation*, September 1943, p. 68.

8 "its objectives were largely non-military": ibid., p. 69.

9 "Trained in Canada Scheme": Hatch, *Aerodrome of Democracy*, p. 6.

9 "revitalized training . . . would increase the flow of air crew": Robert Leckie, "Notes on the Proposal to Establish a Flying Training School in Canada," *Roundel II*, December 1949, pp. 14-15.

9 "prepared to have our own establishments": Mackenzie King, *Senate Debates*, June 14, 1938, 521, and *House of Commons, Debates*, July 1, 1938, 4523-32.

11 "autonomy in air crew training": Hatch, *The Aerodrome of Democracy*, pp. 11-12.

11 "the discussion turned to Canada's role": ibid., p. 13.

12 "Canada might be able to make a decisive contribution": Norman Hillmer, "Vincent Massey and the Origins of the British Commonwealth Air Training Plan," *Canadian Defence Quarterly*, Spring 1987, quoting *What's Past Is Prologue: the Memoirs of the Right Honourable Vincent Massey* (Toronto: Macmillan, 1963), pp. 303-6.

12 "a scheme whereby . . . air forces should be training in Canada": Hillmer article quoting "Minutes of a Meeting Held at Dominions Office," September 16, 1939, PRO, *Dominions Office Records*, 121/6.

12 "we trust . . . that this co-operative method": Dominions Secretary to Secretary of State for External Affairs, September 26, 1939, *Documents on Canadian External Relations*, VII: 1939-1941 (Ottawa: Queen's Printer, 1974), pp. 549-51.

13 "was not Canada's war": Mackenzie King, quoted by Hatch, *Aerodrome of Democracy*, p. 17.

13 "given the highest priority in Canada": ibid.

14 "essential step forward in our joint war effort": Dominions Secretary to Secretary of State for External Affairs, November 27, 1939, *Documents on Canadian External Relations VII*, pp. 622-23.

14 "the air training plan should take priority": Minutes of Emergency Council, November 14, 1939, ibid., pp. 604-6.

15 "the ministry would refuse RCAF designation": Hatch, *Aerodrome of Democracy*, p. 24.

15 "Canadian pupils when passing out from the training scheme": Quoted in C.P. Stacey, *Arms, Men and Governments: The War Policies of Canada, 1939-1945* (Ottawa: Queen's Printer, 1970), p. 27.

15 "in making provision for this vast undertaking": Leslie Roberts, *Canada's War in the Air* (Montreal: Alvah M. Beatty, 1942), p. 29.

16 "certainly a memorable birthday": King diary quoted in article by F.J. Hatch, "The British Commonwealth Air Training Plan," *Canadian Aviation Historical Society Journal*, Winter 1982, p. 100.

CHAPTER TWO – COUNTDOWN TO ZERO DAY

page

19 "a germ spreading": Jack Meadows, "Clustered Skies," manuscript, Surrey, B.C., 1991. Used with permission.

20 "the British dirigible R100 motored overhead": Hugh Halliday, "The Flight of the R-100," *Canadian Aviation Historical Society Journal*, Fall 1967, p. 64.

20 "Amelia Earhart stopped in Halifax": Amelia Earhart, "20 Hours, 40 Minutes: Our Flight in the Friendship," *Canadian Aeronautics Chronology* (New York: G.P. Putnam, 1928).

21 "Balbo's aerial armada": Claudio G. Segre, *Italo Balbo: A Fascist Life* (Los Angeles: University of California Press, 1987), p. 242.

22 "luck was with me": Alan Stirton, correspondence, April/May 1991, Moose Jaw, Saskatchewan.

25 "May's mercy mission . . . captured world attention": Michael Hartley, *The Challenge of the Skies* (Edmonton: Puckrin, 1981), pp. 92-121 and 144-55.

25 "the first pilot to fly over the Arctic Circle": Philip H. Godsell, *Pilots of the Purple Twilight* (Toronto: Ryerson Press, 1955). Robert St. G. Gray, "Punch Dickins: A Legend in His Time," *JR News* (quarterly corporate newsmagazine of James Richardson & Sons Ltd.), Winnipeg, Fall 1990.

26 "Woollett flew some of the first survey crews": W. Babe Woollett, *Have a Banana!* (North Battleford, Saskatchewan: Turner-Warwick Publications, 1989).

26 "the air observer has the most . . . exacting task": Quoted in Hatch, The United Kingdom, Air Ministry Pamphlet 133, "Aircrew Training: Abridged Report of the Conference held in the United Kingdom, January/February 1942," May 1942, 13, "The British Commonwealth Air Training Plan," HQ 927-1-1, VI, DHist 80/408.

26 "my main concern became finding my way home": Woollett, *Have a Banana!*, p. 52.

27 "flying in the backwoods": Babe Woollett, correspondence, May 14, 1991, Honolulu, Hawaii.

27 "Douglas explained that . . . they were going to call": Babe Woollett, letter to Keith Rich, Toronto, September 8, 1981.

28 "civilian companies had to hire civilian pilots": Hatch, "The British Commonwealth Air Training Plan," p. 164.

28 "We gathered in Ottawa": Babe Woollett, correspondence, May 1, 1991, Honolulu, Hawaii.

29 "our group had to wind up our effort": Woollett, *Have a Banana!*, p. 476-77.

29 "he called us back in": Woollett letter to Keith Rich.

29 "they opened No. 1 AOS at Malton": Woollett, *Have a Banana!*, p. 478, and letter to Keith Rich.

31 "he'd seen the fleet of ten Martin B-10 bombers": R. Murray Shortill, "Memories of Blatchford Field," *Canadian Aviation Historical Society Journal*, Winter 1979.

32 "its flying arsenal consisted of 270 aircraft": Edmond Cloutier, RCAF Logbook, *A Chronological Outline of the Origin, Growth and Achievement of the Royal Canadian Air Force* (Ottawa: Air Historical Section, King's Printer, January 1949), p. 58.

32*n* "sudden demand for aircraft skis": Bill Colborne, correspondence, August 4, 1991, Thunder Bay, Ontario.

33 "three-quarters of a million blueprints": Hatch, *The Aerodrome of Democracy*, p. 34.

33 "Rivers, Manitoba . . . compared the arrival of the BCATP": *The Gazette*, Rivers, Manitoba, December 5, 1940.

34 "the greatest single achievement": Roberts, *Canada's War in the Air*, p. 10.

36 "in mid-September we received the first four": Don Rogers, correspondence, May 1, 1991, Islington, Ontario.

37 "we tied an inner tube": Al Martin, "Len Trippe, Pioneer Instructor," *Canadian Aviation Historical Society Journal*, Summer 1964.

37 "in 1939, the government came to Leavens Brothers": ibid.

37 "for us as instructors": Rogers correspondence.

39 "the Fraser was rammed and sunk": Tony German, *The Sea Is at Our Gates: The History of the Canadian Navy* (Toronto: McClelland and Stewart, 1990), p. 78.

CHAPTER THREE – ABANDON HOPE ALL YE WHO ENTER HERE

page

43 "British Blenheim reconnaissance bomber flew": Middlebrook and Everitt, *The Bomber Command War Diaries*, p. 19.

43 "Bomber Command recorded its first casualties"; ibid., p. 22.

43 "German bombers made their first attack on British territory": Charles Messenger, *World War Two Chronological Atlas* (London: Bloomsbury, 1989), p. 26.

44 "pilots made 996 daylight sorties": ibid., p. 30.

45 "a pupil in an Anson": Jack Meadows, "Clustered Skies."

47 "one little chap went up in the Gyro": Ken Leavens, "Walt Leavens, The Last Barnstormer," *Canadian Aviation Historical Society Journal*, Spring 1992, p. 8.

48 "each morning [they were] hosing down the bullpen": Ken Smith, "One Man's War," diary, Toronto, Ontario, p. 1. Quoted with permission.

49 "cock and ball lectures": Wilf Sutherland, interview, December 17, 1990, Islington, Ontario.

52 "if each procedure were . . . followed to the letter": Jeff Mellon, interview, January 2, 1991.

52 "they had to pay close attention to DROs": John Bigham, correspondence, April/May 1991, Burlington, Ontario.

52 "if it was on the ground": Wilf Sutherland, interview, December 17, 1990, Islington, Ontario.

55 "we never knew what we were doing": George Bain, interview, June 2, 1991, Oakland, Mahone Bay, Nova Scotia.

57 "its strength had doubled": Cloutier, *RCAF Logbook, A Chronological Outline*, p. 62.

57 "the first of forty-eight RCAF squadrons": G.A. Fuller, J.A. Griffin, K.M. Molson, *125 Years of Canadian Aeronautics: A Chronology 1840-1965*, (Toronto: Canadian Aviation Historical Society, 1983), p. 209.

58 "a pay increase from $1.70 a day": *Pay and Allowance Regulations for the Royal Canadian Air Force*, including amendments to November 1, 1939 (Ottawa: J.O. Patenaude, I.S.O., The King's Printer, 1939).

59 "Will I make a pilot?": Malcolm Logan, *Flying Simply Explained* (Toronto: Sir Isaac Pitman & Sons, 1941), p. 5.

59 "some of the more jealous non-air crew types": Don Suthers, correspondence, January to April 1991, Burlington, Ontario.

59 "Edwin Link had grown up during the 1920s": "Edwin Albert Link," *Current Biography*, 1974, p. 238.

60 "an unheard-of order at the time": Jack Charleson, transcript of speech given to Toronto chapter of the Canadian Aviation Historical Society, November 2, 1977.

63 "Dat goddam bird de Link": Carrol W. McLeod, *Dat H'ampire H'air Train Plan* (Toronto: Gaylord Printing, 1943), p. 15.

65 "began the repetitive ritual": Fred Lundell, correspondence, July 1991, Montreal, Quebec.

CHAPTER FOUR – A GREAT TIDE OF AIRMEN

page

67 "rendering the most meritorious service": Alice Gibson Sutherland, *Canada's Aviation Pioneers, Fifty Years of McKee Trophy Winners* (Toronto: McGraw-Hill Ryerson, 1978), p. 7.

68 "This scheme had three goals": Murton Seymour, *Canadian Aviation*, March 1942, quoted in Sutherland, *Canada's Aviation Pioneers*, pp. 115-6.

68 "the government would provide two airplanes": ibid.

69 "the number totalled 41,000": ibid., p. 118.

70 "his salary jumped to $40 a week": Jack Williams, *Wings Over Niagara, Aviation in the Niagara District, 1911-1944* (St. Catharines: Niagara Aviation Pioneers, no date), p. 23.

70 "claimed to have flown in 500 dogfights": William E. Corfield, Wings Over London, Our Aviation Heritage (London: Webco Publications, 1982), p. 98.

71 "killing both the pilot and his passenger": Williams, *Wings Over Niagara*, p. 24.

72 "seven of the ten had qualified": Corporal Stan Helleur, "A Story of Ten GDs," Wings, RCAF magazine, July 1943, pp. 5 and 12.

72 "the RAF spotted German ships steaming north": Messenger, *World War Two Chronological Atlas*, p. 20.

75 "diplomatic contacts in Washington and Montreal": Gerry Beauchamp, "Hawks of Norway," *Canadian Aviation Historical Society Journal*, Winter 1977, p. 116.

75 "organizers of the Norwegian training camp": "The History of Little Norway in Canada" (Ottawa: Royal Norwegian Embassy, 1987).

77 "about $20 million worth of aircraft": RNAF training film, "Wings for Norway," photographed and edited by members of the Royal Norwegian Air Force, c1943.

77 "And five-year-old Prince Harald": ibid.

77 "the risks of aviation over the bay": Dr. Smirle Lawson, Chief Coroner of Toronto, quoted in article "Coroner Fears Airplane May Fall in City Street If Flying Not Controlled," *Toronto Telegram*, July 12, 1941.

78 "and watch the Norwegians fly": Beauchamp, "Hawks of Norway," p. 116.

78 "they used to order extra bread": Herbert Whittaker and Arnold Edinborough, *Winston's: The Life and Times of a Great Restaurant* (Toronto: Stoddart, 1988), p. 32.

78 "a young Norwegian aircraft engineer": "Viggo Ullmann," *Current Biography*, 1973.

79 "the seaplane was taking a long time": Fred Dickie, quoted in "Coroner Fears Airplane May Fall in City Street if Flying Not Controlled," *Toronto Telegram*, July 12, 1941.

80 "disappeared in ten or fifteen seconds": Captain Ernest Straker, quoted in "Would Not Happen Again in 100 Years," *Toronto Star*, July 12, 1941.

80 "one of those rare things": Lieutenant-Commander Haahon Joergensen, ibid.

80 "the part the Norwegian flyers are playing": Jury verdict, ibid.

80 "the great metropolis proved too much": Kid Pedersen, "Little Norway: May She Always Be Free," *The Forester*, August 19, 1981, p. 2.

81 "we saw a tremendously high bow": Smith, "One Man's War," p. 5.

82 "200 ships and 177 aircraft had been lost": Messenger, *World War Two Chronological Atlas*, p. 34.

83 "we can defend ourselves for some time": Churchill, quoted in I. Norman Smith, *The British Commonwealth Air Training Plan* (Toronto: Macmillan, 1941), p. 7.

84 "Stirton had a bad habit of undershooting": Alan Stirton, correspondence, April/May 1991, Moose Jaw, Saskatchewan.

CHAPTER FIVE – COCKPIT CLASSROOM

page

93 "the backbone of the training plan": Eric Johnston, interview, August 4, 1991, Scugog Point, Ontario.

94 "the Fleet Finch's tail section was modified": Ron Page and William Cumming, *Meet: The Flying Years* (Erin, Ontario: Boston Mills Press, 1990), p. 72.

94*n* "more than 25,000 air crewmen were lost": Andrew Brookes, *Crash!: Military Aircraft Disasters, Accidents and Incidents* (Shepperton, Surrey: Ian Allan, 1991) p. 37.

95 "the RCAF recorded its first battle casualty": Fuller, Griffin, Molson, *125 Years of Canadian Aeronautics*, p. 211.

97 "the original eight-week syllabus included": W.A.B. Douglas, *The Creation of a National Air Force, The Official History of the Royal Canadian Air Force*, vol 2 (Toronto: University of Toronto Press, 1986), pp. 242-3.

97 "God watches over first solos": Stan Castle, interview, November 28, 1991, Picton, Ontario.

98 "now, see if you can get it down": Hugh Godefroy, *Lucky Thirteen* (Stittsville, Ontario: Canada's Wings, 1983), p. 23.

98 "my first solo lasted only ten minutes": Bill Olmstead, *Blue Skies* (Toronto: Stoddart Publishing Co. Ltd., 1987), p. 8.

98 "I twisted twice to look into the empty back seat": Len Morgan, *The AT-6 Harvard* (New York: Arco, Famous Aircraft Series, 1965), n.p.

99 "feet didn't hit the ground for hours": Charlie Purcell, interview, September 14, 1990, Hamilton, Ontario.

99 "aloft solo and revelling in the experience": F. Robert Letson, correspondence, May 1991, Etobicoke, Ontario.

101 "the masterful manner in which you averted": citation signed by No. 7 EFTS Windsor manager, Cyril Cooper.

106 "I learned more from you than I've learned since": Art Browne, letter to Pallett, August 21, 1942.

106 "I owe you plenty": Dave Duffy, letter to Pallett, April 1, 1941.

109 "Oh! I have slipped the surly bonds of earth": John Gillespie Magee, "High Flight," from an article by A.H. Lankester, "John Magee: the Pilot Poet," *This England*, Winter 1982.

110 "was in a flight of seven Spits": Al Stirton, correspondence, April 9, 1991, Moose Jaw, Saskatchewan.

110 "out of a total of 203 Canadians": Douglas, *The Creation of a National Air Force*, p. 237.

CHAPTER SIX – RECRUITING AT THE WALDORF

page

111 "the RCAF had purchased thirty Harvard trainers": David C. Fletcher and Doug MacPhail, *Harvard! The North American Trainers in Canada* (Dundas, Ontario, DCF Flying Books, 1990), p. 16.

112 "Some of the aircraft already had RCAF markings on them": M.L. McIntyre, "The Aylmer Story," from *I'll Never Forget . . . Canadian Aviation in the Second World War*, a selection of articles from the *Canadian Aviation Historical Society Journal*, Willowdale, 1979, p. 68.

114 "there were 6,129 Americans": Douglas, *The Creation of a National Air Force*, p. 240.

116 "arsenal of democracy": Joseph P. Lash, *Roosevelt and Churchill, 1939-1941: The Partnership that Saved the West* (New York: Norton, 1976), pp. 63-74.

116 "321 American recruits": Douglas, *The Creation of a National Air Force*, p. 635.

117 "air chauffeurs": Hatch, *Aerodrome of Democracy*, p. 90.

118 "No. 1 B&GS at Jarvis, Ontario, reported": Robert Schweyer, "Jarvis . . . The First Three Years," in *Canadian Aviation Historical Society Journal*, Winter 1978, p. 105.

118 "scored a perfect zero": George Penfold, correspondence, November 10, 1990, Don Mills, Ontario.

120 "Royal California Air Force": Morgan, *The AT-6 Harvard*, n.p.

120 "Pague took his training with the Navy": Brick Bradford, interview, May 18, 1991, Richmond, British Columbia.

123 "a God-send to the Plan": Babe Woollett, letter to Keith Rich, September 8, 1981.

123 "among them was . . . Jim Hamilton": Fred Hotson, "On Staying Civilian," in Larry Milberry and Hugh Halliday, *The Royal Canadian Air Force At War 1939-1945* (Toronto: Canav Books, 1990), pp. 72-74.

123 "aerial truck drivers": W.A. Bishop, *Winged Peace* (Toronto: Macmillan, 1944), p. 118.

124 "Bennett and his group of Atfero ferry pilots": ibid., p. 119.

125 "*Coventrieren*": Messenger, *World War Two Chronological Atlas*, p. 43.

125 "chaos reigned": Ernest "Jack" Hunt, correspondence, May 4, 1991, Elmira, Ontario.

126 "the place was all connected": Roy Legassicke, correspondence, September 1991, Keene, Ontario.

127 "quarantine ward for several hundred recruits": Don Suthers, correspondence, April 22, 1991, Burlington, Ontario.

131 "seeing every prospective graduate": Rev. W.C. Sellars, correspondence, August 11, 1991, Ottawa, Ontario.

CHAPTER SEVEN – HOLLYWOOD HEROES

page

134*n* "critic Howard Barnes wrote": Hector Arce, *The Secret Life of Tyrone Power* (New York: Bantam Books, 1980), pp. 144-150.

135 "the whole plan . . . with its schedules": Norman Ward, ed., *The Memoirs of Chubby Power, A Party Politician* (Toronto: Macmillan, 1966), p. 209.

136 "Canada's Open Secret": *The Saturday Evening Post*, February 1, 1941.

136 "the RCAF's biggest promotional scheme": A.W. O'Brien, "Inside Story of RCAF Film Epic," *Montreal Standard*, March 7, 1942.

136 "the effect on the sick man": ibid.

137 "Warners had also demonstrated their sympathies": Rudy Mauro, "The Making of Captains of the Clouds, Part I," *Canadian Aviation Historical Society Journal*, Summer 1991, pp. 41-42.

137 "to illustrate the gallant work": Hal B. Wallis and Charles Higham, *Starmaker, The Autobiography of Hal Wallis* (New York: Macmillan, 1980), p. 75.

137 "bush pilots at work": ibid.

138 "rob them from Billy Bishop's office": Mauro, "The Making of Captains of the Clouds, Part I," p. 42.

139 "I suppose a picture can be made": ibid.

140 "by far the most extensive and difficult venture": Wallis and Higham, *Starmaker*, p. 76.

141 "the place to apply for the air force": *Captains of the Clouds* dialogue from screenplay by Norman Reilly Raine, Arthur T. Horman, and Richard MacAulay.

143 "at least one of you will be killed": Art Badland, correspondence, July 1991, Roche's Point, Ontario.

143 "he did it splendidly without much time to learn it": William Arthur Bishop Jr., *The Courage of the Early Morning: The Story of Billy Bishop* (Toronto, McClelland and Stewart, 1965), p. 193.

143 "our script called for a plane": Wallis and Higham, *Starmaker*, p. 77.

144 "a ceremony at which His Excellency accepted an RCAF flag": "Training School at Uplands Receives RCAF Flag," Ottawa *Evening Citizen*, July 22, 1941.

144 "the trouble was there were no aircraft": Bishop, Jr., *The Courage of the Early Morning*, p. 192.

144 "we finally had to piece together fragments": Wallis and Higham, *Starmaker*, p. 77.

145 "a Red Cross fund-raiser": stories from Ottawa *Evening Citizen*, July 1941.

146 "taxiing Harvards in a giant circle": Len Schryer, correspondence, July 14, 1991, Nanaimo, British Columbia.

148 "the change from a twenty-dollar bill": Charlie Konvalinka, interview, December 5, 1990, Toronto, Ontario.

149 "doubling for Brenda Marshall": "City Girl is Praised For Work," North Bay *Nugget*, August 21, 1941, p. 1.

149 "the stars were forced to use homing pigeons": pigeon fancier Harry Mulligan quoted in North Bay *Nugget*, March 6, 1942, p. 12.

150 "things grew tense when Fox requested": Rudy Mauro, "The Making of Captains of the Clouds, Part II," *Canadian Aviation Historical Society Journal*, Fall 1991, p. 90.

151 "the scenes of RCAF training are impressive": Bosley Crowther review, *New York Times*, February 13, 1942.

151 "socko air adventure with timely patriotic appeal": *Variety*, February 1942.

151 "the flying scenes are breath-taking": New York *Herald-Tribune*, February 1942.

151 "the Capital Theatre enjoyed a city record": Rudy Mauro, "When Hollywood came to North Bay," North Bay *Nugget*, March 1, 1991.

152 "they even hinted that a Captains sequel": Jack Karr, Toronto Daily Star, March 11, 1942.

152*n* "the Westland Whirlwind fighter . . . was a contemporary of the Spitfire": Victor F. Bingham, *Whirlwind, the Westland Whirlwind Fighter* (England: Airlife, 1987).

153 "the plan is proceeding": Chubby Power, *House of Commons Debates*, 1940, III, 2108.

CHAPTER EIGHT – YELLOW PERILS

page

155 "opening of the Rainbow Bridge": George A. Seibel, *Bridges over the Niagara Gorge* (Niagara Falls: Niagara Falls Bridge Commission, 1991), p. 199.

156 "I was particularly fortunate in having Sergeant Cap Foster": Bill Olmstead, *Blue Skies* (Toronto: Stoddart, 1987), p. 10.

157 "the feat was even more amazing": ibid., p. 257.

158 "the French armed forces ordered 230 Yales": David C. Fletcher and Doug McPhail, *Harvard, The North American Trainers in Canada* (Dundas: DCF Flying Books, 1990), pp. 36-39.

160 "five crashes involved mid-air collisions": Robert Schweyer, "RCAF Dunnville: The Story of No. 6 SFTS," *Canadian Aviation Historical Society Journal*, Fall 1989, p. 88.

160 "the training wing consisted of 168 students": Hatch, *Aerodrome of Democracy*, p. 141.

161*n* "course length at SFTS fluctuated": Douglas, *The Creation of a National Air Force*, pp. 233, 241.

164 "the torque . . . often pulled the aircraft to one side": Jeff Mellon, interview, January 2, 1991, Richmond Hill, Ontario.

164 "the earliest Harvard Is became notorious": Charlie Konvalinka, interview, December 5, 1990, Toronto, Ontario.

166 "I looked around to the left": Bill Hill, quoted in Dunnville station publication *Mentioned in Despatches*, September 1943.

166 "Hill was found to have three gashes": Schweyer, "RCAF Dunnville, The Story of No. 6 SFTS," p. 82.

170 "at No. 7 EFTS Windsor, eight pilots resigned": Frank Vines, interview, December 1, 1990, Etobicoke, Ontario.

170 "entering one end of the train as an RCAF flight lieutenant": Maury Dillingham, interview, July 1991, San Antonio, Texas.

171 "one was accidentally shot down by an RAF night fighter": Messenger, *World War Two Chronological Atlas*, p. 43.

175 "chant magic alphabetical incantations": Murray Peden, *A Thousand Shall Fall* (Stittsville, Ontario: Canada's Wings, 1982) p. 58.

175 "I must not approach to land with undercarriage retracted": ibid., p. 63.

175 "rolling an aircraft wheel around the perimeter": Bob Hesketh, interview, January 23, 1991, North York, Ontario.

177 "*pilotage sans visibilité*": Sir Basil Embry, *Mission Completed* (London: Methuen, 1957), p. 65-69.

179 "used the wrong rudder one time": Bill Lennox, interview, January 23, 1991, North York, Ontario.

180 "mad Australian Gussie Grimmer": Fred Lundell, correspondence, July 1991, Montreal, Quebec.

183 "death-defying feats and mortal peril": John Campsie, correspondence, May 10, 1992, Toronto, Ontario.

184 "in the future, there will be no instructor to correct your faults": Iris Barr, correspondence, November 3, 1991, New Westminster, British Columbia.

184*n* "Lehman trained with the RCAF": Allan Nevins, *Lehman and His Era* (New York, Scribner, 1963), p. 243.

CHAPTER NINE – TOO VALUABLE TO RISK

page

189 "on the home front in Canada": Jean Bruce, *Back the Attack!* (Toronto: Macmillan, 1985), pp. 1-20.

191 "a conference in which all of the United Nations": Canadian Minister in the United States to Secretary of State for External Affairs, April 16, 1942, "Air Training Conference," HQ 55-1-0, PAC, RG 24, vol. 5388.

192 "the plan's projected output": Hatch, *Aerodrome of Democracy*, pp. 105-106.

193 "the ticket out of instructing was insubordination": Norman Phibbs, interview, August 29, 1990, Burlington, Ontario.

194 "in front of [the CFI's] horrified eyes": Olmstead, *Blue Skies*, p. 14.

194 "may not have been appreciated at the time": ibid., p. 13.

196 "the war had done nothing but provide me": John Evans, "A Johnny Canuck of the Twentieth Century," unpublished diary, Toronto, Ontario. Used with permission.

200 "I wanted to fly bigger aircraft": Maury Dillingham, correspondence, July 1991, San Antonio, Texas.

202 "Dahl had enlisted in the USAAF in 1931": Whitey Dahl biographical information supplied by his daughter, Stevie Cameron, April 25, 1992, Toronto, Ontario.

202 "Dahl was 'more aggressive'": Sterling Seagrave, *Soldiers of Fortune* (Virginia: Time-Life Books, 1981), p. 54.

202 "we have been married only eight months": ibid., p. 63.

100 "mission to promote goodwill and comradeship": Bill Sargent, *Sgt. Sargent's Trenton, The War Years 1941-1945* (Belleville: The Hangar Bookshelf, 1985), p. 22.

207 "Lawrence Welk discovered Estes": Bill Hill, correspondence, January/August 1991, Hanover, Ontario.

212 "this man is considered too valuable": John Bigham, correspondence, November 1990, Burlington, Ontario.

214 "in one of the instructor's courses here": Graduation lecture from the papers of John Bryan Kelshall, with permission from Anneliese Kelshall, correspondence, May 5, 1991, San Fernando, Trinidad.

CHAPTER TEN – TO THE EDGE OF THE WORLD

page

218 "hundreds of fighter aircraft assembled": Terence Robertson, *The Shame and the Glory* (Toronto: McClelland & Stewart, 1962), p. 204.

218 "one of the greatest air battles of the war": ibid., p. 389.

218 "scores of BCATP graduates took part": Milberry and Halliday, *The Royal Canadian Air Force At War*, pp. 179, 180, 206, 216, 218.

219 "planes were coming out of the skies": Bob Bowman, interviewed by Bill McNeil, "Voice of the Pioneer" broadcast, 1991.

219 "the graduates of Little Norway": Kal Pedersen, "Little Norway, May She Always Be Free," *The Forester*, August 19, 1981, p. 2.

220 "for reasons not explained to us": Jim Askew, correspondence, July and August 1991, Calgary, Alberta.

221 "guilty of betraying our families": Michael Foster, "Cold Weather—Warm Welcome," *Airforce Magazine*, Vol. 13, No. 4, Jan/Feb/March 1990, p. 12.

222 "three grain elevators and a Chinese laundry": ibid., p. 12.

227 "Pennie made two ominous entries": Archie Pennie, correspondence, February 3, 1991, Ottawa, Ontario.

228 "westerly winds gusting from the Rockies": Bill Lennox, interview, January 23, 1991, North York, Ontario.

228 "all hands scrambled out to the airstrip": Len Schryer, correspondence, July 14, 1991, Nanaimo, British Columbia.

229 "instructors at Carberry suddenly faced": Doug Lomas, interview, March 28, 1991, Bowmanville, Ontario.

229 "on the windward side of the control tower": Charlie Konvalinka, interview, December 5, 1990, Toronto, Ontario.

229 "I was shaken by an enormous bang": Meadows, "Clustered Skies," n.p.

230 "my first flight into Portage": Kenneth McDonald, correspondence, April 26, 1991, Willowdale, Ontario.

231 "I was under the hood": Don Suthers, correspondence, April 22, 1991, Burlington, Ontario.

232 "he was producing the RCAF 'Blackouts'": Toronto *Star*, December 16, 1982.

232 "to photograph her house": Arthur Hailey, quoted in *The Canadians at War, 1939-45* (Montreal: Reader's Digest, 1969), p. 97.

233 "Burton's air force career in Canada": John Cottrell and Fergus Cashin, *Richard Burton, An Intimate Biography* (London: Barker, 1971), pp. 85-88.

233 "the *Argentina's* guns fired on a U-boat": Ren Henderson, unpublished diary, May/June 1942.

235 "we didn't come here to scrub floors": Frank Montgomery, interview, September 3, 1991, Peterborough, Ontario.

235 "the chief flying instructor, a RAF Squadron Leader": Robert Fowler, "Our Canadian Airmen in Allied Air Forces 1939-45," speech delivered at Annual General Meeting of the Canadian Aviation Historical Society, June 1, 1991, Toronto, Ontario.

237 "it will bring about 1,000 men here": Yorkton *Enterprise*, August 8, 1940, quoted in "The Impact of the British Commonwealth Air Training Plan on Western Canada: Some Saskatchewan Case Studies," by Brereton Greenhous and Norman Hillmer, in *Journal of Canadian Studies*, Vol. 16, Nos. 3&4, Fall-Winter 1981, p. 134.

237 "the first winter was a bit grim": Eileen Topham, "Wives in the War," *Dafoe Digest*, November 8, 1990.

238 "to people coming from wartime England": Vernon McLeod, quoted in Rod Nixon, *The History of Greenwood 1942-1990* (Greenwood: CFB Greenwood, 1990), n.p.

238 "in absorbing this influx": ibid.

238 "she took a job in the airmen's mess": Charlotte Tyerman Anderson, correspondence, November 26, 1990, Goderich, Ontario.

239 "Jackie Gaudette at No. 9 AOS St. Jean, Quebec": Jackie Gaudette Dysart, correspondence, November 28, 1990, Espanola, Ontario.

239 "Betty met RAF pilot Ernest Shadbolt": Betty Ross McFetridge, correspondence, 1992, Oakville, Ontario.

241 "at about 3:30 on March 12, 1944": Robert Schweyer, "RCAF Dunnville; The Story of No. 6 SFTS," *Canadian Aviation Historical Society Journal*, Fall 1989, pp. 84-86.

241 "we contacted them . . . and were invited to Uxbridge": Jock Evans, correspondence, December 29, 1991, Welland, Ontario.

243 "the Harvard . . . ploughed into the hill": "New Zealand Flyer Dies After Air Crash," *Uxbridge Times-Journal*, August 31, 1944.

244 "local people treated us with great kindness": Jock Evans, correspondence.

CHAPTER ELEVEN – THE SURVIVAL DIVIDEND

page

245 "a grand total of 8,014 aircraft": Leslie Roberts quoted by Brian Nolan in *King's War, Mackenzie King and the Politics of War 1939-1945* (Toronto: Fawcett Crest, 1988), p. 116.

246 "it drives one mad to think": Goebbels quoted by Ralph Allen in *Ordeal By Fire* (Toronto: Doubleday, 1961), p. 421.

246 "would be kind enough to do a draft": L.B. Pearson, *Mike, The Memoirs of the Right Honorable Lester B. Pearson* (Toronto: University of Toronto Press I, 1972), p. 208.

250 "the number of hours flown per fatality": Hatch, *Aerodrome of Democracy*, p. xviii.

251*n* "it was my first familiarization flight": Hardie Gray, correspondence, December 1990, Toronto, Ontario.

254 "on April 22 . . . they ran into heavy weather": Rita McCloskey Carey, correspondence, November 1990 and June 1991, Kingston, Ontario.

255 "I remember going to one of the hospitality dances": John Evans, "A Johnny Canuck of the Twentieth Century."

256 "one sunny day, in Bournemouth": John Neal, "The Diary of an Airman," unpublished diary, Calgary, Alberta. Used with permission.

264 "I was flying as captain over the North Sea": Malcolm Davies, correspondence, January 1991, Gloucester, Ontario.

267 "in seconds, there was the drum beat of shrapnel": Erik Nielsen, *The House is not a Home* (Toronto: Macmillan, 1989), p. 35-36.

269 "typical of one of these 'Flower' operations": Russ Bannock, interview, December 12, 1990, Toronto, Ontario; and Bannock from "The Intruders, 418 Squadron," *Canadian Aviation Historical Society Journal*, Fall 1982, p. 74-75.

270 "a Jewish Billy Bishop": Dave McIntosh, *Terror in the Starboard Seat* (Toronto: Beaufort, 1980), p. 34.

273 "Brick Bradford survived a Spitfire flight deep into China": *Critical Moments, Profiles of Members of the Greater Vancouver Branch of the Aircrew Association* (Vancouver: Aircrew Association, 1989), p. 297-298.

276 "the above information is secret": No. 150 Wing News Bulletin, 85 Group. No. 18. June 6, 1944, Newchurch, England. Courtesy of Ren Henderson.

CHAPTER TWELVE – THEY GOT NO GONGS

page

283 "dashing heroes were needed overseas": Jeff Mellon, interview, January 2, 1991, Richmond Hill, Ontario.

288 "more than 13,000 operational casualties": Larry Milberry and Hugh Halliday, *The Royal Canadian Air Force At War 1939-1945* (Toronto: Canav Books, 1990), p. 468.

288 "an instructor killed in a crash at the hands of an inexperienced student": Stan Castle, interview, November 28, 1991, Picton, Ontario.

290 "Heroes, such as the unflappable F/Sgt Boyd": Bill Davies, correspondence, March 19, 1991, Toronto, Ontario.

290 "I experienced a starboard engine failure": Alan Wingate, correspondence, July 16, 1991, Toronto, Ontario.

291 "having spent many hours in the Link trainer": John Bertram, correspondence, April 22, 1991, Cavan, Ontario.

293 "many people were highly decorated for far less": Babe Woollett, interview, May 31, 1991, Toronto, Ontario; and correspondence, 1991, Honolulu, Hawaii.

294 "women would be allowed to work as clerks, cooks": Jean Bruce, *Back the Attack!* (Toronto: Macmillan, 1985), p. 75.

299 "Len Schryer couldn't understand why": Len Schryer, correspondence, July 14, 1991, Nanaimo, B.C.

299 "we didn't win the war by ourselves": Al Stirton, correspondence, April/May 1991, Moose Jaw, Saskatchewan.

299*n* "overseas services is not essential": H. Reginald Hardy, "Overseas Service," High River *Herald*, February 22, 1941.

300 "Recommendations Re: Instructor Discrimination": Wilf Sutherland, correspondence, December 28, 1990, Toronto, Ontario.

301 "I gave my name in": Bill Topham, correspondence, December 27, 1990, Brighton, Ontario.

302 "if they had only sent airmen over, even for one day": Alan Wigby, quoted by Bill Topham in correspondence.

302 "wangled his way onto one Lancaster bomber mission": Lynne Bowen, correspondence, June 9, 1992, Nanaimo, British Columbia.

306 "some figures at Trenton's Central Flying School reveal": "British Commonwealth Air Training Plan, Flying Training," Section Two, Part Three, Instructors, DHist 181.009 (D89A); Daily Diaries, 1,2 and 3 FIS, DHist.

306 "Department of National Defence records show": "The British Commonwealth Air Training Plan," DHist 73/1558, X, p. 55.

307 "total number of fatalities . . . was approximately 3,000": Kenneth B. Conn and Fred Hitchins, committee chairmen, *The RCAF Overseas: The Sixth Year* (Toronto: Oxford, 1949), p. 511.

307 "throughout these great movements of men and material": "Unending Flow from Canada," *The Times*, December 17, 1942.

307 "when No. 38 SFTS at Estevan, Saskatchewan, shut down": *Estevan Mercury*, February 17, 1944.

307 "the station commander at No. 8 OTU at Greenwood": Rod Nixon, *The History of Greenwood* 1942-1990, n.p.

308 "some of the pupils . . . were not allowed to graduate": Jim Askew, correspondence, August 19, 1991, Calgary, Alberta.

309 "people in Weyburn who . . . found it difficult to sleep": Greenhous and Hillmer, "The Impact of the British Commonwealth Air Training Plan on Western Canada: Some Saskatchewan Case Studies," p. 143.

312 "we are today dedicating an enduring monument": *The British Commonwealth Air Training Plan 1939-1945: a Historical Sketch and Record of the Ceremony at RCAF Station Trenton* (Ottawa: King's Printer, 1949), p. 39.

312 "Their shoulders held the sky suspended": A.E. Housman, "Epitaph on an Army of Mercenaries."

Ranks in the RCAF are as follows:

Aircraftman 2nd Class (AC2)
Aircraftman 1st Class (AC1)
Leading Aircraftman (LAC)
Corporal (Cpl); Sergeant (Sgt)
Flight Sergeant (Flt Sgt)
Warrant Officer (WO)
Pilot Officer (P/O)
Flying Officer (F/O)
Flight Lieutenant (F/L)
Squadron Leader (S/L)
Wing Commander (W/C)
Group Captain (G/C)
Air Commodore (A/C)
Air Vice-Marshal (A/V/M)
Air Marshal (A/M)
Air Chief Marshal (A/C/M).

Sources

INTERVIEWS

Craig Ainslie, May 1, 1991, Comber, Ontario.
Joel Aldred, September 16, 1991, Port Perry, Ontario.
Gerry Anglin, April 6, 1991, Thornhill, Ontario.
Hadley Armstrong, December 13, 1990, Port Hope, Ontario.
Ted Arnold, February 3 and July 22, 1991, Naples, Florida, and Uxbridge, Ontario.
John Bailey, January 1992, Scarborough, Ontario.
George Bain, June 2, 1991, Oakland, Mahone Bay, Nova Scotia.
Russ Bannock, December 12, 1990, Toronto, Ontario.
George Barrett, November 2, 1990, Galt, Ontario.
Gordon Bassett, May 5, 1991, Barrie, Ontario.
Les Baxter, November 1990, Islington, Ontario.
Gary Bekkevold, March 1991, Toronto, Ontario.
Bill Benbow, September 14, 1990, Charmhaven, New South Wales, Australia.
Gus Bennett, December 1, 1990, Mississauga, Ontario.
John Berven, June 30, 1992, Winnipeg, Manitoba.
Eleanor Bone Dahl, December 28, 1991, Markham, Ontario.
Jack Bowers, interviewed by Margaret Gammon, September 1, 1991, Ripley, Ontario.
Ab Bowman, April 20, 1991, Stratford, Ontario.
Brick Bradford, May 18, 1991, Richmond, British Columbia.
Jim Buchanan, September 14, 1990, Dickerson, Maryland.
Harold Calford, August 1991, Oshawa, Ontario.
John Campsie, July 17, 1991, Toronto, Ontario.
Howard Carr, December 1990, Mississauga, Ontario.
Stan Castle, November 28, 1991, Picton, Ontario.
Desmond Chorley, October 1991, Agincourt, Ontario.
Terry Clifton, December 5, 1990, Kingston, Ontario.

John Clinton, January 9, 1991, Mississauga, Ontario.
Willy Clymer, December 11, 1990, Scarborough, Ontario.
Stan Colborne, August 29, 1991, Nanaimo, British Columbia.
Anne-Marie Couchman Fairweather, February 24, 1991, Toronto, Ontario.
Jim Coyne, June 1, 1991, Wiarton, Ontario.
Bob Davidson, April 28, 1991, North York, Ontario.
Art de Breyne, May 1991, St. Lambert, Quebec.
Punch Dickins, July 29, 1991, Don Mills, Ontario.
Dorothy Dove Bogden, February 24, 1991, Toronto, Ontario.
George Dunbar, March 27, 1991, St. Catharines, Ontario.
Bill Dunphy, April 17, 1991, Etobicoke, Ontario.
Paul Emery, February 16, 1992, Scarborough, Ontario.
Don Evans, April 24, 1991, Toronto, Ontario.
Jan Falkowski, September 28, 1991, Peterborough, Ontario.
Bob Fallis, May 1991, London, Ontario.
Wally Ford, September 14, 1990, Williamston, Michigan.
Livingston "Cap" Foster, January 4, 1991, Smiths Falls, Ontario.
Charley Fox, August 28, 1990, London, Ontario.
Bill Frost, December 20, 1990, North York, Ontario.
Alwyn Geen, September 1991, Belleville, Ontario.
Henry Gordon, December 19, 1990, Thornhill, Ontario.
Ernie Guzzo, September 15, 1991, Sault Ste. Marie, Ontario.
Wade Hampton, September 17, 1990, Toronto, Ontario.
Jack Harris, August 28, 1990, Oakville, Ontario.
Art Harrison, September 14, 1990, Owen Sound, Ontario.
Norm Harrison, February 18, 1991, Scarborough, Ontario.
Tom Hawkins, May 9, 1991, London, Ontario.
Len Head, July 31, 1991, Horning Mills, Ontario.
Ren Henderson, November 30, 1990, Clarkson, Ontario.
Bob Hesketh, January 23, 1991, North York, Ontario.
Fred Hotson, April 30, 1991, Mississauga, Ontario.
Harold Jackson, July 21, 1991, St. Thomas, Ontario.
Madge Janes Trull, June 20, 1991, Mississauga, Ontario.
Harald Jensen, March 12, 1991, Don Mills, Ontario.
Eric Johnston, August 4, 1991, Scugog Point, Ontario.
Elmer Keating, April 1992, Hamilton, Ontario.
Charlie Konvalinka, December 5, 1990, Toronto, Ontario.
Charlie Krause, August 28, 1990, Toronto, Ontario.
Gordon Kydd, November 29, 1990, Uxbridge, Ontario.
Don Lamont, January 26, 1991, Brampton, Ontario.
Harold Lancaster, January 30, 1991, West Lorne, Ontario.
Z. Lewis Leigh, August 21, 1991, Grimsby, Ontario.
Bill Lennox, January 23, 1991, North York, Ontario.

W.J. "Mike" Lewis, May 31, 1992, Etobicoke, Ontario.
Herb Liebman, August 27, 1991, Willowdale, Ontario.
Margaret Littlewood, interviewed by Byron Christopher, January 20, 1991, Edmonton, Alberta.
Fridtjov Loberg, March 12, 1991, Toronto, Ontario.
Doug Lomas, March 28, 1991, Bowmanville, Ontario.
Walter Loucks, April 24, 1991, Etobicoke, Ontario.
Fred Macdonell, January 3, 1991, Ottawa, Ontario.
Larry D. Mann, August 14, 1991, Tarzana, California.
Rudy Mauro, December 1990, London, Ontario.
Bill McCauley, December 29, 1990, Don Mills, Ontario.
Chuck McCausland, October 28, 1990, Guelph, Ontario.
Iris McDonald Barr, November 3, 1991, New Westminster, British Columbia.
Dave McIntosh, June 7, 1992, Ottawa, Ontario.
Wess McIntosh, March 12, 1991, Oakville, Ontario.
Pat McLean, September 25, 1990, Cambridge, Ontario.
Stan McMillan, May 4, 1981, Edmonton, Alberta.
Jeff Mellon, January 2, 1991, Richmond Hill, Ontario.
Frank Montgomery, September 3, 1991, Peterborough, Ontario.
Jeanne Muldoon, May 9, 1991, London, Ontario.
Bill Munro, January 4, 1991, Ottawa, Ontario.
Noel Ogilvie, September 10, 1990, Grimsby, Ontario.
Marion Orr, July 14, 1991, Peterborough, Ontario.
Joe Ouellette, October 1990, Don Mills, Ontario.
Dick Pallet, Jeff Pallett, Joyce Pallett, June 21, 1991, Dixie, Ontario.
Charlie Parkin, January 8, 1991, Brampton, Ontario.
Jim Peat, April 1992, Oakville, Ontario.
Norman Phibbs, August 29, 1990, Burlington, Ontario.
Charlie Purcell, September 14, 1990, San Antonio, Texas.
Carl Puterbough, November 26, 1990, Uxbridge, Ontario.
Jackie Rae, August 14 and December 27, 1990, Toronto, Ontario.
Ted Relf, October 6, 1991, Woodville, Ontario.
Valori Richard, April 20, 1991, Ottawa, Ontario.
Cliff Robb, October, 1990, Uxbridge, Ontario.
Dick Ross, October 20, 1990, Markham, Ontario.
Cy Roberts, December 17, 1990, Islington, Ontario.
Clyde Russell, April 28, 1991, North Bay, Ontario.
Allister Rutherford, August 14, 1991, Scarborough, Ontario.
Len Ryder, October 19, 1990, Tuakau, New Zealand.
Bill Sargeant, December 8, 1990, Don Mills, Ontario.
Norm Shrive, November 26, 1990, Burlington, Ontario.
Don Skene, winter 1991, Kingston, Ontario.
Betty and Bill Spence, September 22, 1991, Toronto, Ontario.

Charlie Spurgeon, June 1, 1991, London, Ontario.
Jack Stephens, May 8, 1991, London, Ontario.
Ken Summerville, September 14, 1990, Deerfield Beach, Florida.
Wilf Sutherland, December 17, 1990, Islington, Ontario.
Dick Tarshis, June 9, 1991, Toronto, Ontario.
Maurice "Tommy" Thompson, January 1991, Toronto, Ontario.
Bill Tilt, May 5, 1991, Willowdale, Ontario.
Harvey Timberlake, February 16, 1991, Toronto, Ontario.
Ross Truemner, January 3, 1991, Ottawa, Ontario.
John Trull, June 20, 1991, Mississauga, Ontario.
Gordon Venables, Fall, 1991, West Hill, Ontario.
Frank Vines, December 1, 1990, Etobicoke, Ontario.
Gene Vollick, September 14, 1990, Plant City, Florida.
Bill Walker, July 28, 1991, Oakville, Ontario.
Larry Walker, May 8, 1991, Chatham, Ontario.
Tom Wallnutt, June 15, 1992, Colorado Springs, Colorado.
Max Ward, November 3, 1991, Toronto, Ontario.
Helen Webster Barnett and Marjorie Webster Kerr, October 10, 1990, Agincourt, Ontario.
Les Wilkinson, January 26, 1991, Toronto, Ontario.
Roger Wilson, June 10, 1992, Toronto, Ontario.
Babe Woollett, May 31, 1991, Honolulu, Hawaii.

CORRESPONDENCE

Rick Arnold, December 4, 1990, Roseneath, Ontario.
Jim Askew, July and August 1991, Calgary, Alberta.
Art Badland, July 1991, Roche's Point, Ontario.
Robert Baker, December 13, 1990, Sunderland, Ontario.
John Bertram, April 22, 1991, Cavan, Ontario.
John Bigham, November 1990, April to May 1991, Burlington, Ontario.
Lynne Bowen, June 9, 1992, Nanaimo, British Columbia.
G. Burton Brown, November 14, 1990, English River, Ontario.
Bob Buchan, October 16, 1991, Ottawa, Ontario.
Peter Burnett, February 10, 1991, Etobicoke, Ontario.
A. Helena Campbell, November 10, 1990, Simcoe, Ontario.
Rita McCloskey Carey, November 1990 and June 1991, Kingston, Ontario.
Doug Carr, November 25, 1990, Ingersoll, Ontario.
Joseph A.P. Clark, May 13, 1991, King, Ontario.
Bill Colborne, August 4, 1991, Thunder Bay, Ontario.
John Cooper, April 29, 1991, Oakville, Ontario.
William Corfield, February 26, 1992, London, Ontario.

Bill Davies, March 19, 1991, Toronto, Ontario.
Malcolm Davies, January 1991, Gloucester, Ontario.
Maury Dillingham, July 1991, San Antonio, Texas.
Harry Elder, January 29, 1991, Burlington, Ontario.
Paul Emery, February 18, 1992, Scarborough, Ontario.
Jock Evans, December 29, 1991, Welland, Ontario.
John Evans, May 30, 1991, Toronto, Ontario.
George Flinders, November 26, 1990, Acton, Ontario.
Robert Fowler, June 1, 1991, Weston, Ontario.
Jack Fry, January 29, 1991, Long Sault, Ontario.
Jackie Gaudette Dysart, November 28, 1990, Espanola, Ontario.
Hardie Gray, December 1990, Toronto, Ontario.
Hugh Halliday, November 25, 1990 and June 1992, Orleans, Ontario.
Bill Hill, January and August 1991, Hanover, Ontario.
Norman Hillmer, February 1991, Ottawa, Ontario.
Brian Howard, February 4, 1991, St. Catharines, Ontario.
Ernest "Jack" Hunt, May 4, 1991, Elmira, Ontario.
Bill Hutchins, February 8, 1991, Etobicoke, Ontario.
Ralph Jago, April 4, 1992, Brockville, Ontario.
Peg Johnson, December 1991, Edmonton, Alberta.
Anneliese Kelshall, May 24, 1991, Trinidad, West Indies.
Marion E. Kennedy, November 25, 1990, Haliburton, Ontario.
Roy Legassicke, September 1991, Keene, Ontario.
Robert Letson, May 27, 1991, Etobicoke, Ontario.
Fred Lundell, July 1991, Montreal, Quebec.
Allan Mather, July 25, 1991, Keene, Ontario
Neil McArthur, August 1991, Markham, Ontario.
Mark McDermott, November 14, 1990, Hamilton, Ontario.
Iris McDonald Barr, November 3, 1991, New Westminster, B.C.
Kenneth McDonald, April 26, 1991, Willowdale, Ontario.
John McMillan, May 7, 1991, Weston, Ontario.
Jack Meadows, July 9 and 17, 1991, White Rock, British Columbia.
Gifford Mitchell, July 21, 1991, and February 24, 1992, Kingston, Ontario.
Mildred Morland Gorman, May 4, 1991, Mississauga, Ontario.
John Neal, October 25, 1991, Calgary, Alberta.
Mrs. A.T. Nicholls, March 31, 1991, Woodstock, Ontario.
Vic Nielsen, June 6, 1991, North Bay, Ontario.
Art Parry, April 12, 1992, Islington, Ontario.
Pat Paterson Boyer, November 19, 1990, Islington, Ontario.
George Penfold, November 10, 1990, Don Mills, Ontario.
Archie Pennie, February 3, 1991, Ottawa, Ontario.
Charlie Purcell, October 21, 1991, San Antonio, Texas
Joyce Putnam, November 10, 1990, Kingston, Ontario.

Don Rogers, May 1, 1991, Islington, Ontario.
Betty Ross McFetridge, March 1992, Oakville, Ontario.
Len Schryer, July 14, 1991, Nanaimo, British Columbia.
Rob Schweyer, October 1991, Jarvis, Ontario.
Rev. Walter C. "Paddy" Sellars, August 11, 1991, Ottawa, Ontario.
Ken Smith, September 1991, Toronto, Ontario.
Shirley Smith Mills, August to September 1991, Victoria Harbour, Ontario.
Alan Stirton, April to May 1991, Moose Jaw, Saskatchewan.
Don Suthers, January and April 1991, Burlington, Ontario.
Jessie Thompson, December 12, 1991, St. Catharines, Ontario.
Bill Topham, December 27, 1990, Brighton, Ontario.
Alan Tustin, November 19, 1990, Niagara Falls, Ontario.
Charlotte Tyerman Anderson, November 26, 1990, Goderich, Ontario.
Dyson Webb, January 18, 1991, Toronto, Ontario.
Ken West, January 16, 1991, London, Ontario.
Alan Wingate, July 16, 1991, Toronto, Ontario.
Babe Woollett, May 14, 1991, Honolulu, Hawaii.
Janet Wright, May 15, 1991, Edmonton, Alberta.

Photograph Credits

page

1 Autogyro courtesy Ken Leavens; R100 Library and Archives Canada PA-136594; RCAF poster Library and Archives Canada PL-3028; Directorate of Works and Buildings National Defence PMR 79-133

2 Manning Depot shots all Ken Smith Collection

3 St. Catharines EFTS crew courtesy Joyce Pallett; Stirton courtesy Al & Bernice Stirton; St. Catharines air field courtesy Eric Johnston

4 Windsor EFTS crew courtesy Brick Bradford; Finch crash courtesy Syd Hutnick Collection; Truemner courtesy Ross Truemner

5 Malton AOS staff courtesy Babe Woollett; ferry Library and Archives Canada PA-136046

6 Riggers Library and Archives Canada PL-14880; fitters Library and Archives Canada PL-1041

7 Paulson B&G Western Canada Pictorial Index 1281-38355 FP; gunner Library and Archives Canada PL-964; airborne gunnery National Defence PMR 81-212

8 Cagney and Bishop Library and Archives Canada PL-5065; Wallnutt wings courtesy Tom Wallnutt; Cagney wings courtesy Tom Wallnutt

9 Buzzing wings parade Library and Archives Canada PL-5036; Konvalinka courtesy Lorraine Konvalinka; Strand Theatre Library and Archives Canada PL-6839

10 Link class National Defence PMR 81-213; Littlewood courtesy Margaret Littlewood; wireless class National Defence PMR 81-148

11 Harvards over Parliament National Defence PMR 74-494; buzzing trucks courtesy Elmer Eadie

12 Wood funeral courtesy Ted Arnold; under the hood Library and Archives Canada PA-163736; Fox courtesy Charley Fox

13 Ansons over Alberta National Defence RE 64-9843; Anson crash courtesy Norm Shrive; Harrison courtesy Norm Harrison; observer students Library and Archives Canada PL-3740

14 Trenton CFS National Defence PMR 79-279; Bannock courtesy Russ Bannock; Finch crash courtesy Maury Dillingham

15 Dauphin SFTS Western Canada Pictorial Index 1281-38356 FP; observers at Rivers Library and Archives Canada PL-3722; Winnipeg arrival and Campsie courtesy John Campsie

16 Bournemouth Personnel Reception Centre National Defence PMR 72-459; Foster courtesy Cap Foster; Danish gift courtesy Eric Johnston

Index

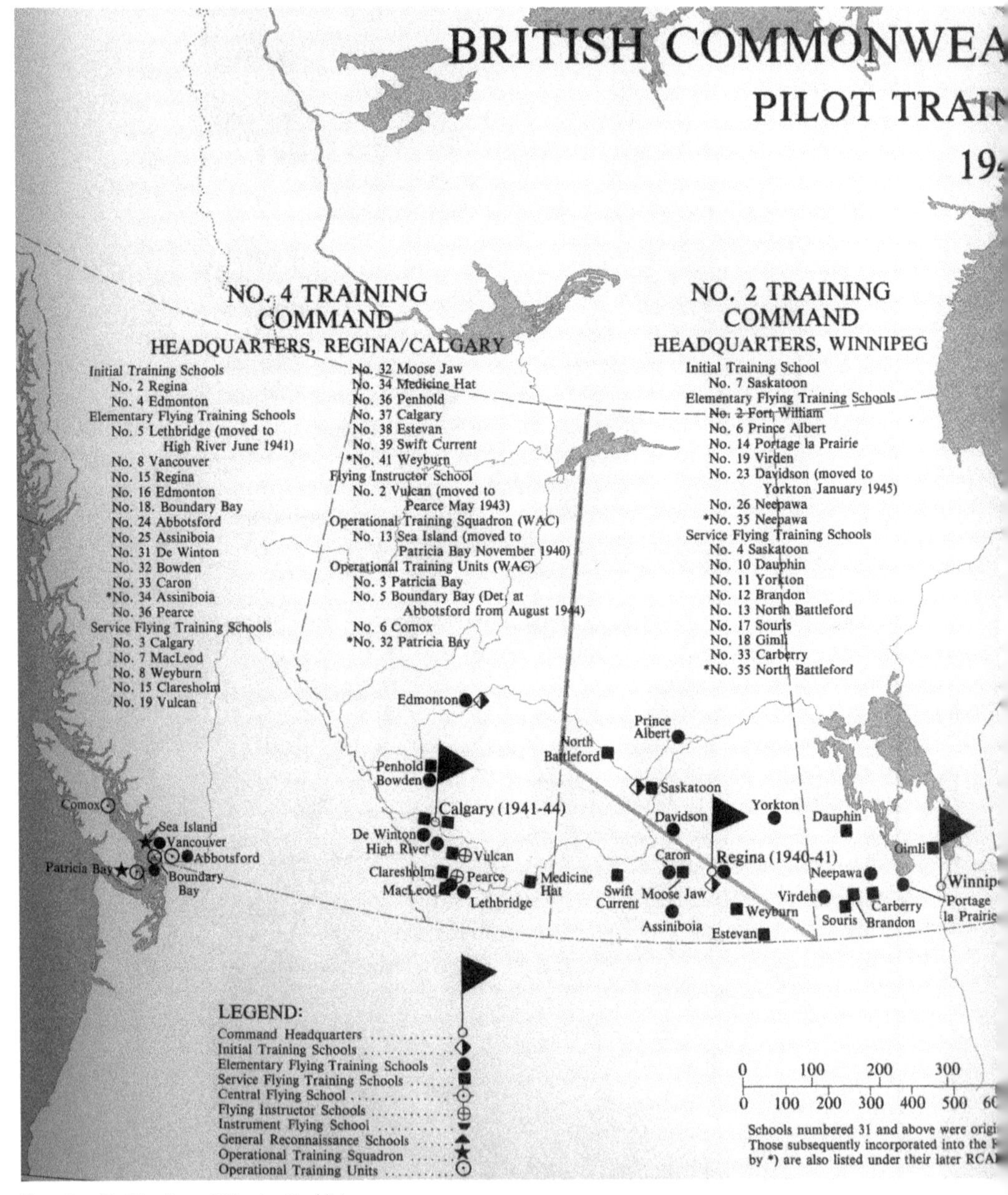

Reproduced by Mapping and Charting Establishment.

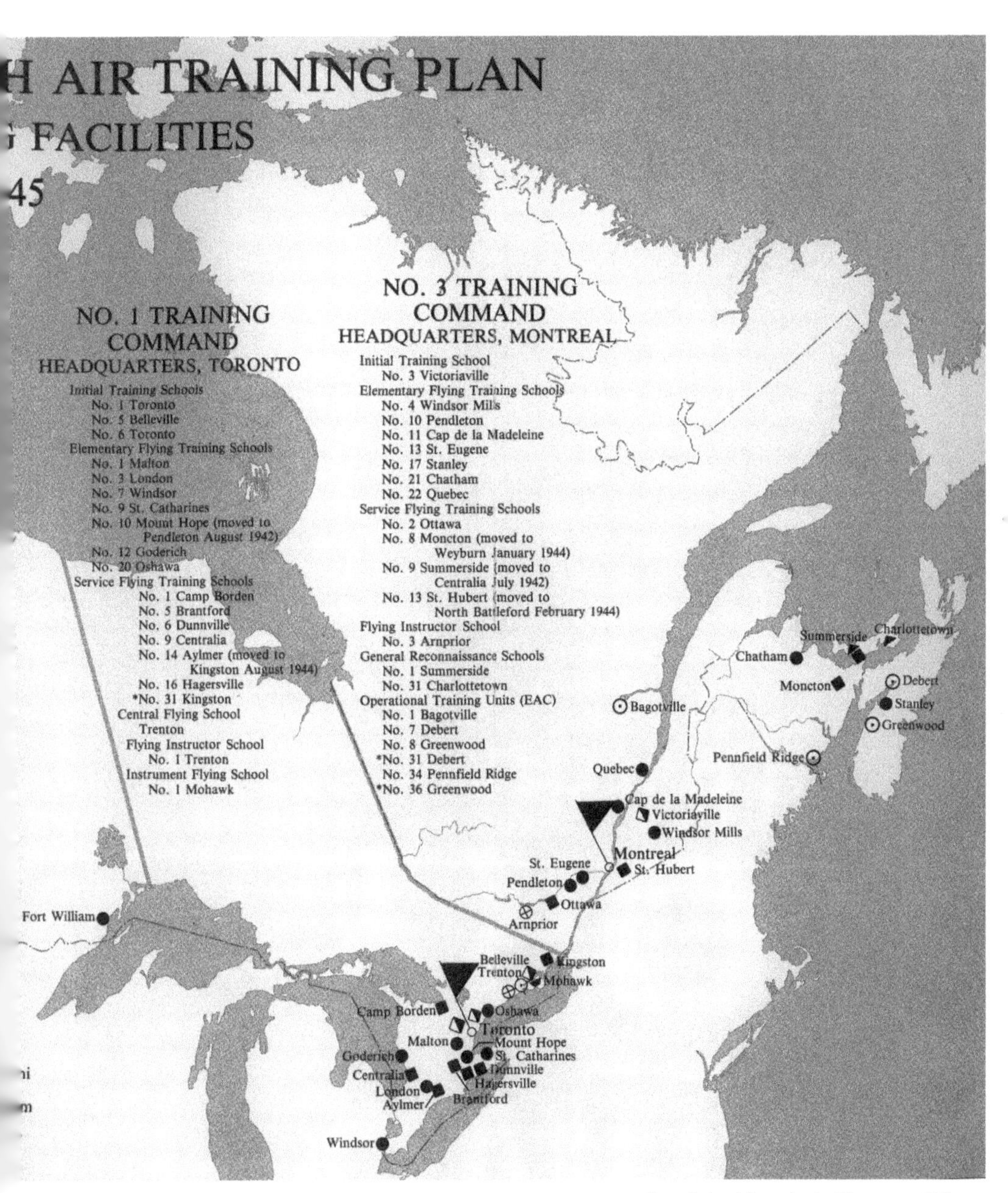

Compiled and drawn by the Directorate of History.